The
Executive's
Guide to
Information
Technology

The
Executive's
Guide to
Information
Technology

John Baschab

Jon Piot

Foreword by Lynda M. Applegate
Henry R. Byers Professor of Business Administration
Harvard Business School

WILEY

John Wiley & Sons, Inc.

About the Cover: We have chosen the legend of Sisyphus as the theme for our cover. In Greek mythology, Sisyphus was condemned by the gods to push a massive boulder uphill. Upon reaching the summit, the boulder would slip and roll back to the bottom, and Sisyphus would be forced to repeat the effort endlessly. This tremendous, but futile and neverending effort is, unfortunately, an apt metaphor for the hard reality facing many IT managers. We hope that the approaches and techniques in this book help the IT director break free of the Sisyphean cycle. This original cover art was created by Dale O'Dell, an artist with over 20 years of experience in digital artwork design. Dale O'Dell Photography & Digital Illustration is online at www.dalephoto.com.

For general information on our other products and services please contact our Customer Care Department within the United States at (800) 762-2974, outside the United States at (317) 572-3993 or fax (317) 572-4002.

Wiley also publishes its books in a variety of electronic formats. Some content that appears in print may not be available in electronic books. For more information about Wiley products, visit our web site at www.wiley.com.

ISBN 0-471-26609-4

Printed in the United States of America.

10   9   8   7   6   5   4   3   2   1

Foreword

Information technology (IT) has always been a wildcard in business, a source of opportunity and uncertainty, of advantage and risk. Business executives often view the IT function with apprehension, as the province of technocrats primarily interested in new features that may have little relevance to real-world business problems. Technology executives, on the other hand, often consider business managers to be shortsighted, lacking the vision to exploit all that technology has to offer. Both struggle as they attempt to implement increasingly complex systems in the face of rapid change in business and technology.

Yet, we have, since the inception of business computing, tightened our embrace of IT for good reason. Despite exasperating moments, technology transforms how we do business. Over the past 30 years, IT has become embedded in the way we define and execute strategy, how we organize, and how we create and deliver value for stakeholders.

The recent decade has added considerably to the mystique and the magic of IT. Something dramatic happened to technology in the 1990s, although it is probably too early to discern the full impact. Many of us remember the first time we opened a browser and gained access to the World Wide Web. For some executives who had lived their lives avoiding technology, a light went on, and they glimpsed the potential of what previously had lain deep within the silicon switches that processed data in the basement of the organization.

Then came the boom of the late 1990s, when the capital markets caught the fever. Stories of "20-something" billionaires, who only a few years earlier plotted their business ideas on napkins, grabbed our attention. As the new century dawned, the bubble burst and the tech-heavy NASDAQ lost more than half its value within months as spending for IT equipment and services dropped. The world economy headed into a downward spiral, and executives young and old found themselves in pretty much the same situation, as they attempted to make sense of which opportunities were real and which were nothing more than hype.

Yet, some things are clear. The world is forever changed. IT has burst forth from its safe containment in the basements of corporations. Business executives have begun to wrest control from IT executives who have failed to step up to the challenge of running IT units as a business. Technology has become a core enabler and, in some cases, the primary channel through which business is done. The world is smaller and the "global village" is quickly becoming a reality. Physical location matters less than it did. Borders and boundaries, ownership, and control have become less rigid. And, more importantly, there are still new frontiers to explore, new challenges to meet, and new magic in store.

The objective of this book is to help business executives who are struggling to identify and capitalize on the full potential of IT. The book offers practical insight from two authors who have helped guide clients in building highly effective IT departments. The book is based on real-world, hands-on experience, and the frameworks and recommendations have been developed through practical experience across a wide variety of industries, company sizes, and technology environments. The authors have clearly documented their insight and have worked hard to highlight prescriptive solutions to share with the reader.

This book helps the CEO, CFO, CIO, technology consultants, and newly promoted IT directors effectively navigate the whitewaters of IT. For the CEO and CFO, this book offers an opportunity to learn how to choose and work with an IT leader. More importantly, they will learn the right questions to ask and the appropriate level of oversight necessary to ensure that IT becomes a competitive advantage for the company or, at a minimum, a well-run internal service department. For the CIO and IT management, this book offers an opportunity to more effectively lead IT as a member of the senior management team and as the operating head of the IT business within the business.

In summary, this book is important reading. It offers practical, real-world insight and pragmatic no-nonsense approaches for people who have a stake in corporate IT. In today's rapidly changing and highly competitive environment, the more effectively you exploit and manage IT in your business, the more successful your company will be. I hope you enjoy the book.

LYNDA M. APPLEGATE
Henry R. Byers Professor of Business Administration
Harvard Business School

Preface

The bulk of our experience in the technology field has been in consulting to companies of all sizes and across a wide variety of industries, and helping them to improve the effectiveness of their IT departments. We have worked with many struggling information technology (IT) departments and have been fortunate enough to help many of them transform themselves into highly effective, fine-tuned organizations, which deliver the highest return on investment to the companies in which they operate. We have observed a consistent pattern of symptoms and causes in the IT departments experiencing difficulties. We have captured these lessons learned and the tools, techniques, and practices that can revive a struggling IT organization.

This book is a sophisticated and comprehensive guide to running a cost-effective and efficient corporate IT unit. While we spend time describing the challenges facing IT departments, our primary aim is to prescribe a course of action for senior managers and IT staff. To that end, we provide sharply defined, specific policies, approaches, and tools for each important aspect of managing the IT function, from human resources to operations to vendor selection to project prioritization.

The techniques covered in this book will facilitate a detailed assessment of current operations, and development of a step-by-step improvement plan designed to save companies significant IT expenditures, while providing measurable productivity improvements. Further, the book will help IT managers and directors improve individual performance in their organizations or consulting companies by identifying common areas of friction and miscommunication between IT departments and the business, and addressing ways to overcome these dysfunctions.

The accompanying CD-ROM contains specific spreadsheets, documents, and checklists for use in planning and decision making.

The reader will gain valuable skills, including:

- Understanding the main sources of wasted IT dollars and identifying specific areas where IT managers can reduce costs.
- Identifying the industry average IT spending.
- Identifying the main management areas of a successful IT operation.
- Distinguishing the *business* of managing IT from the technical aspects.

- Understanding symptoms and sources of IT department inefficiencies.
- Learning critical improvement steps in each of the main IT management areas.
- Learning how to make better decisions in technology direction setting, project management, human resources management, risk management, and technology strategy setting.

In addition, consultants can build new consulting services for companies who are in need of these practices and cost reductions; they will be able to propose additional engagements and services to clients based on the techniques they learn in this book, as well as bring new thinking to existing projects. Companies can attain higher utilization from their existing IT assets and avoid unnecessary IT expenditures in the future. CEOs and CFOs can gain a better understanding of how to work with their top IT executives.

How This Book Is Organized

Each chapter in the book stands on its own. Therefore, some minor overlap of content from chapter to chapter occurs. We work to be prescriptive and specific instead of conceptual and theoretical. We attempt to show not just *what* to do but also *why* to do it. We also try to follow each *should* with a *because*. The book is arranged in three parts and an appendix.

Part I: The Effective IT Organization

Part I examines the ongoing dilemma that effective management of the IT function has presented for both technical and nontechnical managers. IT management is consistently considered a "neither fish-nor-fowl" business area. Few of the constraints or management considerations that apply to a normal business functional area, such as finance or human resources, apply to IT, but neither do the natural efficiencies and incentives that affect the practices of a P&L-driven business unit.

This situation has been exacerbated by the fact that nontechnical managers are confounded by the combination of business and technical skills required to manage IT, and many IT managers lack the business training and experience to bring the P&L mind-set to the function. The result is long-term dissatisfaction from all concerned—senior managers, business users, and the IT department. In many cases, businesses have an ongoing dysfunctional, mildly hostile relationship with their IT departments, and, in the worst cases, IT departments spin out of control, damaging the business with inappropriate spending, squandered opportunities, and other forms of waste.

Part II: Managing the IT Department

Part II explains in detail the key practices, policies, and strategies for effectively managing the IT department across all activities. Unlike many other treatments of this topic, we focus on the *business* of managing an IT shop, rather than focusing on a specific technology area or a niche topic. This section is geared to the IT manager, director, or CIO who wants to understand how to get the best out of their people, vendors, systems, and budget. This comprehensive, detailed guide provides concrete, specific approaches for all aspects of managing IT, as well as real-world "war stories" from a variety of organizations.

Part III: Senior Executive IT Management

Part III covers executive decision-making tools and processes for senior executives and IT managers. The traditional difficulties managing the relationship between IT and the business users can be overcome. Similarly difficulties setting company-wide priorities and ensuring that IT is executing against these priorities is critical to the executive team's success. These topics are discussed including working with the business, IT budgeting and cost management, risk management, IT demand management, effective IT benchmarking systems, and the IT steering committee. The topics and processes described will assist the executive in managing those areas that are critical to IT success and its alignment with the company both financially and strategically.

Appendix: IT Toolkit

The appendix lists the tools discussed in Parts I through III, including project prioritization matrices and project estimating tools, IT steering committee charters, hiring checklists, project charters, and other documents mentioned throughout the book.

Terminology

We use specific terminology repeatedly throughout the book. These terms are used inside IT departments at many companies:

TERM	DEFINITION
The business	Business managers and users who are part of the company but are not part of the IT team.
Business units	Units within the corporation whose functions are in line with revenue- and profit-generating activities.

TERM	DEFINITION
Functional group	Overhead departments in the company that support operations, not including IT, for example, human resources, finance, marketing.
Infrastructure	Used synonymously with the term *operations* (see definition for *operations*). Infrastructure is the breadth of utility services an IT department provides, for example, e-mail, network access, file storage, printing. Infrastructure can be contrasted with *applications,* which are software-based business transaction and analysis systems.
IT	Information technology or the IT department itself.
IT department	The main IT unit in the company. Also called *information systems (IS) group, IT group, IT, MIS department.*
IT director	The top information technology officer in the company; used interchangeably with Chief Information Officier (*CIO*).
IT initiatives	Information technology improvement programs that include multiple projects for completing a single goal.
IT management	The group of top managers in the IT department, usually the IT director and his or her direct reports.
Operations	The full breadth of utility services in an IT department includes the entire infrastructure. Chapter 7 is devoted to this subject and contains a comprehensive definition.
ROI	Return on investment, a method of financial analysis to estimate financial impact of an investment.
Senior management /senior managers	Everyone who manages a business unit or function and executive officers. Typically includes the top two layers of management in an organization and all C-level officers, for example, CEO, CFO, COO.
System	Computer systems and applications.
Technology	The full range of hardware, software, infrastructure, and telecommunications systems that the IT department has control over. The broadest sense of items and services that the IT department controls and is responsible for.
Vendor	Any outside provider of hardware, software, products, or services to the IT department.

Acknowledgments

An endeavor of this scope is the result of countless investments by mentors, clients, friends, family, and teachers. Although it is impossible to fully thank this "cast of thousands," we acknowledge the contributions of those who have had a direct role in providing content, review, critique, and support during the creation of this book: Scott Anderson, Lynda Applegate, Teresa Chao, Leslie Lee, John Martin, Scott Mastbrook, Darren Morrison, Katy R. Scott, and John Rosenbaum.

We also thank our agent, Neil Salkind, and the team at Studio B, as well as Matt Holt, our senior editor at John Wiley & Sons. They were both kind enough to guide two first-time authors through the trials of translating our experiences helping clients into something we could share.

We would also like to thank our teams at Booz-Allen & Hamilton and Impact Innovations Group who made many client successes possible.

Last, and most important, we thank our families, Mary, Emily, and Will Baschab; and Susan, Lauren, Allison, and Will Piot without whose patience and support neither this book, nor the careers which provided its content, would be possible.

About the Authors

The authors have a combined 30 years of experience in information technology management at Fortune 500 companies and middle-market companies operating in industries ranging from retailing to services to manufacturing. They have combined their real-world experience with academic business education on dozens of consulting engagements focused on IT effectiveness and turnarounds for distressed IT departments.

JOHN BASCHAB began his career with a degree in MIS from the University of Alabama. He received the prestigious Seebeck award for achievement in computer science. John continued his career in the IT department of BellSouth and in the technology and finance department of computer hardware and software manufacturer, Intergraph Corp. After receiving his MBA with honors in behavioral science from the University of Chicago Graduate School of Business, John worked as a technology consultant to Fortune 500 companies in the Chicago office of Booz-Allen & Hamilton. John is currently senior vice president with Impact Innovations Group, a privately held management and technology consulting firm, employing more than 600 consultants, with offices in Dallas, Atlanta, and Washington, DC. E-mail: jbascha@gsbalum.uchicago.edu.

JON PIOT received his degree in computer science from Southern Methodist University, and joined Andersen Consulting, developing computer applications and providing technology-consulting services to Fortune 500 companies. Jon continued his career as vice president of DMACS International, a software company whose international software rights of Fox Software products were later acquired by Microsoft. After receiving his MBA from the Harvard Business School, Jon joined the information technology strategy group of management consultancy Booz-Allen & Hamilton. Jon cofounded Impact Innovations Group. E-mail: jpiot@mba1995.hbs.edu.

Contents

xiii

PART I

The Effective
IT Organization

1

The IT Dilemma

Dilemma: A situation that requires a choice between options that are or seem equally unfavorable or mutually exclusive.

—*American Heritage Dictionary*[1]

". . . you're damned if you do, and damned if you don't."

—Eleanor Roosevelt [2]

In January 2001, we were taking a brief vacation with our families in Phoenix. Like any good technology consultants, we were never more than a few yards from our mobile phones. The call came from an acquaintance, the chief operating officer of a medium-size company based in the Southeast. He knew we were on vacation, but he really wanted to talk . . . now. His story came out in a rush:

> I tell you, I've completely had it with my IT department. We have a tremendous number of business initiatives that rely on technology projects in the IT department. Not only have we lost the chance to get ahead of the competition, but we are falling behind because the IT department can't seem to finish anything. We have a list of over 150 projects and no one seems to know what the status is or who is in charge. I can't remember the last time one was completed. The entire executive team has lost confidence in IT.
>
> Every time I ask how I can help the IT department, they come back with additional headcount or capital expenditure requests. Now the IT budget is twice what it was two years ago, and the headcount has doubled, too. I think our costs are way out of line. I can't see a light at the end of the tunnel, but I don't know enough about technology to understand the issues and get out of this mess either.

We responded with some anecdotes from previous work with clients in similar situations. After listening to a few of these, the COO responded, "It's almost like you were here. This is a relief—the fact that you are so familiar with the symptoms means you probably know the cure. See you Monday."

This was not the first, nor the last, call that we received from an exasperated senior executive whose IT department had grown into an uncontrollable tar pit of backed-up projects, miserable staffers, and frustrated business users—all set against a backdrop of never-ending spending increases for additional staff, services, equipment, and software. This scenario, with no light at the end of the tunnel, is usually when we hear from senior managers who later become our best clients.

This call resulted in an engagement that allowed us to help the client dramatically, measurably improving the company's IT operations and project completion rate, while, at the same time, reducing their overall IT spending significantly. That project, and the multiple similar engagements that preceded and followed it, were the basis for some serious contemplation. We had been fortunate enough to help lead a variety of clients through the improvement of their IT departments. Our client base covers a disparate array of geographies, industries, and technologies. Nevertheless, in each case the symptoms and causes of problems in the IT department are nearly always the same.

Our experiences begged the questions: What is it about IT departments that seem to so often result in such dysfunctional relationships with senior management? Why do successful corporate senior management teams, who manage every other aspect of their businesses with incredible acumen and ability, turn into confused neophytes when it comes to managing IT? Why do IT managers have so much trouble communicating with the senior management team? If IT departments are so bad, why are they tolerated and even given enormous spending power? And, most importantly, how can IT managers learn to avoid being the victims of this phenomenon, and how can senior managers learn to work with the IT team so that the organization can avoid all of the torment and pain we had observed?

Our insights on these questions, and a set of specific, actionable prescriptions, are the subject of this book. We have based this book on our experiences working with clients with 1,000-member IT departments and 10-member IT departments; from industries ranging from retailing, to manufacturing, to services; and from IT budgets ranging from under $1 million to well over $100 million. We are fortunate to have had smart, forward-thinking, action-oriented clients who have moved aggressively with us to implement our recommendations; therefore, we can claim with field-tested confidence that our methods produce real, quantifiable results. We hope that you derive as much enjoyment and value from our findings and approaches as we have had in creating and documenting them.

What Good Is Information Technology?

Most companies ought to have an IT department. This appears to be an obvious observation. However, it is worth recognizing that, in the memories of more than half the working population of the United States, a company department organized solely around information technology was unheard of. The IT department has evolved from a narrowly focused data processing element of the accounting department to a function that supports and, in many cases, drives, nearly every area of a company. This has happened in a mere 40 years. Stand-alone IT departments are a relatively recent development. The number of people working in technology-related jobs grew six times faster between 1983 and 1998 than the U.S. workforce at large. Information technology-related industries doubled their share of the U.S. economy between 1977 and 1998. Practically overnight, technology-related services have become a global, trillion-dollar industry.[3]

The principle driver behind this remarkable, rapid creation of a vibrant, sophisticated, and enormous industry and the attendant inclusion of a department dedicated to it in every credible company, is the quest for business productivity improvement.

The notion of technology investments as a driver of United States business productivity has a controversial history. The benefits of technology investments (and IT departments) were not always so apparent. Productivity growth in the United States faltered from the mid-1970s through the early 1990s,[4] in spite of large technology investments from most major U.S. corporations. The disconnect between heavy capital and expense investment and the theoretically associated improvements in productivity led to a so-called *productivity paradox*. In reaction to the failure of such large investments to produce the expected productivity gains, MIT Nobel Laureate Robert Solow famously remarked in 1987, "You can see the computer age everywhere but in the productivity statistics."[5] More recent research suggests that the productivity benefits from the deployment of technology have had a massive, albeit delayed, impact on the U.S. and world economy.[6]

A variety of researchers have concluded that investments in IT have been instrumental in the improved productivity seen in the U.S. economy beginning in the mid-1990s. In early 2000, the Federal Reserve gave information technology investments credit for approximately $50 billion in productivity improvement, which represents more than 65 percent of the total $70 billion in productivity gains seen by businesses in the United States in the last half of the 1990s[7] (see Exhibit 1.1).

The Federal Reserve staff report, by Kevin J. Stiroh, concluded, "Industry-level data show a broad productivity resurgence that reflects both the production and the use of IT. The most IT-intensive industries experienced significantly larger productivity gains than other industries." The report went even further, attributing most of the productivity improvement to technology. "Results show that virtually all of the aggregate productivity acceleration can be traced to the industries that either produce IT or use IT most intensively."[8]

In 2001, *Business 2.0* magazine summarized the turnabout in top economic thinkers' viewpoints on the productivity gains from technology, saying that those gains:

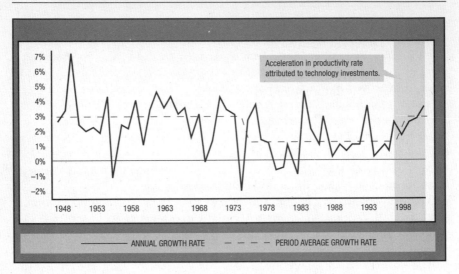

Exhibit 1.1   U.S. Productivity Growth, 1947 to 2000

. . . materialized in force beginning in 1995. What followed was a five-year run in which productivity grew an astonishing 2.8 percent a year, or double the rate of the previous two decades. (The numbers may sound small, but at 2.8 percent, living standards double every 25 years; at 1.4 percent, they double every 50.)[9]

Solow went on record saying that his paradox had finally been solved, and Alan Greenspan's Federal Reserve concluded that information technology had raised the economy's long-term speed limit.[10]

Laura D'Andrea Tyson, dean of the Haas School of Business at the University of California, and former National Economic Advisor in the Clinton administration, emphasizes this point as well, writing in *BusinessWeek:*

The productivity numbers tell the most convincing story. According to a recent study by the Council of Economic Advisors, labor productivity accelerated by 1.6 percentage points from 1995 to 2000, compared with its growth from 1973 to 1995. The lion's share of this acceleration stemmed from more investment in information technology and the efficiency improvements made possible by this technology.[11]

In a March 2000 speech before the Boston College Conference on the New Economy, Federal Reserve Chairman Alan Greenspan, a former skeptic, remarked that the "source of [the U.S. markets'] spectacular performance [is] the revolution in information technology."[12] Former Secretary of Labor Robert Reich says that it should now be obvious that "the extraordinary productivity improvement [is] generated primarily by information technology," which has been "the driving force behind this economy."[13]

Leading researcher Eric Brynjolfsson of the Massachusetts Institute of Technology has spent nearly a decade researching the link between technology investment and business benefit. Along with Lorin Hitt of the Wharton School at the University of Pennsylvania, Brynjolfsson has also concluded that investment in information technology has been responsible for major productivity improvements in corporate environments. Brynjolfsson says that "firms that invest more in IT have greater productivity improvements, and productivity continues to improve over time."[14]

Senior managers do not have to rely merely on the economists or on abstract concepts such as productivity gains in the U.S. economy for confirmation that IT investments produce results for corporations. The quantitative, specific results that companies who invest in information technology have enjoyed are easy to inventory.

Significantly improved sales forecasting, rapid month-end closings, shortened supply chains, tightened inventories, and streamlined customer communication are just a few of the results of the combination of hardware, software, and effort expended over the past two decades.

A few anecdotes from the field demonstrate the quantifiable improvements brought about by the deployment of corporate technology:

- General Electric, through a systems-based push to monitor all of its business activities more effectively, has created capabilities and reporting systems which allow it to respond in hours to events which previously took weeks or even months. Business managers have real-time dashboards or "digital cockpits" that highlight important aspects of their operation—sales results, inventory levels and order status. The systems have not only helped the company improve response times to trouble areas, but also reduce cycle times and improve risk management. Overall systems implementations have helped GE rack up impressive savings numbers: $100 million from inventory, accounts payable and receivables, $680 million saved in procurement through on-line auction purchasing, $3 million saved on payroll costs in the plastics division, a 5 percent improvement in inventory turns at GE Power Systems and a 100 percent improvement in required sales staff per customer. GE estimates total savings as a result of "digitization" at a staggering $1.6 billion.[15]

- Weirton Steel, a $1.3-billion steel manufacturer, has lowered labor hours per ton of steel from 6.5 hours to 1.3; the CEO attributes the cost improvements directly to the deployment of technology.[16]

- Roadway Express, a $2.8 billion freight hauler, implemented systems which provided detailed tracking for all internal operations down to the most minute detail. This allowed the systems to track the true cost-to-serve for all processes using Activity Based Costing (ABC). The system not only helped them identify process improvement and cost reduction opportunities, but also understand the true cost of serving customers, allowing them to turn away unprofitable business. Based on these IT initiatives, the company was able to improve their operating yields, with revenue-per-ton up 4 percent in 2001, in an environment where their competitors were struggling to merely maintain existing margins.[17]

- United Health Group, an $18-billion insurer, used technology-driven reengineering to produce large productivity gains and reduce overhead costs by more than $300,000 annually.[18]

- KIAH, a financial services firm, reduced its mortgage approval process from four days to 10 minutes, all based on technology deployment.[19]

- Tsutaya, Japan's largest CD and video retailer used a combination of customer relationship management systems, data warehousing, and wireless technology to begin offering new services to customers through their subsidiary, Tsutaya On Line (TOL). By taking advantage of the large number of wireless phone subscribers in Japan, TOL achieved a subscriber base of over 2.15 million in a few short years. TOL builds an assessment of subscribers personal entertainment preferences and provides content to their wireless phones, including music clips, movie reviews, and film recommendations. TOL customers who use the mobile service spend 9 percent more with Tsutaya than non-TOL customers. Based on their sophisticated delivery of personalized content, TOL has grown profits by more than 48 percent, in an ailing Japanese economy.[20]

Even the Internet, which the hindsight of the dot-com era shows us was obviously oversold, is still a revolutionary achievement. Certainly, it has not lived up to the price/earnings expectations reflected in the NASDAQ of the late 1990s, but, on the other hand, would anyone care to do without it?

In short, no reasonable person today contemplates a life without corporate systems supporting every business function, from manufacturing, to finance, to sales and customer support, to say nothing of desktop office-automation products such as spreadsheets and word processors. Corporations have adopted technology to improve productivity, reduce costs, drive revenues, offer new capabilities to customers and suppliers, and maintain competitive parity. Researchers, educators, economists, and, most importantly, business managers agree that investments in information technology are not only unavoidable, but, in fact, are undisputedly and universally beneficial. What is immensely perplexing, then, is that studies of business satisfaction with IT and IT initiatives have produced surprisingly negative results.

Information Technology Misery

In spite of the impressive results from business investment in technology, the IT department is the source of tremendous frustration, missed opportunity, and inefficiency in companies. Corporate management is at odds with the IT department more often than not. The revolving door in the top IT management spot at so many companies has led to the only half-joking interpretation by some that the CIO title stands for "Career Is Over." This level of cynicism is not something you generally hear directed at the individuals who have risen to similar levels of responsibility in a corporation in other functions or business units. Something is clearly amiss with IT departments.

A host of evidence backs this position. One important snapshot of the failures of IT is provided by the Standish Group, a technology research group and consultancy, which has performed an exhaustive analysis of the outcomes of more than seven years of corporate IT projects. The researchers at the Standish Group have performed periodic studies on the results of corporate IT initiatives since 1994. In their widely publicized, groundbreaking research, they found that IT initiatives had surprisingly high failure rates. They found that more than one-half (53 percent) of IT projects had overrun their schedules and budgets. Thirty-one percent of IT projects were cancelled. The average time overrun on projects was 222 percent of the original estimate. It is impossible to calculate the opportunity cost of the failed projects.[21]

Incredibly, Standish found that a scant 16 percent of projects were completed within the original time frames and budget constraints. The group found that the percentage of completion in larger companies was even lower, at 9 percent. Of projects that were completed, only 42 percent delivered the original planned benefits.[22]

The investment stakes for projects and information technology initiatives are high. Standish has estimated that the average cost of a development project for a large company is well over $2 million, and even small companies invest over $400,000. Others confirm a high level of investment in IT. *Information Week* has completed an annual survey of IT costs in companies, which run from 2 percent to 9 percent of total revenues, depending on industry, which is an average of 3 percent to 4 percent of revenues.[23]

Standish is not alone in its findings. Consultants KPMG found that 87 percent of projects surveyed went 50 percent over their budget. They also found that 45 percent of projects failed to produce the expected benefits and that nearly 90 percent went over schedule.[24]

If statistics and research results aren't proof enough, observers need look no further than some of the high-profile IT failures of the past few years. A review of a few of these provides ample empirical evidence of how difficult IT projects can be and the tremendous amount of damage they can cause when they go awry:

- *Denver International Airport:* A new state-of-the-art automated baggage handling system was planned to improve baggage management speed, accuracy, and throughput by implementing information technology support to automate the entire system. The sophisticated system was to be controlled by more than 300 computers and be composed of more than 4,000 unmanned baggage cars running over 21 miles of track. Difficulties with the project, which required an investment of more than $230 million, delayed the opening of the airport by 11 months. The delayed opening of the airport cost the city more than $1 million per day while system shortcomings were corrected, with a net result of costs higher than the original investment in the project over the course of the delay. Ultimately, the airport installed a $51-million conventional baggage handling belt system so that the airport could open for business.[25]

- *Hershey Foods:* Three up-to-date programs designed to increase productivity, cut costs, enhance customer-relations management, and improve logistics were arranged to replace Hershey's legacy system simultaneously. Despite that, glitches during peak buying season resulted in sales decreases of 12.4 percent, yielding a dismal third-quarter report.[26]

- *Nike:* New software was implemented to manage Nike's supply chain production line. However, the software failed to adequately match supply with consumer demand, resulting in shortages in some product lines and overproduction in others. Nike blamed its $100-million quarter-to-quarter revenue drop on i2 Technology's software, a part of a larger software project, which ultimately cost Nike more than $400 million.[27]

- *Washington State Department of Licensing:* A new program was implemented to provide a fully automated system for vehicle registration and renewal. The program was expected to cost $41.8 million and take five years to execute. However, difficulties after only three years increased the cost to more than $51 million. The project was terminated seven years after its initiation. Consequently, $40 million had been wasted because of bad management and poor guidelines.[28]

- *Mississippi Department of Information Technology Services (ITS):* The original $11-million contract called for a consulting firm to build an automated tax system to collect 36 taxes for the state's tax commission during a 40-month period. However, "not a single tax was implemented during the 64-month term of the contract," according to an ITS statement. Settlement attempts failed, the case made it to trial, and a jury in August 2000 awarded the state of Mississippi $475 million in actual and punitive damages. Post-verdict negotiations between the parties reduced the settlement to $185 million over several years.[29]

- *Cisco Systems:* A modern forecasting system was produced as a major strategic competitive advantage. However, management's trust in the system allowed a large economic turndown to go unnoticed, which, in turn, led to write-offs totaling $2.2 billion, 8,500 layoffs, and a decrease of $68.37 per share in its stock.[30]

- *FoxMeyer Drug:* A top-of-the-line enterprise resource planning (ERP) program, anticipated to cost $65 million, was facilitated to boost the drug distributor's productivity. Release of the software was pushed forward 90 days, sacrificing valuable module test time and eliminating the opportunity to reengineer business processes. Software glitches and inaccurate inventory forecasting resulted in bankruptcy.[31]

- *Tri Valley Growers:* A modern software program was designed to cut costs and improve productivity. The system cost more than $6 million; however, no expectations were met and some of the software could not even be installed. After investing $20 million in the implementation, Tri Valley refused to pay its vendor and stopped using the software. When Tri Valley filed a $20 million lawsuit, its software provider countersued for breach of contract.[32]

- *W. W. Grainger Inc.:* A software system was implemented to optimize profit and cut costs. The system, costing at least $9 million, repeatedly overcounted warehouse inventory, which led to inventory shrinkage. As a result, Grainger experienced $23 million in reduced earnings and a loss of $19 million in sales.[33]

- *Snap-On Inc.:* A new order-entry system was established to increase order ease and increase profits. The system took three years to implement and created delayed orders and miscounted inventory, resulting in second quarter earnings 40 percent below previous year levels.

These high-profile IT project failures are simply those highlighted in the technology press. The Standish Group statistics imply that such anecdotes are the rule, not the exception.

Dissatisfaction with the IT department, however, extends far beyond these high-profile project flameouts. There is also well-documented dissatisfaction with all levels of corporate IT departments, from help desk support, to operations, to management. Marcy Lacity and Rudy Hirscheim documented this in their research for *Information Systems Outsourcing: Myths, Metaphors, and Realities,* finding that "only two of the thirteen companies that participated in the study agree that their IS departments are critical to corporate success. The remaining eleven companies all see their IT department as a necessary, but burdensome, cost pit."[34]

The proverbial surly, supercilious, and contemptuous "tech guy" from the IT department has become such a common corporate stereotype that *Saturday Night Live* immortalized the character in the form of "Nick Burns: Your Company's Computer Guy."

The character of Nick certainly goes over the top, with comments such as "They teach this kind of stuff on 'Blue's Clues'"; "[so] it's the e-mail that's stupid, not you, right?"; "I was trying to help those morons on the third floor. They're trying to run RealPlayer behind a firewall without the proxy set—can you believe that?"; and (responding to his ever-beeping pager) "It's those goofs over in Organizational Development—they make you guys look like brainiacs over there." Much of the effectiveness and humor of the skit comes from the fact that everyone seems to know a Nick Burns in his or her own organization.

The image of technology workers is so negative that even the federal government got into the act. In a September 2000 publication, *The Digital Work Force: Building Infotech Skills at the Speed of Innovation,* Carol Ann Meares and John Sargent, senior policy analysts in the Office of Technology Policy in the U.S. Department of Commerce, concluded, "Many people have a distorted, negative image of IT workers," and recommended remediation in the media of the IT profession image to attract additional workers to the field.[35]

The result is that IT has, in many companies, been relegated to a backwater operation, in spite of its clearly recognized importance to operations and productivity. As a former CIO writing under the pseudonym "Anonymous" writes in *CIO Magazine,* "As far as most people at your company are concerned, [the] IT staff operates . . . somewhere apart from the 'real' company."[36]

In a March 2002 article, "IT's Rodney Dangerfield Complex," *InformationWeek* highlighted the result of business frustration with IT, quoting a CIO from a major corporation: "[IT] gets no respect [from the other departments]." The article goes on to say that IT was "left out of business process or technology-related discussions" and that the department "was fragmented and the organization lacked consistency in project management, processes, and production."[37]

The Standish Group goes one step further, saying that in the computer industry, "failures are covered up, ignored and/or rationalized."[38] The unfortunate reality is that the "Rodney Dangerfield complex" describes the position of the IT department at a considerable number of corporations.

A Burning Platform

For more than a decade, *Information Week* magazine has conducted a survey on IT spending in top U.S. corporations. The results are telling. Most U.S. companies spend between 2 percent and 9 percent of their annual revenues on IT-related expenditures. The rate varies by industry, but median spending is somewhere between 4 percent and 5 percent.[39] Exhibit 1.2 outlines the spending by industry, as a percentage of corporate revenue. Although the benchmark IT spending as a percentage of revenue varies from industry to industry, the majority of industries spend between 2 percent and 5 percent of revenues on technology.

Exhibit 1.3 shows the trend in the *Information Week* data over the past few years. The average spent on technology by companies has risen steadily, in spite of the well-known pullback in 2001.

The problems outlined in the previous section should be of material interest to corporations. The amount of spending and investment by corporations,

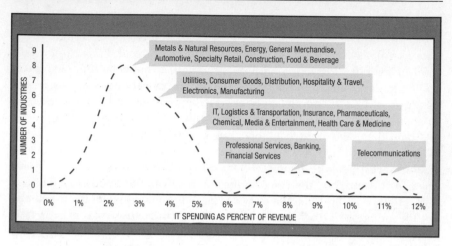

Exhibit 1.2   IT Spending as a Percent of Revenue by Aggregate Industry Group

even those investing in IT at the low end of the scale, means that the problems in IT have to be addressed. At 4 percent to 5 percent of revenues, the IT costs in a company must be managed effectively. At this average range, IT costs are usually one of the largest nondirect expenditures in a company. In comparison, according to studies performed by The Hackett Group, world-class companies on average spend only 0.75 percent of revenues on finance.[40] Clearly both the benefits to be achieved, and the high level of investment required by IT justify close attention from senior management to ensure that IT is effective and producing the right results.

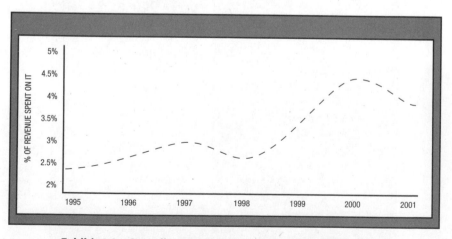

Exhibit 1.3   Spending as a Percent of Revenues, 1995 to 2001

Information Technology Satisfaction?

One useful way of rating corporations' effective use of IT is to plot their level of overall satisfaction with IT—the sum of customer service levels, cost reductions, improved business operations, or other relevant aggregate measures of benefits produced by the IT department. Exhibit 1.4 compares this satisfaction with the level of cost relative to peer companies.

Companies with limited IT operations begin in the southwest quadrant. While their satisfaction with IT is low, it is not surprising given their low level of investment. To improve IT operations and achieve the benefits outlined in this chapter, the company begins investing in technology. This migrates them northward on the matrix. The senior management team generally has the intention of finding a way to migrate to the southeast corner where IT costs are kept at reasonable levels expected for the company, and higher satisfaction is achieved.

In many companies, the increased investments in IT do not produce the expected benefits. Satisfaction stagnates, or even diminishes, based on the high expectations set from the incremental investment. Often, at best, companies achieve large improvements in their level of satisfaction, but the baseline steady state of IT investment never levels off, or it goes back to previous levels. As Exhibit 1.5 demonstrates, the fate of many companies is at best a

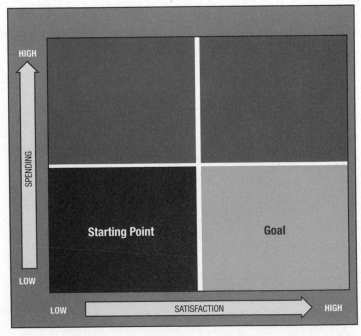

Exhibit 1.4   IT Satisfaction versus IT Spending

permanent residence in the northeast quadrant and, at worst, the northwest "high-spending, low-satisfaction" corner.

This combination of IT dissatisfaction and high spending has created a burning platform for the improvement of the IT department.

The Information Technology Dilemma

Why, then, if IT is an absolute requirement in any company today, is corporate senior management's satisfaction with such a critical function so startlingly low? Why is the actual and perceived satisfaction of the end customer so low? Why is the IT department's satisfaction with consultants, applications providers, and hardware vendors similarly low? How can IT shake the "Nick Burns" stereotype and thrive as an integral, vital function in a company?

Most importantly, why do companies spend as much as 9 percent of their annual revenues on a function that didn't exist 40 years ago and, while achieving incredible benefits, still so often fail to derive full value or satisfaction from their investment?

These are intriguing questions, and, more importantly, ones that senior management teams ignore at their peril. Many companies appear to be caught in a perplexing dilemma. They must invest in information technology, if not for productivity gain, at least for competitive parity. Technology investments have created major productivity gains over the past two decades.

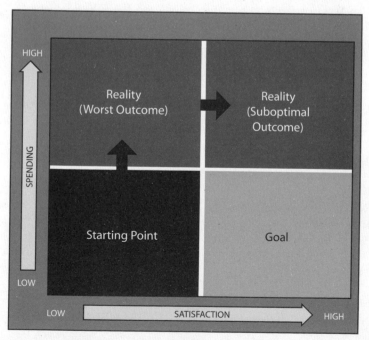

Exhibit 1.5 Typical Company Progression

Research and anecdotal evidence, however, also make it clear that the failures of IT departments to produce cost-effective, satisfactory results have produced misery on a massive scale for corporations and IT department personnel alike.

Every company spending money on an IT department has no choice but to grapple with these issues. Many organizations continue to throw money at the problem, escalating the issue even further. Ignoring the issues, or treating them with superficial infusions of additional investment, does not change the underlying problems. In fact, it is the primary reason companies find themselves in the northwest corner of the IT spending and satisfaction matrix.

Chapter 2 outlines some of the symptoms and causes of the IT dilemma and attempts to answer some of these questions. The remainder of this book presents the building blocks of effective IT management, which we have used to help so many of our own clients move to the southeast corner of the matrix.

NOTES

1. *American Heritage Dictionary,* 4th ed. (Boston: Houghton Mifflin, 2000).
2. Eleanor Roosevelt, "How to Take Criticism," *Ladies' Home Journal* (January, 1944). All rights reserved. Reprinted with permission.
3. U.S. Department of Commerce, Office of Technology Policy, *Update: The Digital Workforce* (Washington, DC: U.S.Government Printing Office, September 2000).
4. Kevin J. Stiroh, "Information Technology and the U.S. Productivity Revival: What Do the Industry Data Say?" Federal Reserve Bank of New York, staff reports, no. 115 (January 24, 2001).
5. Robert M. Solow, "We'd Better Watch Out," *New York Times Book Review* (July 12, 1987), p. 36.
6. See note 4.
7. "It's Official: IT Adds Up," *Information Week* (April 17, 2000). All rights reserved. Reprinted with permission.
8. See note 4.
9. Jerry Useem, "And Then, Just When You Thought the 'New Economy' Was Dead," *Business 2.0* (August 2001).
10. See note 4.
11. Laura D'Andrea Tyson, "Why the New Economy Is Here to Stay," *BusinessWeek* (April 30, 2001).
12. Alan Greenspan, "The Revolution in Information Technology" (March 6, 2000). Available from http://www.federalreserve.gov/boarddocs/speeches/2000 /20000306.htm.
13. See note 7.
14. See note 7.
15. Dave Lindorff, "General Electric CO's Drive to Real Time," *CIO Insight* (November 2000).

16. See note 7.

17. Edward Cone and David F. Carr, "Unloading on the Competition," *Baseline* (October 2002).

18. See note 7.

19. See note 7.

20. Alexandra Harney, "Always On," *CIO Insight* (February 2002).

21. The Standish Group, *The Chaos Report* (Yarmouthport, MA: The Standish Group International Inc., 1994). Available from http://www.standishgroup.com /sample_research/chaos_1994_1.php.

22. See note 21.

23. KPMG Project Risk Management and Information Risk Management http://www .kpmg.co.uk/kpmg/uk/IMAGE/PRMFINAL.PDF (1998).

24. See note 23.

25. See note 21.

26. Polly Schneider, "Another Trip to Hell," *CIO Magazine* (February 15, 2000). Copyright © 2002 CXO Media, Inc. Reprinted with permission.

27. Martha Heller, "Sound Off. Taking Sides on Critical IT Issues," *CIO Magazine* (March 29, 2001). Copyright © 2002 CXO Media, Inc. Reprinted with permission.

28. Tom Field, David Pearson, and Polly Schneider, "To Hell and Back," *CIO Magazine* (December 1, 1998). Copyright © 2002 CXO Media, Inc. Reprinted with permission.

29. Ann Bednarz, "IT Malpractice," *Network World* (April 8, 2002).

30. Scott Berinato, "What Went Wrong at Cisco," *CIO Magazine* (August 1, 2001). Copyright © 2002 CXO Media, Inc. Reprinted with permission.

31. Malcom Wheatley, "ERP Training Stinks," *CIO Magazine* (June 1, 2000). Copyright © 2002 CXO Media, Inc. Reprinted with permission.

32. Dawn Kawamoto and Wylie Wong, "Case Study: Oracle Customers Pay the Price," *ZDNet News* (June 28, 2001).

33. Craig Stedman, "ERP Woes Cut Grainger Profits," *ComputerWorld* (January 7, 2000).

34. See note 34.

35. See note 3.

36. Anonymous, "No Satisfaction," *CIO Magazine* (January 15, 2001). Copyright © 2002 CXO Media, Inc. Reprinted with permission.

37. "IT's Rodney Dangerfield Complex," *Information Week* (March 28, 2002). All Rights Reserved. Reprinted with permission.

38. See note 21.

39. "Snap-On Retools Amid IT Problems," *Information Week* (July 6, 1998). All Rights Reserved. Reprinted with permission.

40. "2003 Book of Numbers" (Hudson, OH: The Hackett Group, 2003).

2

Sources and Causes of IT Ineffectiveness

I think it is an immutable law in business that words are words, explanations are explanations, promises are promises—but only performance is reality. Performance alone is the best measure of your confidence, competence and courage. Only performance gives you the freedom to grow as yourself.

Just remember that: Performance is your reality. Forget everything else. That is why my definition of a manager is what it is: one who turns in the performance. No alibis to others or to one's self will change that. And when you have performed well, the world will remember it, when everything else is forgotten. And, most importantly, so will you.

—Harold Geneen, CEO, ITT[1]

In the previous chapter, we outlined the fundamental IT effectiveness dilemma facing both IT managers and the senior management team in a corporation. This chapter focuses on the symptoms that manifest themselves in ineffective IT departments, the proximate causes of those issues, and the ultimate cause of IT dysfunction: the leadership gap caused by inadequate preparation for the management responsibilities a career in IT gives to future managers.

In our careers, we have been fortunate to have worked in dozens of IT departments, in a variety of roles—technical support staff, developers, managers, consultants, and advisors. Over time, we have observed a common set of symptoms of an ineffective, struggling IT department. Most of these phenomena have very little to do with the specific technology deployed, the industry the corporation participates in, the external market conditions, or the size of the organization. Instead, regardless of those factors, the same sets of issues emerge repeatedly.

In this chapter, we broadly categorize these indicators and inventory them for the reader. With these identified, we begin to answer the question raised in Chapter 1: What are the ultimate causes of ineffective IT departments?

Symptoms of IT Distress

Although the symptoms are wide-ranging, we have identified four main categories of symptoms of trouble we have seen in distressed IT departments. A brief description of the four areas follows:

1. *Business satisfaction:* Level of satisfaction and confidence in the IT department on the part of the business.
2. *Budgeting:* IT spending, including internal resource costs, services, and capital expenditures.
3. *Projects:* IT support for business projects; internal software and hardware deployments.
4. *Staffing:* IT human resources management, team morale, and IT organization.

This chapter covers some of the symptoms we have seen in each of these categories. While this list is lengthy, it is certainly not comprehensive. The symptoms of a distressed, ineffective IT department show up in many ways. However, most manifest themselves in one of the previous categories, primarily business satisfaction, which is the ultimate arbiter of the effectiveness of the IT department.

Symptom: Business Satisfaction

The most important category by which to measure IT is satisfaction rate from the business. This, of course, presumes a well-run company where members of the senior management team and business unit heads are motivated to run their businesses with the best efficiency to produce economic gain for the company and shareholders. This "invisible hand," which keeps the business units motivated toward the right goals, in turn, puts pressure on the IT department to provide infrastructure, applications, service levels, and initiatives to help the business drive revenues, reduce costs, or achieve better control. It also assumes that business unit managers understand how IT can be used to drive those goals and generate business value. Given the statistics in Chapter 1 on level of investment in IT for the past 25 years, this, too, is a reasonable assumption. Therefore, if the business unit managers are highly motivated to drive company revenues and profits, and they clearly understand how IT can help them do so, the business will recognize if the IT department is not living up to those goals.

Many companies suffer from an enormous disconnect between the IT department and the business. This has led to the negative image of IT departments and staff as covered in the previous chapter. This IT-business disconnect and lack of satisfaction with IT services manifest in a variety of common symptoms:

- Business unit leaders (and functional heads) are dissatisfied with the performance of IT and the support for their initiatives and day-to-day requirements.
- Business managers lack confidence in IT when IT commits to a deadline or business managers discount the probability of completion.
- Business users are frustrated by their lack of control over IT; they perceive that IT "doesn't listen."
- Business doesn't believe that IT has the same goals as the overall business, most easily evidenced in the perception that IT "doesn't care about helping" the business succeed.
- Business users either don't know or don't understand priorities in the IT department.
- IT claims the business "doesn't respect them" and/or "ignores IT" and leaves IT out of decision-making processes.
- In response to IT shortcomings (real or perceived), business units hire their own, separate IT teams, which they control.
- Business units blame IT shortcomings for missed business opportunities or failed projects.
- Business units create and implement systems without input or help from IT.
- Business units bring IT into decision making that affects systems at the last minute (or not at all).
- IT department insulates itself from the rest of the organization and does not communicate or socialize with business units or other functional areas.

Symptom: Spending/Budgeting

The second potential area of weakness in the IT department is costs. Properly managing IT investment (and measuring the return on the investment) is treated in several chapters in this book. In discussing IT spending, we include not just the actual IT budget but all spending on technology in the company, including technology spending in the business units, on any technology related labor, technology consumables, outside technology services, hardware, software, and other capital.

We have observed that often IT managers and staff have trouble showing sensitivity to the effect of cost on the bottom line. The "customer" of the IT department, usually a business unit manager, is quite familiar with assessing costs in terms of how they affect the bottom line profitability of their division or organization. This means, given average profit margins of 10 percent for a company, that the business unit manager, both intellectually and, most importantly, viscerally, understands that spending a dollar on something "costs" approximately $10 in revenue to cover it. This P&L-focused view of costing means that incremental investments in staff, services, or equipment are carefully and clinically scrutinized, and that the business unit manager makes the investment only after he or she is convinced that it is essential and that it will return more to the business than it costs. Further, they will monitor the investments and projects to be sure that the promised business returns are realized.

We have not found this keen awareness of the "cost of costs" to be present in IT managers and staff, who have generally not had experience in a line role where they are responsible for managing both the costs and revenue sides of a profit-and-loss statement. For example, a junior manager over a 15-person IT shop had submitted a requisition for a server that cost more than $20,000. Although it was clear that a less robust, less powerful model would suit just as well, her response to the notion of a downgrade was "Look, its only $20,000; we have over $100 million in revenues." This, unfortunately, is often the perspective from IT. We reminded the manager that to "cover" the cost of the server would require a sales team to sell (and successfully deliver) more than $200,000 in products and services.

There is ample evidence of this behavior at the end of the fiscal year in many companies in the mad scramble by IT personnel to spend unused IT budget dollars on items that may or may not be good investments for the company. Typically the money is consumed in overpurchasing goods and services from vendors who are trying to make year-end sales goals. The vendor entices the IT staff with discounts and incentives on items like disk storage and software licenses that have only marginal benefit for the company. These funds are also used on training that may have no relevance to the skills needed to run IT or complete upcoming projects. Unfortunately, the IT budget is viewed as "monopoly money" and not real dollars that might be better spent in other parts of the company, for instance, funding for an additional salesperson or dollars sent back to the company treasury to preserve operating cash.

This phenomenon leads companies to see IT as an endless sink for resources. As observed in the previous chapter, this spendthrift flippancy by IT concerning costs has contributed to the attitude of the many companies. In an IT satisfaction survey by researchers Lacity and Hirscheim, the majority of the companies "see their IT department as a necessary, but burdensome, cost pit."[2]

Although less common, the reverse problem can happen as well. IT departments can be underinvesting. This is often caused by timidity on the part of the IT managers who do not work to push their agendas through, or by business unit managers and a senior management team who do not "believe" in the value of technology. The effect of underinvestment on a company can be just as corrosive as out-of-control spending. Companies can fail to achieve the benefits attendant with the quality use of technology; after all, investments in technology have accounted for more than two-thirds of the productivity growth in the past half-decade. Companies who consistently underinvest in technology are at risk for higher than necessary cost structures, missed opportunities in new markets, and erosion of share in existing markets by aggressive competitors who find ways to serve their customers better with technology. Ironically, companies in this position often get caught in a downward spiral; their unwillingness to make smart technology investments drives away the talented technology professionals who could potentially help them realize gains from well-executed IT spending.

Typical symptoms of an IT department that is out of control on spending or is underinvesting include:

- Spending more than peer group companies on IT (percentage of revenue or other relevant measure).
- Large quarter-to-quarter or year-to-year expansion of IT budgets without associated expansion of business volumes.
- Large quarter-to-quarter or year-to-year expansion of capital expenditure without associated business imperative or retirement of capital being replaced.
- High levels of outside purchasing, particularly services or consultants.
- Company failing to cover or exceed cost of capital on IT projects or other capital spending (IT dollars not achieving same value as they could in other parts of the company).
- Continuous flow of "emergency" requisitions from IT for headcount, services, equipment, or software.
- IT management has difficulty forecasting IT costs annually or quarterly.
- Ongoing large budget variances (positive or negative) in IT department; high budget variances in top-level categories of IT budget (staff, services, capital expenditures). Chapter 3 outlines the key drivers of IT spending and provides a starter set of benchmarks by which companies may measure themselves.
- Technology infrastructure does not have capacity or capability to support business initiatives.

Symptom: Projects

One of the best measures of the overall competence of an IT department is its ability to successfully manage projects. Poor project execution by IT is one of the largest complaints from business users. Although many IT managers and team members are often exposed to, or are even well versed in, the mechanics of project management, the actual results do not reflect their supposed capabilities.

IT departments usually are part of projects that are internal to IT (they involve no one outside the department; e.g., server upgrades, e-mail system rollouts) or external (involve some level of coordination with areas outside IT; e.g., financial package implementations, sales force automation software implementations). We have not observed any appreciable differences between the success rates between these internally directed projects and those that involve significant external coordination. This implies that IT managers struggle with the fundamentals of good project management.

We have found that these struggles are not contained to any particular piece of the project management discipline, but instead run the spectrum from project scoping, ROI calculation and business value justification, requirements gathering, business process mapping, team building, planning, execution, tracking, and completion.

A major source of project ineffectiveness is the overall management of project demand within the IT—creating potential project inventories, prioritizing the projects, determining the baseline project capacity of the IT department, and ensuring that only the number of projects supported by that capacity are allowed to be open simultaneously.

Some of the trouble in IT departments, particularly concerning project completion, is due to the notion, propagated for quite some time, that the business is a "customer" of the IT department. While there is some merit to this notion, it has led IT teams to adopt a "customer is always right philosophy." Without negotiation (or even protest), the IT team continues to absorb a barrage of project requests and to-do items from the business. Business managers quite reasonably assume that the capacity to complete the projects is available, or the IT management would reject the request. Instead, IT signs up for yet another project that, as 200th on a list of 200, is doomed before it begins. Four months later, on the project due date, a very unhappy business manager reminds the IT department that they are the "customer" and the cycle continues.

The typical IT department we are asked to assist easily has more than 100 projects "on the books." These projects are at every level of magnitude (with projects such as "repair the system clock on the backup server" aggregated at the same level as "migrate servers from Windows NT to Windows XP"). IT managers often confuse their to-do lists and their projects lists, hopelessly comingling both.

Most often, there is significant overlap in the project inventory. What may be listed as a project in one part of the inventory is actually a substep of yet another project in the inventory. In one client engagement, just based on overlap elimination alone, we reduced the project list from more than 160 projects to fewer than 50. For example, auditing and purchasing server licenses and upgrading server memory could both be substeps in a larger project to migrate the servers to a new operating system.

Aggravating matters further, the projects have widely varying creation dates, or worse, no date. Rarely has the business rationale, or business owner, for the project been documented, to say nothing of a cost benefit or return-on-investment analysis. This makes culling projects whose relevance has long passed challenging.

Finally, each of the projects is "underway," each in varying stages of completion, but far from 100 percent. In a misguided effort to please the business, IT departments often fail to complete one project before starting another. The result is a quagmire of multiple, often contradictory, efforts that, in aggregate, never seem to be completed.

Common symptoms of an IT department struggling with project management issues include:

- No clear successes to point to on the project front; no record of the last successful project completed.
- Multiple project inventories; no consolidated project list.
- No distinction between "internal" IT projects versus those that must coordinate with the business.
- Confusion between to-do lists and projects.
- Large numbers of projects (greater than 100).
- No project charters for projects underway.
- Slight progress on the entire list of projects in inventory instead of substantial and real progress on a limited subset of priority projects.
- No relationship between IT team capacity to execute projects matched to the number of projects (and required labor capacity) allowed to be underway simultaneously. IT team capacity to execute projects has not been calculated.
- Multiple, simultaneous, uncoordinated projects underway.
- No framework (or even attempt) to prioritize projects based on business value, risk, existing system adequacy, ease of completion, or other relevant factors.
- No clearly set individual responsibility for project management or completion (responsibility at team level only or responsibility split between two or more people).
- Project documentation (scope, requirements, work plans, and deliverables) incomplete or missing.
- System projects that are completed have poor quality and reliability and require constant patching and rework.

Symptom: Staffing

An often overlooked set of symptoms of a struggling IT department manifests itself in the human resources and staffing area. Often, the first refuge of a beleaguered IT manager in charge of a distressed IT department is the addition of staff.

As so famously outlined in Fredrick P. Brooks' classic text on technology project management and organization, *The Mythical Man-Month,* adding capacity to an already disorganized, chaotic, mismanaged environment is simply the recipe for more cost, not better results.[3] The addition of capacity in these cases often obscures the issues even further. It is difficult for organizations to absorb a high number of new staff in a short period and still be productive.

Because the IT director in a distressed department is, by definition, having difficulty managing, they most often, ironically, also have trouble identifying the very talent most likely to be of use in turning the situation around. The result is that new staff are of average or below quality, or at best, deficient in the very skills and knowledge most needed. Often, the IT managers turn to their social circle for sourcing of new candidates. This complicates matters even further because of the negative consequences from the mixing of business and personal agendas in the office.

Because the capacity additions are made as part of a panicked response, they are not part of a clear, well-thought-out plan and, therefore, do not have clearly defined roles and responsibilities. The resulting distorted organization chart creates responsibility gaps and overlaps that lead to even further chaos. Inexperienced new managers struggle with the inherent ambiguity of a rapidly changing organization, and seasoned staffers have trouble keeping track of the rapidly changing plan.

The final blow to the IT departments comes as the best players realize that the situation is hopeless. Morale among those seasoned staff that are "in the know" sinks rapidly. High morale is found only among the newest team members who have not yet had time to grasp the situation. Those with options outside the company (again, ironically, the very team members who are most likely to have the highest positive impact) begin to flee. The resulting replacement hiring continues to lower the average ability in the department and contributes further to the issues attendant with large numbers of new staff.

The IT director begins spending more time behind closed doors hoping for a miracle. Eventually, the issues in IT become a burning platform for senior management, and a major housecleaning ensues.

This pattern of failure, reflected in the following staffing symptoms, is one that we have observed in multiple clients struggling with IT challenges:

- No ownership of results by IT, particularly IT management.
- Worried IT staff.
- Large number of recent hires (greater than 30 percent of staff members have less than one year of tenure).
- Organization chart not clearly defined (or entirely missing) as to operations support and application support.

- Disparate titles; no standardization of roles and responsibilities; no clearly documented job responsibilities at any level of the IT organization.
- High (or no) attrition in IT department; attrition disproportionately high among tenured staff.
- Large volume of gossip in IT department.
- Inadequate (or unsatisfying) interaction between IT staff and rest of company.
- Strong morale dichotomy: newest staff members with adequate or high morale; exceedingly low morale among staff with most tenure.
- Inexperienced IT managers (no previous management experience, or experience in only a subset of the disciplines within IT).
- Little or no screening of new hires to department (in-person interview screening only).
- Sourcing of candidates from social circles (friends and family members of managers or other IT team members; from same neighborhood or other nonbusiness association).
- Excessive consumption of vacation time or sick leave by tenured staff.
- Inordinate number of team members "working from home."
- Disengaged management (IT director or managers difficult to find, behind closed doors, taking excessive vacation, or other offsite activities).
- Constant infighting and bickering between business and IT and within IT.

Proximate and Ultimate Causes of IT Ineffectiveness

In most departments, there are nearly as many obvious causes as symptoms. With every failure, it is easy to spot a multitude of potential causes (e.g., "The implementation project failed because the team never clearly defined scope and didn't do requirements gathering before selecting a vendor").

The most common categories of causes of ineffectiveness are:

- *Business turmoil:* Changes to the business because of external or internal pressures that manifest themselves in radical changes in demand on the IT department:
  - —Changes to the business model: New lines of business, new operating models, new sales and distribution channels.
  - —Changes to external entities: More customers or suppliers, or more transactions with customers and suppliers.

—Merger and acquisition activity: New business units to be integrated, along with associated staff, applications, data, customers, suppliers.

—Divestiture: Business units being carved off; disaggregating of data and separation of systems.

—Changes to business profitability: Higher profitability driving investment in IT and increased pressure on increased IT capability; lower profitability driving cost pressures to IT.

—Rapid revenue growth of the company requiring new/rapid response to changes from IT.

—Additional support for disparate geographies required from IT, particularly requiring international support.

—Multiple technologies in place for operations, development, and database creating "technology chaos" and slowing down every initiative.

- *Vendor management:* Use of hardware, software, and services vendors not capable of supporting the business; poor selection and weak ongoing management of vendors:

—Vendors and service providers that were appropriate for a smaller company, but have not scaled with growth in the company.

—Poorly performed vendor selection and implementation.

—Weak management of vendors.

—Weak or nonexistent standard setting; wide variety of disparate technologies and vendors creating a chaotic, heterogeneous environment.

- *Staffing and communications:* Inexperienced and insular management style alienates the IT team and business; business uses IT ineffectiveness as an excuse for its own shortcomings:

—Business unit leaders take no interest in IT and use it to finger point and lay blame.

—IT makes little or no effort to socialize with the business.

—IT leadership is usually in the role for the first time; IT director has limited experience managing people, growth, and setting technology direction.

—IT director is unable to identify good new hires and resorts to personal contacts for sourcing.

—Department lacks ability to attract the "right" talent; issue goes beyond technical capabilities to inability to recruit team-oriented achievers.

—Poor staff management, hiring; unclear organization and roles/responsibilities.

—Rapid growth in IT department—large numbers of staff with fewer than one to two years with the company and/or fewer than two to three years in technology.

—Each decision approached as a one-off proposition resulting in suboptimal decision making for the department at large.

- *Financial and risk management:* Team does not understand the critical link between expenditures on IT and the benefits, cost-reduction, or incremental revenue; team does not make (or even contemplate) effective cost-benefit trade-offs:

    —No attempt to calculate or document return on investment for projects or other IT expenditures.

    —No record of ROI for previous projects; no analysis of ROI for proposed projects.

    —No understanding of cost of additional expenditures to company profits; no comprehension of marginal-spend versus marginal-benefit.

    —IT managers consistently "overinsure" system engineering at significant expense.

    —IT managers engage in "sunk cost fallacy" and continue to plow additional money into clearly losing projects or technologies.

    —IT director focuses on optimizing each project on a one-off basis instead of the overall company.

All of these causes provide some level of explanation for failings in the IT department. However, they also share a common thread. Evolutionary biologists have a behavior model for how organisms adapt. This model, first presented by Ernst Mayr in *Science* in 1961, makes a distinction between *proximate* causes—the most obvious explanations for behavioral phenomena—and *ultimate* causes—root causes that are the behind-the-scenes driver of the proximate causes.[4]

This behavior model is particularly relevant in the case of the dysfunctional IT department. In attempting to "fix" the IT department, the senior management team (and sometimes IT leadership) gets caught up in chasing the proximate causes to problems, such as those previously inventoried. This can be confusing and demoralizing, because new proximate causes continually emanate from what we believe are the ultimate causes—lack of experienced leadership from IT management and lack of engagement from senior management.

Most new IT managers are woefully inadequately prepared to begin taking on their new responsibilities. The skills and competencies required to survive, let alone excel, at managing a functional department in a corporation are quite different from those required to excel as a staff member in that same department. In few professions is the gap between doing and managing so profound as in IT.

One of the primary causes of this difficulty is the internal split between the functions that the IT manager must successfully oversee. As Chapter 4 shows, most IT departments are organized into two large activity areas split between operations and applications. IT managers usually have been trained and promoted from one or the other of these two areas and, therefore, have had little experience managing (or even interacting) with team members outside their subfunction.

In addition to lacking experience with half of the IT functions that the novice manager is newly responsible for, the skills and knowledge required to be effective are vastly different. Exhibit 2.1 summarizes the skills developed and mastered by IT professionals before promotion to IT management levels, as contrasted with the list of skills required for success as an IT director or manager shown in Exhibit 2.2.

This gap between the pre-promotion skills learned as an applications manager, developer, or operations specialist and the skills required to succeed as an IT director is the root cause of many of the woes discussed in this and the preceding chapter.

Newly minted IT directors find themselves in an entirely different role, with high expectations from their senior management team. To exacerbate matters, the new manager is usually reporting to a nontechnical professional, most often the corporate CFO. This means that at the very moment the IT director needs the most guidance and support, it is unavailable.

This finding has been the primary diagnosis in many of the IT turnarounds that we have completed in the past few years. For many of the senior managers we work with, the notion that something as simple as leadership can be the ultimate cause of problems in the IT department can be difficult to swallow. A simple answer to what seems to be an impossible-to-solve knot of issues is particularly tough to believe when many of the issues, at the surface, appear to be technical in nature.

PRE-PROMOTION SKILLS
System requirements gathering and analysis.
Programming and systems development.
Application design and management.
System configuration.
Business process documentation.
Technology implementation.
Systems administration.
Systems performance management.
Technical, data, and applications architecture design and management.
Limited project management.
Upward reporting relationship with technical manager.

Exhibit 2.1 Skills Developed Pre-Promotion

POST-PROMOTION SKILLS
Management of both applications and operations portions of IT function.
Vendor selection, negotiation, and management.
Hiring, evaluating, managing, motivating, developing, promoting, and firing team members.
Decision making.
Cost containment.
Cost/benefit estimating; project economics estimation.
Budgeting.
Risk management.
Communications with business units and senior management.
Resource and project prioritization.
IT organizational design.
Standard setting and enforcement.
IT measurement and effectiveness.
Coordination of multiple, disparate projects, and initiatives across business units and internal functions.
Determining best use of scarce economic resources (staff, budget, time).
Maintenance of *steady-state* service levels for basic IT services.
Upward reporting relationship to nontechnical business manager, COO, or CFO.

Exhibit 2.2   Skills Required Post-Promotion

If these arguments are not compelling enough on their own, we usually point to the empirical evidence we have gathered as part of the IT effectiveness. We have seen repeatedly that most of the proximate issues resolve themselves quite rapidly once the IT leadership challenges have been solved. Two client examples illustrate this:

1. Our client, a software development company, relied on the IT department for not only internal applications support, but also development of the company's core product. Over the year before our work with the client, the IT department had trebled in size. Many projects were at a standstill, with little hope of near-term completion. The product itself was producing inaccurate results, and even outright operating failures. The internal and external customer frustration with the IT group had reached a fever pitch. In response, IT had become defensive and belligerent. The impasse between business and IT seemed truly unbridgeable.

Working with the client senior management team and the technical team, in short order, we implemented the leadership, cost-containment, organization, demand management, and vendor management principles outlined in this book. Within three months, the IT staff had been reduced by more than 70 percent, containing the out-of-control costs. Not only had the product accuracy and failure issues been fixed, but also the performance of the product itself had been measurably improved, much to the delight of the customer base.

2. A mid-sized manufacturing company, already under intense cost pressure, was informed by IT management that the hardware on which all of the corporate systems were running had to be replaced due to capacity constraints. The company's peak order season was threatened. System capacity issues from previous seasons had nearly capsized the business, and the anticipated increases in order volumes might very well result in complete systems failure. The company could ill afford the nearly $1 million in capital expenditures it would take to completely replace its systems hardware, to say nothing of the business disruption and risk that are part of any major systems overhaul.

When the client retained us to assume management of the IT department, our first task was to identify opportunities to reduce systems load. In the previous four years of systems capacity issues, many ideas had been considered, but no testing or attempts at implementation had been made. Within a few short weeks, the IT team had identified a combination of data purging, database tuning, tight-loop code rewrites, and usage smoothing that reduced the overall system load by more than 40 percent, creating more than enough room to make it smoothly through the peak season and beyond.

What makes these client examples both interesting and highly relevant is that the fundamental changes were made in the leadership and management of the IT department. In every case, the major elements in the IT department remained the same: the same systems, the same technology, the same hardware, the same infrastructure, the same business users, and most importantly, the same technical staff. The only variable introduced was the management of the IT staff, which produced measurable and dramatic results in surprisingly short order.

While laying most of the responsibility for IT ineffectiveness at the feet of IT managers (or more accurately, at the lack of preparation most IT managers receive), it would be remiss to remain silent on the contribution of senior management to the situation.

We have found that, although IT is rightly considered a *function*, along with departments such as human resources, finance, accounting, and marketing, it also has hallmarks of a business unit. More so than any other functional department, IT is required to interact with, and understand the processes of, every business unit and every functional unit. IT departments are, in many ways, the nerve center of the entire company.

Further, as outlined in Chapter 1, technology, as deployed by corporate IT departments, has been the largest driver of productivity for corporations. It is a key component for most company initiatives focused on cost reduction or revenue building. At best, IT is a source of competitive advantage, productivity gains, and new capabilities and, at a minimum, the largest nondirect expense for most companies. In every case, it cannot be ignored. Yet, in many cases, senior management refuses to engage with IT, and so it remains managed as neither a function nor a business unit. This happens for a variety of reasons, including disinterest, uncertainty of how to manage technology issues, or no understanding of how IT can help the business. In every case, it is demoralizing to IT and produces a resentful, marginalized IT management team.

In working with one client, we were having particular difficulty convincing the senior team to pay attention to IT issues. To draw their attention to the importance of the IT department, we took the budgets of each of the eight strategic business units in descending order of size. We then inserted the IT department into its proper part of the sequence according to budget size. If considered a business unit, IT would be fourth largest in the company, well ahead of the smaller business units. Faced with this analysis, all agreed that, in proportion to its cost to the company, IT certainly did not receive enough attention from senior management.

Steps to Effective IT Management

Although our complete prescription for implementing effective management of the IT department is covered in this book, we are often asked for the short version of our program. A checklist of specific steps across five broad areas that can be taken in dysfunctional IT departments to improve performance and begin reaping the rewards of a productive relationship with the business follows:

1. Improve IT management:
    - Implement an IT steering committee as a "virtual CIO" to provide advice and leadership to the IT director and help speedily resolve issues between business and IT.
    - The committee should be composed of the top 5 to 10 senior managers in the business; they should be required to attend every meeting.
    - Upgrade management talent in the IT department by hiring the right director.
    - The IT steering committee should source the candidates and hire the new director as a senior manager instead of a senior programmer.
    - Clean up the IT organization chart; this means no "floating boxes" and clean, clear lines of responsibility between applications management and operations without gaps or overlaps in coverage.
    - Every staff member should have a shorter-than-one-page roles and responsibilities document posted at his or her desk.

2. Add basic project management disciplines:
   - Establish a single, well-documented master inventory of projects.
   - Determine the ROI or business benefits for each project.
   - Projects that do not improve revenues, reduce costs, or improve control over the business should be ignored.
   - Prioritize projects by their benefits, difficulty, and adequacy of the current systems, generating a force-ranked list.
   - Determine the intrinsic project capacity of the IT department.
   - Limit the number of open projects to that capacity.
   - Expect this number to be shockingly small and disconcerting, but be comforted by the notion that the projects will actually be accomplished.
   - Assign a specific person from the IT department to be responsible for the management and execution of the project, and have them report progress in a five-minute update to the IT steering committee on a weekly basis.
   - Each team lead must develop a clear work plan for accomplishing the assigned project, with work tasks, time lines, deliverables, dependencies, and required resources clearly defined.
3. Manage vendors:
   - Determine which vendors are good, productive partners and which are sapping the IT budget with bloated fees and unproductive products, services, or billable hours.
   - Migrate business to the former and dismiss the latter.
   - Insist on favorable contracts and pricing in return for vendor exclusivity.
   - Migrate the technology platform in the department to homogeneity to facilitate ease of management and project execution.
   - Negotiate hard with vendors for best pricing, and aggressively manage them after the sale.
   - Ask vendors how they measure their own client-satisfaction performance internally, and require them to produce a report card on themselves at reasonable intervals.
   - If they don't know how to measure themselves internally, get them out.
   - If they do, hold them to the periodic reporting and help them improve their services with clear feedback.
4. Fiscal management/budgeting:
   - Recognize that most companies must generate $10 in revenues to cover every $1 spent in IT.
   - Build a reputation for saving the company money by "making do" and reserve capital expenditure requests for must-have items. Although

more difficult, IT directors must become a business resource for the senior management team by suggesting ways to lower the company's overall operational costs through use of IT.

- If budget variances appear, proactively explain them to senior management and provide fair warning for surprise capital or operating expenditures.
- Build trust with the CFO by avoiding typical agency issues that accompany the budgeting process which give IT teams a bad reputation for being focused on the constant acquisition of new toys.

5. Improve relationship with the business:
  - Reduce finger pointing between IT and business users by initiating a "seat rotation" that has key IT staff members sitting with the businesses they support one to two days per week.
  - IT director should have a quota of two lunches per week with business unit managers, functional managers, or members of the IT steering committee.
  - Add effective business-user relationship management to the appraisal process for all IT team members.

With the right leadership in place and enthusiastic engagement from the senior management team, the IT department can lead the company in management excellence.

As evidence that the IT department can lead the entire company toward excellence, we share a note received from the CFO of a client for whom we had previously completed an extensive IT effectiveness engagement:

> We are a totally different company today than when you were here last year. It all started with the IT area. [Based on the work completed there,] we have reorganized every phase of our operations and continue to refine our processes.

NOTES

1. Harold S. Geneen and Alvin Moscow, *Managing* (New York: Doubleday, 1984), p. 285.
2. Marcy Lacity and Rudy Hirschheim, *Information Systems Outsourcing, Myths, Metaphors and Realities* (Chichester, England: John Wiley & Sons, 1993).
3. Frederick P. Brooks, *The Mythical Man-Month* (Reading, MA: Addison-Wesley, 1995).
4. Ernst Mayr, "Cause and Effect in Biology," *Science*, vol. 134 (November 10, 1961).

3

Information Technology Costs

You cannot ask us to take sides against arithmetic.

—Winston Churchill[1]

There are only two qualities in the world: efficiency and inefficiency, and only two sorts of people; the efficient and the inefficient.

—George Bernard Shaw, *John Bull's Other Island,* 1904, Act IV[2]

This chapter outlines the process for benchmarking IT spending in a corporation. It suggests general determinants and targets for IT spending and presents multiple methods of calculating benchmarks as well as the pros and cons of each. It also introduces historical IT spending trends in aggregate and by industry.

The chapter is organized around the IT cost benchmarking process. First, we introduce some of the historical spending levels of U.S. corporations. Second, we outline the various methods for benchmarking and discuss key IT cost drivers, which can affect IT spending, and the subsequent attempt to benchmark spending. Finally, we analyze scale economies that can be achieved as a company grows and then provide recommendations for aligning IT spending with the corporate business strategy.

Benchmarking approaches discussed here are intended to be guidelines for spending—not a specific recommendation as to the precise amount for a given company to spend on IT. First, the data provided by industry group is a blunt metric. The IT manager must perform some independent analysis to gather peer group information to add additional meaning and context to the data. Second, the analysis provided here is best used as a reasonableness test. That is, is the current level of spending reasonable in light of factors such as industry, peer group spending, and other company-specific attributes? The bottom line is that the IT manager must justify all spending on technology in relation to the benefits it generates for the business.

This chapter highlights the importance of the proper management of IT expenses, as one of the largest components of spending in organizations, yet one of the most mismanaged areas.

Why This Topic Is Important

In the final analysis, the IT manager is evaluated on the level of output from the IT department compared to the input required to produce the results. In this case, the output is effective technology that drives productivity, profits, user satisfaction, competitive advantage, and new revenue streams. The input is capital in terms of labor and dollars.

Unfortunately for the IT manager, the measurement of both variables has traditionally been poor. The input in terms of expenses required to fund the IT department is generally readily available; however, the true total input requires some investigation of IT spending outside the IT department and is typically overlooked. The output is also not measured rigorously. The result is a seemingly clear but understated knowledge of IT spending paired with almost no knowledge of benefits (output), making justification of the spending, or a precise linkage between the spending and business benefits difficult.

The next step in the process is a justification of IT spending based on the industry benchmark, but as we discuss later, this process can be flawed and result in widely different ratios and recommendations for IT spending.

Compounding the issue is the fact that peer spending information on IT is difficult to find. As a result, companies are often left with no basis to create or adjust the IT budget and resort to the baseline set by the previous year's budget. Meanwhile, the company is challenged by a technologically advanced competitor that is reaping huge cost savings from being fully integrated with its customers and suppliers.

It is vitally important that the IT manager understand how to benchmark IT spending and develop recommendations for general spending levels to achieve the company's strategic objectives.

This chapter presents to the IT manager:

- Different methods used to benchmark IT spending.
- How to calculate ranges of appropriate IT spending.
- Key drivers of IT spending and their effect on the IT budget.
- Historical IT spending as a percent of revenue.
- What is included in the definition of *IT spending*.
- Direct or indirect IT costs generally unaccounted for—the "hidden" costs of IT.

- Spending statistics by expense category.
- Technologies and activities that benefit from economies of scale.
- Aligning IT spending with business goals.

Chapter 15 further outlines calculating the business value of projects or IT initiatives based on their costs and benefits.

Introduction to Benchmarking IT Spending

By any measure, U.S. corporations have been faced with ever-escalating information technology spending. "In 1999 alone, U.S. firms invested $393 billion in [hardware, software, and telecommunications equipment] which accounted for more than 30 percent of all nonresidential fixed investment," according to Kevin Stiroh of the Federal Reserve Bank of New York.[3] At the same time, executives are attempting to determine the benefit of this spending in terms of productivity, profits, and competitive advantage. As Chapter 1 illustrates, after years of questioning the linkage between IT spending and business productivity, economists are finally beginning to see the link between IT spending and higher productivity.

The frustration with increased costs and the lack of a clear correspondence between IT expenditures and profits as well as the proportionally large operating expense outlays, are the reasons IT costs are a major concern for senior executives in U.S. corporations and have led to the IT dilemma outlined in Chapter 1. IT spending can range anywhere from 1 percent to 10 percent of overall company revenues, depending on the dynamics of the industry and the specific situation of the company. For example, a company turning $1 billion in annual revenue might spend anywhere from $10 million to $100 million on information technology each year. This order of magnitude difference in what is the "right" level of IT spending is explained by a variety of macroeconomic factors, including industry, size, competitive environment, and customer concentration.

In spite of significant expenditures and corresponding financial exposure, many companies do not have a clear understanding of actual dollar amounts of direct IT costs, much less hidden IT costs scattered throughout their organization. Further, there is a lack of understanding of how to benchmark their IT spending—whether they are overspending or underspending in the area.

Company senior managers do not generally know how to determine what their IT costs should be. What should be considered reasonable expense in information technology? What are the key predictive variables that drive IT costs? The senior manager in a company often has only the historical IT budget and trends as a test of reasonableness of spending.

The operating budget for IT is not only one of the largest expenses for companies, but also is becoming the single largest capital expense for corporations. Information technology was 30 percent of the capital expense budget in 2000, according to Gartner Group. Gartner predicts IT to be 50 percent of the capital expense budget by 2010.[4]

Major drivers of increased spending in the past decade include client-server conversions, Year 2000 remediation, enterprise resource planning (ERP) package implementations, e-commerce, Internet, customer resource management (CRM), and mobile computing and wireless initiatives. Over the past eight years, savings in declining hardware prices have been outweighed by increased spending on personnel, increased software costs, and spending on outside service providers, as the benefits from IT have increased and the IT operating environment has become more complex.

Understanding current spending on IT is critically important as a first step for assessing whether a company is overspending or underspending on IT. Developing appropriate benchmarks is difficult and takes careful analysis and context setting. A simple benchmark such as the average IT spending-to-revenue ratio, should serve only as a starting point for further study. There are multiple factors that should be considered, and we highlight some of the most important ones in this chapter.

Paul Strassman, a leading thinker on the valuation of business IT investments and a regular columnist in *ComputerWorld*, emphasized this point in his article, "Misleading Metric":

> IT spending is not a characteristic of an industry, but a unique attribute of how a particular firm operates. CIOs should stop taking an easy (and easily manipulated) path for explaining their spending plans. Don't ask what others tell you is the "right" spending, but commit to what profits you can deliver for the company, whatever the cost.[5]

However, based on these top-level benchmarks, the IT director can at least determine some ranges of spending in which the IT department should be operating.

IT Spending—Trends, Comparisons, and Benchmarking

In this section, we examine IT investment trends and spending comparisons from leading IT research companies. We present historical IT spending of sample companies and make predictions on future spending. As we have noted, IT managers should determine the applicability and relevance to their companies and specific situations.

Additionally, we present an approach for benchmarking IT spending within a company. We discuss multiple methods, including comparisons versus peer groups based on revenue, employees, expense ratio, and other factors.

The section also examines how to measure the return on IT spending, identifying hidden IT costs, and presents average IT spending metrics by budget category (hardware, software, services, resources).

The IT Capital Budget

The capital budget is used for allocating the costs of long-term outlays for assets that depreciate over a long period of time to the periods over which the asset is used. For example, a piece of manufacturing equipment, which may have a useful life of 15 years, is a capital budget item that affects cash and the balance sheet. Capital budget items affect the income statement only as the asset is depreciated over time. Capital assets are usually long-term assets that are not bought or sold in the normal course of business. In general, the term includes fixed assets, such as land, building, equipment, furniture, and fixtures.

For the IT department, capital expenditures could include hardware, equipment, purchases of packaged software, and, in some cases, application development. In many cases, accounting rules allow most of the expenses for large projects, whose value will be realized over a long period of time, to be capitalized. Chapter 15 discusses this process in further detail.

Because these are large cash outlays for corporations, it is worth examining the trend in spending for capital assets. Further, the IT portion of the capital budget is usually associated with large projects, such as hardware replacements, desktop rollouts, or other systems renewal efforts.

Exhibit 3.1 demonstrates that the percentage of IT spending devoted to the IT capital budget varies by industry. It covers a period of 20 years—from 1990 to 2010—and shows that the IT capital budget is projected to consume nearly one-half percent of the corporate capital budget by 2010. Corporations are obviously anticipating large payoffs from investments in technology and systems—and are allocating their expenditures correspondingly.[6]

While capital spending trends by industry provide some benchmarking information, the IT manager should treat each purchase hitting the capital budget as they would any other corporate investment. That is, it must generate financial value for the company and generate benefits in excess of the costs, producing a rate of return greater than the hurdle rate set for company investments, or for other possible projects or investments within the company. If the investment cannot stand on its own merit, it should not be an investment in your portfolio. The fact that a competitor is spending significant dollars on new hardware or an ERP system has only tangential relevancy to the company's needs. It is useful to know where competitors are investing,

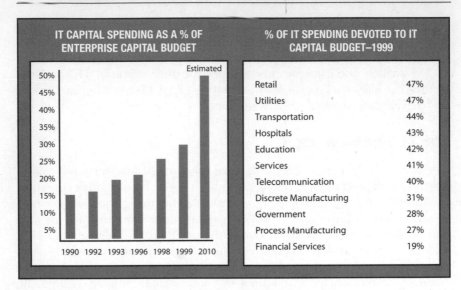

IT CAPITAL SPENDING AS A % OF ENTERPRISE CAPITAL BUDGET	% OF IT SPENDING DEVOTED TO IT CAPITAL BUDGET–1999	
	Retail	47%
	Utilities	47%
	Transportation	44%
	Hospitals	43%
	Education	42%
	Services	41%
	Telecommunication	40%
	Discrete Manufacturing	31%
	Government	28%
	Process Manufacturing	27%
	Financial Services	19%

Exhibit 3.1   IT Capital Budgeting

and what they believe their outlay will mean for their costs, pricing, and services they can deliver to customers. However, the company may or may not need to make and equivalent investment given the employee base, specific services offered, vendor services, and so on.

Total IT Spending

IT spending over the past two decades has risen dramatically as a percentage of revenue for North American companies. Exhibit 3.2 illustrates this growth and the major technology industry events during the period. Over time, this growth in spending has been driven by continuing advances in technology that have enabled IT departments to deliver new capabilities to their companies.[7]

In the early 1980s, personal computing, office automation capabilities on the desktop, and the advent of client server systems drove large investments in IT spending. This was followed by enormous spending in ERP software in the mid-1990s; remediation for the year 2000 technical problem; the rush to the Web; and the frenzy in spending on e-commerce, CRM and wireless platforms in the late 1990s and early 2000s. The current trend, beginning in 2001 and denoted by the dashed line on the exhibit, appears to be that IT investments will flatten, or even decline in the coming years. After the tremendous waves of investment over the past two decades, this may come as no surprise. At the end of the tremendous market gains of the 1990s and the following economic doldrums, companies may need time to fully absorb the impact of the previous IT investments and retrench. Our best estimate is that the

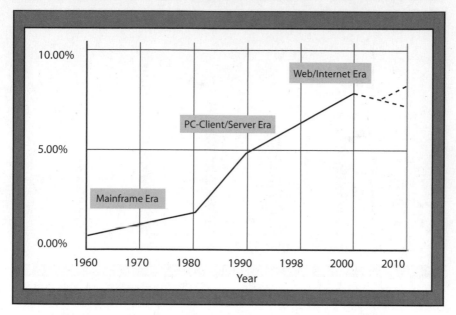

Exhibit 3.2   North American IT Spending as a Percent of Revenue

percent of spending as a percentage of revenue will decline in the near term and is likely to descend below the 7.5 percent mark.

Supporting this assertion is a survey by the META Group and Metricnet showing that IT spending may have peaked for now. Exhibit 3.3 highlights the results of that survey.[8]

This survey was composed of about 1,800 companies from various industries and sizes and reflects similar results from other surveys forecasting spending in U.S. companies. Because large companies, particularly in industries such as financial services, traditionally have heavy IT spending and elevate the averages, it is important for the user of these statistics to control for industry and size effects to properly analyze the information.

Further validation appeared in a survey of CIOs conducted by Morgan Stanley released in December of 2002. In the survey, 44 percent of CIOs described the coming year as "a year of cost containment" and 16 percent as "a year of cost reduction." Only 19 percent of respondents planned for 2003 to be "a year of new project investment." Based on the survey results, Morgan Stanley forecast IT budget growth of only 2 to 3 percent.[9]

The Quality of IT Spending

Clearly, IT spending cannot be assessed in a vacuum. There must be some return for the dollars you spend on IT. The ultimate goal is to spend on IT so long as each incremental dollar generates an appropriate return for the business.

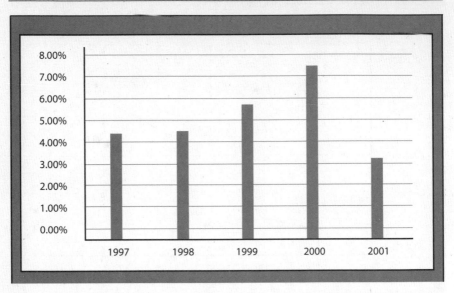

Exhibit 3.3   U.S. Corporation IT Spending as a Percent of Revenue

To help in benchmarking IT spending effectiveness, a variety of analyses may be undertaken, including:

- User satisfaction.
- Financial cost/benefit analysis.
- Financial performance versus peer group.
- Return on investment/return on assets (overall and for specific projects).
- Level of senior management objectives met.

IT spending mapped to your IT effectiveness score can illustrate the quality of your IT spending. Exhibit 3.4 is an example of this mapping.

It is acceptable to be very efficient (low cost) and have relatively lower user satisfaction if there is a conscious strategic underinvestment decision made by the company. It is unacceptable to have high costs and low user satisfaction and effectiveness. There should usually be a correspondence between IT spending and overall user satisfaction (e.g., points A and C in Exhibit 3.4). Companies that find themselves off of this linear relationship (points B and D in Exhibit 3.4) may either have unusually effective or ineffective IT departments.

Understanding where your company currently falls on this graph is a worthwhile exercise. Ensuring that a tight linkage between IT spending and user satisfaction and what levels are either required or acceptable to the company are critical in building an overall strategy for IT.

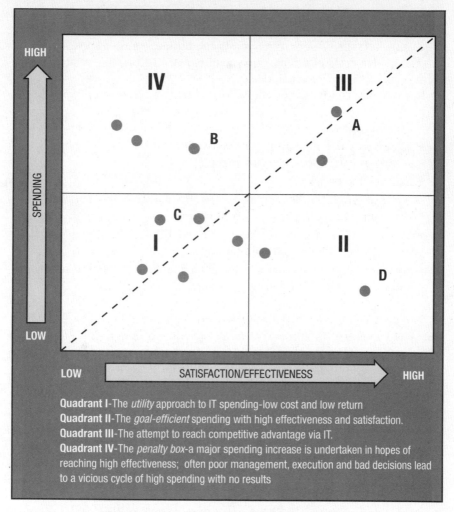

Exhibit 3.4   IT Satisfaction versus IT Spending

Other benchmarks for ensuring that IT spending is generating the proper return for the company are covered throughout this book. Other chapters specifically addressing the topic of return on IT investment include Chapters 10, 13, and 15. Chapter 16 addresses issues in measuring quality of service, user satisfaction, and other performance metrics in IT.

Defining IT Spending and Identifying Hidden Costs

Making IT spend comparisons and trend analyses even more challenging is the fact that the assessment of what comprises IT spending varies substantially from company to company and even within companies. Should the measure of IT spending include capital expenses or just income statement expenses? Does it include the IT department costs and business unit IT spending? What are the hidden costs of technology spending? Are technology-related expenditures such as telephony included?

In this analysis, we include the following when we refer to *IT spending:*

- Capital expenditures for IT projects, hardware, software, and services.
- IT services and outsourcing: Expenses for external IT services (IT consulting, research services, hosting, etc.).
- Salaries and benefits.
- Applications: Cost of implementing and enhancing application systems that support existing business systems.
- Maintenance and administration: Cost of IT staff functions plus baseline costs of running and maintaining systems.
- Voice telecommunications are usually not included except in small companies (less than $100 million revenues).[10]

The next factor that makes analysis difficult is hidden IT spending. As much as 10 percent to 20 percent of IT spending occurs outside the IT department in business unit budgets. This occurs because ineffective IT departments cause a bottleneck for projects and technology investment. Business units go around IT to complete their critical initiatives, often creating mini IT departments, additional IT vendor spend, as well as investments in hardware and software that do not show up in the IT budget. This hides a portion of IT spending and aggravates the IT ineffectiveness issues because of inconsistent technology choices.

Overall, the IT budget, plus the hidden IT costs buried in the business units or functions, provides a good measure of the total IT spend in a company.

In late 2001, we were involved in assisting a $400-million media company in calculating their IT budgets. After combing through the centralized information systems budget, we ascertained that IT spending was roughly 5 percent of revenue. We then embarked on a mission to discuss IT spending with each of 12 business units. During the fact-finding effort, we asked one question of the business unit general managers that would prove enlightening: "What percent of your business unit revenue do you spend on technology, for example, applications or programming? Do not include services that the IT department provides for you." Almost every general manager came back with the following answer: "About 5 percent." After sifting through business unit organization charts and financial statements, we determined that the general managers were right at about 4 percent to 5 percent of spending on various services, applications, and hardware. The final result was a company with an

IT budget of only 5 percent of revenue, but a total IT spend of about 9 percent of revenue. The 9 percent measure was definitely outside the range of reasonable spending for their company and helped drive them to take a hard look at the effectiveness of their IT spending. The analysis ultimately resulted in a successful cost reduction effort.

This effect pervades most companies. Gartner Group estimates that the average spend outside the IT budget for IT-related products and services is 16 percent of the companies' total IT spend.[11]

There is a wide variety of these hidden expenses that should be considered as part of the IT budget to get an enterprise-wide view of total IT spending. A sampling of these include:

- IT staffers embedded in business units or functional departments (e.g., Web developer working for the marketing department, database programmers working in the finance department, desktop support staff within a business unit).
- Outside service vendors (e.g., IT contractors, Web site hosting, technology consulting company implementing systems or software within a business unit or function with no reliance on IT).
- Software (e.g., marketing group orders Adobe Illustrator on a credit card or marketing purchase order).
- Hardware/IT fixed assets (e.g., VP of manufacturing doesn't like the standard laptop and orders one on a credit card).

There are several drivers of "hidden" IT spend. Hidden IT spending will be higher in companies where these characteristics are present:

- Loose integration between IT and business units; infrequent communication of needs and priorities.
- Subpar service levels delivered by IT, forcing business to seek alternatives.
- Slow decision making and purchasing processes in IT, creating a bottleneck for projects, hardware acquisition, and other business requests.
- Poor adherence to corporate standards for technology (software, hardware, desktops).
- Loose corporate procurement processes and standards.
- Decentralized, geographically disparate business operations.
- Weak leadership in IT.

Well-managed companies work diligently to aggregate IT spending within IT, or at least ensure that all components of IT spending can be identified and, therefore, managed. Cisco Systems estimates that only 5 percent of its total IT spend is outside the IT budget.[12] In Cisco's case, business units prioritize and approve application projects.

How to Estimate Appropriate IT Spending Levels

The popular IT press is filled with spending survey results. Reviewing these generalized IT investment trends is helpful to understand the macroeconomic activity occurring at large, however, trends are of limited use in helping determine what each individual company should plan on spending themselves. Measurement against peer groups of companies or other methodologies, as well as incorporating idiosyncratic company information, will help arrive at a more accurate answer.

While there is no industry consensus on a single correct way to estimate the appropriate level of IT spending, there are several different industry-accepted approaches that can provide a starting point for the executive:

- Comparison of IT spending as a percent of revenue against peer group of companies (industry or other comparative).
- Comparison of IT budget by company size (revenues).
- Comparison of IT spending per employee against peer group of companies (industry or other comparative).
- Formula developed by leading IT investment researcher Paul Strassman based on key drivers of IT spending.[13]

Regardless of the approach used, the initial steps to estimating target IT spending levels for a company are the same:

1. Baseline current IT spending. Because this analysis is based on current expenditures, it can be thorough and should include:
   a. Baseline IT costs: Current fixed portion of the IT budget.
   b. Variable IT costs: The variable portion of the IT budget—that changes depending on the level of business demand, service level requirements, and project work currently approved.
   c. All IT costs borne by the business units and functions in the company (see previous definition of hidden IT spending).
2. Allocate the costs to budget categories. The high-level major categories of spending may include hardware, software, staff (salaries, benefits, training), and outside services. Other breakouts may be appropriate, depending on the specific company and IT department situation. Costs aggregated in major categories will facilitate later analysis of appropriate ratios between categories (e.g., hardware to software spend ratio, staff costs to hardware spend ratio). Chapter 13 addresses this topic further.
3. Select a peer group of companies based on similarity across relevant factors such as company size, industry, geographic footprint, or business operations. Where possible, selecting public companies will often

provide for better revenue and spending data, as it may be disclosed as part of the companies' required financial filings.

After this preliminary data gathering is complete, any of the previous four comparison methods may be used. We address each of these in turn.

BENCHMARKING USING IT SPENDING AS A PERCENT OF REVENUE. IT spending averages about 3.5 percent of revenue across all industries. However, results show "for a particular industry, there does not exist a required ratio for IT spending to remain competitive."[14] Various research groups, most notably *Information Week* and the Gartner Group, have put significant effort into determining IT spending as a percent of revenue by industry group. This type of high-level estimate is useful as a starting point for determining appropriate IT spending for a specific company; the specific situations for a given industry, competitive landscape, and financial position have a significant impact on the actual number. If the peer group developed in the previous step can be used as a comparison, instead of the industry as a whole, more precision can be achieved. Senior management should not automatically increase or decrease IT budgets based on these calculations, but instead use them as a general benchmark for understanding why the right spending should be more or less in their company. Exhibit 3.5 shows IT spending as a percentage of revenue by a major industry group.

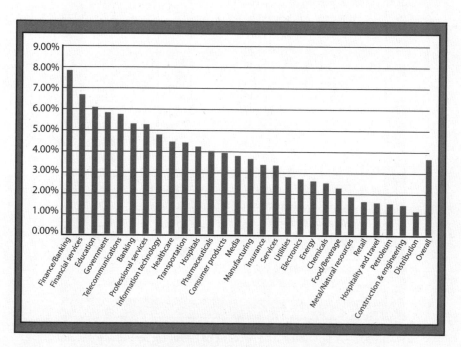

Exhibit 3.5   IT Spending as a Percent of Revenue by Industry

The overall industry average IT spending as a percent of revenue from this information is about 3.55 percent.[15] Some industry-level trends are shown in Exhibit 3.6.[16]

Several observations are worth noting from these exhibits:

- Industries with heavy concentration of knowledge workers have higher IT spending as a percent of revenue.
- Conversely, industries with a large number of physical labor employees have lower IT spending.
- Industries that are data analysis or technology intensive have high IT spending as a percent of revenue (e.g., financial services).
- High profit margin industries (financial services) have higher IT budgets than lower profit margin industries (e.g., distribution).

	Actual 2001	Estimate 2002
Financial Services	6.56	6.64
Telecommunications	5.66	6.40
Banking	5.16	5.37
Professional Services	5.13	5.12
Information Technology	4.78	5.13
Health Care	4.28	4.42
Transportation	4.25	4.17
Pharmaceuticals	4.02	3.91
Manufacturing	3.96	3.60
Consumer Products	3.94	3.64
Media	3.85	4.13
Overall	3.58	3.61
Insurance	3.54	3.49
Utilities	2.83	2.43
Electronics	2.80	2.95
Energy	2.72	2.20
Chemicals	2.66	2.68
Food/Beverage Processing	2.36	2.13
Metals/Natural Resources	1.93	2.01
Retail	1.69	1.63
Hospitality & Travel	1.62	1.55
Construction & Engineering	1.46	1.43

Exhibit 3.6   IT Spending as a Percent of Revenue by Industry Trends

Benchmarking Using IT Spending per Employee. This approach assumes that IT costs are driven by the number of knowledge workers, professionals, or individuals that use computing resources in your company.

Exhibit 3.7 shows IT spending per employee by industry, which provides the IT team another basis for comparison of existing or planned IT spending.[17]

	IT Spending Per Employee
Financial Services	$137,538
Insurance	$34,721
Energy	$25,365
Utilities	$24,509
Telecommunications	$20,002
Information Technology	$17,489
Banking	$16,612
Healthcare	$14,187
Manufacturing	$13,652
Consumer Products	$13,510
Pharmaceuticals	$13,270
Hospitality and Travel	$11,406
Chemicals	$10,822
Media	$10,006
Transportation	$9,887
Retail	$8,846
Food/Beverage	$6,884
Electronics	$5,998
Metals/Natural Resources	$5,846
Professional Services	$5,098
Construction & Engineering	$4,003
Overall	$13,968

Exhibit 3.7   IT Spending per Employee by Industry

Several observations are worth noting:

- Industries with heavy concentration of knowledge workers have higher IT spending per employee.
- Financial services is by far the heaviest spender of IT per employee.
- This metric does take into account the fact that, in many industries (e.g., retail), the majority of the workers provide physical labor and are not knowledge workers. Calculating on an end-user basis can be more relevant.
- The average spending on IT per employee across all industries is just under $14,000; the average is heavily skewed by the large spenders.

Another related analysis is to calculate the ratio of IT employees in your company as a percent of the total employee count. While this should not drive any spending considerations, it gives you a rough idea of the number of IT employees it takes to support a company. There are a number of caveats, especially as they relate to outsourcing. Many companies outsource functions, including IT. Outsourced employees are not included in the calculations shown in Exhibit 3.8 and, thus, skew the analysis.[18] We have seen averages for this ratio across all industries range from 2.2 percent to the 4.6 percent shown in Exhibit 3.9.[19] Also noteworthy is the clear staff scale economies for the IT function in larger companies. Exhibit 3.9 shows this ratio grouped by industry; as expected, information-intensive industries, such as financial services and insurance, have a high ratio.

BENCHMARKING AGAINST PEER GROUP USING COMPANY SIZE. As the company being assessed diminishes in size, it gets more difficult to compare industry averages as a measure of correct IT spending, because most of

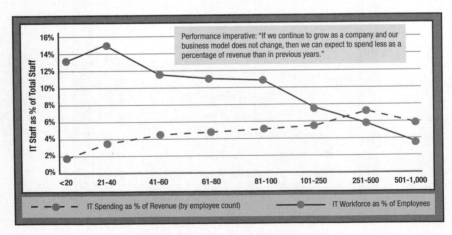

Exhibit 3.8   IT Staff by Company Size

the data is driven by public companies. Public companies are generally large in terms of employee count and revenue. As IT budgets and staff increase with company size, the company begins to enjoy economies of scale across a wide variety of IT spending categories, as well as the ability to leverage fixed costs over a larger pool of employees and operations. This makes comparison of the data presented earlier more difficult for a mid-size company that has, for example, $30 million in revenue or less.

Measuring against a peer group using company size is generally more applicable for small companies. The data presented in Exhibit 3.8 show some benchmarks for spending at a variety of business sizes.[20]

	IT Employees % of Total
Financial Services	19.90%
Insurance	11.88%
Information Technology	7.56%
Banking	7.35%
Telecommunications	7.34%
Media	6.58%
Hospitality and Travel	5.91%
Utilities	5.47%
Healthcare	4.53%
Pharmaceuticals	4.37%
Energy	4.23%
Consumer Products	3.61%
Electronics	3.28%
Chemicals	2.84%
Retail	2.54%
Professional Services	2.39%
Manufacturing	2.37%
Construction & Engineering	2.31%
Food/Beverage	2.16%
Metals/Natural Resources	2.08%
Transportation	1.90%
Overall	4.63%

Exhibit 3.9   IT Employees in Organization as a Percent of Total Employee Population

Several observations are worth noting:

- Most of the industry surveys on IT spending are made up of Fortune 1000 companies (small businesses cannot achieve economies of scale in IT spending); this measure may be more applicable.
- Small- to mid-size businesses have different spending patterns and IT needs and therefore company size should be considered in any benchmarking exercise.
- Companies begin to see benefits of economies of scale in IT after they reach approximately 500 employees.
- The average company with fewer than 20 employees spends approximately 1.7 percent of revenue on IT.
- An average company with 100 employees spends approximately 4.7 percent of revenue on IT. The number of employees drives increased IT spending.
- Companies between 251 and 500 employees spend approximately 6.7 percent of revenue on IT.
- Companies between 501 and 1,000 employees spend approximately 5.4 percent of revenue on IT.

BENCHMARKING USING LINEAR EQUATION BASED ON KEY DRIVERS OF IT SPENDING. In his book, *The Squandered Computer,* Paul Strassman, the former CIO of Xerox and a leading thinker on the value of corporate investment in IT, outlines an alternate method for calculating IT spending. His method is based on regression analysis of specific business attributes that drive IT spending.[21] Strassman proposes that a small number of variables can actually predict appropriate levels of IT spending when companies have common characteristics and similar employment structures. Employment structures include ratios of professional, clerical, and factory workers.

Strassman's linear equation method is:

$$\text{IT Budget} = K + (A \times SG\&A) + (B \times \text{Profit after tax}) + (C \times \text{Desktops}) + (D \times \text{Professionals}) - (E \times \text{Officials})$$

In this equation, the estimated IT budget can be calculated based on the variables:

K = Fixed IT budget—that which is nonvariable.

A, B, C, D, E = Weighting of each category appropriate to the peer group.

$SG\&A$ = Company's sales, general, and administrative expenses.

Desktops = Number of desktop computers (includes laptops for this purpose) deployed throughout the company.

Professionals = Number of knowledge workers employed by the company.

Officials = Number of executive officers in the company.

This equation implies a number of conclusions. First, supplying computers to all information professionals in the company, and supporting them, is a major driver of IT cost. Second, officers are not heavy users of IT and thus their costs (salaries and bonuses) should not be a driver of IT costs as included in SG&A.

IT managers must determine the values of the variables required by the formula to calculate for the applicable IT budget, which may pose a challenge. However, Strassman's methodology is based on extensive research and is worth investigation. Before using this method, or to investigate further how companies can derive optimum benefit from their IT spending, we recommend Strassman's book.

Key IT Cost Drivers

We touched on a few key IT cost drivers earlier in the chapter. However, there are many factors to consider when analyzing corporate IT spending and attempting to understand what factors should drive the appropriate amount of IT expenditure for the company. Exhibit 3.10 highlights some of these factors.

Scale Economies

Scale economies have a major impact on spending levels and are therefore an important consideration when estimating appropriate IT spend. Economies of scale occur when size provides efficiencies and purchasing power, which drive down costs. This is important to the IT spend estimating process for several reasons. First, when planning an IT budget, it is critical to know if and when the company will achieve economies of scale in spending. Second, company growth (and therefore IT growth) can help lower overall spending as a percentage of revenue, but it will likely increase overall spending. Technologies and IT activities with scale economies include:

- *ERP systems:* These systems have high entry costs. As companies grow, the systems can support the increased volume of activity with little or no incremental costs, reducing IT cost as a percentage of total spending. Additionally, vendor discounts on enterprisewide licenses help lower costs further as you get larger.
- *Help-desk infrastructure:* In large organizations, the help-desk fixed cost—particularly the infrastructure—is spread across a larger user base. Incremental growth in support representatives is the only variable cost component as the company grows.
- *Management team:* As the firm produces more goods and revenue increases, the fixed cost of the IT management team is leveraged across a larger organization.

IT COST DRIVER	COMMENTS	AREAS AFFECTED
Industry	• Some industries dictate higher IT spending e.g., transportation—airline reservation systems	• General spending
Company size (sales, profitability, # of end users, type of end users)	• Company revenue • Number of knowledge workers • Number of professionals	• General spending • Support • Capital items
Number of computers per knowledge worker	• IT costs rise with the number of personal computers deployed	• Purchase of PCs • Support
Complexity of internal operations	• Outsourcing functions should lower IT costs since no longer have to support. Cost will show up in services • Computational intensive environments will increase IT costs	• Personnel • Hardware • Maintenance • Integration
Historical capital spending	• Historical CapEx spending does not drive increased cost however increased depreciation expense will affect the IT budget, e.g. purchasing Mainframe will affect depreciation for 3–5 years or useful life of the equipment	• Depreciation • Capital expenditures
Current economic/ marketplace condition	• Economic pressures will increase need to cut IT spending • Profitable companies tend to spend more on IT	• Personnel • Overhead
Competitive initiatives	• Major business transformation projects such as supply chain reengineering will precipitate major IT expenses to support	• Personnel • Software • Hardware
Demands from customers or suppliers	• Pressure from customers or suppliers for electronic information flows and other types of computer related messaging can drive up IT expenditures in the short term	• Software

Merger and acquisition activity	• Acquisitions and mergers acquisitions will drive IT integration costs • Potential economies of scale in the long term	• Personnel • Integration
Age of infrastructure	• As age of infrastructure increases, cost to support generally increases	• Maintenance
Central versus decentralized IT operations	• Decentralized IT operations tend to increase IT spending due to lack of controls and volume discounts	• Personnel • Software • Hardware
Number of platforms	• Costs increase in relation to the number of supported platforms • Standardization of environments lowers IT costs	• Personnel • Maintenance
Application complexity	• Application complexity drives higher support costs	• Maintenance
Application age	• Application age drives higher support costs	• Maintenance
Central versus decentralized purchasing	• Decentralized purchasing tends to increase IT spending due to lack of controls and inability to leverage purchasing volume	• Personnel • Software • Hardware
Standardization	• Standardization of environment, technical platform and tools reduces IT spending	• Hardware • Support/Maintenance
Chargeback mechanism employed	• Chargeback mechanism can lower IT spending by driving more rationale behavior with business units, e.g., market pricing	• General spending

Exhibit 3.10   Key Drivers of IT Costs

- *Purchasing:* Larger firms gain benefits by consolidating purchasing and receiving deeper vendor discounts in return for volume.
- *Tool sets for development and infrastructure management:* Development tools and their infrastructure are leveraged for a larger team with little or no incremental costs.

The following variable cost items are worth noting since they usually do not experience scale economies, and most often grow with employee headcount:

- *Desktops:* Prices may drop because of discounts, but the company will still acquire additional equipment for employees.
- *Network:* As the employee base grows, the network will require additional capacity and investment.
- *Telecom:* Additional phone lines, bandwidth, and voice mail capacity may be required as employee count increases.
- *E-mail servers:* Additional server, bandwidth, and backup capacity required.
- *End-user license fees:* New licenses or seats required as employee count or business volume increases.
- *End-user desktop support:* New IT capacity for end-user desktop support required as employee base grows.

It is also important to note that diseconomies of scale can occur (e.g., average costs go up) if the IT environment is overly complicated (e.g., multiple complex platforms and lack of standards). Chapter 6 covers these issues in detail.

Exhibit 3.11 provides evidence of scale enjoyed by larger companies.[22]

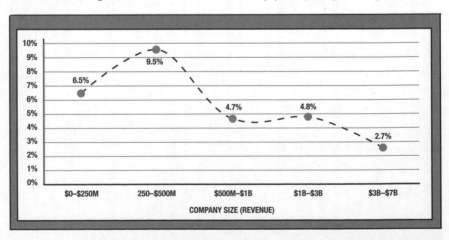

Exhibit 3.11   IT Spending by Company Revenue Range

Aligning IT Spending with Business Strategy

An important reason for benchmarking is to provide context from which measurements and recommendations can be made to senior management and the IT steering committee. One of the main considerations should be the business strategy executed by the senior leadership of the company and endorsed by the board of directors and shareholders.

An assessment that indicates that corporate technology spending is low compared to competitors who are in build mode, while the company strategy is harvesting profits mode, does not necessarily indicate that IT spending should rise in response. A minimal spending approach may make the most sense for a company in low-growth mode, regardless of what competitors are planning.

Therefore, the IT manager, when presenting benchmarking data, should consider the business strategy of the company and attempt to compare spending with companies with similar business attributes and, ideally, similar business strategies. In any case, the IT manager should adjust their benchmarking to account for specific business strategy.

Taking Action Based on Spending Benchmarks

After accounting for all the caveats outlined previously, the IT manager, in conjunction with the IT steering committee, can begin to take action based on the benchmarking results. If the ranges of spending computed are close to the current spending levels, no action may be necessary. If the ranges of spending are significantly higher or lower than the current spending, further action should be investigated.

- If benchmark spending is significantly higher, the company may elect to undertake an aggressive review of technology requests or potential investments on the basis of their business value. Clearly, every technology investment still must stand on its own merit. However, senior management and IT may have been slow to approve technology initiatives or additional capacity in the past, which may explain why the company is significantly outside the peer group.
- If benchmark spending is significantly lower, senior management should begin a detailed analysis and prioritization of IT costs, while investigating ways to improve productivity and eliminate excess spending. While it may be tempting for companies to begin chopping IT costs rapidly, a higher-than-peer benchmark simply indicates that there may be opportunities to reduce spending, and the company should take a hard look at its technology spend.

IT Spending Decisions: Summary

Estimating and benchmarking IT spending provide focus and validation of an organization's IT spending and investment strategy. It also educates IT management and the steering committee on the spending levels and strategies of peer companies. Additionally, it provides deeper insight into company-specific IT spending and puts into clear focus the actual total dollars spent on IT in your company. Regardless of the outcome of the exercise, companies should only invest in projects that meet all the criteria for business value and prioritization laid out in Chapter 15.

NOTES

1. Winston Spencer Churchill, speech in House of Commons (August 31, 1926).

2. George Bernard Shaw, *John Bull's Other Island,* act IV (1904).

3. Kevin J. Stiroh, "Information Technology and the U.S. Productivity Revival: What Do the Industry Data Say?" Federal Reserve Bank of New York, staff reports, no. 115 (January 24, 2001).

4. Kurt Potter and Carolyn LeVasseur, "IT Spending: Its History and Future" (Stamford, CT: Gartner Measurement Services, 2002).

5. Paul Strassman, "Misleading Metric," *ComputerWorld* (July 1, 2002).

6. See note 4.

7. See note 4.

8. Howard Rubin and Margaret Johnson, "What's Going On in IT?" (META Group & Metricnet, 2002).

9. Charles Phillips and Ryan Rathman, "Morgan Stanley CIO Survey Series: Release 3.8" (Morgan Stanley Equity Research North America, December 9, 2002).

10. "Data—Frequently Asked Questions" (Metricnet a Division of META Group, 2002).

11. Kurt Potter and Carolyn LeVasseur, "IT Spending Budget Practices, beyond Service-Level Agreements" (Stamford, CT: Gartner Measurement Services, 2002).

12. Tad Leahy, "Pay to Play @ Cisco," *Business Finance* (January 2002).

13. Paul Strassman, *The Squandered Computer* (New Canaan, CT: Information Economics Press, 1997), p. 320.

14. See note 13.

15. See note 4.

16. "IT Spending as a Percentage of Revenue" (Metricnet a Division of META Group, 2000–2001).

17. "IT Spending Per Employee by Industry" (Metricnet a Division of META Group, 2001).

18. Barbara Gomolski, "Mid-Size Company Summit" (Stamford, CT: Gartner Measurement Services, 2002).

19. "Percentage of IT Employees in a Company" (META Group and Rubin Systems, 1998).

20. See note 18.

21. See note 5.

22. See note 18.

PART II

Managing the IT Department

4

The IT Organization

You will find that the State is the kind of organization which, though it does big things badly, does small things badly too.

—John Kenneth Galbraith[1]

This chapter identifies the organizational components of the IT department and defines the roles and responsibilities of the IT staff and the interdepartmental and intradepartmental interactions necessary to complete IT projects on time while successfully running the existing systems and applications. While there are a wide variety of ways to structure an IT organization, we recommend a specific structure that has proven successful across many companies. This chapter addresses two major aspects of the IT organization—the structure of the organization and the division of labor within the structure.

The wide variety of roles and responsibilities in an IT organization can be difficult to fully understand for those in the organization and completely baffling to those outside the IT department. The myriad of technologies and their complicated interactions require a complex organization that can support the business while managing sophisticated technology environments and achieving the highest levels of service. Creating an organization that can achieve this is a daunting task. The inputs to this organization come from every direction, ranging from the IT organization working to maintain the systems day-to-day and solve customer problems; the business from user questions to system problems to the endless stream of requests to enhance the systems; and externally through vendor-driven software or hardware upgrades, maintenance and security requirements, and new technology evaluations. This can make priorities difficult to establish, and the balance between maintaining existing systems and satisfying perpetual requests from the business a significant challenge.

Why This Topic Is Important

The organization of the IT department directly impacts the success or failure of IT to meet the mission-critical business needs. An IT organization that is well structured and coordinated can manage the complexities and adapt to new business requirements, while maintaining service levels and successfully completing priority projects. On the other hand, a poorly structured and uncoordinated IT organization is a major liability because of its inflexibility for rapidly solving problems and its inability to deliver new capabilities to the business.

One of the most common symptoms we have seen in underachieving IT departments is a poorly designed organization. The result is a confused staff and confused business users. The overlaps and gaps in roles and responsibilities present a disorganized face to the business and cause endless turmoil within the IT department. The organizational chaos hampers the team's ability to effectively execute projects, prioritize demand on the IT department, manage vendors, or even maintain the most basic service level commitments to the business or external partners.

Inevitably, the confusion and fuzziness of roles and responsibilities leads to multiple staff members' providing overlapping coverage for similar unclear duties, resulting in unauthorized pet projects, slack time, and coverage gaps. Unfortunately, this leaves fewer resources for the most important duties. It also destroys any form of accountability.

Understanding successful organizational structures, establishing well-defined roles and responsibilities, and actively managing and measuring performance are the same approaches used by other parts of the business. All too frequently, IT managers are promoted because of their technical expertise, and few have developed the managerial skills needed to lead an organization. The result is a director who understands the technologies but fails to understand the business; how to communicate with the business; how to organize, manage, and motivate teams; and how to organize the department. Chapters 2 and 5 discuss this phenomenon further.

Further complicating matters is the fact that many newly promoted IT managers have come from either the operations or applications area of the department and do not have enough exposure to the subtleties required to skillfully manage all parts of the department. While it is common for a manager to have an extensive knowledge of one or two areas and a general understanding of others, it is very uncommon for an individual to have an extensive knowledge of all IT areas. In addition, maintaining detailed knowledge in one or two areas requires considerable reading, training, and on-the-job experience with new technologies. It is common for a manager to change positions in the IT organization and no longer be considered an expert in his or her previous area of expertise in fewer than 18 months. Systems hardware, applications, and networks are continuously changing, and it is difficult for managers to have more than a limited understanding of all the technologies deployed in a large department, putting even more pressure on achieving an effective organizational structure.

This chapter focuses on the organizational structure of the IT unit in a company. Roles and responsibilities must be clear so that the team can work together effectively to deliver all of the IT capabilities required by the business.

The chapter discusses:

- Common components of an IT organization.
- The most effective ways to structure an IT organization to produce optimal performance.
- Roles in each IT group.
- Key responsibilities and typical promotion paths for each role.
- Dangers and benefits of mixing IT development and IT operations.
- The importance of well-defined roles and accountability for achieving results.
- Effective use and integration of outside consultants.

IT Organization Overview

A major source of IT department inefficiency is poor organization of staff and lack of clear roles, responsibilities, and accountability. The resulting chaos causes responsibility gaps and overlaps, unclear roles, and difficulty holding individuals accountable for their results. This section highlights a standard approach to organizing IT and delineates key components in an IT department: management, operations, applications, development, help desk, infrastructure support, and administrative support. We then discuss how each of these areas should interact with the others and the business, and describe optimal ways to organize each area.

The costs of an ineffective IT department are high. As discussed in Chapter 2, while a disorganized department is another symptom of poor IT leadership, the symptom can lead to a variety of other failings. One of our most memorable client anecdotes occurred while we were restructuring a particularly poorly organized IT department. Because of the multiple overlapping responsibilities and unclear role definitions, it was difficult to account for which staff members were actually responsible for any given project or system. The cost to the client was driven home for us during a lunch meeting with an acquaintance who happened to own a small business in the same town. He remarked that we must be quite busy making changes at the client, because the three IT staffers from the client who usually came to his office three afternoons a week to moonlight for him had not had time recently for their extracurricular activities.

Missed project deadlines, frequent unplanned system and "maintenance" outages, unmanned help-desk lines, abundance of slack time, and pet projects are symptoms of poor organization and accountability.

IT Department Organization Structure

Exhibit 4.1 provides a standard structure for the major components of the IT department. Depending on the size of the business, the IT director or CIO may report to a vice president, CFO, COO, or directly to the CEO.

At the simplest level, the IT department consists of two areas: infrastructure (called IT Operations and Infrastructure) and applications (called Application Management or Applications Development and Support). Correspondingly, the IT organization structure relies on two managers with a direct reporting relationship to the IT director: the manager of operations and infrastructure and the manager of applications management. The structure assumes strong leadership and managerial skills for the people in these two key positions. The operations manager is responsible for all day-to-day management of the computing environment, maintenance and upgrades, and security. The application manager is responsible for all work associated with the business applications, enhancements, and upgrades.

We have observed a tendency for the IT director to maintain too many direct reporting relationships. Often we will, as part of an IT assessment, find an IT director with five or more direct reports, such as application development, user support, operations, network administration, and telecommunications administration. An IT director with too many direct reports typically spends a disproportionately large amount of time dealing with day-to-day "fire drills" and very little time working and communicating with the leaders of the other business organizations (e.g., sales, manufacturing), setting the long-term architecture and strategy for the IT organization, and monitoring and reporting the status of projects with significant long-term business benefits to key executives. While the director may feel busy, he or she is working on the wrong issues.

Within the operations and application organizations, specialized groups exist around specific technologies or functions. The operations group consists of the help desk, end-user support teams, data network administrators, system administrators, and telecommunications network administrators. The applications group has application development teams, testing teams, database administrators, electronic data interchange (EDI) specialists, and business analysts. Each of these roles is examined in detail in this chapter.

The organization outlined here establishes a clear division of labor, but because of multiple touch points between the two main component organizations, over time, the organizational boundaries often become blurred. Monitoring and measuring each of the groups is critical to ensure that each

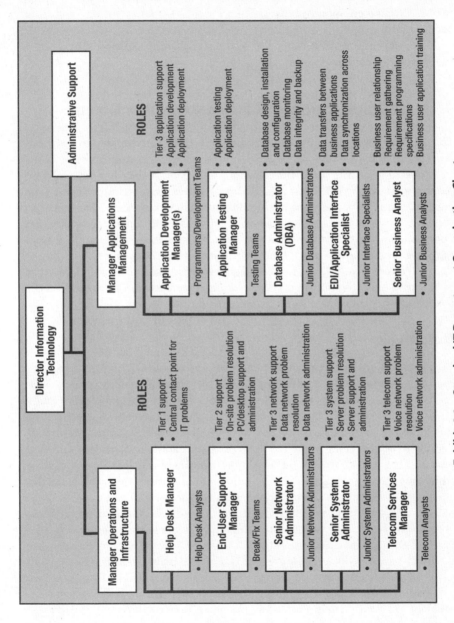

Director Information Technology

Administrative Support

Manager Operations and Infrastructure

ROLES

Help Desk Manager
- Tier 1 support
- Central contact point for IT problems
  - Help Desk Analysts

End-User Support Manager
- Tier 2 support
- On-site problem resolution
- PC/desktop support and administration
  - Break/Fix Teams

Senior Network Administrator
- Tier 3 network support
- Data network problem resolution
- Data network administration
  - Junior Network Administrators

Senior System Administrator
- Tier 3 system support
- Server problem resolution
- Server support and administration
  - Junior System Administrators

Telecom Services Manager
- Tier 3 telecom support
- Voice network problem resolution
- Voice network administration
  - Telecom Analysts

Manager Applications Management

ROLES

Application Development Manager(s)
- Tier 3 application support
- Application development
- Application deployment
  - Programmers/Development Teams

Application Testing Manager
- Application testing
- Application deployment
  - Testing Teams

Database Administrator (DBA)
- Database design, installation and configuration
- Database monitoring
- Data integrity and backup
  - Junior Database Administrators

EDI/Application Interface Specialist
- Data transfers between business applications
- Data synchronization across locations
  - Junior Interface Specialists

Senior Business Analyst
- Business user relationship
- Requirement gathering
- Requirement programming specifications
- Business user application training
  - Junior Business Analysts

Exhibit 4.1   Standard IT Department Organization Chart

67

is accomplishing its stated goals and not simply passing responsibilities to other groups. The managers and members of the specialized groups must understand that they are accountable for the success or failure of their teams. Variable compensation and other incentives can be used to reinforce accountability.

Roles and responsibilities of each of these two subgroups are discussed in the remainder of this chapter.

IT Operations and Infrastructure Group

The IT Operations Group is responsible for maintaining the day-to-day functionality of the IT systems. Because of the utility nature of these systems (desktops, e-mail, file and print services, networks), this group has an enormous impact on the overall satisfaction level of the business user. The IT operations group is typically organized into five major areas: help desk, end-user support, network management, systems administration and operations, and telecommunications services. Each of these groups focuses on either a function or a technology in the IT organization. Larger companies (i.e., greater than 1,000 employees) may further segment the group into additional areas. Some commonly split out functions including operators, security management, change control, disaster recovery, and demand management.

Help Desk

The help desk is the IT group that company employees initially contact when they have a computing question or a problem. From a business perspective, the help desk represents the IT department's face to most employees and is closely identified with the customer experience—regardless of whether this should be the case. From an IT perspective, the help desk is the first line of defense to address and resolve as many problems and questions from users as possible. It is the central point where most business user problems are identified and tracked. It facilitates communication between the users and other components of the operations group, resulting in a rapid response to major outages and critical problems and a timely, coordinated response to less important problems. The help desk is frequently referred to as the *first tier* for problem management and resolution.

Broad-based skills are required of the help-desk staff to triage the wide variety of questions that inundate any help-desk team. The staff must adhere to a methodology that systematically eliminates the possible causes of a problem. After the help-desk staff member understands and isolates the problem, he should have the ability and authority to resolve it or assign it to the next tier of support for resolution. Frequently, this requires interaction and cooperation with another IT operations group, as well as the end users.

In a typical service request, a business user might call the help desk and report, "I cannot access the customer order system." What appears to be a simple request—fix the customer order system access—actually requires a fairly complex diagnostic process to understand which one (or more) of a host of interacting systems components might be causing the problem.

The problem may be with the PC on the business user's desk, it may be with the network connecting the business user's PC to the server, or it may be with the server itself. When accounting for the complexities of different types of hardware, software, and configuration differences, it is easy to understand why the help desk may not be able to solve a problem over the phone. The help desk must coordinate the efforts of other teams to correctly identify and eliminate the business user's problem as rapidly as possible, depending on the severity of the issue.

Optimizing the help desk is the primary role of the help-desk manager. This process begins by establishing a single help desk as the point of contact for the business user. Introducing multiple help desks almost always results in confusion for the business user about which help desk to call and the perception of finger pointing in the IT department. The costs of coordination of multiple help desks, even when organized by technology, geography, or problem type are quite high. An important characteristic of help desks is close geographic and physical proximity, to provide on-the-job training, the ability to quickly spot trends (e.g., several "down e-mail calls" coming in simultaneously helps in the diagnosis), and simple camaraderie on the help-desk team. The result of multiple points of contact is a frustrated business user and difficulty tracking problem trends and help-desk performance for the IT manager.

The help desk should strive to resolve as many questions or problems on the first contact with the customer as possible. This not only reduces the burden on the IT department but also results in dramatically increased end-user satisfaction. Simply taking problem information and forwarding it to another part of the organization for resolution creates numerous problems. The help desk must correctly diagnose the problem and send it to the appropriate group; after it is sent, there is an agency problem with no clear ownership for resolution of the end-user problem. Problem resolution statistics can be used to measure and improve first-contact resolution in addition to identifying the most common calls and developing a course of action to reduce the number of those calls.

Medium and large businesses normally elect to use an inbound call routing system (e.g., "Press 1 for a computing problem, press 2 for a telephone or voicemail problem, press 3 for a new account"). In mid-size companies, this is typically a less-expensive, automated call distributor (ACD); in large companies, it may be a fully configured, full-featured phone switch (see the Telecommunications Services Group section discussion). Use of this type of system enables the business user to self-route to the person most likely to be able to help, and it provides call statistics, which can be analyzed for trends. The ACD can also be changed to update status messages and inform the business users who call the help desk during a major outage. While usage of these systems in larger companies can result in productivity gains for the help-desk team, the systems should be deployed intelligently, as they can also overinsulate the IT team from the end user and make the help desk too difficult to reach.

Management of help-desk activities is best facilitated through the use of full-featured help-desk application software that can manage customer calls, track progress on resolution, ensure that issues are closed, escalate urgent issues, automatically update end users on issue status, and provide reporting on help-desk performance. Whether a package-based or manual system is used, basic issue information must be captured to communicate with the business user experiencing the problem.

In addition, IT-specific categorizations are also necessary, such as the initial diagnosis of the problem, the scale of the business impact, user urgency, and the final problem resolution. The initial diagnosis of the problem identifies the tests performed to troubleshoot and narrow the possible causes and the group responsible for resolution if the help desk cannot resolve the problem. The scale of the business impact dictates the urgency and the resources that should be applied, with priority given to system or networkwide problems over most individual business user problems. The help-desk staff must identify when they are receiving multiple individual phone calls for what turns out to be a systemwide or networkwide problem. The final resolution should also be captured because it is critical for quantifying problems that are misdiagnosed initially, and it enables additional root cause analysis for future problem elimination or best practice documentation for resolving a particular problem.

A variety of help-desk applications are available that provide a wide range of functionality from simple to highly sophisticated. At the lower end of the scale, the pricing is quite reasonable and should not pose a significant hurdle for even small IT departments. The improved coordination, communication, user satisfaction, and root-cause analysis provided by more sophisticated packages usually makes the benefits far outweigh the implementation costs.

The help desk is often used as a training ground for new IT employees. These employees gain a broad exposure to all the systems and applications in use by the business, as well as the overall IT and corporate organization and the business of the company. However, the rapid transactional nature of a help-desk position does not enable the employee to learn the details of any one system or application. New IT staff can spend anywhere from one month to one year working on the help desk, depending on the business circumstances. The intensity of the daily experience on the help desk can quickly lead to staff burnout—properly setting goals, expectations, and a date to transfer into other parts of the IT organization can mitigate some of the burnout risk and provide a motivational goal for harried help-desk staff. Ultimately, the help-desk manager must monitor all of the staff and their performance levels with the business users.

While this experience can be very valuable in rapidly developing broad skill sets for new IT team members, it can be frustrating to the business users calling the help desk when they cannot get first-call resolution to their problems because of lack of knowledge or experience. Mixing experienced help-desk staff with new IT employees provides mentor resources that can be referenced by junior staff to accelerate learning and reduce the probability of business user frustration. To the extent practical, periodic rotations through different help-desk support areas for help-desk team members (or other staff, if possible) can ensure that the repetitive nature of the job does not become too onerous. The interaction with the more experienced staff is the key to rapid learning for the new help-desk employees.

When a help-desk employee cannot fix and close out a problem with the business user over the phone, he or she must hand off the issue to additional IT operations resources to assist in the problem diagnosis and resolution. These groups may include end-user support, network administration, system administration, application support, or telecommunications services.

End-User Support/Break-Fix Group

The end-user support/break-fix group is responsible for physical computer repair and field visits to customer (end-user) locations. This group is considered the second tier for problem management and resolution. Depending on the size of the group, number of employees, geographic footprint of the company, and complexity of calls and call volume, a manager typically organizes the staff into teams, which may be assigned to support a specific location, technology, application, or business group. These teams can be co-located with the business users to minimize the time required to get to users' desks, and to provide a better interface between users and the IT department. In large companies, each of the teams requires a team leader with responsibility for the performance of that team.

As with the help desk, a variety of technical skills, spanning all operations and applications areas, are necessary for the end-user support staff. The same type of problem-solving skills, methodology, and logical approach that systematically eliminates the possible causes of the problem is critical here as well. Exposure to the standard systems, applications, and networks is necessary to provide the insight required to execute the on-the-fly technical testing used to identify the cause of the business user's IT problem. The systems experience required is focused on the hardware and software on the business user's desk, as opposed to the server systems behind the scene. Ultimately, the end-user support group is responsible for all the equipment, client-side applications, and local software that operate on the business user's desktop computer. Responsibilities frequently include deployment of new equipment, maintenance of existing equipment, and upgrades to desktop equipment and software. As discussed in Chapter 6 (IT Direction and Standard Setting), the level of standardization of hardware, systems software, and applications across the organization is one of the largest drivers of effort for both the help-desk and end-user support staff. Highly heterogeneous environments are challenging to support and usually require much higher than average staffing levels to provide adequate service to the end user.

In addition to technical skills associated with the systems supported, customer handling skills and the ability to develop productive working relationships with the business users are as important as technical knowledge for ensuring a positive customer experience. End-user support staff may find that problems encountered result from lack of training for the business user; therefore, it is common for the end-user support staff to train the business user at their desk on various applications to reduce the likelihood of additional problem calls.

Furthermore, the demeanor and approach of the support staff is as important as their technical skills. Unfortunately, IT professionals often have a reputation for supercilious and arrogant treatment of end users. This not only damages the IT-business relationship, but also ultimately impairs the effective delivery of the IT service, as the staff members fail to help users learn to solve basic problems on their own. Operations managers should work to ensure that soft skills are a key screening criterion during the hiring process, are part of the ongoing appraisal process, are required for promotion within the department.

In weak IT organizations, it is common to find that business users circumvent the standard process of going through the help desk and consistently call the top team members in the end-user support group directly. This circumstance has obvious drawbacks and eventually erodes the morale and patience of the professionals that the IT team most needs to retain. This phenomenon highlights the importance of continually ensuring that reliable, customer-focused staff are on the break-fix team.

Occasionally, companies place their end-user support teams under the reporting umbrella of the business unit or department they support. The goal is to make IT more responsive to the needs of the business. While this can be an appropriate temporary fix, it is also usually indicative of serious problems within the IT department. As one client remarked, "The sales department is in the business of sales. I don't want to run my own IT shop, but I will if the IT department is incapable of providing the level of service required."

Establishment of this type of shadow IT support staff in business units or departments can create security and administration issues outside the control of IT. It also creates a new level of coordination and communication requirements for system changes. Not only must the business users be notified of an impending change, but also the shadow support staff must be briefed on the details and may be required to implement or test the changes. This promotes finger pointing and turf issues when modifications and system changes go awry. Further, the business loses out on any scale economies available in this area, as well as career track and training and development benefits for the team. In summary, the presence of shadow IT functions embedded in business units is a major indicator of IT department ineffectiveness and, when addressed, can usually provide major cost savings and service-level improvements. The benefits of such models are typically outweighed by negative impacts, including higher costs and lack of coordination and communication.

Typical staff progression in the IT organization transitions people with 12 to 24 months of experience at the help desk into the end-user support group. Normally, the end-user support staff then spends two to five more years developing detailed skills and knowledge about the systems, applications, and networks used by the company. After they have gained enough experience, staff members may be considered for team leadership or other lateral moves in the organization, typically after three to six years. The end-user support manager is normally promoted from the team leaders.

Network Administration Group

The network administration group manages all data network communication capabilities required by the business. Network responsibilities are typically separated into two broad categories—local area networks (LANs) and wide area networks (WANs). LANs are typically defined as network connections within a particular business location, and WANs are the network connections between business locations. For example, a LAN connects all of the PCs, servers, printers, and peripherals in the Dallas facility, while a WAN connects Dallas with Chicago. We use this terminology because it is the simplified, generally accepted view. Different technologies can be used to network a specific area; for instance, there are LANs connected with wires and cables and others that are wireless—both of which may be in use in the same location. Similarly, WANs can be created from frame relay connections, public Internet VPNs, point-to-point connections, and so on.

The network administrators are responsible for all wiring, hubs, and security for the LANs and the leased lines, routers, gateways, firewalls, and security for the WANs. They monitor network performance and upgrade capacity before the traffic on the network increases to the point that it begins to affect systems performance. To accomplish this requires a specialized skill set with knowledge of networking hardware, networking mediums (different types of cables with different capacities and performance characteristics), networking protocols (which define how messages are passed between computers), encryption techniques for secure messaging, and firewall security. The extensive hardware, application, and configuration knowledge required by a network administrator takes considerable time, experience and training to build.

Networking hardware, software, and services costs can represent a large portion of the annual IT budget, particularly for companies with a large number of geographically disparate locations. Connecting remote sites via a WAN requires leasing a data line from a telecommunications company with enough capacity to handle all of the company data traffic. A good senior network administrator thoroughly investigates all application access and data transfers that will occur over the WAN. Using this information, the network administrator determines the best medium and capacity for the situation and negotiates the contract with the telecommunication vendors. Proper needs assessment, capacity planning, and postimplementation traffic shaping can result in significant monthly savings in leased line costs.

Large numbers of vendors are often involved in networking infrastructure (e.g., local loop, local telco, frame-relay provider, and ISP), making it challenging to determine the exact costs and usage of the network. Compounding the issue is the complexity of the typical billing statements and the difficulty of tying the statements to the actual services provided. A recent analysis performed for one large client revealed that their network administrators could not identify the number of leased lines in use, the capacity of the leased lines, or the total monthly cost. They simply received monthly bills for their leased lines and paid them, without verifying any linkage to actual lines or services consumed.

Typical career paths begin with the junior network administrator who works at the LAN level. It takes several years to build the skills to master the many different types of technologies, mediums, and protocols. Progression to senior network administrator with responsibility for the WAN and teams of junior network administrators typically occurs after five to seven years of experience, and the completion of specialized network training.

In a small to mid-size corporate environment, the system administrator may also serve as the network administrator. As the computing environment grows in size and complexity, more specialized skill sets and additional capacity are needed to ensure reliable operation and system availability.

System Administration and Computer Operations Group

The system administration and computer operations group manages, monitors, tunes, and administers all of the IT servers and systems software that comprise the infrastructure on which the applications and data used to run the company reside. These systems include e-mail servers, file servers, Web servers, print servers, and development, test, production, and failover application servers. Each of these servers may be based on different technologies depending on the requirements and standards established by the organization. For example, the e-mail server may use Microsoft technology, the Web servers might be UNIX-based systems, the file and print servers might be Novell-based, and the production applications may reside on a mainframe server.

System administration encompasses all the efforts required to manage each of the business servers. Duties include deployment of new equipment, maintenance of existing equipment, upgrades to server equipment and operating systems or systems software, creation of regular backups of critical enterprise data, capacity planning, disaster recovery planning, user profile management, user changes, and system security. It takes highly detailed knowledge of how system software works to manage these tasks for the critical business infrastructure components. This is particularly true for diagnosing complex systems failures and to effectively close holes in security.

The best system administrators proactively manage their server systems to minimize the possibility of server problems during production hours and security breaches at any time via system monitoring tools and participation in Internet discussion groups and sites dedicated to the technologies that they support. Administrators also monitor system performance, track increases in server workload, and anticipate the need for additional capacity before performance shortfalls impact business performance. As a result, system administrator responsibilities require double duty—they must be on site during production hours to immediately address any server problems, and they must perform all maintenance work and upgrades after production hours and on weekends.

Few system administrators, in small or large companies, regularly install the software patches provided between major system upgrades that are necessary to close the system security holes. If an administrator postpones patches until a major upgrade is released, and these occur only once every 12 to 18 months, the environment has a considerable amount of exposure to hackers who attempt to enter systems for fun (control and bragging rights) or profit (data theft). These people know the security patches for each operating system and systematically search for machines where the patches have not been installed and configured properly so that they can gain access. Combined with the fact that it takes time to configure, test, and install a major operating system upgrade with the existing business applications, the exposure may last as long as two or three years.

Scheduled maintenance and upgrades must be carefully coordinated with the business units and other departments to ensure that production systems are available during critical times after normal business hours. For example, business users at a client company recently expressed frustration that the systems were unavailable when they had to work overtime one weekend. The business users had no idea whom to contact in the IT department and, therefore, IT received no notification of the business need. The IT department indicated that if they had known about the weekend work, they would have been able to reschedule their maintenance for another time.

This is a typical example of the lack of communication of process, roles, and responsibilities from IT to the business, and one of the most common complaints about IT departments that are struggling with communications issues. Because upgrades are complex and risky, and require significant advance planning and effort to complete, it can be easy to neglect informing the user community of the associated system impacts or outages. Each systems project that may cause downtime should be clearly communicated well in advance to business users.

The system administration and computer operations group also coordinates the introduction of new technology into the production environment. Senior system administrators are very cautious by both training and experience, and carefully plan tests to ensure that transitions to new technologies are performed in a controlled manner that does not adversely impact the operation of the production environment or disrupt the business. The ultimate goal is to ensure that all servers work 100 percent of the time so that their function is transparent to the business. The introduction of system changes into the production environment involves the process called change management discussed in Chapter 7. System administrators manage the process, ensuring that all changes have been tested and that rollback procedures (i.e., a method to restore the environment if necessary) are in place.

The support of server hardware and systems software is complex and, like many of the other third-tier IT operations functions, requires a specialized skill set to understand the details of the systems in use. It is not uncommon for an organization to require a specialist for each type of server used—for example, understanding the inner-workings of a UNIX-based system well enough to "tune a kernel" is very different from understanding how to "gen" a mainframe system; and it is a rare individual who has an extensive working knowledge of both. However, in smaller businesses it may not be cost effective to break responsibilities down to this level. We recommend including additional costs of skilled labor capacity in all purchasing decisions and minimizing the number of different computing platforms in the organization to minimize the different skill sets and staff required. The staff capacity issues can be further mitigated by cross-training the system administrators or using contractors on an as-needed basis to minimize the costs.

In larger organizations, a group of operators may be included in the systems operations group. The operators are responsible for managing system operations functions such as printing, batch jobs, and user online sessions. Operators manage various jobs (print, batch, or online processes) on servers to ensure the correct processing power is available to the most critical resources and that the functions are executing and completing correctly. A critical component of the operators job is to ensure that processing capacity is available for applications. For example, if it is the Friday on the last day of a month and most orders come in that day, the operator can divert computer processing power to online sales sessions so that computer resources can quickly process the orders. Additionally, operators may prioritize application print jobs for critical reports such as invoices. Operators are necessary to maximize CPU usage and other computing resources and ensure a smoothly operating application. In smaller companies, the server typically auto-prioritizes various requests eliminating the need for full-time staff to perform this function.

Typical career paths for system administrators involve initial training to build a foundation of knowledge about the servers they will support. These junior system administrators typically work in an apprentice role under the close supervision of a senior team member to gradually shift responsibilities for the systems and build experience and confidence. Simply "turning over the keys" puts the organization at risk because the junior administrator needs time to understand the processes that minimize the risks of any system changes and the subtleties of the specific system configurations, which can vary from machine to machine at the server level.

Depending on the complexity of the server computing environment and the desired level of cross-training, it typically requires four to seven years of experience as a junior system administrator before consideration for a senior administrator role is warranted. Senior system administrators manage a team of junior administrators, and in larger organizations, a manager may be required to coordinate the efforts of the senior system administrators across multiple locations.

Telecommunications Services Group

Many businesses find it cost effective to purchase and operate their own telephone systems. The telecommunications group manages all telephony and related services. Services include telephones, voicemail systems, fax machines, and video conferencing systems. The group must monitor system use, bandwidth consumption, and network security for the voice and video networks in a manner similar to the procedures used by the network administration group for the data network.

Telecommunications services requires knowledge of telephony switch hardware (PBXs) and software configuration; wiring in buildings and demarcation facilities; trunk line capacities; call center configuration; voicemail system configuration and management; video conferencing equipment, and voice/video bandwidth requirements. Individuals without the appropriate knowledge can quickly interrupt telephone service.

The help desk normally handles inbound problem calls and requests for service to maintain the single point of contact for the business user. However, few help-desk staff members have the knowledge, experience, or authority to make changes to these systems, and the voice telecom requests are immediately routed to the telecommunications services group. In some larger companies, the telecommunications services group may assign one of its team members to rotate onto the help desk to address telecom requests and problems. In many cases, the skills required are highly specialized, and telecom support is fully or partially outsourced to a specialized provider. In these cases, the help desk may serve as the first line of defense for phone system questions but have the authority to schedule the contracted outside provider to rapidly fix the problems.

Telecom services analysts begin by supporting the wiring in buildings and develop expertise in the other areas over a period of several years. Specialized training from the PBX vendor is typically required to establish a basic understanding of the systems used by the business. On-the-job training with direct senior-level oversight is used to build on the foundation. Junior-level telecom analysts transition to senior-level telecom analysts after four to seven years.

Operations Manager

The operations manager is responsible for the performance of all the teams in the IT operations group. The operations manager must have a basic understanding of the technologies used in each of the areas managed, but the critical skills are the organization and management of the teams. Planning, setting reasonable service levels, managing staff, and actively participating as a "doer" are all part of the typical responsibilities of the operations manager.

The IT operations manager oversees the day-to-day performance of the IT systems to maximize availability and address user problems. Having a manager in this role enables the IT director to focus on the strategic direction that confronts an IT department, instead of worrying about "putting out the fires" on a daily basis. Because shortfalls in operations are highly noticeable to the entire organization (it affects everyone in the company when phones are out, e-mail is down, or the network printers are not working), the IT operations manager plays a critical role in ensuring that the utility functions provided by the department operate smoothly and do not negatively impact the business.

Very small organizations may have the system/network administrator also serve as the operations manager. As businesses grow, a dedicated management resource at this level is important to maintain the control and direction of the IT operations organization and reduce the number of managers and team leads reporting to the IT director. If an IT director has more than four direct reports, it is time to consider creating an IT operations manager position.

Process Responsibility in IT Operations

The IT Operations Group is responsible for all the processes described in Chapter 7. Some of the key operations processes overlap groups. A description of the process responsibility alignment follows:

1. IT operations manager is responsible for:
   *a. Systems demand management process.
   *b. Disaster recovery function.
   c. All management processes.

2. Help-desk manager is responsible for:
   a. Help-desk function.
   b. Problem management process.
   c. Input to changes in standard operating procedure/problem diagnosis process.
3. End-user support manager is responsible for:
   a. Problem management process (break-fix portion).
   b. Fixed asset management process.
4. Senior network administrator is responsible for:
   a. Problem management process (Tier 3 network support portion).
   b. LAN/WAN management process.
   *c. Security management process (overall).
5. Senior system administrator is responsible for:
   a. Problem management process (Tier 3 system support portion).
   b. Systems administration process.
   c. E-mail administration process.
   d. Operators.
   e. Change control process.
   f. Asset management process (server equipment portion).
   g. Login management (add, change, delete).
   h. Security (server portion).
6. Telecom services manager is responsible for:
   a. Telecom administration.
   b. Problem management process (Tier 3 telecom support portion).
   c. Security (telecom portion).

Processes with an asterisk may actually be divided into a wholly separate group depending on the size of the company and the complexity of the systems. For example, many IT operations managers in large companies will have a single manager dedicated to security.

Key Drivers for IT Operations Structure and Staffing Levels

Five key drivers determine IT staffing levels:

1. Number of end users supported.
2. Number of systems supported.
3. Number of sites supported and geographic dispersion.

RESOURCE	COMPANY SIZE (NO. OF EMPLOYEES)				
	0–25	25–50	50–100	100–200	200–400
CIO/IT director	—	.25	.5	.75	1
Network/Systems engineer	—	.5	.75	1	1.5
Network/Systems administrator	.25	.5	.75	1	2
Helpdesk supervisor	—	—	.5	1	1
Jr. Network/Systems administrator	.5	1	1.5	2	3
Helpdesk/Desktop support	1	2	3	4	6

**Exhibit 4.2 Typical IT Operations Resources
Required for Small and Mid-Sized IT Departments**

4. Support requirements (e.g., 5 days a week, 8 hours a day, or 7 days a week, 24 hours a day).
5. Complexity of the computing environment—number of different types of applications, systems, and networks.

Exhibit 4.2, which is based on our experience with businesses across many industries, provides a rough estimate for staffing IT operations at small to mid-size companies and is based on the number of end users supported. These figures are estimates; investigate other industry research to better understand if the company is above or below peers and how staff signing impacts cost structure and long-term competitiveness. A more detailed method of calculating staffing levels for larger organizations is described in Chapter 7.

In smaller organizations, it is not cost effective to hire an individual for each position, and the complexity of the computing environment will usually not warrant doing so. As the business gets larger and the computing environment gets more complex, additional resources will be needed to properly manage and maintain the computing environment.

Application Development and Support

The application development and support group maintains all the critical business applications that are layered on top of the infrastructure provided by the operations group. The application group supports the production applications, gathers requirements for enhancements or additional functionality, develops specifications, programs the new system functions, tests the interaction of the old and new code, and integrates the changes into the production environment. The group is also in charge of managing, upgrading, configuring, troubleshooting and tuning all business applications. Because the majority of the large business-oriented projects are planned and delivered by this group, the management of the group requires a skillful balancing act of new development and baseline application support.

The IT application development and support group is typically organized into five to six major areas: application development, application support (may be combined with application development in some organizations), application testing, database administration, EDI/application interface specialists, and business analysts. Each of these groups focuses on an application, function, or a technology required by the business.

Application Development Teams

The application development team provides enhancements and support for business applications, based on the requirements gathered and documented by the business analyst team. In smaller organizations, the business analyst and application developer roles are often played by the same team members. The business applications may be custom developed in-house, or they may be packages purchased from third-party vendors and configured and customized for the specific business.

Application developers typically specialize in specific technologies and software development technologies such as object-based, Web-oriented, client/server development, enterprise application configuration and customization (e.g., ERP, CRM), and electronic data interchange and application interface development (application integration).

The IT development group is typically organized around applications in three broad categories. Each category may use a variety of technologies to deliver all of the business functionality required. These categories are:

1. *Customer-facing applications,* which may include Web-based customer access systems, order-entry and order-processing systems, and internal customer service systems.
2. *Production support,* the set of supply chain applications, such as procurement, manufacturing, warehousing, inventory, and logistics.
3. *Business support,* which typically incorporates systems completely internal to the business, such as human resources and accounting.

An application development team member typically joins the staff with skills in different technologies to manage and enhance the business applications in one of the three areas. This team is responsible for the creation of new capabilities within existing business applications, upgrading and patching third-party applications, testing existing and new application functionality before deployment in production, and support for the business application after it is in production. As the business system size and complexity increase, it may be necessary to dedicate staff to a particular application in one of the three categories and to have the team work together on cross-application interfaces.

Establishing a team for each business application enables cross-training multiple staff members to support specific applications. The danger is a potential lack of ownership for the application; therefore, clear ownership and responsibility for delivery of the application enhancements and overall management of the applications must be established for each system deployed.

The IT development group must schedule and clearly communicate to the IT department, steering committee, and business users committed dates for deployment of new system capabilities. Communication must occur within the IT organization and the business organizations to ensure that everyone is aware of the timing and the functionality that will be provided. Major changes to applications should, in every case, be coordinated through the IT steering committee.

In addition, deployment of new system capabilities must show sensitivity to business cycles and should be timed to minimize disruption to the busiest business cycles. For example, one of our clients generates 70 percent of its business during the holiday season in the months of November and December. The IT application developers are required by the business to have system changes in place by the end of September to adequately prepare for the holiday rush. No additional system or application enhancements are allowed until after the end-of-year busy season.

We have witnessed a more recent trend among our clients of reducing or eliminating the business-specific customization of third-party software applications. The most notable areas are around enterprise resource planning (ERP) systems such as SAP, JD Edwards, or PeopleSoft, and customer relationship management (CRM) systems such as Siebel. Businesses are increasingly finding that the costs of customization are very high for these packages because of significant investment in time and resources. More troubling is discovering that the expensive customizations do not work with the annual upgrades to these third-party products, and they face the choice of maintaining an older system after the vendor stops support or investing additional time and resources to remove the customizations, install the upgrade or patch, and recreate the customizations in the latest software release.

As a result, clients are installing new third-party software in as close to the standard, off-the-shelf form as possible. In some extreme cases, companies that have made investments to customize applications are backing out selected customizations and choosing to change the business processes to match the software instead. This has been to the mutual benefit of both software vendors and their customers.

Application Support Group

Mid-size organizations may have an application support group that is separate from the application development teams. The application support group is responsible for the day-to-day operation of critical business applications. The organization of the application support group typically parallels the structure of the development group to ensure ownership and accountability of production applications.

In large companies, separate groups may exist for the development and support of a particular application. In smaller organizations, the responsibility for supporting an application can reside with either the end-user support group or the application development group. As discussed previously, the operations help-desk and end-user support teams provide the first and second tiers of support. The third tier of support for business applications comes from the application support team.

The development group is responsible for identifying, developing, testing, and deploying new functionality to enhance the IT capabilities of the business through increased efficiency or creation of technologies and provide differentiation from the competition. While the development group focuses on new capabilities, the support group maintains the existing version and fields tier-three requests described previously. This separation of support and development has several positive effects for the organization. First, it eliminates distractions for the development staff so they can concentrate on new development. Otherwise, development is consistently being taken away from new duties to address the support requests. This inevitably leads to delays in the development cycle and pushes out the milestone and agreed on delivery dates. It also eliminates the lack of accountability that can occur when the two functions are integrated. It becomes easy to blame support requests for missed deadlines if a single group is performing both functions. It also becomes easy to provide poor service to users if personnel are dedicating too much time to new development activities and not enough time to support. By dividing the two functions into two groups, the accountability is clear and the groups typically work with better effectiveness. Having two groups also provides career paths from the support group to the development group for staff.

Application Testing

The application testing team is responsible for testing changes and upgrades to business application modules with the goal of eliminating problems and ensuring compatibility with other modules. Application testing occurs on multiple levels: Developers test the code in their modules as they are developing it, the application testing team combines groups of modules and tests for the interaction of their functionality, and, finally, the entire application is put together and tested in its entirety, along with its interfaces to other internal and external systems. These tests are typically called *unit, integration,* and *system testing,* respectively.

Few development organizations allow adequate time for full testing of business applications before deployment. Testing often begins in the week before the system goes live—resulting in a system that is not thoroughly tested, which makes it susceptible to problems when it is placed in production. Successful application development groups allocate as much as 30 percent of their development time to application testing. The groups that do this are rewarded with significantly fewer major problems after the application is put into production and easier ongoing management of the production systems in the postimplementation environment.

The application testing team should also incorporate business users to test the functionality of the applications. Business user participation in the testing ensures that the most commonly used functions are tested for system problems. In addition, providing business users with access to the new system before placing it in production creates familiarity and instills confidence and ownership in the new system.

Another critical aspect of testing the entire application is stress testing to identify system scalability, volume limitations, and catastrophic failure points. Knowledge of these stress points prior to production deployment will dramatically aide system performance monitoring and avert disastrous situations. Well-defined stress points enable system administrators and application developers to address the limitations before reaching them instead of after the thresholds have been crossed and have brought the business to a standstill.

In smaller application development groups, the application testing team may be a subset of the developers, database administrators, and system administrators. Larger businesses, or smaller companies engaged in a significant system rollout, may be able to afford a separate individual or team of individuals to perform the full testing of the application.

Database Administrator

Database administrators (DBAs) design the database architecture, install and configure the database software, participate in design and development activities with the development team, ensure data integrity, and monitor and optimize the database performance for the underlying database software used by the business applications. They are responsible for the databases in both the production environment and the development environment. Large-scale relational databases are highly sophisticated systems, and the DBA role is one of the highest technology skill positions on an IT team.

Because of the complexity of relational databases, specific skill sets are required, depending on the database technology used by the business. Like the system administrators on the operations side of the IT department, DBAs are required to understand the most intimate details of their database to control, manage, and tune it effectively. Finding an expert in one database, such as an Oracle DBA, is not as difficult as finding an expert who is knowledgeable about Oracle, Informix, Sybase, and DB2. Performance tuning a database can have enormous impacts on systems performance and can often be the difference between viable systems and those that fail.

In larger organizations, the DBA role is often split between a development and production DBA. In these cases, the development DBA is focused on the structural changes to existing databases required to support projects and enhancements, as well as the design of new database models for emerging applications. Production DBAs work to monitor and tune existing database performance and ensure that the integrity of the production database is maintained.

Electronic Data Interchange/Application Interface Specialist

The electronic data interchange (EDI) specialist is responsible for ensuring the accurate, timely, and speedy transport of data between applications inside the company and with strategic partners outside the company walls. Application integration is a critical component of streamlining system communication and databases across the business and across business partners. Each business system and application requires data in specific formats. Interapplication interfaces may be triggered by events and pass data on an as-needed basis (asynchronously) or on a given schedule, transferring a number of transactions (batch). The EDI specialist is a master at translating information so that it can be understood by the receiving system. In addition, he or she must maintain a schedule of data transfers to ensure that large data transfers do not all occur at the same time and cause slow performance or data transfer failures because of the load placed on a particular machine, database, or network. Application interface specialists are skilled in various tools that provide messaging management or systems connectivity. As the rate of business transactions increase and time pressures advance, more asynchronous, real-time communication between systems is necessary.

Multiple tools are now available that allow the construction of sophisticated cross-application, cross-platform asynchronous communications. These systems provide a common set of protocols, formats, and triggers for all applications to use for interfacing with each other. This enables the group to develop only one interface for each application (from the application to the messaging system) in a many-to-one relationship versus a many-to-many relationship. The messaging system then manages the timing and flow of all messages between applications.

Business Analyst Group

The business analysts work directly with the business users to understand how the systems are used and identify the enhancements that will provide the greatest benefit to the business. The responsibilities of a business analyst are divided equally between two major constituencies: the business users and the IT department application developers.

Business analysts develop relationships with the business users and maintain these relationships through regular meetings and requirements gathering sessions. They must understand the internal business processes and how IT applications are used in the process, including how the IT applications streamline or inhibit the process. The business analyst must proactively solicit, gather, and document information and requirements to drive high-value enhancements, customizations, and upgrades to the business systems. In addition, the business analysts must track and help prioritize all requests for application changes or enhancements. Integrating the business user into the prioritization of system changes as well as the testing before deployment ensures that the highest value items are addressed and the systems work as requested.

The most challenging aspect of the business analyst's job is understanding both business processes and the supporting applications and technology well enough to anticipate, identify, inventory, and articulate system changes that the business user may need but does not expressly request. For instance, a slight change in the system functionality, such as automatically populating customer information fields, may change the process the business users use and save them several minutes per order transaction. The business users may not know that this is possible; therefore, it is incumbent on the business analyst to identify the change and bring it up for discussion and evaluation.

The business analysts also work closely with the application development teams. Business analysts are responsible for authoring the high-level requirements documentation used by the programmers to create detailed programming specifications. The requirements documentation process is complex and requires a high degree of detailed documentation before any actual systems development activity occurs. Multiple iterations and refinements are required that include meetings with the business users and application developers to ensure the accuracy of the request and the documented systems specifications.

Manager of Applications Management

The manager of the applications management group is responsible for the performance of all the teams in the application development and support group. The application manager must have a complete understanding of the business systems used in each of the areas managed, but the most critical skills are the organization and management of the team. Setting priorities, managing the team, and completing project work are all part of the responsibilities of the application manager.

The application manager directs the applications teams according to the overall project priorities set by the IT steering committee. This manager oversees the delivery of the medium-term direction of the IT business systems to enhance capabilities, streamline processes, and successfully deliver priority projects to the business on time and on budget. Having a manager in this role enables the IT director to focus on the strategic direction of IT in the entire business and address the funding issues that confront an IT department, instead of worrying about delivering the next round of functional enhancements in three months.

Very small organizations may have a lead developer/tester also serve as the application manager. As businesses grow, a dedicated management resource at this level is important to maintain the control and direction of the IT application organization and reduce the number of managers and team leaders reporting directly to the IT director. If the IT director has more than four direct reports, it is time to consider creating an application management position.

Key Drivers for IT Development Structure and Staffing Levels

There are five key drivers for determining the staffing levels for the IT application groups:

1. Number of applications.
2. Number of systems.
3. Number of different technologies used (e.g., databases, operating systems, interface tools).
4. Number and complexity of systems interfaces.
5. Number and complexity of systems changes requested or required.

In most environments, as the number and complexity of different applications, systems, and technologies grow, higher numbers of skilled people are required to maintain and enhance those business applications. This assumes that the systems are relatively stable. Often, complex systems are riddled with subtle, difficult-to-diagnose errors, increasing again the number of skilled staff to provide baseline support. The number of staff needed is based on several key drivers. For example, one developer may be able to support multiple applications if they are on similar systems, use the same underlying technologies, and are stable. However, because of the high number of cross-system interactions, the introduction of differing technologies may increase the number of staff required on both the old and new systems.

IT application development groups frequently claim that they need more staff. The real question to be decided by the IT director and the IT steering committee is the appropriate level of staff to provide cost-effective service to the business and to execute the priority projects required in the IT area.

As discussed throughout this book, the "right" level of staffing is dependent on a wide variety of factors: Are the application enhancements so critical to the business that an additional person is required? Are new technologies being introduced into the organization? Are the underlying systems and skill sets necessary in the IT organization changing?

If the answers are yes, the staffing levels and skill sets should be closely examined to determine if it is appropriate to add staff. Rapid growth in staffing levels and frequent requests by IT for additional headcount are the warning signs of an IT department in trouble. This is particularly true where the usual drivers of staff size, such as business growth or technology platform complexity, have not changed. In this instance, the IT steering committee should ensure that the IT director is not overwhelmed, which is often the case. Ultimately the staffing level should be developed from the bottom up by estimating in hours the required time for the development projects approved and the hours required for system support based on the average number of support requests received.

Separation of Responsibilities between Operations and Applications Groups

We have uncovered a common practice among small and mid-size businesses of mixing the responsibilities of the IT application development group with those of the operations group in the IT department organization structure.

The effects of this lack of separation begins with confused priorities for the application developers. Should they work on the production problem of the day or focus their energies on the enhancements they are developing for the next major release? Major production problems must be addressed immediately, but business users are often persuasive in adding minor tasks to the immediate fix project plan. This inevitably leads to missed development deadlines because of reductions in the resources allocated to creation of the new capabilities because of the constant fire fighting. In addition, time is also lost because of switching costs associated with orienting a programmer to a particular problem and then reorienting him or her on the development assignment. Finally, it provides a convenient excuse for the development organization to miss the next release deadline or underdeliver on the functionality.

Avoid this scenario by adhering to the application development process and incorporating the most important requests into the regularly scheduled enhancement releases. Communicating the priority and availability of the enhancement requested is also critical to demonstrate that IT is responsive to the business user's needs and that he or she does not need to circumvent the IT process to get things done.

As we discuss in Chapter 9, while clearly defining the responsibilities of each group and keeping them from overlapping is the right policy, there are times when the application team may act as extra capacity in the operations area. The skill sets can overlap, and having built-in surge capacity available in the application area can allow the operations team to staff to its average level of demand instead of the peak demand, reducing overall IT costs. The cost of this approach may be some project slippage in instances where the application team is called on to assist the operations team, but the cost tradeoff is usually favorable. This approach is particularly appropriate for smaller organizations where the cost impact of saving one or two full-time employees is most noticeable.

IT Director and Administrative Support

The IT Director is responsible for all aspects of the IT organization, from day-to-day operations to long-term strategies, the IT architecture, and customized development. The position requires a unique combination of technology understanding, leadership and managerial skills, and business knowledge. The critical nature of this position requires an in-depth discussion, which is provided in Chapter 5.

Administrative support is important in the IT department, just as in any other business department. While a secretary with limited technology skills may be acceptable in a small IT organization, as the organization becomes larger, an assistant with some interest in and knowledge of technology becomes very valuable to the IT director and his or her staff. One well-run organization we encountered provided a career path for administrative assistants into the end-user support groups after they had acquired the appropriate experience, training, and tenure.

Other IT Organizational Issues

Mix of Contract and Employee IT Personnel

Use of contract IT personnel is becoming more common because of the difficulty of hiring individuals with knowledge of new technologies. The topic is covered in more detail in Chapter 9. The decision to use contract staffing is usually based on one or both of two rationales: the provision of additional capacity so that priority projects can be completed or the provision of unique skill sets not found on the existing IT team.

In the first case, managers often find that high-priority projects mandated for completion by the IT steering committee cannot be completed without the addition of team capacity. In these cases, temporary capacity is added with outside contractors. In some cases, the outside contractors are used for specific roles in a project (e.g., testing, requirements gathering), or they may be deployed to provide baseline support for existing systems so that the full-time team members can spend the majority of their time completing the high-priority projects.

In the second case, managers often find that new projects involve technologies that are new to the market, or at least to the existing IT team. The temporary engagement of skilled professionals with experience in the new technology can provide both capacity and on-the-job training for the existing IT team.

In every case, the IT manager should work to ensure that he or she maintains control of the projects and technologies being deployed. This can be accomplished by selectively hiring contractors for short terms (i.e., 3 to 12 months), targeting skills unavailable in the current organization, ensuring cross-training of employees to avoid dependency on a specific contractor or vendor, and establishing milestones to measure productivity and quality standards for performance. The manager should also establish clear reporting relationships between contractors and the full-time IT team members, and measure contractors by appropriate standards to ensure that the company is receiving full value for the services provided.

IT Accountability

The key drivers for accountability are different in the IT operations group and the IT application development group. The IT operations manager must:

1. Establish well-defined roles and responsibilities, a single point of end-user contact to prevent the end user from being forced to navigate the IT organization to obtain an answer or solution, clear ownership for end-user problems, problem status communication procedures (e.g., application outages, end-user problems, systems changes), clear problem hand off criteria and new ownership acceptance criteria, and problem closure and user acceptance parameters.

2. Measure help-desk response times, end-user problems (types and resolution times), end-user satisfaction via service ratings, and outages for systems, networks, and applications.

3. Recognize and reward rapid end-user problem resolution, identification and elimination of root causes of problems, and minimization of nonscheduled outages.

The IT application development manager must:

1. Establish well-defined roles and responsibilities, ownership for individual applications and new development initiatives, aggressive time lines and increases in application capabilities, deployment dates, testing time required, development time available (working backward from the deployment date to establish checkpoints and milestones), and ensure that the appropriate amount of time is allocated to testing.

2. Measure milestones and checkpoints met, functionality delivered, problems found in preproduction, and problems found in production.

3. Recognize and reward maintaining the time line commitments, meeting key milestones, minimizing problems with newly developed code.

4. Promote and ensure the use of an application development methodology to reduce risk, improve quality, and improve and ensure accuracy of workload estimates.

5. Ensure that IT demand management principles are adhered to in setting application development and enhancement priorities (see Chapter 15).

Large Company Considerations

While the organization structure and roles described in this chapter are relevant for any size of company, large companies dictate more division of labor because of the complexity and sheer size. Some of the more common additional considerations include:

1. *Architecture:* Information architecture, technology (infrastructure) architecture, and application architecture definition are the implied responsibilities of the IT director and his or her direct reports in small to mid-size companies. Larger organizations typically separate this responsibility into another position usually called the chief technology officer (CTO). CTOs are focused on defining and developing the three- to five-year future architecture of internal systems. The architecture is then handed to various managers to "execute" and make reality over that time period. All systems built or implemented by the IT department attempt to adhere to the architecture road map. For companies in technology industries (e.g., software firms), the CTO may not reside in the IT department but may report directly to the CEO and be strategically focused on architecture for customer-facing technology or "products" that are actually sold to customers.

2. *Security:* Security management may be a full-time position in some companies depending on the number of systems and access points into the company network and the industry the company operates within. Financial services companies, for example, should have a separate, full-time security position that may or may not reside in the IT department. Security personnel are responsible for implementing controls to limit the potential of unauthorized users from entering the company networks. This includes implementing firewall equipment, security monitoring software, encryption policies, access policies, password policies, physical access limitations, and detection and monitoring of fraud from internal staff.

3. *Audit/accounting control/project office:* Large IT organizations must have additional command and control as a separate function from regular management to avoid agency issues. Companies that process financial transactions, such as banks, must also protect against fraud protection from internal employees. This group may report to the IT director/CIO or to the finance/audit department. This function reviews project approval requests, reviews project plans, and tracks project progress versus original project plans. It also serves as a risk management function to ensure that large projects are following the approved methodologies to reduce project risk and reviews security practices on projects that involve sensitive systems. Project audits are both scheduled and random to catch fraud.

4. *Centralization versus decentralization:* There is a constant tension in large organizations between centralizing versus decentralizing IT operations. Centralizing results in increased control and lower costs for IT within the corporate IT entity while decentralizing results in more control at the business unit level and potentially at the user level. While the right balance requires careful analysis the two models are best used in specific situations. When business units require similar technologies, a high level of quality, coordination, standardization, and consistency in operation more centralization is preferred. Additionally when the business wants to operate IT at its lowest possible operating cost and share capital intensive infrastructure and personnel, centralization works best. For companies that have dissimilar business units that require vastly different technologies and operate in an environment where time to market is the most critical component of delivering IT systems, decentralization is preferred. Decentralization works well when business units have a high level of independence, complex customers and products, and less leveragability of technology for other business units to share. In most organizations IT operations can be centralized without much argument while the IT application development organizations will be determined by the best fit option.

5. *Organization by business functions, application types, business units, departments, and/or geography:* With the application development and maintenance organization, the application team can be organized multiple ways. One way was presented in the previous discussion. The larger the company, the more possible permutations. Some companies organize the application team into its functional areas (e.g., finance applications, and supply chain applications). Others organize based on business units (e.g., online catalog, retail, and wholesale). Others organize by geography (e.g., East Coast, West Coast, Europe, South America). A combination of methods may also be used. The decision on the organization will hinge on cost, technology expertise required,

level of industry knowledge required, level of functional knowledge required, size of the organization, and the needs and location of the end users.

Summary

The optimal organization of the IT department should adhere to a split between applications support and operations support. IT directors should avoid any blurring of the lines between roles and responsibilities between and within groups. A disorganized IT department with competing roles and gaps in service coverage continually finds itself behind in project delivery and user satisfaction. The proper organization and clearly delineated roles in the IT department rank equally with proper IT leadership, IT demand management, technology standards, vendor management, risk management, and financial management as a crucial lever for creating the effective IT department.

RESOURCES

Harris Kern, Stuart Galup, and Guy Nemiro, *IT Organization: Building a Worldclass Infrastructure* (Upper Saddle River, NJ: Prentice Hall, February 15, 2000).

Lynda M. Applegate, F. Warren McFarlan, and James L. McKenney, *Corporate Information Systems Management* (New York: McGraw-Hill/Irwin, February 23, 1999).

NOTE

1. Attributed to John Kenneth Galbraith.

5

The IT Director

Organization doesn't really accomplish anything. Plans don't accomplish anything, either. Theories of management don't much matter. Endeavors succeed or fail because of the people involved. Only by attracting the best people will you accomplish great deeds.

—General Colin Powell, Chairman (Ret.), Joint Chiefs of Staff, U.S. Secretary of State[1]

This chapter highlights the importance of the IT director or CIO in building and managing the effective IT department. Topics include scope of the role of the IT director and CIO, impact of the position on the productivity and capability of the IT department, skills and experience found in the most effective IT directors, and how those managers allocate their time. For IT department staff members, the chapter outlines the skills needed for promotion to IT director or CIO. The chapter also contains advice for senior managers seeking to hire or promote a new IT director or CIO, and explores how IT directors and CIOs can go astray and become disconnected from the business imperatives, as well as how to use effectively the IT steering committee to substitute or augment the IT director and CIO. Throughout the chapter, we use the term *IT director* and *CIO* interchangeably, except where specifically noted.

Why This Topic Is Important

We have found that the quality of the individual in the role of IT director or CIO has the single largest impact on the overall effectiveness of the IT department. Whether that role is called the *CIO*, the *vice president of information systems*, or simply the *IT director*, this person is usually responsible for one of the largest operations in a corporation in terms of costs and the only operation that interacts with virtually every point in the organization. To be effective in this role, the person must have a wide range of management skills, communications skills, motivational ability, and political savvy. Leadership in this position is critical to the success of the IT department. As observed in

94

Chapter 2, IT departments can, in best cases, be a source of competitive advantage and positively impact overall company productivity. In the worst cases, they can be endless sinkholes for corporate time and budgets. In the latter case, the ultimate cause of many of the problems plaguing troubled IT departments—failed projects, wasted dollars, and lost opportunities—is a lack of leadership from the top IT manager.

Because of the unique combination of technical and nontechnical skills required, the process of identifying the ideal candidate for the role is challenging and can be particularly vexing for the nontechnical senior management team members.

Internal promotion candidates are often technically skilled, but lacking in the requisite management expertise and communication skills. External candidates can be expensive and difficult to attract, particularly for smaller mid-market companies. Even after the right candidate is identified and hired, the position can often lead to conflicts of interest and agency problems that can be detrimental to the overall organization. The incentives and motivations of "star" IT managers are often incongruent with the incentives of the company overall. This chapter provides guidance for identifying, selecting, and motivating the right individual for this crucial role. Topics include:

- Impact of leadership on the effectiveness of IT departments.
- Scope of skills and capabilities required in the ideal IT director.
- Challenges in identifying and recruiting appropriate candidates for IT director.
- Approaches for identifying, evaluating, attracting, and successfully hiring IT directors.
- How successful IT directors allocate their time.
- How the role of IT director changes based on company size, geographic footprint, and type of business.
- What IT staff must do to be good candidates for promotion to IT director.
- What IT directors and CIOs must do to be good candidates for promotion out of the IT function.
- Role of the IT steering committee in IT leadership.
- How the IT director or CIO should be evaluated by senior management on an ongoing basis.

Critical Role of the IT Director

As observed by David Foote, managing partner of Foote Partners, a technology research and management consultancy, "The pressure on CIOs today is just tremendous. In many ways it is the toughest executive job. IT cuts across the entire business and [the CIO has] to be responsive to a wide variety of business and business styles."[2]

This rings true; next to the CEO, the IT director has the most highly visible and politically complicated position in most organizations. The responsibilities of the IT director cover a wide swath of territory—management of the utility functions that allow the business to conduct its basic operations (network, desktop computer support, e-mail), the applications that are used to plan and manage the business (forecasting, manufacturing, finance systems), as well as applications used to grow the business and gain competitive advantage (customer-facing systems, customer relationship management applications). This far-ranging set of responsibilities also means that, while the role can be challenging, the IT director is uniquely positioned to actually lead the company and effect real change.

In spite of the inherent potential of the position, and because of the intense pressure and visibility, the IT director is one of the most often maligned corporate professionals. According to numerous technology authorities like the Industry Advisory Council and *Baseline Magazine,* the average turnover rate for CIOs is between 33 percent and 50 percent annually.[3] As outlined in Chapter 2, technology spending is the largest nondirect cost in most corporations, and it has driven many of the productivity gains in the U.S. economy over the past five years. In spite of this, IT departments in general, and IT projects specifically, have gained an often well-deserved reputation for being endless money pits associated with few real business results. While there are many proximate causes to this ineffectiveness, the ultimate cause is a lack of leadership and focus in the IT department.

Our most frequent consulting engagements have been focused on helping IT leadership improve, and they have provided volumes of empirical evidence for these assertions. Invariably, our clients' IT departments improve after the IT director is effectively coached or, failing that, replaced, and a solid strategic plan for IT is put in place.

In case after case, the only variable being changed in the newly improved IT department is the manager or top level of managers; the technology in place is the same, the staff is the same, the vendors are the same. Consistently the focus of the department improves, the processes and procedures improve, and the ultimate execution of the overall department is superior. This repeated "controlled experiment" has proven without a doubt that IT leadership is the principle determinant of the overall success of the department.

The Talent Challenge

One of the most difficult challenges facing IT directors is that the traditional path to promotion has been from inside the IT department. The skills and disciplines that make a top performer in the IT operations or applications area are not the ones that best serve the IT director. In fact, although internal promotion candidates appear to be the most logical choice for IT director, they have been the type that we have seen fail most often, as they have had the most difficulty adapting to the new role and skills required.

The pre-promotion role for most IT director candidates consists of managing applications (i.e., director of applications or senior project manager) or operations (i.e., director of operations or senior network manager) where in-depth technology knowledge is required and where the individual reports to a manager with a similar technical background. Post-promotion skills are of an entirely different nature, with an emphasis on leadership, communication, planning, financial control, selling, and management. Exhibit 5.1 outlines several of the skills required or developed in the pre-promotion role, and Exhibit 5.2, the post-promotion role. Furthermore, the newly promoted IT director most often reports to a nontechnical executive, either the CFO or COO. Naturally, the combination of different required skills, new job pressures, a changed reporting relationship, and the inherent difficulty of the role lead to the high failure rates we have observed.

Based on these internal skill-set issues, many companies attempt to hire an IT director from outside. This approach has some difficulties as well. Large companies easily become victims of other companies' hiring mistakes when interviewing outside candidates. Candidates who have been promoted to a level of incompetence leave their company and actually get a "promotion" by being hired at another firm. After a two-year tenure and prior to discovery of their incompetence, they again embark on the job hunt for another unsuspecting company readily willing to hire and "promote."

Mid-market companies often have difficulty attracting the best talent. Their IT departments are smaller, and they have fewer dollars to invest in them. If a high-caliber business leader had all the experience and abilities

PRE-PROMOTION SKILLS
System requirements gathering and analysis.
Programming and systems development.
Application design and management.
System configuration.
Business process documentation.
Technology implementation.
Systems administration.
Systems performance management.
Technical, data, and applications architecture design and management.
Limited project management.
Upward reporting relationship with technical manager.

Exhibit 5.1   Skills Developed Pre-Promotion

POST-PROMOTION SKILLS
Management of both applications and operations portions of IT function.
Vendor selection, negotiation, and management.
Hiring, evaluating, managing, motivating, developing, promoting, and firing team members.
Decision making.
Cost containment.
Cost/benefit estimating; project economics estimation.
Budgeting.
Risk management.
Communications with business units and senior management.
Resource and project prioritization.
IT organizational design.
Standard setting and enforcement.
IT measurement and effectiveness.
Coordination of multiple, disparate projects, and initiatives across business units and internal functions.
Determining best use of scarce economic resources (staff, budget, time).
Maintenance of *steady-state* service levels for basic IT services.
Upward reporting relationship to nontechnical business manager, COO, or CFO.

Exhibit 5.2   Skills Required Post-Promotion

listed in the exhibits, it is not likely he or she would want to come to work in a small to mid-size IT department—even as the director. Most small to mid-size companies simply cannot offer the level of responsibility and opportunities to attract the best professional from outside. A potential high-performance candidate may feel that he or she would not obtain enough visibility to make a difference in the organization.

Larger companies often have this difficulty as well, suffering from the poor reputation of IT and the perception that a career in the IT department offers little room for advancement to senior management. Only 7 percent of Fortune 500 companies placed CIOs in their group of five highest-paid officers.[4] Although the budgetary and staff responsibilities are significant enough to attract high-quality IT directors, they often lack upward mobility and a chance to be promoted to senior business roles (e.g., COO, CEO, SVP of unit).

We have dubbed this the *Groucho Marx* problem. Marx once famously quipped "I don't want to belong to any club that would have me as a member." Applied to the IT director, it means that any individual willing to accept the job is, by definition, likely the wrong person, particularly in the instance of mid-market companies. An individual who would take a job with little corporate influence or with very little opportunity for upward advancement may be looking for a sinecure, or is simply not savvy enough to understand the implications of the position. To attract the best talent, senior management should ensure that the IT department is a "club" where an A player would want to belong. Further, the senior management team should be aware of the inherent transition difficulties for internal promotions, and they should work with the internally promoted IT directors to help them develop the skills they need to be successful in the role.

Another phenomenon we have observed in companies that have been successful in creating an attractive role for the IT director is the salary equation. After a company has attracted the right individual for the IT director role, it has trouble offering the right level of compensation to close the offer. For many small or mid-size companies, this ideal IT director, who can ensure the creation and management of a highly effective IT department, requires a higher compensation level than some members of the senior management team. Companies have worked around this issue by hiring relatively expensive "turnaround specialists" as temporary CIOs to improve or stabilize the department, then hiring an IT director to follow the temporary CIO in a caretaker role.

In every case, senior management must understand that in addition to providing an attractive environment, the salary structure must be competitive to ensure that the best candidates are available. A dollar invested in a high-quality IT director is returned to the company many times over from the effective management of IT.

Finally, companies should guard carefully against the agency problems implicit in the IT director role. Companies that successfully clear these hurdles, having attracted a top-flight IT director at a reasonable salary, often find themselves in a further dilemma. Aggressive, career-oriented IT directors are often *builders* who want to create new systems, build staff levels, and implement or enhance systems. In the worst case, we have seen IT directors who simply see their current position as a stepping-stone in their careers. In these cases, the IT directors made decisions that put their career interests over the best interests of the business. They worked hard spending corporate resources to expand their portfolio of experience in building systems and managing large-scale initiatives, regardless of the outcome for the business, in the hopes of departing for positions in other companies with even larger budgets and salary expectations. In other cases, we have seen the CEO or CFO restrict technology spending for business reasons and request a strategy of pure "system maintenance" in IT. In these cases, the companies had little chance of retaining or attracting A players to IT management.

As demonstrated throughout this book, ROI-focused growth of the IT department can create enormous value for the company. However, we have often seen out-of-control spending predicated on the *building* that improperly motivated IT directors feel is their mandate. Ensuring that the IT director's incentives are in line with those of the senior management team is critical in avoiding this trap. IT directors should be rewarded for providing the most appropriate level of service for the least cost to the organization, and ensuring that every effort of the IT department is focused on reducing costs, improving revenues, or affording more control over the business. It is up to the senior management team and the IT director to work together so that the *build* incentives are secondary to the priorities of the business or that the "maintain" strategy is readily accepted and understood by those in IT.

The skills required, difficulty of attracting the best candidates, salary constraints, and agency issues add up to a "talent challenge" that must be addressed by senior management. While this requires more than customary attention be paid to IT by senior management and a rethinking of the role of the IT director in many companies, it also provides the most important building block of the effective IT department: the right IT director.

Responsibilities and Skills Needed

The director is responsible for overall IT policy and the alignment of information systems across the business units. Gartner Group has researched the director role extensively and created the following outline of responsibilities:

- *Business technology planning process:* Sponsor collaborative planning processes.
- *Applications development:* New and existing for enterprise initiatives and overall coordination for business unit/divisional initiatives.
- *IT infrastructure and architecture:* Running as well as ensuring that ongoing investments are made.
- *Sourcing:* Make-versus-buy decisions relative to outsourcing versus in-house provisioning of IT services and skills.
- *Partnerships:* Establishing strategic relationships with key IT suppliers and consultants.
- *Technology transfer:* Provide enabling technologies that make it easier for customers and suppliers to do business with our enterprise as well as increase revenue and profitability.
- *Customer satisfaction:* Interact with internal and external clients to ensure continuous customer satisfaction.
- *Training:* Provide training for all IT users to ensure productive use of existing and new systems.[5]

Much of the complexity of the IT director role comes from the wide variety of business constituencies, outside suppliers, and staff that he or she must deal with on an ongoing basis. The director needs to understand, communicate with, negotiate with, and influence a wide and diverse group, including:

- Senior management.
- Business unit general managers.
- Outside business partners/customers/suppliers.
- Functional vice presidents.
- Business process managers.
- Professional IT staff.
- End users.
- Vendors and service providers.

Each of these groups may have very different needs and conflicting agendas. In addition, each of these groups may require very different sets of communications skills to effectively manage interaction. The IT director must be able to reconcile differing agendas to properly align the role of technology throughout the corporation. This reconciliation requires experience in presentation, negotiation, conflict resolution, personnel management, and political conciliation.

A new IT director must be able to hit the ground running and immediately gain an understanding of the range of agendas presented by various stakeholder groups. Unfortunately, many IT directors are put into their positions because of their technical knowledge as opposed to their management savvy. Without prior management experience and expert communications skills, a new IT director is likely to encounter serious problems that cascade and grow exponentially over time. These problems can lead to many of the outward signs of IT distress discussed in Chapter 2. Eventually, these signs of distress can lead to true business failures and result in enough senior management dissatisfaction to lead to major restructuring of IT, most often involving the departure of the IT director. As we noted earlier, it is no surprise that many IT professionals only half-jokingly claim that the *CIO* acronym stands for "Career Is Over."

A successful IT director typically has a unique combination of business strategy understanding, business/people management experience, financial planning/budgeting experience, communication and selling skills, and a broad understanding of business technology. Without this combination, there are bound to be holes in the director's skills that prevent him or her from being effective.

The IT director should have a strong understanding of the company's business strategy, competitive landscape and industry trends, business unit organization, business partners, major initiatives, and key corporate processes. This understanding usually comes after working in an organization for some time, but a new IT director needs to quickly grasp this information and become fluent in the organization's business context. Previous positions in business development in the industry, and strategy consulting experience can provide the bird's-eye view that helps facilitate the needed understanding.

The IT director must have extensive experience in project and people management. He or she should have significant experience in all the areas highlighted as skills required for the IT director in Exhibit 5.2. In addition, the IT director should have previously managed 5 to 10 technology-related projects from beginning to end, and proven that he or she can deliver expected results on time and within budget. At least some of those projects should have crossed over multiple business units, functional groups, and outside partners.

Another key factor of success for an IT director is business line management and responsibility for profit and loss (P&L). Without experience managing P&L, many functional managers have trouble showing sensitivity to the effects of costs on the bottom line. The best way to gain this sensitivity and understanding is for a manager to spend some time in a role where he or she has direct responsibility for bringing in revenues and is accountable for delivering bottom line results. Having this experience also helps the IT director gain instant credibility with other business unit heads. Ideally, the IT director should also have an MBA that firmly focuses his or her thinking and skills on business imperatives. Although it is not a necessity for success in the position, the classical business concepts (e.g., negotiations, investment analysis) learned in an MBA program can be extremely useful.

Finally, the IT director should usually have some fairly deep understanding of a wide range of technologies in terms of their costs/benefits, pros/cons, and overall business value. While an IT director doesn't need to know how to write code or administer a database server, he or she should know the advantages and disadvantages of using particular platforms and how these will affect the business. The IT director should be able to quickly understand how any proposed technology solution will increase revenues, cut costs, or provide more management control over the business (and reduce risk). Ideally, the IT director should have previously been involved in a dozen or more projects involving technology evaluation, technology selection, build/buy decisions, system implementation, and ongoing operations management. Preferably, the IT director's experience should have spanned multiple business units, functions, and technology platforms.

Above all, the IT director should have impeccable communication and time management skills. The communications skills include a strong ability to listen to the needs of different groups, ability to make persuasive presentations, ability to inspire key potential employees, ability to effectively negotiate with a wide variety of stakeholders, ability to sell ideas, and general ability to develop amicable relations with a wide range of different personalities. Because of the immense pressures and changing responsibilities given to an IT director, he or she must also be able to effectively manage his or her time among various constituencies. Time management is a fundamental skill that must be carried out through efficient prioritization, meetings, delegation, and people management.

How Successful Managers
Allocate Their Time

Studies of the most successful IT directors and CIOs have reached similar conclusions: Winning IT directors spend the majority of their time planning and communicating and the minority of their time "doing." Because the role can be challenging, particularly for the newly promoted, many directors retreat to managing and executing the tasks they find most comfortable, usually the tactical execution of projects or enhancements. While having the capability for hands-on execution is certainly a strength and part of the skillset of the ideal IT director, it is often a refuge for the overwhelmed director.

IT directors should allocate the bulk of their time to communication with business unit managers, IT direction setting, and staff management. The best IT directors hire "A" players to lead their teams, avoiding the daily minutiae of managing the department by delegating the tasks that can be accomplished by a quality team. This frees up time for the IT director to develop the larger picture agenda and ensures that he or she develops the trusted relationship with the business required to accomplish that agenda.

A successful IT manager we know goes jogging at lunch every day with a group of business unit managers from his company. His close relationship with the business users, a natural result of half-an-hour per day spent with the management team, has resulted in a highly effective IT department that keeps the priorities of the business first.

New IT directors should spend the first 30 days in the position completing a full assessment of the department. The assessment should be fully documented and provide an unbiased review of all components (e.g., the organization, technical architecture, application architecture, projects, budget). The second 30 days can then be spent developing the three-year strategic plan. During this first 60-day period, a full schedule of interviews with each of the business unit and functional department leaders should occur. This develops a complete picture of the current satisfaction level throughout the business, as well as the technologies required by the business. Finally, the new IT director must sell the plan to the IT steering committee and the business, then develop an implementation plan to improve the department in critical gap areas to achieve targets in the strategic plan.

On an ongoing basis, the time allocation among competing activities differs depending on the size of the company and the IT organization. The IT directors' time can be divided into five categories:

1. Administrative and financial.
2. "Doing" technical work or managing projects.
3. Cultivating relationships with senior management.
4. Communicating, marketing, and selling the IT department to the rest of the organization.
5. Leading and developing senior IT staff.

While all categories are important at one time or another, the IT director can gain the most leverage and make the largest difference by cultivating relationships with senior management and participating in the company's overall business management, while delegating many of the other activities to high-quality direct reports.

Financial and administrative matters can seem very important; however, they are never the catalyst of great success. If done badly, they can lead to very poor performance; however, successful directors learn to optimize and reduce time spent on such matters yet still execute well. No one should spend more than 10 percent of their time here if they are to excel.

Spending time doing technical work or managing projects depends greatly on the size of the company and organization. In a small company, an IT director may be forced to contribute in a hands-on role because of budgetary constraints. In such instances, the IT director should spend no more than 40 percent of their time "doing," otherwise they cease being an IT director and more of a glorified manager. Much of the strategic IT function will likely fall or reside in the CFO, or whoever is ultimately responsible for IT. The IT department in these cases will never perform well and the IT director will never be valued and, more importantly, will be blamed for the poor performance. In mid-sized IT organizations—staff greater than 15—the amount of time spent "doing" by the IT director should approach 0 percent and never be greater than 10 percent. Why 10 percent? IT directors must keep abreast of technology and close to those they lead. By keeping this edge they continue to earn the respect of those they wish to lead. While "doing" is not a highly leveraged use of time, it helps keep the IT director close to the work in their unit.

Cultivating relationships with senior management is important in order for the IT director to be involved with the business. If the IT director does not build respect with the business unit leaders, he or she cannot be a good leader. During this activity, the IT director can continue to learn the business as well as sell ideas to improve revenue or reduce costs in the business units. By doing this, the IT director becomes a valuable member of the company's senior leadership team. This time can also be used to continuously test the priorities of the business units to ensure the IT priorities are aligned and to perform quality assurance. In most cases, this activity takes 30 percent to 50 percent of the IT director's time.

Communicating, marketing, and selling the IT organization to the company is critical for the IT department to gain the respect of the entire organization. The IT director can also gain leverage by teaching others in the IT organization who to "sell" the department to. Promoting a culture of over-communication and relationship building will help the IT director accomplish this. Typically, this function can be well fulfilled spending 10 percent to 20 percent of time here.

Leading and developing senior IT staff is a high-value activity. The better the direct reports perform, the more leverage the IT director will gain from his or her staff. The performance of the IT department can be greatly increased by improving senior staff. Here the IT director sets direction for the staff, provides a vision, creates management frameworks, and helps the staff solve *their* problems. Finally, the IT director holds the staff accountable and either makes them better through coaching or counsels them out of the company when they are performing poorly. IT directors devote 20 percent to 30 percent of the work week to this activity depending on the size of the organization.

Obviously the percentages vary by company size and by individual skill; however, the IT director should review each of the five categories and determine what time allocation provides the best use of time on high-value and leveraged activities. Time spent outside the company (e.g., developing relationships with peers, within the industry, with clients, and with vendors) is also important and should not be neglected, but should not be a significant time sink either.

Recruiting and Retaining the Ideal Candidate

Recruiting and retaining the ideal IT director candidate can be difficult. The job must be constructed in a way that is attractive to the best candidates, and this often requires members of the senior management team to rethink the scope and influence of the role. Senior executives should ask themselves, "Would I take this job?" If the answer is no, there is no reason to believe that the best candidates would. Just because the job is technology-related doesn't mean that the candidates lack any of the career ambitions or interests of their counterparts on the senior management team. In fact, the reverse is true. The best candidates want to understand how their careers can advance, and they want to be in a position to influence decision making in their companies.

As outlined earlier, successful candidates have a solid base of technical skills, and they will have worked in an IT department, preferably with exposure to both applications management and IT operations. The best candidates have enhanced this basic experience with team management, staff development, business training, and a proven ability to deliver quantifiable results.

Many IT director recruitment processes fail because of an overemphasis on finding an exact match of technical skills required instead of the leadership, business, communication, and management background found in an ideal candidate. While specific knowledge of the operating systems, applications, and other pieces of the technical environment in a given company are helpful, such knowledge should always take a back seat to the candidate's proven ability to deliver results, prioritize work, communicate with the business, and manage people.

Another common failing in the recruiting process, particularly for growing companies, is to focus on candidates who have "built" an organization. One candidate we were interviewing had most recently held the role of CTO/CIO at a failed startup. The company had been extraordinarily well funded and was highly reliant on technology for internal use, as well as for its main product line. The candidate had been responsible for all technology. When asked about his most important achievement while there, he proudly boasted, "I built an IT department of over 300 people inside of one year!" Too many CIO candidates are focused on what they "built" as opposed to how they use their budget, staff, and capabilities to drive revenues and reduce costs for their company. A good recruiting process identifies candidates who can generate these results for their companies, regardless of what they are asked to "build."

When interviewing potential candidates for an IT director position, a scorecard can be used to help drive the selection process and to ensure that the candidate has technology-specific knowledge. Subjective criteria covering all of the previously mentioned areas can be included on the scorecard along with weighting for each criterion based on the value necessary for the organization. Exhibit 5.3 is an example of a scorecard for evaluating potential IT director candidates.

Reference and background screening of candidates should not be overlooked. Often, when recruiting from the outside, in the rush to complete the sourcing, interviewing, and closing of offers, companies neglect to perform

CRITERIA	SCORE
• IT operations management experience.	
• IT applications management experience.	
• Custom development (requirements gathering through deployment).	
• Project management/team leadership.	
• Profit and loss responsibility.	
• Departmental budgetary responsibility.	
• Non-IT business management responsibility.	
• Staff management (no. of staff managed).	
• Vendor management experience.	
• Vendor selection experience.	
• Business training (advanced degree, other).	
• Undergraduate and post-graduate degree training.	
• Verbal and written communication.	
• Senior management team participation.	

Exhibit 5.3   Example IT Director Evaluation Scorecard

the most basic screening for the IT director position. Candidates should have their references and educational backgrounds verified, as well as the normal background screening that can encompass credit checks, criminal background screens, and so on. This process can usually be coordinated through the corporate human resources (HR) department, who most often have standard processes in place for completing background screening. Other highly valuable screening techniques include IQ testing (to determine raw intelligence capability), psychological and behavioral testing (to determine fit with senior management team), and situational interviews (to determine decision making patterns). In all cases, the CEO, CFO, or manager of the IT director should spend time in a social setting (e.g., lunch, dinner, golf, or ballgame) with the finalists to make sure the person is likeable and a good cultural fit for the organization.

Other Factors Impacting the IT Director's Role

The role of the IT director gradually changes over time with changes in the business. The role is primarily affected by the size of the company, scope of operations, and its geographic footprint. As the company grows and changes, so, too, does the role of the IT director and the skills he or she requires to be successful.

For smaller companies with a relatively small scope of operations, the IT department is usually smaller in size (10 to 50 people) and budget ($1 to $5 million). At this size, the IT director can be more focused on individual project management and can take greater ownership of specific initiatives as discussed earlier. An advantage of having a department of this size is that the IT director can generally have more personal relationships with all the heads of the business and functional units. When the steering committee is evaluating potential candidates for these positions, they can make tradeoffs between experience levels and compensation. They can be less stringent on higher level requirements such as P&L experience and extensive program management. This can help expand the pool of candidates and lower the overall compensation costs.

As a company expands through either organic growth or acquisitions, the IT department will likely expand in size (50 to 200 people) and scope ($5 to $20 million). At this point, the IT director needs to gain key skills to remain effective, including:

- *Learning to get things done through people.* The IT director needs to modify his or her organizational structure to more effectively delegate responsibility to senior managers within the group. If the director cannot master this skill of delegation, he or she will likely fall into the trap of being cramped for time and not be able to focus on the more important high-level issues. In addition, he or she may not be able to stay in sync with senior management.

- *Learning to judge people and attract the best professionals.* As growth accelerates, the IT director will not have the time to get to know every candidate. He must spend less time with each potential new hire. For this reason, he or she must learn how to judge and evaluate people using objective measures and outside help from HR professionals.

- *Developing and managing people.* The IT director needs to become even more focused on the development needs of his or her staff. This includes ensuring that the best members are rewarded and that the poor performers are eliminated.

- *Focus on the majors.* While the IT director could get into the details of specific projects with a small IT department, he or she needs to keep his or her head above the trees to avoid getting stuck in minute details as the department grows and larger issues surface.

- *Ensuring all projects are productive.* The IT director needs to continually ensure that all projects are focused on at least one of three objectives: (1) cost reduction, (2) revenue improvement, and/or (3) increased control of the business (risk reduction).

- *Developing partnerships with management.* Through diligent use of the IT steering committee and informal meetings, the IT director needs to build stronger relationships with the lines of business to stay on top of ever-changing and growing needs.

Eventually, the IT department may increase to over 200 people with a budget over $50 million per year. At this stage, the company is probably large in terms of geographic footprint, as well as diversity of operating divisions. As growth continues, the IT director should more closely reflect the image of the "ideal IT director." The focus of his or her work should shift from that of a large program administrator to that of a true business leader. The job will include less and less internal management, but more and more external coordination and bridge building within and outside the enterprise.

As the enterprise grows and changes, the role of the IT director must change. The IT steering committee should determine if the current IT director (1) wants to change his or her role and (2) has the requisite skills and experience needed to make the change. If the answer to either of these questions is no, time should not be wasted trying to "get by" until there is a serious problem. The steering committee should take a proactive position on finding a new IT director who is suitable for the role.

Other major factors influencing the type of IT director who is successful include industry and geographic footprint. The skills required of the successful IT director in education and government differ somewhat from the skills required for a private-sector IT director. The budgeting process for federal and state government and educational institutions is a different process than for private sector companies. The IT mission is also often different. Further, in federal or state agencies, the top official is often a political appointee with an agenda that may vary from the career professionals in the agency.

As observed in a General Accounting Office (GAO) study, "Implementing Effective CIO Organizations,"[6] "Agency . . . executives are political appointees who are often more focused on national policy issues than building capabilities essential for achieving the desired strategic and program outcomes," and "the federal budget process can create funding challenges for the federal CIO that are not found in the private sector," and, finally, "the relative inflexibility of federal pay scales makes it difficult to attract and retain the highly skilled IT professionals required to develop and support the systems being proposed." It is an understatement to say that the role of the federal IT executive is challenging. We recommend two GAO-created reports on the role of the CIO as reading for state or federal government IT directors—"Executive Guide: Maximizing the Success of Chief Information Officers" (GAO-01-376G) and "Chief Information Officers: Implementing Effective CIO Organizations" (T-AIMD-00-128).

In every case, the ideal IT directors for these organizations have exposure to, and understanding of, the budgetary and political factors that impact their jobs. Although the skills in the private sector tend not to vary from industry to industry, an understanding of the specific industry is always important for the IT director.

Getting Promoted

Because of the skills gap noted in this chapter, the promotion to IT director can be a traumatic, and often career-ending, experience for the new manager. The well-prepared new director can avoid being the victim of his or her new role by rapidly working to develop the core skills described. As we have too often observed, the newly promoted manager clings to his or her previous role as a "doer," and ignores the new skills needed to succeed in this role.

The first goal of the newly promoted IT director is to fill in the gaps in his or her knowledge of the business, senior management priorities, and the business itself. The director should work hard to establish understanding of the portions of the IT department where he or she has not had sufficient exposure, whether operations or applications. The IT director should next begin understanding the priorities of the senior management team. This can be done informally through lunch meetings and formally through the vehicle of the IT steering committee. Finally, the IT director should work to understand the components of the business and how they fit with the IT department goals. For example, the IT director in a manufacturing company should understand how forecasting, order management, manufacturing, shipping, and finance interact at a detailed level.

The Role of the IT Steering Committee

The role of the IT steering committee is described fully in Chapter 17. However, it is important to note that the committee is the most important vehicle for helping the IT director succeed and for ensuring that the priorities of the business are reflected in the IT department's projects, service levels, staffing, and budgets.

In companies where the IT director is weak or absent, the IT steering committee can be an effective prop in the interim until the right director can be found, serving as a "virtual CIO." In many cases, the IT steering committee works in conjunction with an outside consultant who serves as a temporary CIO.

In every case, the presence of an IT steering committee helps potential IT director candidates feel assured that the proper management of the IT function is a top priority for senior management and is viewed as a business enabler rather than a cost pit. The potential candidate can feel confident that his or her views are respected in the organization by both senior management and the functional and business unit leaders.

Evaluating the IT Director

To keep the IT director from overfocusing on systems growth and initiatives to the detriment of the overall business, incentives can be developed. Holding the IT director strictly accountable for value-increasing performance measures such as ROI helps keep the focus in the right areas; however, it may not be enough to prevent the director from crafting projects to justify unneeded expenditures. Incentive compensation should be tied directly to measures (e.g., reduction in company paper use, increase revenue per employee as productivity indicator, ROI achievement) that are collected independently through the ongoing IT performance measurement program. These incentives can help alleviate the agency problem by rewarding the director for increasing value and punishing the director for destroying value.

Examples of key performance measures (KPIs) are described in Chapter 16. These should be measured on an ongoing basis and used as inputs for an incentive compensation scheme developed in conjunction with an HR compensation specialist.

As the IT director gains tenure in the organization, he or she should be building relationships throughout the company to effectively and efficiently fulfill his or her mission. In addition to performing well against standard measurement indicators, the IT director should also be judged against the quantity and quality of relationships developed with major stakeholders. One of the themes of this book emphasizes the need for better alignment between IT and business/functional units. To achieve this end, personal relationships must be developed between the IT director and stakeholders. The organization meets the IT director halfway through the formation of the steering committee, but the director needs to make the effort to ensure that the relationships are forged and maintained.

One way the IT director can accomplish this is to perform a regular (quarterly) self-audit. Questions to be considered include:

- Have you read the latest company financial reports?
- Can you list key financial metrics (e.g., revenues, profits)?
- Can you list the company's top five customers?
- Do you understand the business strategy of the company's top five competitors?
- Can you list the top five key trends in the industry?
- Can you draw the top three layers of the company's organizational chart?
- Have you met or spoken with a customer in the past month?
- Do you know the secretaries/receptionists of stakeholders by name?
- Have you met in person, one-on-one, at least once with all of the business unit leaders in the past month?

If the IT director cannot answer all of these questions with a yes or an appropriate answer, he or she needs to start making additional concerted efforts to build relationships and enhance his or her strategic view of the organization.

NOTES

1. Collin Powell, *My American Journey* (New York: Random House, 1995).
2. Mindy Blodgett, "The CIO Starter Kit," *CIO Magazine* (May 15, 1999). Copyright © 2002 CXO Media, Inc. Reprinted with permission.
3. Kim Nash, "How CIOs Reach the Top," *Baseline Magazine* (September 4, 2002); "IAC/CIO Task Force Report" (Industry Advisory Council, July 15, 1996).
4. See note 3.
5. "The Mission of the CIO," *CIO Executive Research Center* (Stamford, CT: Gartner Measurement Services, April 23, 1999). Copyright © 2002 CXO Media, Inc. Reprinted with permission.
6. David L. McClure, "Chief Information Officers: Implementing Effective CIO Organizations," GAO/T-AIMD-00-128 (Washington, DC: U.S. General Accounting Office, March 24, 2000).

6

IT Direction and Standard Setting

"Would you tell me, please, which way I ought to go from here?" asked Alice.
"That depends a good deal on where you want to get to," said the Cat.
"I don't much care where—" said Alice.
"Then it doesn't matter which way you go," said the Cat.
"—so long as I get somewhere," Alice added.
"Oh, you're sure to do that," said the Cat, "if only you walk long enough."

—Lewis Carroll, *Alice in Wonderland*[1]

IT standard and direction setting includes the creation, documentation, propagation, and adherence to a set of standards for all elements of the technology platform in an organization—including hardware, software, peripherals, development languages, operating systems, desktop systems, network protocols, and telephony.

IT standard and direction setting often gets lost in the shuffle of myriad other decisions made in the day-to-day operation of the IT department, yet it is a decision area that has one of the largest impacts on the efficiency and overall productivity of the IT department—the flexibility of the department to handle changes in the business and new requirements. Furthermore, the IT standards model generally dictates a large part of the underlying cost model for the organization in terms of both labor and capital expense.

However, making choices around IT standards and setting overall technology direction can be challenging for IT leadership. A wide variety of factors and constraints impede the ability to see around corners. Technologies interact in different ways and are at different points in the technology life cycle, mastering the fundamentals of varying technologies that cover ground from hardware to development languages to network protocols is challenging, and it is difficult to discern real vendor products from "smoke and mirrors" and competing agendas from within and outside the IT department.

Compounding the issue of building a cohesive, standardized IT environment is the fact that most systems are built incrementally versus emerging as a fully articulated complete environment at once. The level of technical diversity is particularly high in companies that have had technology in place for a long time or have seen large changes to their business model. Therefore, the IT director's ability to control the existing footprint, as well as the timing of any future changes, adds to the already formidable challenge.

This means that technology direction and standard setting always falls short of the perfection, or even near perfection wished for by the IT manager; instead, IT managers are forced to "satisfice" in this area. Although the task is challenging, the manager must devise an approach that attempts to maximize the effectiveness of the IT department, but focuses on creating, documenting, promulgating, and adhering to an overall technology plan that includes standards for all technology departments.

Why This Topic Is Important

The decisions made around standards have a tremendous impact on the capabilities and productivity of the department. During an IT effectiveness engagement, we saw many of the typical complaints about the efficacy of the IT department from the client's senior management team; in particular, there was always a variety of excuses for being late with projects. When we interviewed the director of IT, he had this to say:

> Well, we try hard to get projects done but never seem to get any traction. We plan our projects well and follow all the normal project management disciplines. We have a dedicated staff, clear project goals, and the backing of the business. The number one thing getting in our way is the complexity of our environment. We have two accounting systems, two CRM systems—one for sales force automation, and one for help desk systems—as well as custom systems for production management and Web sites written in both Java and ASP. We also have several operating systems—Solaris, Linux, Windows, and OS/2. All of the systems are interfaced with custom code and batch jobs. Every time we start a new project, despite our best planning, there are cases of unintended consequences resulting in system outages or errors, as well as unexpected delays because of the intricacies of the system interactions. This draws out even the simplest projects and makes complex projects nearly impossible. We spend so much of our time dealing with the project-related issues and downtime that we will never find a way to migrate to systems that we can manage.

We immediately understood why the IT department was having trouble getting its projects completed.

Although, as you would expect, this is a more commonplace occurrence with larger companies; we have seen this phenomenon nearly as often in smaller companies, with less complex requirements and technology environments. In this example, the client was a small company with less than $70 million in annual revenues. Ultimately, they found ways to reduce the chaos that had been created and get to a set of technology standards that was the right balance of capability, flexibility, and cost for their organization.

Although IT direction setting, via standards, is an important piece of the puzzle in an overall IT strategy and smoothly functioning IT department, it is not the only piece. Project prioritization and management, IT organization design, budgeting and cost analysis, vendor selection, and staffing are all equally important concepts for developing an overall technology strategy and are discussed in other chapters. These topics can all rightly be considered part of an overall IT direction; this chapter addresses the issues of establishing standard technology platforms to be used by the IT department, the migration of existing platforms, and the acquisition of new technology. Issues discussed in this chapter include:

- Why technology standards are important and the consequences of technology chaos.
- What technology areas should be covered by standards.
- Frameworks for creating and documenting technology standards.
- Life-cycle evaluation of existing and new technology platforms.
- How to achieve acceptance of standards by the business.
- How to enforce and perpetuate standards in the IT and business organization.
- Management of the procurement process to ensure adherence to the standards.
- When and how to make technology standard exceptions.
- How to keep the technology direction and standards up to date.
- How to survive after inheriting a highly heterogeneous environment.

Standard Setting for Technology Areas

Standards should be set for any piece of technology deployed in the organization, particularly those for which the IT department is responsible.

Often, technology standards decisions are made based on grouping dependent and interrelated technologies. The choice of a certain operating system dictates the network protocol used; the choice of a certain CRM package narrows the field of hardware on which it will run. In these cases, it is important to recognize and make explicit the technology decisions that are being made in areas outside the area under consideration, so that the grouping of technology can be treated in its entirety.

Typically, the technologies involved fall into a few broad categories. A sample inventory is shown in Exhibit 6.1. This list varies widely by company,

CATEGORY	TECHNOLOGIES
Computing hardware and servers	Desktops Laptops PDAs Network attached storage/SAN Servers
Application software	Package software (ERP, CRM, other point solutions) Custom developed software Application integration/middleware E-mail
Systems software	Operating system Virus detection/elimination System monitoring System performance management Configuration management Web services
Development	Development languages Databases Database design standards (normalization rules) Coding conventions
Infrastructure and facilities	Cabling Equipment storage (racks/shelves) Environmental controls
Network	Routers Hubs Firewall Patch panels
Peripherals	UPS Network printers Desktop printers Tape backup Media burner (CDRW/DVDRW)
Outside services	Consulting (by application/technology area) LAN/WAN cabling

Exhibit 6.1   Sample Technology Inventory

and the sample inventory here should be considered a starting point for the creation of a custom inventory plan for a specific organization.

Framework for Setting Technology Standards

We have developed a baseline framework for use by organizations in developing their own technology standards. Because each organization is different, this framework may require some customization for an improved fit, but it should provide a useful start for any technology manager. Exhibit 6.2 outlines the overall process.

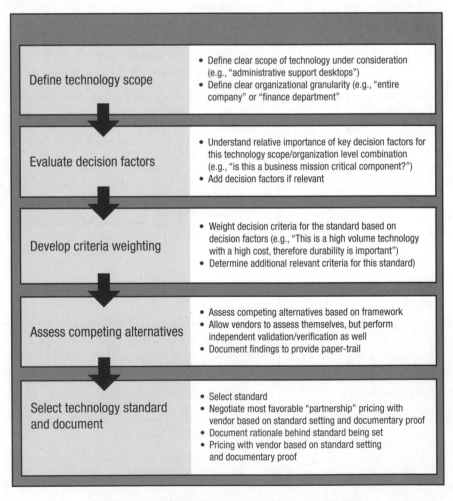

Define technology scope
- Define clear scope of technology under consideration (e.g., "administrative support desktops")
- Define clear organizational granularity (e.g., "entire company" or "finance department"

Evaluate decision factors
- Understand relative importance of key decision factors for this technology scope/organization level combination (e.g., "is this a business mission critical component?")
- Add decision factors if relevant

Develop criteria weighting
- Weight decision criteria for the standard based on decision factors (e.g., "This is a high volume technology with a high cost, therefore durability is important")
- Determine additional relevant criteria for this standard)

Assess competing alternatives
- Assess competing alternatives based on framework
- Allow vendors to assess themselves, but perform independent validation/verification as well
- Document findings to provide paper-trail

Select technology standard and document
- Select standard
- Negotiate most favorable "partnership" pricing with vendor based on standard setting and documentary proof
- Document rationale behind standard being set
- Pricing with vendor based on standard setting and documentary proof

Exhibit 6.2   IT Standard Setting Process Overview

The process begins by selecting the organizational scope and specific technology under consideration. The appropriate level of granularity for this task varies but should be at a high enough level for the standard to have meaning (e.g., the *standard desktop* should be defined at the company level versus having a potentially differing standard for each department, while the standard set for servers may vary at the individual server level depending on what applications the server supports).

After the technology grouping is determined, the decision factors for the standard are evaluated. These factors are the key pieces of information that drive the criteria used in setting the technology standard. For instance, if the technology under consideration is the server for a company-wide ERP system, the mission-critical nature of the deployment dictates that the standard set for such servers includes high reliability. However, if the technology being considered is a "dumb terminal" for use by dozens of data entry clerks, cost and durability become more heavily weighted than reliability. Exhibit 6.3 contains a detailed description of each of the potential decision factors.

The decision factor analysis determines which criteria are important for the standard. While the criteria should be kept the same for each assessment, their relative importance varies greatly according to the decision factors. Exhibit 6.4 outlines the criteria that may be considered in setting the standard, based on the relevant decision factors.

After the criteria weighting is complete, the analysis becomes a relatively simple comparison of competing alternatives, with a single choice emerging for the subgrouping of technology being considered. Exhibit 6.5 shows how the decision factors impact the importance and weighting of the technology standard criteria.

The remainder of this section outlines examples of technologies by factor and explains the weightings shown in Exhibit 6.5.

Decision Factor: Mission Criticality

Examples: Manufacturing planning and management system, warehouse picking and shipping systems, and hardware for running ERP system.

Primary Considerations
- *Reliability:* If the business cannot run when the system is down, reliability is of primary concern.
- *Labor availability:* A well-trained, fungible labor pool for the technology must be available to ensure continued operations.
- *Upgrade path:* A clear vendor path for continued upgrades/enhancements is necessary; if the system is of central importance for running the business, easy-to-implement, low-risk vendor upgrades supporting new hardware and business capabilities are important.

FACTOR	DESCRIPTION
Mission criticality	• Level on which the business depends on the system being up and functional. Mission critical systems are generally the application systems, which drive core parts of the business, such as order entry, manufacturing management, or customer service. Examples of other common nonapplication mission critical systems include telephony, LAN/WAN connectivity, and e-mail. • Systems that are considered "mission critical" vary from company to company. Determining the criticality of the systems requires a detailed understanding of both the business operations and the technology component.
Unit volume	• The number of units of the technology that will be acquired for the business and supported by IT. • Generally will be most applicable for hardware such as desktops, laptops, printers, PDAs, or other handheld computing platforms, as well as high-volume desktop-based software components (office automation, call center tools, etc.). • Low volumes imply that the factors such as unit cost or durability may not be important. • High volumes generally indicate that unit cost, ease-of-use, and industry adoption will be important decision criteria.
Stability of area supported	• Rate of change in the business unit or organization using the technology (e.g., core business unit with processes unchanged for years, vs. "startup" environment with undefined and rapidly changing requirements). • Drives level of importance of criteria such as industry adoption, consistency with existing systems, and upgrade path, which becomes less important if requirements change rapidly. • Drives higher level of importance for flexibility—system can react to changes in the business and can be adapted for other uses.

Exhibit 6.3   Decision Factors for Determining IT Standards

FACTOR	DESCRIPTION
Expected asset lifetime	• How long the asset is expected to last. • Payback period for system or low-lifetime estimates for assets that wear out over time, such as printers; rapid turnover for consumables such as printer paper or toner cartridges. • Implies ability to change standard over time for assets with shorter life spans and dictates level of effort spent on standard analysis. • If asset lifetime is low (consumables), cost and rapid availability become a primary consideration. • If asset lifetime is expected to be high, physical durability and manageability become primary considerations.
Level of customization	• Measure of the amount (cost) of additional labor effort required to deploy the system. • Examples: High: desktops that require large number of customizations to work in target environment or systems management software that requires ongoing configuration to operate properly; low: plug and play peripherals such as printers or mice.
Interfaces with other systems	• Number, frequency, complexity, and volume of interfaces between this technology component and other systems. • Applies particularly to application components, as well as interfaces outside the organization with suppliers or customers. • Examples: High-frequency, high-volume interfaces such as required EDI transactions to exchange inventory positions with suppliers for cooperative forecasting; low-volume/complexity/frequency: annual printout of depreciation schedule from fixed asset system for manual keying on monthly basis to general ledger system. *(continued)*

Exhibit 6.3 *Continued*

FACTOR	DESCRIPTION
Current and future transaction volume required	• Volume, frequency, and complexity of transactions to be carried out by system. • Current requirements as well as future estimated requirements. • Implications for scalability and reliability on high side and cost on low side. • Examples: High-volume: printers used for statement creation by a consumer-oriented company, such as a bank; low-volume: periodic ad-hoc MS Excel extracts of previous period sales data for marketing department analysis.
Organization growth plans	• Strategic plan for growth by the business. • Includes geographic expansion, acquisition of competing firms, vertical integration through the acquisition of suppliers or customers, or divestiture by selling off business units or entire company. • Implications for level of customization for systems to reduce integration costs in event of acquisition or sales. • Implications for level of cross-business-unit integration of systems in event of spinning-off separate business units.
Size/type of user base	• Order-of-magnitude estimate of total volume of users. • Type of users (technically sophisticated "power users" or computer neophytes). • Usage profile: Business unit or business function. • Geographic profile: Wide range of geographies or international presence vs. small, concentrated user base. • Implications for technical support requirements, durability, ease-of-use, and cost.

Exhibit 6.3 *Continued*

FACTOR	DESCRIPTION
Cost	• Cost of technology component. • Includes costs of acquisition, installation, training, ongoing maintenance, changes to steady-state cost model, and effect of accelerated depreciation. • Cost details are included in the following section.
Industry adoption	• Level of adoption across the technology industry, or within the industry in which the organization or company competes. • Examples: MS Exchange as a technology-industry-wide standard e-mail platform; JD Edwards as an ERP system oriented to the mid-market manufacturing companies.
Consistency/interoperability	• Level of consistency or interoperability with current technology. • Examples: Selecting MS Internet Information Service (IIS) for Web services given enterprise MS Window 2000 deployment for both servers and desktops. Developing point solution applications in Lotus Notes/Domino based on corporate standard of Lotus Notes for Groupware/e-mail.
Labor availability	• Level of availability and cost of labor for the technology component nationally and in the local marketplace. • Examples: High availability of talented professionals for major ERP systems such as SAP or PeopleSoft; low availability of labor for systems regarded as "dead ends" or uninteresting to technology professionals.
Upgrade path	• Level of vendor and marketplace clarity on upgrade path for technology. • Generally, technologies backed by a major vendor with large number of customers and sophisticated third-party support market will have the most clear upgrade paths. • Upgrade path is often closely linked to the system life cycle; see following section on system life cycle for details. • Examples: Clear upgrade paths to major ERP and CRM systems from vendors such as Siebel, Computer Associates, and SAP; less clear upgrade paths for aging mainframe/legacy applications or for new offerings from unproven vendors.

(continued)

Exhibit 6.4   Criteria for Setting Technology Standards

FACTOR	DESCRIPTION
Current life cycle	• Place in product life cycle of the technology product or service. • Implications for upgrade path, labor availability, cost, and industry adoption.
Reliability	• Number of failures across a variety of measures, depending on the technology component; can be tested as consistent output given a set of inputs, mean-time-between-failures, or other relevant statistics. • Often corresponds to complexity of technology component, particularly for applications that have a significant number of "moving parts." • Can be closely linked with product life cycle (the further into the product life cycle, the higher the reliability). • Examples: High reliability: high-availability, fault-tolerant servers with multiple redundant components (power supplies, disk arrays power supplies, processors, memory units, et al.), such as the Sun Enterprise Server 10000; low(er) reliability: desktop computer intended for general usage.
Scalability	• Ability for the technology component to handle additional volumes of work. • Examples: Consulting service organization having scope of experience and depth of staff to take on additional work in the organization; ability for on-line-transaction-processing system (OLTP) to handle increased volumes of transactions within a given time window.
Flexibility	• Technology components adaptability of different related or unrelated tasks. • Example: Server hardware that can become an e-mail server, a Web server, or an application server.
Timing/availability	• Current availability of technology component. • Lead time required when technology component is requested from vendor. • Highly available: Stock configuration PDAs available via retail or the Web within one-half day; low availability: high-end server requiring four-week manufacturing and configuration order lead time.

Exhibit 6.4 *Continued*

FACTOR	DESCRIPTION
Available support	• Presence of strong vendor-based capability or third-party marketplace for consulting and support services for technology component. • Example: Consulting firms dedicated to implementation and management of Great Plains accounting application.
Customer, supplier, and competitor use	• Extent to which the system/standard is used/adopted by customers, suppliers, and competitors. • Example: Similar forecasting and inventory management system used by supplier facilitates integration.
Ease of use	• Relative complexity of the technology component; end-user perception of difficulty of learning and using the system. • Implies level of technical support required for technology component. • High level of ease: Commercially available e-mail systems; low-level of ease: sophisticated order entry system for highly customized engineering product.
Durability	• Physical durability of the technology (generally hardware) component. • Important for harsh environments (manufacturing floor, marine usage), mobile/heavy travel users. • Example: "Hardened" machines with special casing and filtering to withstand the jostling and dust on a plant manufacturing floor.
Manageability	• Ease of managing the technology component. • Availability of remote management tools, similarity to system already in place to reduce training burden, management of incremental systems with existing tools/processes. • Example: Additional desktop systems that can be administered by existing remote management tools.

Exhibit 6.4 *Continued*

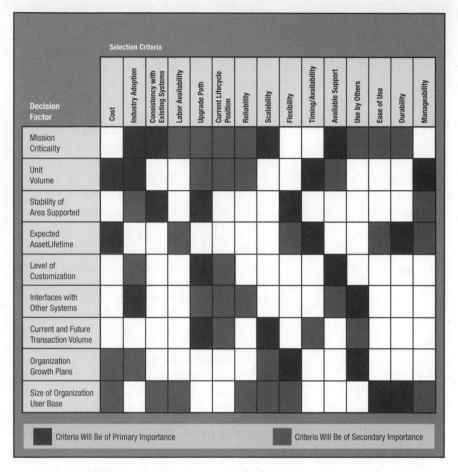

Exhibit 6.5 Decision Factor and Criteria Weighting Matrix

- *Current life-cycle position:* Technologies that are too early or late in their life cycles expose the organization's critical business operations to reliability issues or "dead-end" technologies.
- *Available support:* Existence of a vibrant third-party labor market ensures availability of productivity-enhancing tools and supplemental support, and prevents vendors from enjoying a support monopoly.

Secondary Considerations

- *Industry adoption:* Industry adoption by technologists and multiple businesses in your industry is important for mission-critical systems; the long-term reliability and viability of the system will be impacted by the adoption of the platform as an industry standard by technology departments; a well-established user community for a given technology helps hold vendors accountable for producing reliable systems, forms an objective forum for sharing best practices on system usage, and provides large aggregate funding for additional functionality to the system via ongoing vendor maintenance fees.

- *Consistency/interoperability:* System should be able to interoperate with existing systems to ensure smooth running of overall technology platform (consistent interface incompatibilities, particularly from systems that generate inbound transactions to a core system, spell trouble for a mission-critical system).
- *Scalability:* If changes to the business dictate increased volumes for a given technology component, business mission-critical components that scale appropriately lower the risk to the business by not requiring replacement.
- *Use by competitors:* Use of a given technology by the competition provides secondary validation to the standard under consideration.
- *Ease of use:* A business mission-critical system should have high ease of use to ensure that user community will more easily adopt the system and achieve the highest productivity gains from it.
- *Durability:* Mission-critical systems should be physically durable, particularly if used in mobile, manufacturing, or other harsh environments. Systems that drive the business should either be durable or replacements immediately available and easily deployed with a minimum of configuration and additional labor effort.

Decision Factor: Unit Volume

Examples: Handheld computers for delivery drivers, laptops for consultants in large consulting organization, desktop-level antivirus software, and desktop printers.

Primary Considerations
- *Cost:* Even small variations in unit cost drive high dollar amounts for high unit volume purchases; therefore, achieving the lowest possible pricing per unit is crucial.
- *Industry adoption:* Because the technology will be deployed extensively throughout the organization, cost and effort of replacing the equipment over time will be prohibitive if industry standards change and new capabilities are needed; further, high levels of industry adoption should create, in theory, lower pricing.
- *Timing/availability:* High-volume equipment, particularly hardware, may need frequent replacement/repair; ideally, the units are readily available across a wide variety of geographies from vendor or reseller inventory.

- *Manageability:* The high unit volume magnifies any system management inefficiencies by orders of magnitude; the best high unit volume systems require little management or intervention by IT.

Secondary Considerations

- *Upgrade path:* Because a significant amount of capital is likely to be invested in a high-volume system, it is important that the vendor provide an upgrade path to ensure the highest longevity.
- *Current life-cycle position:* The inevitable changes to system standards, configurations, and costs as systems travel along their life cycles dictate that high unit volume systems are ideally in the "full adoption" or "steady state" segments of the technology life cycle.
- *Reliability:* Even small lapses in reliability create headaches for the IT department when multiplied by hundreds or thousands of individual units.
- *Available support:* Because high-volume units are often deployed across the organization and across disparate geographical areas, the systems should easily be supported remotely or with vendor staff or resellers in each geography; because high unit volume systems are generally a large investment for the organization, the availability of support over the long term is an important consideration.
- *Ease of use:* Many high unit volume systems are end user oriented; in these cases, ease of use should be considered; small improvements in ease of use are multiplied across many users.
- *Durability:* If high unit volume systems are not durable, the IT team can be stuck with an endless supply of broken equipment; further, because purchases are often made in bulk, a lack of durability may show up simultaneously across many units, creating a tidal wave of work for the IT department.

Decision Factor: Stability of Area Supported

Examples: Spectrum of business activity from new business unit or startup with actively evolving business model to stable, mature business with rarely changing business processes and technology requirements.

Primary Considerations

- *Consistency/interoperability with existing or planned systems:* If the business area supported by the technology is stable, the investment made in systems should be consistent with, or interface easily with, existing or planned technologies. The low turnover of requirements on stable business areas means that these systems will be deployed for the long term. Similarly, if the business area is rapidly changing, the IT department may take more latitude in making technology choices, given the likelihood that the business requirements change rapidly.

- *Flexibility:* If the business area supported is subject to considerable change, the flexibility of the systems to be upgraded, reconfigured, customized, or otherwise adapted to those changes is a primary consideration. This ensures that at least some of the technology investment made for the business will be salvageable as the business needs change.
- *Upgrade path:* Likewise, the upgrade path for technologies deployed in changing business areas should be clear. Often in these cases, other customers of a package, service, or product are experiencing the same changes, and the vendor will provide an upgrade based on these new needs.

Secondary Considerations
- *Industry adoption:* Industry adoption influences the long-term costs, upgrade path, related systems integration, and third-party support levels enjoyed by the technology. For stable business areas where the technology is a long-term investment, level of industry adoption should be considered.
- *Manageability:* Manageability is a consideration for technologies deployed in business areas with low rates of change, because the technology will likely be supported for long periods of time in a static, unchanged configuration. This means that easy-to-manage systems pay dividends for IT over a long period.

Decision Factor: Expected Asset Lifetime

Examples: Heavy-duty high-volume printers, color printer cartridges, and handheld computers.

Primary Considerations
- *Cost:* If an asset has a short life span (particularly for consumables), it will likely be purchased repeatedly. In these cases, cost should be a primary consideration.
- *Timing/availability:* If the assets are short lived, the vendor should have short lead times for acquiring replacements and availability to provide them across a wide geographic area.
- *Durability:* If the asset is expected to have a lengthy time in service, it should be durable enough to last through the lifetime with a minimum of maintenance and wear and tear.

Secondary Considerations
- *Labor availability:* If the asset is a long-term asset, the availability of a skilled technical staff in the labor pool should be considered. If the

technology is a short-term asset, labor availability is not an important factor.

- *Flexibility:* If the asset will be in service over a long period, it may be called on to adapt to changing business conditions or serve in different roles, making flexibility and adaptability higher considerations.
- *Ease of use:* High ease of use for assets in place for long periods ensures minimal aggregate user effort.
- *Manageability:* To reduce the support burden on IT, long-term assets should be easy to manage.

Decision Factor: Level of Customization

Examples: Highly customized order entry system for complex, highly engineered product versus "plain-vanilla" install of a general ledger package.

Primary Considerations
- *Labor availability:* If the system is highly customized, a large pool of skilled technical personnel to support and manage the system must be available.
- *Available support (vendor, third party):* Similarly, a large third-party support market ensures that the IT department will be able to bring supplemental resources to bear on a highly customized system.

Secondary Considerations
- *Industry adoption:* High levels of industry adoption ensure that the vendors or suppliers will be able to provide systems that are easier to configure and provide more options for customization.
- *Upgrade path:* For highly customized systems, a vendor upgrade path that supports the customizations with a minimum of new install effort is critical. Software maintenance spending generally entitles the organization to system upgrades; in these cases, the benefits are not available if the upgrade cannot be accomplished because of large amounts of system customization.

Decision Factor: Interfaces with Other Systems

Examples: Forecasting system which shares information with suppliers of ERP system via EDI; inventory system which feeds inventory positions and availability by SKU to customers; and CRM system that receives customer information from external order system.

Primary Considerations
- *Industry adoption:* Level of industry (technology or business) adoption often drives the number of interfaces to other systems created by the

vendor of third parties. If a system becomes a standard in the industry, the vendor will have the resources to ensure that the system interfaces with related hardware or software. Industry adoption also drives suppliers of related systems or third parties to create interfaces or technologies that allow the systems to operate well together.

- *Use by customers, competitors, or suppliers:* If the interfaces with other systems touch outside entities, such as suppliers or customers (e.g., forecast or inventory position exchanges, or other EDI transactions), the systems chosen by those external parties may affect which technology should be chosen. Systems from the same vendor or systems with proven interfaces to the systems used by the external partners will be the front-runners.

Secondary Considerations
- *Upgrade path:* Because the system feeds or receives data from other systems, it should be able to "keep up" as those systems are upgraded or changed. Therefore, the vendor upgrade path for the system should be clear.
- *Current life-cycle position:* Because other downstream systems may rely on triggers or other information from the system being considered, it should be in the mainstream or steady-state portion of the life cycle with a proven ability to handle the transactions.
- *Reliability:* Likewise, to ensure overall platform reliability, the system must be able to hand off and receive data reliably to avoid impacting the other interfaced systems.
- *Available support:* Finally, because of the potential to impact related systems (and the potential for "domino effect" failures), vendor support for creating reliable interfaces should be readily available.

Decision Factor: Current and Future Transaction Volume Required

Examples: Florist with highly seasonal business and high transaction volumes during holidays or special events; nonseasonal producer of commodity product with long lead-time product and little variance in transaction processing volumes.

Primary Considerations
- *Upgrade path:* If the system is subject to high future transaction volume, a clear upgrade path from the vendor for adding additional capacity will allow the organization to purchase the amount of capacity needed currently, while maintaining the ability to bring on additional capacity for small amounts of incremental cost.

- *Scalability:* The system should be able to handle current required transaction volumes with ease, including transaction volume spikes because of seasonality or other factors. The system should also be able to handle long-term increases in the baseline number of transactions as well. Clear proof of scalability across all technology components (e.g., order processing software and the hardware it runs on: CPU, processor, memory, and network capacity) should be analyzed to avoid bottlenecking at low thresholds in one particular element of the technology.

Secondary Considerations

- *Current life-cycle position:* Products in the mature portion of the life cycle have higher field-proven ability to handle large transaction volumes.
- *Timing/availability:* Upgrades to the system or product should be easily available in the case of unexpected incremental volume or rapid changes in the baseline volume.
- *Use by customers, competitors, or suppliers:* Use of the product, service, or system by competitors with similar usage patterns or volumes is indicative of the technology's actual ability to scale appropriately.

Decision Factor: Organization Growth Plans

Examples: Acquisition of competing firms or suppliers with differing business-supporting technologies; geographic expansion of business; aggressive organic growth plans.

Primary Considerations

- *Flexibility:* If the organization plans include acquisition of competitors, geographic expansion, vertical integration, or other business model changes, the systems supporting the business should have the adaptability and flexibility to support the changes while minimizing impact to existing business and incremental investment to add new portions of the business.
- *Use by customers, competitors, or suppliers:* If likely acquisition targets (or buyers) use a particular set of technologies, the purchase of the same, or similar, technologies will facilitate future business integration or partnerships.

Secondary Considerations

- *Cost:* If business expansion plans involve adding incremental capacity to existing systems or rollout of additional systems (e.g., new laptop computers for sales force of acquired competitor), the cost of incremental processing capacity or unit costs should be minimized or guaranteed in advance by the vendor.

- *Industry adoption:* Technologies with high levels of business-industry adoption indicate solutions that have the highest likelihood of being in place at suppliers or competitors or will be most attractive to acquirers, ensuring a minimum of retraining or conversion effort in the event of a business transaction.
- *Scalability:* Key business systems should have the additional transaction processing capacity to support strong expansion plans (geographic, acquisition, or organic growth).

Decision Factor: Size/Type of User Base

Examples: Scale of activity ranging from a large-scale base of heterogeneous users crossing a variety of business units and functions across wide geographies to a small office of a dozen users.

Primary Considerations
- *Ease of use:* Systems that will be deployed across a heterogeneous user base, across disparate geographies, or a large number of users (particularly technically unsophisticated users) should put a premium on ease of use to keep training (and retraining) costs to a minimum and provide the most efficient use of end-user time.
- *Durability:* Systems used by a large number of users, particularly in harsh environments (plant manufacturing floor, delivery trucks, traveling sales), should be durable enough to handle significant wear and tear without breakage or data loss.

Secondary Considerations
- *Cost:* Technologies that will be deployed across a large number of users should seek the least unit cost, particularly for consumables or high-turnover items. In the case of large-scale deployments across a wide variety of users, cost considerations should take a back seat to durability or reliability factors.
- *Consistency/interoperability with existing or planned systems:* Systems should interoperate effectively with existing or planned systems; large unit volume and widespread deployment magnifies any difficulties the system has with interfaces to other corporate systems.
- *Timing/availability:* For remote users or geographically spread users, new or replacement systems should be readily available for vendors or resellers.

- *Labor availability:* A large pool of available technical talent in each required geography should be available; this drives decision making toward well-known vendors and highly standardized technologies.
- *Reliability:* Systems for use in the field or by a large number of users should be highly reliable.
- *Scalability:* Systems should handle large changes in usage or usage spikes; systems deployed across a large number of users that cannot expand to handle additional capacity are difficult (and expensive) to replace rapidly; the initial and ongoing deployment of the technology should ensure that the appropriate processing capacity is in place for planned future business volumes.
- *Flexibility:* Because of the high replacement cost of widely deployed systems, ideal technologies have the flexibility to upgrade or reconfigure inexpensively in response to changes in the business.
- *Manageability:* Large unit-volume systems or widely dispersed systems should be easily managed from a support and configuration standpoint to avoid undue burdens on the IT staff.

The analysis described in this section cuts through the tremendous amount of data available for technology products and services and focuses the decision-making team on gathering and assessing only the relevant pieces of information. To further reduce the data gathering burden, after the decision framework has been established, the competing vendors (or other outside consultants) can be asked to assess themselves on the relevant criteria, subject to independent validation and verification by the team. The combination of a well-thought-out framework, a clearly scoped set of decision criteria, and a willing set of vendors makes for a crisp, rapid standard-setting process.

After the selection is complete, it should be documented as part of the standards manual, along with the decision factors and criteria weighting used in setting the standard. The documentation process is covered in detail in the following sections. Further, the team should commence negotiations with the vendor to achieve partnership pricing levels to keep costs under control. The documentation generated for the standard demonstrates to a vendor that the standard is taken seriously in the customer organization and that follow-on business will be a straightforward process. Vendors are generally willing to share some of their sales-process cost savings with customers based on their selection as a standard.

Technology managers should also concentrate their efforts for standard setting based on a common-sense assessment of the value of standards in each area. Applying the 80–20 rule to standard setting implies that standard-setting efforts should stay focused on the systems components that have the largest impact on the operations of the business, from the standpoint of cost, productivity, and IT effectiveness. A detailed standard around a passing or insignificant technology component is not time well spent.

An example standard-setting process is provided in the Summary section.

Cost as a Criterion

Cost is invariably an important factor in every round of standard setting and purchasing decision making. Often, technology component costing is done as part of an overall project estimation. See Chapter 15, Chapter 10, and Chapter 11, for detailed coverage of project costing and vendor selection and negotiation strategies. Only key considerations for technology component costing, an important part of the technology standard setting, are included here.

To understand the true cost of ownership of a technology component requires more than a superficial analysis of acquisition cost. Instead, a more detailed analysis of the full cost of acquisition and ongoing management should be undertaken. This is often called *total cost of ownership (TCO)*. A complete analysis includes the following cost components:

- *Acquisition cost:* The total cost of original acquisition of all technology components.
- *Install cost:* Incremental labor (internal and external) required to configure, customize, integrate, implement, and deploy the technology component.
- *Vendor maintenance:* Annual fees because vendor is part of maintenance agreement entitling the end user to vendor technical support, upgrades, and input into the product development process, usually for application components.
- *Training cost:* Cost of training for IT staff and end users of technology component.
- *Labor cost:* Likely cost of internal labor (salaries of incremental staff needed) as well as external service providers; if the technology component is required to scale or needs additional support, the cost of incremental internal or external resources is relevant.
- *Steady-state cost model changes:* Any incremental costs (or savings) incurred in the organization, covering all portions of the IT budget. These costs are found across a variety of categories, including labor (additional staff), consumables (e.g., paper, power), facilities (additional space), and capacity (network, processor).
- *Accelerated depreciation:* Occasionally, the implementation of a given technology component makes obsolete an existing system or set of systems. In these cases, depreciation of amounts capitalized from the previous implementation is accelerated and taken as expense after the new

system is deployed; the financial impact and accounting issues around this topic should be addressed in conjunction with the finance department and the chief financial officer.

Product Life-Cycle Analysis and Implications for Technology Standard Setting

An important consideration while setting technology direction is the product life cycle for the technology under consideration.

The product life cycle for most technology products, and the life cycle relationship to cost and reliability, is fairly well understood by most technology managers. The speed at which technology life cycles move varies by product, but is generally rapid. Exhibit 6.6 shows an overview of the typical adoption and retirement cycle for a product or service, and the relationship between adoption level and cost and reliability.

Exhibit 6.6 demonstrates several key dimensions of the typical product life cycle. Most important is the usage curve that shows the aggregate total users (or units deployed) of the technology. Successful technology products, like most other products, typically move from consumer awareness and trial to adoption acceptance and repeated acquisition over time. Users become

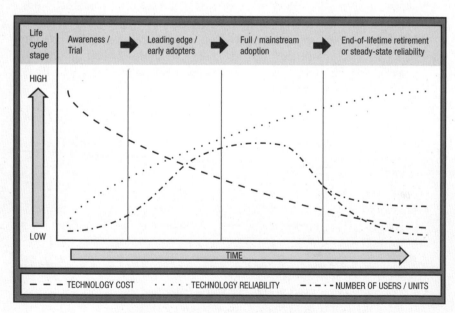

Exhibit 6.6   Existing Technology Life Cycles and Relationship to Cost and Reliability

aware of a new service or product, use or test it in a limited fashion, then push to full adoption as the product is proven. Thus, the primary determinant of where the product is in its life cycle is its level of adoption as measured by number of users or deployed units.

Overall level of adoption and life-cycle stage in turn drive two other key factors. Technology costs decrease as additional volume helps vendors achieve scale economies and generate experience curve effects, which combine to lower overall costs. Costs are also driven down by the entrance of competing products and services. Likewise, reliability increases over time as the product improves with end-consumer feedback and the scale and experience efficiencies begin having a positive impact on manufacturing and delivery.

Most technology vendors are keenly aware of product life cycles and work hard to keep their customers at the appropriate portion of the curve. However, end consumers should satisfy themselves that the products or services are being purchased at the optimal point of reliability, cost, and adoption for their own purposes.

An understanding of these life-cycle fundamentals is useful when setting technology direction and standards. First, the IT manager must understand where on the life cycle all current technology resides so that appropriate investment and retirement decisions can be made for each technology component. Further, as new or replacement technology is added, it is essential to understand where in the life cycle the investment is being made to ensure the highest longevity, least cost, and best reliability and usability of the product or service.

From an internal standpoint, the technology manager (particularly a newly promoted or hired technology manager) should evaluate existing systems to understand where in the life cycle they are. Exhibit 6.7 outlines the framework for such an assessment.

To determine a course of action for each piece of technology currently in place, in some cases, the manager must first group the pieces in chunks that make sense from a business standpoint (e.g., Should the CRM system be considered part of the ERP or as a separate evaluation? Should the hardware that the ERP runs on be grouped with the application or should it be considered separately?). This provides decision outcomes that make common sense and are actionable. For example, a decision that the finance system is at the end of its life cycle should be made in the context of the hardware it runs on and, potentially, the end-user hardware as well.

The appropriate grouping depends on factors such as age of the system, interdependency of systems, system functionality, level of customization, and number of instances of the system. Often, the grouping consists of a single technology, simplifying the analysis greatly. The grouping should be done on a case-by-case basis by the manager.

Next, each technology grouping should be evaluated along two key characteristics, which together suggest a course of action to take for each grouping.

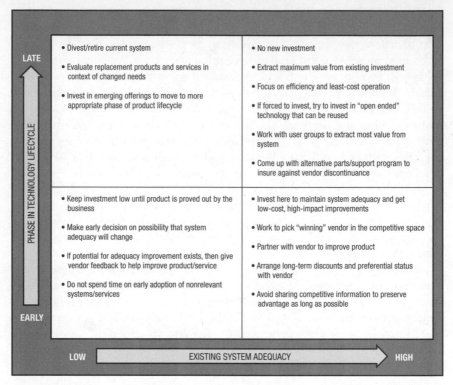

Exhibit 6.7 Existing Technology Life Cycle Assessment Framework

First, the technology grouping is evaluated for where it is in its technology life cycle. The previous exhibits and discussion on this topic should be used as a guide, but this analysis requires the exercise of some judgment on the part of the manager and may be augmented with outside information from vendors, consultants, user groups, research organizations, and industry publications. (See later section in this chapter for Web sites and other sources of information for data gathering in this analysis.) The second characteristic is rating of existing adequacy. The four scenarios for grouping existing technology are:

1. *Early phase/low existing adequacy:* The IT group should minimize investment (training, support, incremental deployment) for these systems. If the system shows promise for improving, the IT group can provide input to the vendor to help the system improve in exchange for future discounting or early looks at beta versions.

2. *Late phase/low existing adequacy:* Systems in this quadrant should be targeted for priority replacement. Replacement services or products should be evaluated to enhance, upgrade, or replace the aging technology.

Potential replacements should be at an earlier point in their life cycles to maximize the lifetime usefulness of the replacement system.

3. *Early phase/high existing adequacy:* Systems in this quadrant are at an ideal point for early investment and partnering with vendors. These systems have the longest "legs," and pushing these systems forward yields the highest business impact with the least cost. The IT department should bias investment dollars for existing systems toward the technologies in this quadrant and partner with the vendors to achieve preferential status, input to the product development process, and long-term discounting.

4. *Late phase/high existing adequacy:* High-adequacy, late-cycle technologies should be "farmed" by the IT department to extract best value, while minimizing new investment. The focus for these systems should be on high-efficiency, least-cost operation so that remaining budget dollars can be invested in high-impact, earlier-cycle products. In many cases, stable systems, which are at the extreme end of their life cycles, can continue to support the business indefinitely. In these instances, vendors may discontinue support for these "sunset" systems.

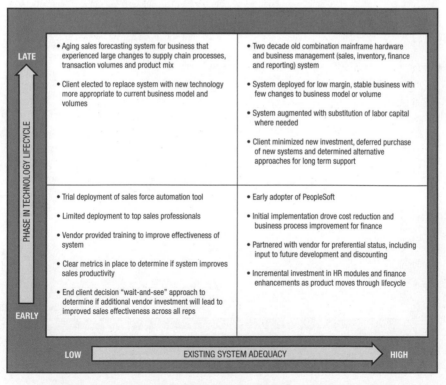

Exhibit 6.8 Client Examples of Existing Technology Assessments

The IT group should create alternate support plans by stocking up on parts, identifying additional sources of technology expertise, and teaming with other organizations to ensure the ability to support the technology through the extreme end of its life cycle.

Exhibit 6.8 shows real-world examples of each of the technology scenarios described and how the client company chose to approach technology and standard setting based on this framework.

The technology product or service life cycle should also be considered as technology managers make decisions about new investments or replacement of technology groups being retired. A framework similar to the existing technology approach is useful in evaluating these investments and their life-cycle position. Exhibit 6.9 shows the approach taken for new investments based on business criticality of the technology component and its relative expense.

This framework uses the level of expense and the impact on business operations to drive decision making on what point in the technology life cycle

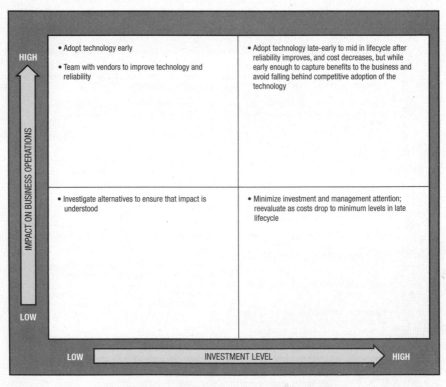

**Exhibit 6.9　New or Replacement Technology
Life Cycle Assessment Framework**

to invest. This analysis can be executed in a fashion similar to the existing technology life-cycle analysis in terms of technology groupings and data gathering.

New systems should be assessed on the left-hand axis according to impact to the business. In general, this should be measured as the systems' contribution to driving revenues, reducing costs, or achieving better control of the business. The bottom axis rates technology grouping options according to their cost, including all relevant cost elements (see costing discussion earlier in this chapter for coverage of technology group costs).

Business impact and investment level can be challenging to assess, particularly for early life-cycle products whose cost-of-ownership and business benefits may be difficult to ascertain. Again, enlisting the assistance of the business for the left-hand axis ensures the most complete analysis. As in the previous analysis, vendors, industry groups, peer companies, publications, and other related sources are useful in making the most complete estimate of cost. The company chief financial officer can also be helpful in understanding the full cost of ownership, as well as where the investment might rank compared to other alternatives for the company's capital. The scenarios for grouping new or replacement investments are:

- *Low impact on operations/low investment level:* The technology should be investigated further to ensure that business impact is properly understood. If the impact on the business operations is low and shows no potential of changing, the technology should not be adopted. Decisions to invest in this area have low risk of damage to the organization because of low costs, but can be distracting for the IT department and run the risk of large opportunity costs for IT.

- *Low impact on operations/high investment level:* Expensive technologies with little impact for the business should be avoided. As the technology moves through its life cycle, costs drop, reliability improves, and product capabilities change, the technology should be reevaluated periodically to determine if it has moved to a different quadrant.

- *High impact on operations/low investment level:* Systems, products, or services that are in the early phase of their life cycles and have no, or inadequate, counterparts in the existing system platform should be further investigated. If the new system shows promise, the IT group should invest time with the emerging system vendor. This can often mean helping the vendor further refine the product or service and serve as a testing ground for a trial implementation of the product. By helping promising vendors early, the gap in system adequacy can be filled sooner, and the organization will have stronger ties with the vendor, ensuring input to the ongoing product development as well as potential early adopter discounts. If the system indeed produces a high impact for the business with low investment, it should be adopted rapidly by the organization.

- *High impact on operations/high investment level:* Most technology choices that have a high impact for the business also require substantial investment to acquire, configure, implement, and deploy. These technologies should be investigated as they mature and followed closely by the IT department, so that adoption plans can mature as the product moves through its life cycle. Understanding the costs and business impact of the technology allow the IT department to determine the ideal inflection point that maximizes business impact and reliability while minimizing cost.

After new or replacement technologies are assessed, the mapping will suggest the appropriate point of entry in the product life cycle for the technology. Exhibit 6.10 provides specific client examples of new/replacement technology assessments.

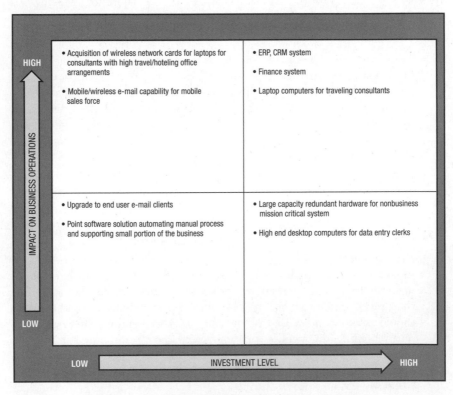

Exhibit 6.10   Client Examples of New or Replacement Technology Assessments

Communicating IT Standards to the Business

After the IT standards have been determined through the previous analyses, they should be clearly documented as a preface to communicating them throughout the organization. The overall process for documenting and communicating the standards is shown in Exhibit 6.11.

The first step after documenting the standards is to have them debated and validated internally by the IT department. This step ensures that the standards are refined, that any potential inconsistencies or surprises in the

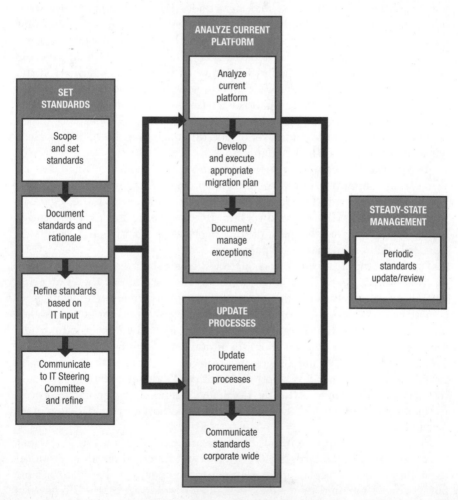

**Exhibit 6.11   IT Standards Documentation,
Communication, and Update Process**

standards are identified by the team closest to the actual technology, and, most importantly, that the IT team feels ownership of the standards. This sense of ownership helps to ensure that every member of the IT department can explain and defend the rationale behind the standards internally and externally. The IT staff is also the first line of defense in ensuring that the overall organization adheres to the standards. The IT review process will likely be an iterative process, requiring several rounds of document refinement and review with the department or subteams.

After the IT department has signed off on the standards document, the next step is the ratification of the standards by the IT steering committee (for more on IT steering committees, see Chapter 17). This round of review ensures that the top business managers understand and support the standards. This step, review and sign-off by the senior managers, is important because it takes the standards from being something by and for IT to being a business decision owned by all departments. The agenda for the IT steering committee meeting should include a review of both the standards and the data gathering and analysis process used to generate the standards. Because adherence to IT standards can have such a tremendous impact on productivity of the department, the committee must understand the importance of the standard setting and the high level of due diligence that the IT department has invested in setting the standards.

As with the IT department review process, the standard setting with the IT steering committee follows an iterative process. The process may surface previously undiscovered pockets of nonstandard technology in the organization, or provoke a debate over direction. In every case, this level of engagement and review on the part of the business is healthy and results in standards that are owned by all parties.

The final step in the review should be a cover sheet approving the standards (or updates to the standards), signed by the members of the IT steering committee or members of the company senior management team. This step is more than a symbolic effort; a highly effective method for getting stakeholders to pay attention is to have documents signed by concerned parties. There is something important about the literal act of signing off on a decision that forces ambiguities and disagreements to the forefront so that they can be solved. We recommend this step for all critical IT documentation, including the standards document. After the document has been revised and approved by the steering committee, it should also be signed off by the IT department members.

Next, IT should work with all business areas dealing with procurement to ensure that IT standards are recognized and followed for all new equipment purchases or replacement purchases. In many small organizations, purchasing is handled by a small, centralized group or by the IT department itself. However, in larger organizations, finding all the points of procurement can be challenging. A critical component of migrating an organization to a homogeneous, standardized environment is finding each of these points and ensuring that the buyers understand the standards and the reasons behind them.

After the standards have been established, a migration plan for the existing technology platform should be evaluated. Technologies or platforms ending their life cycles, or at least their useful lives for the company, represent an opportunity to begin replacing the disparate technologies in a deliberate, consistent fashion. This analysis and process is covered in the Product Life-Cycle Analysis and Implications for Technology Standard Setting section in this chapter.

The final step is keeping standards "evergreen." Today's standards are not static; availability of new technologies, new business initiatives, changes in the competitive marketplace, customer and supplier demands, and technology cost changes all conspire to rapidly make obsolete any set of standards created by IT. The standards process should be revisited on a quarterly basis as part of the overall IT planning process and on an as-needed basis as well. The life-cycle analysis process discussed in this chapter can be a helpful way of prioritizing technology standards to be reviewed. In every case, keeping the IT steering committee and the business engaged and in partnership in the establishment and enforcement of the standards will create the best environment for a least-cost, high-productivity IT department.

Enforcing IT Standards

After standards have been documented and communicated with both IT and the business, the overall approach to standard enforcement should be based on creating an environment where the standards are followed because adhering to them is the easiest course of action. Making it easy for business and IT to follow standards means that the standards must have clearly documented rationale and reasoning, reasonable lead times from vendors, and clear linkages and reinforcement in the approval and procurement processes. Business users have little tolerance for IT standards that they do not understand, that appear arbitrary and capricious, or that get in their way. IT will achieve the benefits of the standards only if they work hard to create a path-of-least-resistance around the standard.

The approach to enforcement should be built on these key principles:

- Clear documentation of the standards distributed to business and IT.
- Clear documentation of the rationale/reasoning behind each standard.
- Purchase approval and procurement processes that support the standards.
- Support of the business senior management for the standards.

- Reinforcement of the standards by periodic recommunication.
- Ensuring that standards stay relevant and respond to changes in the business by frequent revisiting and updating.
- A common-sense approach to making exceptions to the standards.

Rigid enforcement of standards is generally counterproductive. Without good documentation and communication of the standards and no signoff by the business, the purchasing process can escalate into an organizational clash of wills that generally results in a double loss for the IT department: The business prevails in a nonstandard purchase, and IT tarnishes its relationship with a business unit management team. The IT department loses a chance to work with the business to solve a problem and, worse, winds up with the responsibility for supporting a chaotic, heterogeneous environment. In all cases, having the support of the CFO, the purchasing department, and the IT steering committee helps ensure much higher adherence to the standards.

When an exception is made to a standard that has been set, it should be documented, along with the rationale, presented to the IT steering committee and added to the standards document. This increases the perception in IT and with the business that the exception is truly "exceptional" and ensures that the reasons for the exception are preserved for future reference.

The same steps should be followed when IT discovers an exception after the fact. In these cases, any potential changes to cost of ownership or impacts to existing or planned projects should be documented for the IT steering committee as well. The important thing is for the IT department to remain engaged as part of the process and to work in conjunction with the business to achieve the cost-reduction and simplicity goals of the standards without the standards becoming a straitjacket.

Several categories of typical exceptions have emerged through our consulting work with clients. One type of exception is "leading-edge technology products" (read: toys) for senior executives and IT staff. These users are often the early adopters of new technologies and trial products that are interesting or have the potential for providing additional productivity. These tools can be hardware or software. In most cases, these are relatively harmless exceptions to the rule, unless they begin consuming significant amounts of IT attention for support.

Other instances of exceptions are for high-volume products where cost is a factor. For example, one of our clients had established a hardware standard of Dell desktops, laptops, and servers for his or her business units. However, one business unit (a call center) had a large number of employees performing low-intensity, repetitive computing tasks. The combination of low-intensity requirements and high volume led them to adopt a "buy cheapest" approach for their call center computers. To mitigate the support costs and overhead, broken computers were replaced with newer models and retired or repaired at leisure. The overall costs for the business were thus lowered, and a common-sense exception to the hardware standard made.

A final type of exception is one adopted because of customer requirements. For example, a large or important customer may require integration to his or her systems using a certain network protocol or type of software. In these cases, the benefits of pleasing an important customer or of conducting business transactions smoothly with a large number of customers almost always dictates an exception to the standard, or the creation of an additional standard to support the customer base over the long term.

What to Do When You Inherit a "Highly Heterogeneous Environment"

In many cases, the IT manager assuming the role at the same or a new company inherits a "highly heterogeneous environment," or "mess." It is critical for the manager to aggressively address the issues, or the chaos created by the environment will be a tar pit from which neither successful projects nor the manager's career will escape.

Changing a status-quo environment invariably also involves changing the culture in the IT department. This adds to the complexity and risk involved with what is certain to be a large challenge. Further, support from the business may be low, and a large amount of education for both the business and IT is in order. These challenges must be addressed rapidly, however, or the IT manager will die the "death of a thousand cuts." If the cultural and process hindrances cannot be overcome after significant effort, at least the manager will quickly understand that and be able to move on to greener pastures.

Throughout the process, the IT manager should work to enlist the aid of the business unit managers and the finance department/CFO. They can be helpful in understanding the history, constraints, and potential costs and benefits of standards migration. Further, having been part of the process, they will feel additional ownership of the results.

First, Understand "Why"

The first step is to develop a clear understanding of the history of the previous decisions that created the existing environment. An environment filled with exceptions generally emanates from a series of one-off decisions that, taken individually, made sense, but do not fit the overall context for the IT department. Interviewing IT staff, business users, purchasing agents, and finance team about the history behind the standards or purchasing decisions will reveal the "why" behind each of the previous technology decisions. Cases in which off-the-cuff decisions were made also become apparent. Understanding the full scope of the history helps the new manager understand where to tread lightly and where to move ahead with changes. The interviewing and data-gathering process also help the IT manager understand the potential competing agendas within and outside the IT department.

Document Everything

A technology platform covers a lot of territory (hardware, package applications, custom applications, system tools, networks, help desk); understanding the full scope requires writing. Often, the existing system documentation is at varying levels of detail, several years outdated, and available piecemeal. Building your own maps of server footprints, application inventory, and application functions will begin establishing context and ultimately serve as the overall guide for navigating out of the chaos.

Quantify the Implications

After the scope and diversity of the technology environment have been captured, the IT manager should quantify anywhere possible the operating or productivity costs of nonstandard technologies. This should be done by order of magnitude, so that the biggest impacts are identified and explored early. The IT manager should also be selective about the level of detail required; the analysis should be done top-down, sacrificing a few percentage points of accuracy for improved speed.

A typical analysis might be as simple as "having two separate financial systems supporting similar business units requires three extra full-time employees in the IT department for support. Consolidation of financial systems will generate approximately $200,000 annually in savings."

Build a Migration Plan

With the data in place and the costs of the environment quantified, the migration can be planned. The plan should be at an adequate level of detail to understand the timing, dependencies, resources, and costs involved. The plan, however, should not cover in unnecessary detail the migration of pieces that generate small benefit. Priority should be given to steps that produce the highest gain with the least risk and effort. For the top priority projects, a return-on-investment analysis based on costs and benefits should be attached. Chapter 15 discusses project planning and ROI analysis in detail.

Set Expectations

The next step is to set expectations about the IT department's ability to be effective in providing support and successfully completing projects. The discussion should be positioned as expectation setting and should be managed in a cooperative manner. It is easy (and perhaps typical) for communications of this nature to be perceived as "IT whining" by the business; therefore, the manager should have built a quantitative, data-based case for the impact of the environment before expectation setting. It is critical to build a reputation with the business users for being accountable and to avoid any sense of finger pointing, while at the same time driving home the effectiveness implications of the disparate environment.

The primary venue for setting expectations is the IT steering committee, and the environment assessment and plan should be on one of the early agendas.

Finally, the manager should communicate within the IT department the implications of technology chaos and what is being done to fix it. The team will appreciate knowing there is a plan with clear goals and that the migration will allow them to work on helping the business instead of focusing on the next workaround. The IT team should also understand that while the environment may hinder productivity, they should plan their work around it and not use the environment as an excuse for missed deadlines or reduced service levels.

Execute the Plan

After the migration plan has been completed and prioritized and expectations properly set, the migration should begin. There is often a host of constraints, including cost, time, resource capacity, business requirements, and others that prevent a rapid migration. The approach, therefore, should be gradual and opportunistic. The manager should reconcile himself or herself to a slower pace of change and a part-time migration.

In a heterogeneous environment, many times the cost of migration or requirements of the business may make a standards-driven migration impractical. In these cases, the manager should at a minimum conduct a life-cycle analysis and start the standardization efforts with retiring, end-of-life-cycle equipment.

The manager should work with vendors to get the costs down and get free resources to help with the migration. If the vendor believes that the company is serious about establishing its product or service as the standard, the vendor will work hard to help with the migration. If not, this vendor may not be the appropriate vendor.

Summary

Setting IT standards is an exhaustive process which requires significant effort on the part of the IT manager and a clear understanding of the long-term benefits on the part of both IT and the business. The result is a set of standards that allows the IT department to be managed at least cost and highest productivity, and ensures that the technology platform is maintained at the life-cycle point that generates the best return on investment for the business.

Exhibit 6.12 briefly recaps the overall process discussed in this chapter. It shows the main components of standard setting, analyzing the current platform, updating procurement processes, and keeping the standards current.

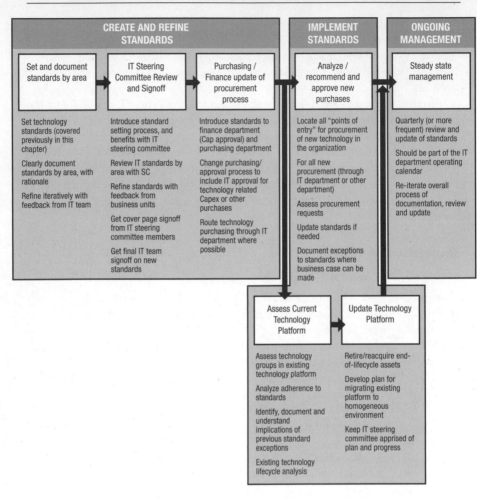

Exhibit 6.12   Start-to-Finish Overview of Standard Setting Process

Sources of Information for Assessing Technology Standards

A variety of research and information sources on which the IT manager should rely to flesh out a set of IT standards can be used. These resources provide recent information to use in performing product life-cycle analysis and in evaluating competing IT standards according to the appropriate criteria:

- *Industry-focused groups:* These are industry groups focused on specific technology areas or on the industry segment in which the organization competes; for example, ERP users groups, manufacturing industry special interest groups.

- *Technology publications/industry publications:* There are dozens of credible, independent publications focused on the technology industry. *InformationWeek* and *CIO* magazine are among the leading publications that address enterprise-level technology management. Others include Baseline and Optimize. Publications focused on the industry in which the organization competes can also be a source of information related to technologies that apply specifically to the business; for example, mobile/handheld computing for direct-store-delivery companies.

- *Vendors:* Technology vendors are an obvious source of information on their own products, and they often will provide additional information on complementary and competing products and services. Although the content and delivery of data is naturally vendor-slanted, the data can still be valuable and help to find the blind spots of competing vendors.

- *Peer companies:* Technology managers from firms in the same industry, or firms with other organization similarity (size—revenues or employees, geography, technology platform), are an often-overlooked source of information and can be particularly valuable for their objectivity. Developing peer relationships with similar companies can provide insight into their decision-making processes and rationale, as well as jump start vendor data gathering.

- *Technology industry-focused Web sites:* A search of Web sites focused on enterprise-level issues in the technology business can turn up additional information. These include:

  —*CIO magazine:* www.cio.com

  —*CMP Media:* www.techweb.com

  —*Computer Business Review:* www.cbronline.com

  —*E-Week:* www.eweek.com

  —*Tech Republic:* www.techrepublic.com

  —*Darwin* magazine: www.darwinmag.com

  —*Analyst Views:* www.analystviews.com

- *End-user Web logs:* Consumer-driven Web logs (blogs) dedicated to monitoring technology trends and technology companies are often a source of unbiased customer experience information, as well as insider information. It can take some effort to separate fact from opinion on the blogs, and the signal-to-noise ratio on a given topic can sometimes be low. Nevertheless, catching up on the undigested news available through these sources should be part of the IT manager's research. Particularly notable are the most popular technology-focused blogs:

  —Slashdot.org

  —Techdirt.com

—f_ _ _edcompany.com

—news.com

—techrepublic.com

—hardocp.com

—anandtech.com

—zdnet.com

—dailytechnews.com

—misweb.com

Because they contain the unedited, unfiltered opinions of end users, these blogs are a highly instructive source of information.

- *Technology research firms:* There is a full-scale mature industry of research firms dedicated to assisting companies in setting technology direction and helping companies understand in which technology standard they should invest. While these sources provide high-quality analysis, their expense can often make them prohibitive, except for decisions involving large capital expenditures. Although this marketplace has dozens of players in it, some of the industry leaders include:

  —Aberdeen Group

  —AMR Research

  —Forrester Research

  —Gartner Group

  —Giga Information Group

  —International Data Corp (IDC)

  —META Group

- *Financial analysts:* Most large investment banks have one or more full-time analysts covering the market in which a given vendor competes. The analysts can be an invaluable source of information about vendors and the overall marketplace, as well as a specific product. Analysts spend considerable time talking with end customers and can be an unbiased source of very up-to-date information. If the company has a banking relationship already, that can be a good place to start. If not, the analysts can often be found lurking in various forums for the product under consideration, soliciting user input.

NOTE

1. Lewis Carroll, *Alice in Wonderland,* Chapter 6, "Pig and Pepper." (New York: Penguin Putnam, 1865).

7

IT Operations

It ain't bragging if you can do it.

—Dizzy Dean[1]

You can't build a reputation on what you are going to do.

—Henry Ford[2]

IT operations refers to the *utility* services provided by the IT department and is used synonymously with the term *IT infrastructure*. IT operations cover management of hardware, network, network security, enterprise security, communications, user administration, and e-mail systems.

This chapter outlines key practices for effectively managing the IT operations department, along with key processes and responsibilities of the department. It details the measures of success and concentrates on key areas that drive user satisfaction and minimize business risk.

Approaches for effectively managing the operations area by implementing standard operating procedures (SOPs) for the most common, repetitive tasks are provided. This chapter also covers techniques for improving quality through process improvement and root cause analysis for diagnosing system problems. Additionally, it covers methods for calculating appropriate staffing levels for the operations areas.

Finally, this chapter outlines ways to raise the IT operations profile and call organizational attention to its successes. As a utility provider, the operations unit most often receives only negative attention when service outages occur, and rarely receives positive recognition. The techniques discussed in this chapter can help raise the visibility, service level, and positive feedback in the organization. Key topics are covered in the following order:

- Scope of IT operations.
- Management approaches for key IT operations areas.
- Techniques to standardize common tasks.

- Setting resource levels.
- Operations process improvement.
- Communicating with users.

Why This Topic Is Important

The IT operations area is one of the two major areas that bifurcate the traditional IT department: operations and applications. The software development and applications area typically receives the predominant share of attention from users and leaders because of users' involvement in application projects and the business driving nature of e-commerce, Web development, and packaged software. In addition, almost no business users are involved in IT infrastructure unless new or updated infrastructure is a prerequisite for a new application. In reality, IT operations have an equal, if not greater, impact on customer satisfaction than application development does. If e-mail or the phone system goes down for a day, the IT operations area receives considerable attention from users at all levels. If EDI or any other type of electronic commerce is suspended for even an hour during a peak business transaction period, the company could be crippled by its inability to process orders.

The IT operations group suffers from a "Cinderella" complex. When the services are running normally, no recognition is offered because satisfactory performance is the expected behavior. There are few events that can occur in the operations area in which a business unit employee would offer praise for the department because the group reaches the pinnacle goal (e.g., no disruptions, fast response time). Similar to Cinderella's stepsisters, the group is asked to "do this, do that"—a multitude of requests to fix everything from PDAs to large mainframe computer systems. A rain of criticism drowns the organization that is not customer service oriented. A service might be stable and running well for 355 days a year, but if it goes down for one day—especially during a critical period, for example, the last day of the quarter—the entire image and satisfaction of the operations group and IT department can be shattered.

Service failures can negatively and rapidly impact large numbers of customers, suppliers, and internal staff. Network outages, server failures, e-mail downtime, and broken desktop computers can significantly reduce the productivity of the entire company.

The nature of the activities managed by the operations function in IT dictates that when the operations team is executing effectively and achieving the most success, it is also invisible. This means that the IT department should engage in proactive public relations around successes in the IT operations area to generate positive recognition for a job well done and bank goodwill with business users. Outages will plague an operations group at some point, so building "goodwill" provides some buffer against the negative public relations impact an outage causes.

Besides system failures, possibly the next single largest driver of customer satisfaction is the IT help desk. The help desk interacts with business users on a constant basis. Response time, courtesy of the representative, level of follow-up and follow-through, and resolution speed are all factors that drive customer satisfaction on a daily basis. It takes only one botched request from a high-level officer in the company to tarnish the reputation of the entire IT department.

Several other areas affect the user base, including user administration, capacity planning, disaster recovery, and security. Significant costs are at stake on a daily basis in the IT operations group, and it should be managed with as much rigor as the applications group typically receives. Concepts discussed in this chapter include:

- Scope of activities and responsibilities in the IT operations area.
- Management approach for each area.
- Techniques for standardizing most common tasks to improve productivity of staff, quality of work, and consistency of operations.
- How to set staffing resource levels appropriately by operations responsibility area.
- Approach for effective troubleshooting and root-cause analysis in IT operations.
- Framework for evaluating capital expenditures or other investment opportunities in the operations area.
- How to communicate operations successes to IT and the overall organization.

Scope of Operations

Operations incorporates the following processes and areas as shown in Exhibit 7.1:

- Problem management (help desk).
- LAN/WAN infrastructure management.
- Systems management.
- Security management.
- E-mail system support.
- Telecom equipment and administration.
- Disaster recovery (business continuity and contingency planning, backup and restore procedures, test plans).

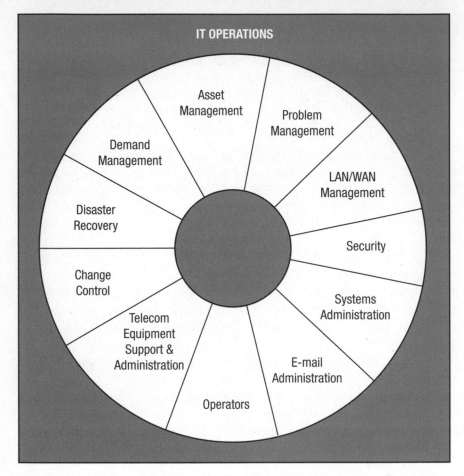

Exhibit 7.1 IT Operations Overview

- Asset management (configuration management, contract and software distribution management, inventory).
- Daily systems operations (cost recovery, facilities, job scheduling, output management performance, production control, quality assurance).
- Change control (change requests, analysis of impact of changes, test plans).
- Demand management (service level management, service request management, workload monitoring).

A brief description, key management practices, and critical success factors of each of these areas are provided in the following sections.

Problem Management

Problem management (e.g., help desk) is the overall support infrastructure, tools, processes, procedures, policies, and organization focused on resolving and reacting to end-user problems or issues. Problem management is generally organized into three distinct tiers, each having very specific tools, processes, and procedures. The first is Tier 1 support, usually made up of help desk personnel answering phone calls and e-mail from end users. Tier 1 support personnel log calls into trouble-ticket tracking software, attempt to resolve common issues over the phone, triage calls to determine who in the IT organization should fix the problem, and provide overall customer support.

Tier 2 support is generally made up of more technically specialized personnel, including programmers (for application problems), network administrators (for network problems), or system administrators (for systems or server related problems). Tier 2 support in most organizations is also responsible for desktop/laptop support and break/fix support. If the Tier 1 support is unable to resolve issues within a given time frame or service level agreement (SLA), the issue is escalated to Tier 2 support.

Tier 3 support is comprised of the most highly skilled IT specialists and may include outside vendor experts and vendor support personnel. Tier 2 personnel are senior analysts while Tier 3 personnel are generally at the highest skill level in a given technology discipline.

The most effective method for managing the issue reporting process is the use of a packaged help desk management application. A wide variety of ticket-tracking and management software is available in the commercial marketplace, and can help an organization ensure that the help desk operates smoothly, and that problems do not go unaddressed. In addition to allowing tight management control of the help desk, these tools can also provide valuable information and statistics to measure the performance of many of the areas in IT operations. Additionally, the systems typically enable other necessary functions within the operations area, such as trend analysis for determining common problems, asset management to assist in managing IT assets, and statistics tracking to understand the workload and demands on the department. Key practices that can help improve operations service levels include:

- Answer incoming help desk calls with a live person. If answering all calls is not possible, then attempt to return calls and e-mails within 30 minutes of receipt. A response to indicate that they have received the user's question and are currently working the situation will greatly improve the customer satisfaction experience for users; ticket-tracking tools can automate the acknowledgment process. Additionally any response should include the anticipated wait time until the problem can be first assessed, as well as an estimate of time to resolution. One method of allowing representatives to answer calls in real time is to install wireless phone sets for the service representatives giving them mobility to perform multiple duties but also answer calls if they are away from their desk.

- Implement a Web self-service portal for the help desk so that users can electronically submit trouble tickets. This will reduce the manual burden on the front-line representatives, as well as give the users immediate feedback on ticket entry and an improved sense control of the process for the user. Additionally, trouble-ticket tracking software can be configured to auto respond to e-mails or self-service tickets and automatically triage the request to the appropriate support personnel.

- Ensure that escalation procedures are clearly documented and updated every six months. Conduct regular training and refresher courses in the escalation process for Tiers 1, 2, and 3 staff. This helps ensure that problems are addressed and solved by the appropriate skilled personnel, and that problems are escalated at the appropriate rate within the operations group. Additionally, it ensures that appropriate business and IT executives are notified in case of emergency situations or when problems are not being addressed in a sufficient time frame. Escalation procedures tend to become outdated over time because of staff turnover, business reorganizations, and business process changes. The processes should be revisited and revised on a regular schedule.

- Execute a customer satisfaction survey on a periodic (usually semi-annual) basis to track and quantify the user community feedback. It is impossible to assess whether the operations group is meeting user expectation if feedback is not solicited. The team should ensure that the survey is statistically relevant. The original survey serves as the baseline and each subsequent survey can indicate the trend of satisfaction and point out areas for improvement, as well as areas that are being well executed. If budget allows, a method for producing credible results is to have a third-party survey organization conduct the satisfaction assessment. There are multiple third-party companies available who can administer these surveys relatively inexpensively.

- Implement a closed-loop process for your trouble tickets. Users become quite frustrated when their ticket is closed yet they are still experiencing the problem. One way to address this issue is to have users close the tickets or acknowledge that the problem is solved.

- Track key help desk metrics and perform trend analysis on the statistics to determine the performance of the teams and individuals. See Chapter 16 for more details on selecting the appropriate metrics.

- Frequent, clear communication with business customers is critical. Provide periodic training to your help desk representatives on topics such as customer service and communication skills. This will help drive a positive customer orientation. Provide information at least once daily to the end user on the status of their open trouble tickets. Also, provide expected wait times for call response and issue resolution.

- Make sure that a single individual has final responsibility for making certain the tickets are completed and closed to the end-user's satisfaction. This should usually be the Tier 1 analyst who first answered the call, regardless of which tier staff member ultimately solves the problem. This will avoid both finger pointing between IT teams, and lost tickets.

- Many larger organizations elect to combine their IT help desk incoming call center with their customer service call center. All calls are answered in a single call center and routed to the appropriate personnel in Tier 2, depending on the type of call (e.g., HR question or IT question).

- Adherence to IT standards greatly increases the productivity of the operations group in general and the help desk group in particular. This includes ensuring that standard disk images are created and either loaded upon receipt of equipment from the manufacturer or, for high-volume purchases, loaded at the manufacturing site.

- Link annual bonuses or other staff incentive compensation to help desk or operations performance metrics. Because help desk ticket statistics are easy to quantify and track, the operations manager can establish compensation or other incentives based on target numbers for the team.

LAN/WAN Network Infrastructure Management

LAN/WAN network infrastructure management incorporates the design, implementation, administration, and monitoring of a company's network infrastructure. Network management involves monitoring to ensure that all components of the network infrastructure (hubs, routers, switches, etc.), as well as any connections or interfaces to outside managed networks (ISPs, frame relay, etc.), are monitored. Network monitoring can help alert the company's network administrator to any potential problems on the network and may be able to help him or her take proactive measures to avoid network downtime or outages.

LAN/WAN network infrastructure also involves management of any dial-up connections, remote access connections, or virtual private networks (VPN) that a company may have. This helps increase company productivity and accessibility of critical information to those who may need it.

Two types of specialists are required—the local-area network specialist (LAN) and the wide-area network specialist (WAN). The LAN specialist has knowledge of network settings in the server and desktop operating systems such as Microsoft Windows XP, required networking protocols, routers, and other network equipment like hubs and bridges. They are responsible for designing and establishing the local network at the office, configuring the internal network addresses, setting up wireless routers and hubs, monitoring the network, and managing capacity.

The WAN specialist has responsibility for connecting networking hardware (routers, bridges) to frame relay, ISP/Internet, and other telecommunications/data vendor networks. The WAN specialist should also have knowledge of network trouble-shooting devices and be adept at working with vendors. They will typically monitor the WAN using third-party tools and be in charge of connecting Web servers and DNS servers to the Internet connection.

The following best practices have been found useful in managing the network:

- Standardize on a network platform. Avoid mixing multiple vendors, hardware, management systems, and protocols if possible; migrate inherited environments running on multiple platforms to a homogeneous environment over time. As outlined in Chapter 6, the benefits of standardizing will typically outweigh the cost of the transition. Running mixed technology complicates both the management of the network as well as increases the potential for hard-to-diagnose errors.

- Ensure that the network support staff employs network monitoring tools that proactively notify them in the event of a network failure or other problems. Not all data centers are staffed 24/7. The technical support personnel can be paged automatically in the event of network issues.

- Change management processes are critical in the network area. If a network configuration (e.g., domain name server, internal IP schema) is inadvertently changed, network chaos can rapidly erupt. Any changes to external IP addresses and DNS servers should be executed with the understanding that these changes take 24 hours to propagate through the Internet. Enforce policies that dictate that all changes to the network configuration are discussed and documented with appropriate rollback procedures.

- Make sure that major changes to the network are made after hours and preferably on a Thursday or Friday evening. (Thursday night allows one business day to correct if there is a problem the network could be down for the entire day.)

- Beware of the streaming video and audio usage from the Internet, as well as peer-to-peer file sharing systems. These activities by users can monopolize the shared network bandwidth. Set a policy to limit or block the use of streaming multimedia on your network. Use firewalls to selectively filter nonbusiness protocols.

- Ensure that network personnel are not only getting the necessary training they need in the network area but are also achieving appropriate certifications. This helps you benchmark their skills and ensure that your internal resources are staying current with the latest advances in networking. Networking technology changes rapidly, and a well-planned training and development program ensures that the networking team can provide the best service for the company.

WAN specialists need a skill set similar to LAN specialists, but also need vendor management skills. Managing telecommunications vendors takes specific experience. Telecommunications vendors will often provide WAN monitoring services; these services can identify (and fix) network issues before internal monitoring. However, careful attention should be paid to service level agreements for vendor-supplied monitoring and uptime, particularly outage penalties. Further, even if the vendor is engaged to monitor uptime, the network team should perform at least rudimentary monitoring to audit vendor performance. It may be necessary to actively manage your telecommunications vendor during outages. If a connection is down, the vendor will open a trouble ticket and notify you when the problem is corrected. However, the network engineer can affect the timing of the fix and get the problem resolved earlier by calling and requesting faster turnaround time from escalating levels of management with the vendor. If the issue is severe, the team should involve a senior manager within the telecom company early on.

The network team should also revisit the telecommunications vendor selection at least every two years and create an RFP for the selection effort. Telecommunication rates change frequently and the company can often save significant dollars through renegotiation. Additionally, revisiting the network architecture to take advantage of lower cost connectivity technologies is recommended at least once a year. Chapters 10 and 11 covers vendor selection and management extensively.

Systems Management

Systems management incorporates the monitoring and administration of a company's systems software and servers. System administrators are responsible for ensuring that systems are running at optimal levels, operating systems are continuously updated with the appropriate patches and releases, server capacity meets business needs, daily backups are performed, and servers do not have unplanned or unexpected outages. In smaller teams without a dedicated security staff, systems administrators will also be in charge of adding, changing, and deleting user information on corporatewide systems, as well as keeping user profiles current. Systems management is important to the business because it ensures that the systems needed to support the business are running efficiently. Proactive management and monitoring servers can help to avoid system downtime:

- To facilitate common processes, the administration team should create checklists and procedures for routine system administration processes (for example, capacity planning, memory usage, CPU usage).

- To ensure that systems are managed consistently and that administrative procedures are adequately documented, the team should create routine procedures for as many systems administration processes as possible.

- In larger departments, system administration resources can be segmented by the technologies they support (for example, mainframe, midrange, Windows NT, UNIX, AS/400, Vax VMS, and others). Simplifying the environment and reducing the number of platforms greatly decreases support costs and simplifies the management of the unit.

Security Management

Security management includes user administration (adding, changing, and deleting system users), security/firewall installation support and monitoring, virus protection, intrusion detection, security policies and procedures, and data transmission encryption.

This function helps ensure that company assets and information are protected from unwanted intruders and unauthorized users. Security management encompasses all activities necessary to secure the network, servers, and applications. It assures computing security by authorizing and enforcing the appropriate level of access to applications and data to internal and external personnel. This function is the primary user and administrator of an enterprisewide security policy. Three critical components of security management include the creation of an effective add, change, delete process for users, firewall implementation, and the rollout and management of virus protection. The primary goal is to provide easy access to systems and applications for authorized users and to allow authorized information to flow in and out of the network unimpeded, while preventing unauthorized activities and programs from taking place or running on internal systems. Security staff best practices include:

- Use network and system management tools for monitoring system access and detecting security breaches.

- Set policies (ID, password length, password renewal period, automated monitoring) on a regular basis and ensure they are enforced.

- Use single sign-on technology when and where possible. This simplifies user administration, end-user experience, and reduces the potential for error in setting user security privileges.

- Use intrusion detection technologies to detect attacks on the internal or external network.

- User management changes and instructions should be tied to and driven by the human resources department (add, change, delete users and profiles), with technology changes and privileges and access levels executed by IT.

- Analyze all access points to systems, applications, and networks throughout the company, and ensure that appropriate access is available, and that unauthorized access has been prevented.
- One to two corporate officers should have access to and knowledge of all IT asset passwords and keys. This prevents the potential of the IT director or systems administrator departing with all the knowledge and presenting a potential server lockout.

In smaller IT departments, the systems security tasks may be split between network administrators (firewall, network security, encryption), systems administrators (virus protection, user management), and applications support staff (application user-level security).

E-Mail System Support

E-mail system support is a unique operations area because of the heavy reliance most companies have on e-mail systems. E-mail systems are often segregated and organized based on geography differences, so that users in a given geography can enjoy the maximum performance from the e-mail system. Each geographic location should have a support plan in place, even in a centralized IT department. The approach for e-mail support is similar to application support, which is discussed in Chapter 8. However, because of unique aspects of e-mail management—such as user administration, security, virus protection, a dedicated e-mail server, and a variety of other unique technical specifications—it is included as a major operations area in this chapter. A number of best practices have emerged in this area:

- Standardize on a single e-mail application (server and client). Adopt new versions of the e-mail application on a trailing basis, to avoid any potential problems with new releases. Lagging the release of a new version by 6 to 12 months is a conservative approach to ensure most critical bugs have been addressed in maintenance releases.
- Users should have access to their e-mail over the Web via a Web client interface. This will help alleviate some of the remote computing issues and help desk support burdens within the company.
- Ensure that a virus protection application is installed on the e-mail system, filtering attachments and detecting e-mail virus activity. If too costly for your company, eliminate potentially dangerous files from being accepted by the e-mail system (for example, .exe files). This can often be done via the firewall or as part of the e-mail server.
- Develop policies for the amount of time e-mail can be saved and put a limit on the size of users' e-mail folders (assuming they save mail on a server and not their client). This will help to reduce the burden on the e-mail application and the server storage requirements.

- Limit file sizes to eliminate large files from clogging the e-mail server. Most companies have a 1 to 2 MB file limit size on their e-mail. Provide other methods for moving and storing large files—public folders, FTP access, or Web-accessible file management systems for moving large files between users.

- Since e-mail is a mission-critical application, spend the money necessary to ensure the server is sized correctly, has the necessary disk space, has back-up power protection, and disaster recovery in place.

- Periodically audit the disaster recovery plan, including validating the backup process and media.

Telecom Equipment and Administration

Telecom equipment and administration is a unique operations area because of its tight integration with outside service providers (local telcos, long-distance providers, and equipment suppliers) and its necessary geographic segregation. Each geographic location generally has its own phone system (key system, PBX, or other switch); thus, a local support plan should be in place to manage each location's telecom needs. The support and management for telecom equipment is based on size and employee footprint of each organization. In some cases, if support size is small, telecom equipment support could be handled by a network administrator or a help desk person. In a large company, or if turnover is high in an organization, more people or a separate unit of people may be needed to manage the telecom changes. Telecom support is needed in an organization to ensure that phone communication is up and available and that phone numbers in a system are accurate. For companies with large numbers of offices with small employee counts, a centralized internal support staff combined with an outside provider that can work in each local office on an as-needed basis works best:

- Telecom user administration should be tied to system user administration and to security. HR initiates a new hire and the request flows to telecom and IT security.

- Negotiate regularly with your telecom provider; often the telecom provider provides bundled services-frame relay, ISP, local telephony, and long distance, necessitating a combined team pricing and contract negotiation process.

Disaster/Recovery

Planning for disaster and subsequent recovery is widely recognized as critical to any company's technology operations. A disaster is generally described as an event that makes the continuation of normal system functions impossible. A *disaster recovery plan,* sometimes called a *business continuity plan,* should be in place to outline steps to take in the event of a disaster. A disaster recovery plan helps to minimize the negative effects and quickly restore critical business functions. A well-designed redundant infrastructure may be the first line of defense to help avoid or recover from a disaster. With fail-safe hardware, backup network services, and redundancy of mission-critical infrastructure either onsite or in a different location, the chance of a seamless system recovery increases significantly. A disaster recovery plan, however, entails much more than redundant hardware and backup procedures. It encapsulates the steps and processes the staff will take to reinstate business functions. A good disaster recovery plan forces the team to think through the specific actions they would take in each anticipated event, so that during the event their focus can be on execution and recovery instead of planning and thinking. The disaster recovery planning process should start with anticipating the range of possible events that can cause service interruptions (e.g., power outage, earthquake, civil unrest, tornado, flood, infrastructure or network failure) and devising a specific response to each potential event. The plan should include the contingencies, as well as the cost for covering the contingency. The IT steering committee can help the team in assessing the likelihood of each event, and the cost/benefit analysis to determine how much risk the company is willing to accept. This in turn dictates the investment the IT team makes to ensure proper recovery. Risk management and planning are covered in detail in Chapter 14.

The IT senior manager should ensure that they have reviewed and signed off (every six months) on the following:

- Disaster recovery plan covering critical IT applications and services.
- Detailed plans, policies, and processes by disaster or event.
- Execution of testing plan to ensure that disaster recovery process is tested periodically.
- Audit of backup procedures to ensure that backup routines and processes are working correctly.
- Training plan to ensure necessary employees are trained on the disaster recovery processes.
- Communication of the plan, costs, and associated risks to the IT steering committee periodically (annually or twice per year).

Asset Management

Asset management is the formal tracking and inventorying of a company's hardware and software assets. However, asset management involves more than just the inventory process of recording the company's assets; it involves procurement of those assets, configuration of the assets, as well as the integration of the accounting for the assets with the company's accounting and financial systems. Asset management is important for tracking the inventory of computer equipment, as well as ensuring that the proper amount of depreciation of the original capital expenditure is being allocated to the operating budget. Additionally, it ensures that the organization stays in compliance with software licensing requirements for software vendors. Proper inventory management can also ensure better pricing from vendors as a true picture of the total number of assets is known:

- Asset management procedures can be standardized easily. Main processes should be documented and standard procedures should be published and followed by the staff.
- Asset management tracking tools can be effective and streamline asset tracking. These are most often a part of the overall financial system implementation, particularly in companies that have invested in large-scale ERP systems. However, an effective procurement and tracking process combined with a simple spreadsheet is a practical, low-cost alternative for small companies.
- Create a closed loop process to ensure all assets enter and exit from one group/location. This entails centralizing the procurement of hardware and software. It also dictates that retired equipment or employee departures are handled by the same group. Periodic inventories can be executed through the use of tools that communicate with devices on the network and ensure that the logical recorded inventory matches with the physical inventory and location. Chapter 6 covers the integration of IT standards and the corporate procurement in detail.
- Periodic reviews of the inventory at the senior management level and periodic audits of the physical inventory and the procurement process can help ensure that the process is being followed.
- Require users to sign an equipment responsibility form that states their agreement to take care of the equipment and make sure it is safely returned to the IT group, particularly for easy-to-transport equipment such as laptop computers.

Daily Systems Operations

Daily operations consist of functions such as batch scheduling and monitoring, managing print queues, physical print distribution, server and printer hardware maintenance, and IT facilities maintenance. Operators are generally responsible for managing all activities in the IT server room, including cabling, maintenance, uninterruptible power supply (UPS), environmental controls, fire prevention/suppression, and flooring. Operators also ensure that the daily reports and jobs are run and distribute reports to the appropriate personnel.

Change Control

Change control is the set of systematic and formalized policies and processes for introducing and implementing changes (hardware or applications) into a managed environment. Controlling any changes made to a business-mission critical production environment is essential to providing uninterrupted, quality service. Managing the process can be tricky, not only because of the inherent risk of rolling out specific technology changes, but also because of the interdependent nature of sophisticated corporate systems. For example, installing a new application on the network may affect other applications adversely. A good change control process incorporates standard tools and methodologies to introduce changes into an environment and involves a gatekeeper who controls what changes are introduced and what changes are not. Change control is important to the business because it helps to reduce the number of unwanted "bugs" or mistakes that get into a production environment. This, in turn, facilitates business continuity and reduction in system outages and downtime:

- Ensure that a change process is in place and has manager approval.
- Create change request forms that require management and end user signoff, to ensure that senior management maintains control of the timing and content of production system changes.
- The IT team should perform an implication analysis for major application, network, hardware, operating system, or infrastructure changes, involving representation from all IT areas potentially impacted.
- Timing and implications of any changes made to systems should be widely communicated to the internal IT team, as well as the end-user community.
- Maintain a document change log that lists all changes in sequential order as well as maintaining a copy of each change request.
- Testing should occur in the testing environment not the production environment and be complete before production environment changes are authorized.
- A rollback plan should be in place for each major change made to production systems.
- Backups of application data and configurations, hardware configuration, and other critical information should be made prior to implementing any large-scale changes.
- Changes should be implemented in off hours (nights and weekends) to minimize disruption to end-user base, as well as provide additional time to roll back changes in the event of unforeseen problems.

Demand Management

Demand management consists of managing demands on operations staff capacity for projects and service from business users. The operations demand management process includes setting expectations for response times, taking action to minimize requests through continual improvements, and moving IT resources to the most highly demanded and mission-critical activities. In addition, IT management must be prepared to work with application managers to consider additional resources or capacity needed to complete a project or request.

Having a formal demand management process in place helps IT management to better account for needed resources and capacity, and ensures that capacity is flowing to the highest value activities. Understanding the metrics (e.g., number of trouble tickets per day, number of user change requests per day, and the current staff numbers) will aid in making decisions on staffing levels and setting appropriate service levels.

An important part of operations demand management is helping the business users understand the trade off between service levels and cost. For instance, if end users are asking for faster response time from the help desk, the trade offs for the business unit executive can be easily quantified (e.g., to reduce response time from four hours to two hours a doubling of the current staff would be required at double the annual cost). Executive management and business leaders can then decide whether they wish to increase investment in the group for the increase in response time. Setting appropriate service levels and managing risk are discussed in Chapter 14. Chapter 15 covers the demand management concept in detail, with a particular focus on application-oriented projects.

Performance Management and Service Level Agreements

Performance management of the operations area is important due to the business-critical nature of the services provided. Most companies have a high reliance on the operations infrastructures that they have created. Outage of telephones, e-mail, file, and print capabilities can cripple a company. This heavy reliance means that extremely high reliability is required of the assets managed by the operations group. To ensure that the services provided by the applications group are being properly met, the group must quantify metrics for measuring their performance. The process for establishing these metrics begins with setting objectives based on business requirements, determining targets, creating a service level agreement, and specifying the targets. Once each service level has been defined and quantified, have each operations area—the CIO and the business—sign-off on the agreed terms. After the service levels have been defined and approved, the operations team tracks and analyzes their performance and makes adjustments in each area depending on the analysis.

Each operations area should be managed on an ongoing basis according to the performance criteria summarized in the service level agreement (SLA). The SLA documents the expected tolerance levels that a particular process should operate within. For example, it may state that the help desk must respond to user requests within four hours of receiving a request. Another example is the WAN must be available and operating 99.8 percent of the time.

The SLA spells out processes, procedures, policies, and targets for each area. It dictates the metrics the IT groups will track (see Chapter 16 on IT Performance Measurement). The SLA is essentially the document that defines the acceptable ranges for each performance metric dictated by the business. Often IT managers implement a "dashboard" as a mechanism of reporting the actual performance results against those metrics in a simplified manner. The dashboard is created by selecting one to two key metrics from the SLA for each IT process. The IT director can also effectively manage each area by providing a one-page dashboard with appropriate SLA metrics.

For the SLA to be effective, it must be created in cooperation between the IT department and the business units. Operations departments that do not have an SLA established with their business users are missing a critical component to providing good service.

Techniques for Standardizing IT Operations

Many of the tasks in the IT operations area, while critical to the functioning of the business, are nevertheless routine and repetitive and thus can be standardized. The organization benefits from creation of standards for these tasks by improving staff productivity, work quality, and consistency, as well as reducing training costs and providing objective measurement standards for setting staffing levels and evaluating staff.

A large number of operations tasks are ideal candidates for standardization, including:

- Employee events: additions, moves, departures.
- Data backup process.
- System shutdown/startup.
- Voice mail password resets.
- Large volume print job management (invoices, payroll checks).
- Capacity management.
- System upgrades.

- Change management.
- New desktop rollout.
- First-round vendor invoice verification.

The operations manager can work with his or her team to identify the full suite of routine tasks that make ideal candidates for standardization. The team then creates standard operating procedures (SOPs) for each of the tasks inventoried. Typically, these tasks are either calendar-driven, periodic tasks (monthly closing process, nightly backup), or asynchronous, event-driven tasks (e.g., new employee administration, a security breach). As part of the operations documentation process, the key driver (period or business event) should be documented and overall volume estimated. Once an SOP for a task has been established, the team can estimate a standard amount of time for completion of the task. Then the combination of SOP labor standards, event volumes, and processing calendar can feed into the resource requirement estimating the process for the operations group. That process is covered later in this chapter.

A variety of benefits are associated with the implementation of SOPs for easily routinized tasks. These have been recognized for years in other task-oriented environments, such as manufacturing. The most significant of these include:

- *Training/staff skills:* Complete documentation of core procedures in the operations area provides a platform for rapidly and easily training new team members or team members moving between roles. Further, it facilitates easy coverage when team members are on vacation or otherwise unavailable.

- *Staff productivity:* When the subtasks needed to complete each work task are clearly understood and easily completed, overall staff productivity goes up. The amount of "scrap" time caused by each piece of work being approached on a one-off basis can be surprisingly large.

- *Work quality:* Because the SOPs are designed and tuned by "experts" who understand the tasks the best, the process and associated checklists produce the best results. By following the SOPs, less-experienced team members are able to achieve the same results as the more expert, experienced team members.

- *Measurement standards:* The idea of work standards for routine tasks has been around since the original time-and-motion studies conducted by Fredrick Taylor in the early 1900s. The same concepts have applicability to the tasks in the IT department. After SOPs have been established, the IT manager is able to set reasonable standards of effort for each task. This gives the manager another useful tool for measuring the performance of team members in the operations area, as well as tools for setting resources.

- *Operations consistency:* The implementation of standards and check-lists for task completion ensures that each task is completed to the same level of detail and in a similar fashion. This improves the consistency of the results from the team member and results in improved customer satisfaction by reducing variability in service.

Exhibit 7.2 outlines the approach for identifying, documenting, and implementing standard procedures in the IT operations area. The following sections describe the processes.

Create Inventory of Routine Tasks

The first step in creating a solid set of SOPs is to identify the full inventory of potential tasks. These tasks should have the following characteristics: clearly defined scope, no large variances in work steps based on decisions that must be made by the operator, reasonable number of subtasks to complete (fewer than 20), and clearly defined inputs and outputs. Defining the inventory of potential task candidates is a relatively straightforward process that can be completed in a brainstorming session with the IT operations team. After the inventory has been identified, it should be prioritized by determining which of the task candidates is generating the highest volume of work and/or producing the highest amount of variability in work quality or performance.

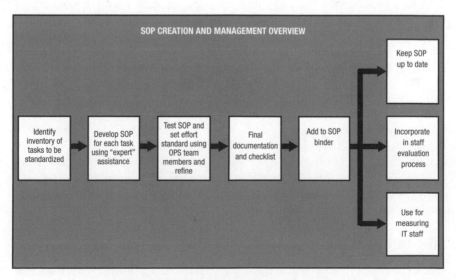

**Exhibit 7.2   Standard Operating Procedure
Creation and Management Overview**

Develop Standard Operating Procedure for Task

For each task identified in the previous step (in priority order), the team should thoroughly document the procedure for completing the task. Each task should be broken into a reasonable number of clearly defined work steps. Each work step should have an easily understood set of inputs and outputs, and the staff member performing the task should be able to easily assess if the work step has been completed correctly before proceeding to the next work step. The ideal way to develop the standard operating procedure is to use a systems expert from the team—most often the operations manager or senior systems administrator.

Test the Standard Operating Procedure

After the preliminary process for the task has been defined, it should be tested under actual operating conditions. Ideally, the testing is done by the staff members who are ultimately responsible for completing the tasks. The testing should be supervised by the creator of the process, who is responsible for gathering feedback and refining the process until the work steps can be completed quickly and easily by the junior team members.

Set Labor Standard for Task

After the process has been tested and refined, a set of labor standards should be created. This standard should document the level of effort (time or other relevant measure) that the task should require. In some cases, the task might have several levels of effort associated with it, depending on the skill of the analyst performing the task.

Create Final Documentation and Checklist

After the process has been defined and labor standards set, the team should create the final SOP documentation. This should include at least two sections: (1) an *abstract* description of the task, which should provide context, show what inputs and outputs are expected from the overall task, and describe not only the *how* or *what* is to be done, but also explain the reasons or *whys* behind the procedure; and (2) a *checklist* to be completed by the analyst as each task is performed. The checklist items should be a sequential subtask list that can be checked off and documented.

Add to SOP Master List and Train

When the SOP is completed, it can be added to the master list of SOPs (most often, a binder organized by IT operations specialty area). The team members responsible for the task area should be trained in the final process and begin using the checklists to manage their work.

Incorporate into Staff Evaluation Processes

To help team members adhere to the SOP and to signal that the SOP is to be taken seriously and used by the team, the appraisal and review process for operations team members should be updated to reflect SOP usage as a key metric for success.

Use for Managing and Measuring Staff

After labor standards have been established, the adherence to SOPs and the team execution of the SOPs within reasonable variance of labor standards can be used as a measure for staff performance. This can be an effective tool for the operations manager and IT director to rapidly identify staff performance issues, as well as help staff members who are struggling.

Update/Refresh SOP

As with any business process, the SOPs should be periodically reviewed to ensure that they are still accurate and relevant. The SOPs should be reviewed annually at a minimum and adjusted based on new information, and the affected staff retrained.

Even more sophisticated tasks such as troubleshooting end-user service requests can be optimized. Basic troubleshooting across all IT support areas can be flowcharted to help guide the Tier 1 support team in diagnosing problems by providing a flowchart or scripted standard set of questions to follow in troubleshooting, along with solutions to the most common problems. For example, the following troubleshooting regimen might apply:

- Is the equipment on? (if no, check power).
- Is the network light lit? (if no, check network connectivity).
- Is the network light green? (if no, check cable or outlet).

This kind of troubleshooting methodology assists the Tier 1 team in making a preliminary diagnosis and even solves some of the easy-to-fix problems. Finally, the SOP can improve the productivity of the next tier support team by requiring the Tier 1 team to gather additional information (computer type, operating system configuration, etc.) before handing off the service request.

Exhibit 7.3 shows an example procedure chart.

Setting Staffing Resource Levels

Setting staffing resource levels correctly within the IT organization operations area is an important part of managing costs and achieving the committed SLAs for the end-user community. Having the appropriate resource

STEP	DESCRIPTION	COMPLETED			
		1st Q	2nd Q	3rd Q	4th Q
1	Initiate SMS software discovery				
2	Prepare software inventory database and configure				
3	Hardware inventory process has been completed previous to this step (confirm)				
4	Validate servers and PCs are logged into network				
5	Examine record and mark complete				
6	Complete for each record				
7	Summarize software asset data				
8	Map actual software inventory to purchased software licenses				
9	Summarize software license gap information				
	Date Performed:				
	Performed by:				
	Signature/Initials:				

Exhibit 7.3   Example Procedure Chart

levels means having the capacity to support both business and IT needs in a cost-effective manner.

One method for estimating the appropriate staffing levels in the operations area is based on the key driver of capacity in the function (e.g., average help desk trouble-ticket volume drives number of staff required for the help desk area). Standard staffing ratios, expressed as the number of IT staff necessary to support the area per some driver, can be determined in each area. Because the driver of activity within each operations area (e.g., systems administration, LAN/WAN support, help desk) is different, each area will have its own staffing ratio. The driver is often the number of end users, but could be other factors that drive the amount of work, such as the number of servers.

For the help desk, this ratio is typically the number of support personnel required per number of end users. A ratio of 1:100 means that one IT support staffer is required for every 100 users. If there were 1,000 users, the company would require 10 IT help desk resources. Developing a staffing ratio for each area assists in determining ongoing staffing levels as the business changes (e.g., number of computer users increases or decreases because of merger and acquisition activity or the number of systems increases because of complexity in the business). The ratio helps determine and justify increases or decreases in IT support personnel.

Statistics for Tiers 1, 2, and 3 of the help desk and the systems administration area are most commonly used and are covered in this chapter. Tier 1 help desk support answers the support phone, e-mail, and other inquiries coming into the help desk. Tier 1 assists users with questions regarding their software, hardware, and network problems. They use a knowledge base (e.g., answers to previously asked questions) and support tools to assist users.

Questions that cannot be answered by Tier 1 are escalated to Tier 2. Tier 2 is sometimes called break/fix or desktop support personnel. Tier 2 personnel generally are dispatched to the user's computer. Additionally, Tier 2 is typically the group that readies new hardware for new users as well as manages inventory of hardware assets. Tier 2 personnel are responsible for installing and configuring, maintenance and upgrades, and fixing user computers and LANs. Tier 2 is responsible for desktop activities up to the point of their connection with other corporate systems (e.g., mainframes, Web servers, backbone networks). Problems that cannot be fixed by Tier 2 or are outside their scope are escalated to Tier 3—system administrators, engineers, and specialists. They have more specialized skills and are segmented between operating systems, networks, and other technical specialties. Tier 3 manages highly complex and critical technical issues. Tier 3 personnel have multiple duties and may spend most of their time on high-skill tasks such as systems administration, standard setting, and architecture.

Tier 1 personnel are typically 100 percent dedicated to operations and the help desk. Tiers 2 and 3 are typically 50 percent dedicated to operations and help-desk related activities and 50 percent dedicated to projects (e.g., rolling out a new version of the e-mail server vs. fixing a computer). This ratio can change depending on the demands of the business.

One way to ensure that the right resource levels are set in the department is to first gather information about past, current, and projected workloads, and then compare the information to a recommended ratio of support personnel to workload from a research specialist such as Gartner Group (Exhibit 7.4). However, the number of help desk personnel needed varies based on

TYPE OF COMPANY	RECOMMENDED RATIO
Companies competing at the cutting edge of innovation	25:1 or 50:1
Companies who compete on full service and overall value	60:1 or 100:1
Companies competing on a thin cost margin and scalability	125:1 or 200:1
Low	12:1

Exhibit 7.4   Help Desk Support Ratios Based on Business/IT Goals

business and IT goals. The ratio is influenced by use of different technologies such as remote access and end-user self-support tools and policies enforced by the IT department. Remote systems management software, for example, can increase the staff leverage within the operations support area.

The ratios include staff for all three levels of help desk support. Since the needs of each organization are different, specific company factors influence the appropriate ratio. A general guide to calculating ratios is described below. The formula considers variables in the working environment to help develop a possible ratio of end users to support staff. To use this formula, start with a base value and add or subtract numbers to come up with a specific ratio tailored to the environment:

- To compute the beginning number, the base value:
  - —If there are a variety of operating systems and no standards for hardware, the base support ratio is about 45:1.
  - —If there is a single operating system and established standards for hardware purchases, the base support ratio is about 70:1.
- Subtractions:
  - —If IT is decentralized and users are allowed to control and adjust their setting, software, and peripherals, then subtract 30:1.
  - —If support personnel must drive or fly to users, divide the support ratio by the ratio of remote users (e.g., if 500 of 1,000 users are remote, reduce the support ratio by 50%).
- Additions:
  - —If IT is centralized and user desktops are locked to eliminate user control of system settings and loading software, add 15:1.
  - —If remote control tools are used to support desktops and install software, add 20:1.
  - —If disk images and configurations are standardized, add 15:1.
  - —If a centralized help desk exists, add 15:1.

This formula provides a general guideline for determining the number of support staff needed. Additional factors affecting staffing ratios include staff attrition levels, standardization, complexity of environment, backlog of work, and required service levels.

Importance of Process Improvement and Root Cause Analysis

The *root cause* of a problem is the fundamental issue that, if corrected, prevents recurrence of the problem. In most IT operations departments, solving problems is not a point of weakness since the team is charged with problem fixes every day. However, most teams do not pursue the root cause of the recurring problems, which, if identified, can be fixed, thereby eliminating the recurring issue.

The operations area of an IT department is the most fertile ground for identifying problem root causes and solving them to reduce overall help desk staff burden. The implementation of a problem tracking system helps identify problem trends. For example, the system might identify a repetitive problem with a given brand and model of desktop computer, helping diagnose a root cause of a manufacturing defect. Often, however, IT departments are caught up in day-to-day problem resolution and do not find time to reduce their overall burden by assessing root causes and taking remedial action.

There are several reasons the root causes of systems problems are not solved:

- When problems arrive at the help desk, the issues are urgent, requiring quick thinking and action.
- The high stress of solving help desk issues can further cloud staff thinking and response.
- IT systems analysts and support personnel are well trained on the technical aspects of systems but not on problem solving and root cause analysis.

One of our clients with a struggling operations department experienced an episode highlighting the issues caused by poor root cause analysis. The client's e-mail service had ceased to work. The IT team rapidly jumped to the conclusion that the WAN link to the Internet was down. The IT department decided that the outage was the "fault" of the outside vendor providing the WAN connection. The telecom vendor providing the link opened a ticket in its system. By the time the ticket traveled through the vendor trouble-ticket system and the vendor service representative called the IT department, 90 critical minutes had passed. In the meantime, the operations staff had not performed additional diagnostics or testing while waiting for the vendor response. The vendor service representative notified the internal operations staff that the T-1 Internet link was running fine, and said that the problem must be with another component of the e-mail system. Time was wasted by a quick jump to an erroneous conclusion. The staff then hurriedly deduced that an internal router table had been modified, causing a link error. Compounding the issue, the company had no change management process in place. Critical questions such as how the table was modified, who modified it, and how the same issue could be prevented in the future were never discussed.

The operations manager can take two actions to improve the capability of the team to correct problems and minimize potential for recurrence, thereby lowering overall IT support costs in the future. First, develop a framework by which system problems must be analyzed, corrected, and documented to minimize recurrence and generate key insights. Second, train systems administrators and operators in hypothesis-driven root cause analysis.

For the purposes of diagnosis and problem solving in the infrastructure and operations area, we advocate adoption of classical root cause analysis, entailing:

- Identification of the problem associated with a particular unwanted situation.
- Identification of the elements that describe what happened in the situation (what barrier or control problems existed).
- For each barrier or control problem, identification of the management elements that permitted the problem and why they existed.
- Description of each of the problems and some brief conclusions on findings and recommendations of how to fix the problem so it does not recur.

To develop a root cause analysis framework:

- Determine the situations that are candidates for root cause analysis. Naturally, removal of the cause must save more than continuing to deal with the symptom.

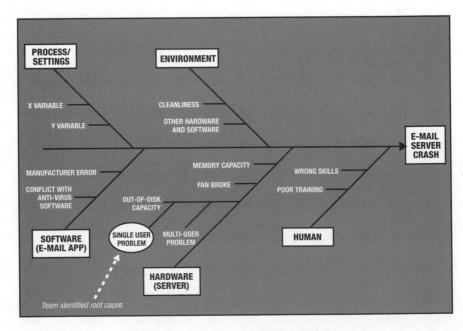

Exhibit 7.5   Conceptual Fish Bone Diagram

- Have the operations staff create fishbone diagrams (Exhibit 7.5) to explain the root cause of issues to IT management. This ensures that staff are thinking critically about the problems.
- Long term, adopt a root cause framework for problem resolution and use it to make adjustments to the operating checklists and management procedures described earlier in the chapter.
- Have root cause analysis training as part of the ongoing education in the operations department.

In the long run, improving the root cause analysis capabilities of the operations team greatly improves the reliability, efficiency, and cost of the support provided to the organization.

Communicating Success

Customer satisfaction with IT operations can be greatly improved by communicating appropriately to the business end users. As observed earlier, the operations area provides an "invisible" service to the business; when the operations team is executing well, they go unnoticed by the business. When operations break down, the team receives negative scrutiny. This phenomenon, combined with the fact that the operations area has an enormous impact on user satisfaction, means that the IT department must proactively engage in public relations efforts to ensure that their operations efforts are properly acknowledged and appreciated by the business team. IT management should ensure that the successes of the IT department are celebrated. In cases where success is measured as service availability, the operations team can point to uptime, systems availability, or other statistics such as speed of service or overachievement of SLAs. In every case, the operations team can select factors that are of material interest to the business and publicize their performance.

There are other ways to ensure that the business users maintain an awareness (and positive perception) of IT successes. First, any major type of application or hardware rollout should have a communication plan. Users should be told when it will commence, when it will be completed, and any potential risks that could disrupt their work. Furthermore, the help desk should set users' expectations for when calls will be responded to, the target time for resolution, when the problem is fixed, and a request of acknowledgment from users.

The communication effort should be an ongoing process for the operations team. Simple efforts such as e-mail communications to the business when milestones have been achieved, or posters and signs highlighting the number of days without unplanned outages can make a difference in the business unit perception of the IT department. Communication devices that can be employed include:

- Periodic IT newsletters detailing service levels, major accomplishments, and upcoming projects relevant to users. The team should keep the newsletter concise.
- Notification of system maintenance at least 5 to 10 days in advance of maintenance. This includes network maintenance, Web site maintenance, e-mail upgrades, operating system upgrades, computer hardware rollouts, and so on. Notifications should be sent out in advance of the maintenance.
- Report major project successes, infrastructure upgrades, and what benefits these will deliver to the users. Claim victory when it is achieved and communicate success regularly.
- Publish frequently asked-question lists covering the top 10 IT help desk questions regularly.
- Submit a brief one-page report to senior management and the IT steering committee on the state of infrastructure once a month (again keep it short).
- Ensure the communication between help desk personnel and users is effective. The help desk should be communicating all of the following: receipt of the trouble ticket, the commencement of work on the ticket, and an estimated time-to-completion. Communicate to the user every 24 hours until the problem is solved.

Communication within the business is perhaps the single most important task the IT operations group can do to affect the perception of performance. By ensuring that IT successes are highlighted, the team can have a major impact on the perception of IT within the organization. In addition to the companywide communication efforts, the IT steering committee provides an excellent venue for IT management to communicate key operations successes. Chapter 12 covers additional ideas for ensuring that the IT department properly communicates successes to the business.

Evaluating Infrastructure Investments

Infrastructure investments are capital expenditures made for division-wide or corporate-wide technologies to support activities in the IT operations area. These investments are usually made in support of a new project to replace existing technology or to enhance technology. Examples of these kinds of investments include:

- Replacing printers for a division.
- Migrating from one e-mail server and client to another companywide.
- Purchasing a new PBX for a branch office.

- Upgrading the communications hardware or speed of the network linkage between offices.
- Replacing employee laptops or desktops with new equipment.
- Implementing new application servers to provide additional processing capacity in support of increased business volumes.
- Implementing an enterprise backup storage solution.

Infrastructure investments are notoriously difficult to evaluate because they exhibit several of the following properties:

- High initial investment costs relative to ongoing costs.
- High level of intangible benefits.
- Indistinct linkage to the actual revenue or cost reduction benefits the investment supports.
- Often a stand-alone project without dependencies on other investments.
- Benefits accrue to multiple groups or divisions within the company (e.g., a shared resource such as a new corporate firewall).
- Benefits accrue over long periods.

These properties make infrastructure investment evaluations distinct from the evaluation that is conducted for investment in software or application development projects discussed in Chapters 10 and 15. Infrastructure investments also tend to be more tactical and require more effort to identify, quantify, and calculate benefits and costs. However, in every case, the infrastructure investments must match closely with a strategic technical architecture plan and set of corporate standards as outlined in Chapter 6. These investments are typically identified as part of the annual planning, IT strategy, or IT architecture efforts.

These investments should go through a rigorous investment evaluation process that aims to make the best use of the firm's capital. Fortunately, much of the evaluation process should be similar to that of projects, as discussed in Chapter 15, including:

- Assessing strategic value.
- Determining the financial value.
- Assessing risk impact on priorities.
- Assessing adequacy of existing infrastructure.
- Determining investment priorities.
- Prioritizing and sequencing of investments.

A major difference between application and infrastructure projects is that many infrastructure investments can be considered in relative isolation, resulting in fewer dependencies and complications. Another major difference is that it may be difficult to readily assess the benefits of a particular initiative because they may accrue to the entire organization. Additionally, there are often many intangible benefits that are difficult to quantify and include in a regular analysis.

In any case, the investment decision can be broken into multiple subdecisions, allowing more time to elapse prior to investment, providing additional information for making the subdecisions. For example, rather than purchase 10,000 new desktop computers for all employees in the company, the IT team purchases them in lots of 500 on an as-needed basis throughout the rollout, providing for pricing negotiation and configuration changes.

Popular Methodologies

There are many popular methods in practice today to evaluate IT investments, along with new methods developed virtually every month by both academics and practitioners. Many of these methods are subsets of traditional capital investment evaluation models, while others are specific to information technology investments. This chapter does not comprehensively evaluate every method but briefly describes the characteristics of the more popular methods to illustrate the wide range of methods used today.

Some of the most common methods are financial approaches that are used in evaluating not just IT investments, but any capital investment made by a firm. At a fundamental level, these are based on the commonly understood concept of weighing costs and benefits. Costs and benefits are quantified over the investment's life cycle using various methods. These are generally combined into a single figure called the net present value (NPV) using an appropriate discount rate over the investment life cycle. The NPV, along with the time period and payback period, is used to calculate the project's return on investment (ROI).

We recommend using an evaluation method that combines speed, ease of use, and communication with various stakeholders while maintaining a firm grounding in analysis and quantitative methods. This method is effective because it can be implemented quickly and provides immediate credibility to the IT organization.

Keep in mind the purpose and goals of investment evaluation when developing an investment evaluation process:

- Prevent investments with high risk of a negative return from being funded.
- Ensure that the best projects receive funding.

- Ensure that the organization understands and follows the evaluation procedure.
- Ensure that the costs and benefits of projects that are funded can be measured to assess the value and effectiveness of the screening process.

An Investment Evaluation Framework

The framework in Exhibit 7.6 outlines the process for identifying, evaluating, screening, approving, managing, and measuring infrastructure investments for the IT operations area:

- *Identification of potential infrastructure investments:* This process can take place through formal requests submitted by business/functional units, deficiencies identified in IT evaluation studies, proposals from the IT department, developed and identified in an approved IT strategy document or in an IT architecture plan. When ready to begin the evaluation process, these potential investments should be presented in a simple

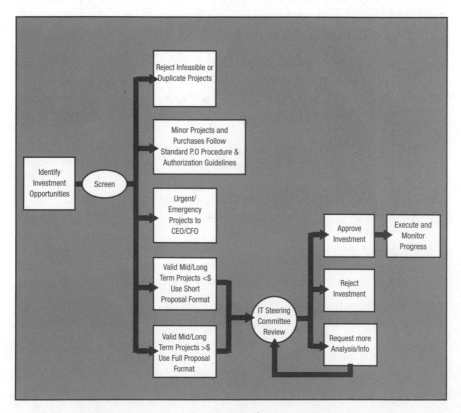

Exhibit 7.6   IT Infrastructure Investment Analysis Framework

single-page summary with a description, estimated costs, proposed benefits, and a "preliminary" financial value calculation.

- *Screening of potential ideas:* Before a full proposal is created, a simple screening process should eliminate ideas that are already being considered, are irrelevant to the organization, violate company policies, are not part of the approved IT standards, or do not otherwise stand up to scrutiny.

- *Prioritization of ideas:* The proposals should be prioritized based on their urgency and potential value to the organization as shown in Exhibit 7.6.

- *Undersized:* If the idea is sufficiently small, it should be redirected to the appropriate sourcing channel in the organization (e.g., central purchasing).

- *Full proposal:* If the proposal is of material cost, it should be sent to the original proposer and/or the IT department to generate a full proposal.

- *Partial proposal:* If the idea falls between an insignificant expenditure and a major expenditure, a partial proposal should be completed. This should follow the same format as a full proposal but without a detailed financial value assessment, and it needs only one alternative to the recommended solution.

- *Urgent approval:* If the investment is especially urgent and critical (e.g., data center replacement because of a catastrophe), it should be sent to the CFO or COO for immediate approval of at least an interim solution. If necessary, a later proposal should be developed for a longer term solution.

- *Review by the steering committee:* Just as project proposals are reviewed by the steering committee, so too, should infrastructure proposals be reviewed.

- *Investment management:* If the project is approved, it should be managed and tracked throughout its life cycle to ensure that all the proposed benefits are realized.

- *Ongoing measurement:* Any lost benefits or extra benefits should be recorded and reported to the IT steering committee. This will help to verify that the investment evaluation process is working correctly.

For financial value assessment, a model should be created that calculates the financial value of the proposed project. The inputs to the model should include the project's benefits, costs, and discount rate. Chapter 15 discusses methods for calculating financial value of a given investment.

The benefits of a particular project should include any value produced by a particular investment. In their book *Smart Business,* David Chapman and Barry Sheehy provide an exhaustive list of potential benefits that should be identified and quantified. The following is adapted from their list:

- Improvement in revenue, gross margin, time to profitability, and profit margin.
- Improved quality of customer products and services.
- Improvement in overall customer costs.
- Improved implementation of products and services.
- Reduction in overhead costs and cost to serve.
- Avoidance of costs.
- Displacement of costs.
- Increase in cash flow.
- Reduction in cost of information technology.
- Reduction in skill requirements.
- Improvement in new product cycle time.
- Acceleration of new knowledge, experience, and opportunity to improve performance.
- Provides new knowledge that gives a competitive advantage.
- Reduces overall capital expense.[3]

Estimates should be made for any identified benefit as both an initial (one-time) benefit and an ongoing benefit over time. For each benefit, a point estimate should be provided *plus* either a probability distribution or a range that can be used to determine the risk of the project. In addition, for each benefit, references should be included in the proposal that explain the source of the data and methods used to estimate the range or probability distribution. The proposer should also ensure that potential benefits are not duplicated in the model.

If there is significant strategic value embedded in the project that cannot be captured through standard benefit discovery, real options analysis (ROA) should be considered to identify and value the flexibility that is provided to the organization. Real options analysis provides a way to identify and properly value strategic features that can be included with the benefits of the investment.

Costs of the investment should be just as carefully estimated as the benefits. These costs should include every cost that would be considered in a total cost of ownership (TCO) analysis:

- Capital equipment investment (e.g., hardware).
- Software.
- Management and planning.
- Installation and testing.
- Training.
- Connectivity.

- Technical support.
- Maintenance.
- Required upgrades.
- Increased overhead.
- Increased cost to serve.
- Negative effect on any operating variables (e.g., gross margin, profit margin).
- Negative effect on any capabilities (e.g., ability/speed of customer service).

All of these variables should be considered for both the initial cost and ongoing cost in the future. Just as for benefits, for each cost, a point estimate should be provided *plus* either a probability distribution or a range that can be used to determine the risk of the project. In addition, for each cost, references should be included in the proposal that explain the source of the data and methods used to estimate the range or probability distribution. The proposer should ensure that potential costs are not duplicated in the model.

The cost of capital should be developed coordinating with an analyst from the company's finance group based on the firm's weighted average cost of capital and the discount rate of a company that shares risks that are similar to the proposed investment.

In addition to the financial assessment, the proposal should include a strategic assessment that qualitatively addresses the value and position of the project within the strategic framework of the company. Items to be addressed in the strategic assessment include:

- *Strategic match:* How well does the investment support the strategic plans in the company?
- *Competitive advantage:* If the investment will provide some competitive advantage to the company, how significant will it be?
- *Management information:* How will the investment provide more control over the organization?
- *Competitive response:* How long can the investment be delayed without a significant reduction in the company's competitive strengths?
- *Strategic architecture:* How well does the investment fit in with the company's IT standards, policies, and enterprise architecture?

These items should be judged qualitatively and have a short text description that backs up the qualitative assessment. If desired, they can be weighted and scored for ranking purposes.

Finally, a high-level risk assessment should be included. The financial assessment should already implicitly include a risk assessment by having a range or distribution for the input variables, and thus a range or distribution for the output variables, including financial value. This section should address a qualitative risk assessment that includes:

- *Project and organization risk:* How capable is the organization of carrying out the investment?
- *Definitional risk:* How much uncertainty is there regarding all the costs and benefits associated with the investment?
- *Technology risk:* How technically prepared is the company to implement and use the IT investment?

Summary

The IT operations area typically receives less attention than the applications portion of the IT department. Yet, it often accounts for more than half of the spending in the department, and provides the tools and infrastructure that users see most often. The help desk is the only interaction and communication with the IT department for many corporate users. Therefore, an effective operations department is critical to good customer service, the perception of a well-run IT department, and a high level of customer satisfaction. By implementing standard operating procedures, service level agreements, process control, root cause analysis, and infrastructure investment assessment methodologies, IT managers can greatly improve the performance of the operation team and the infrastructure they manage.

RESOURCES

Useful Web site resources for operations:

IT Infrastructure Library (ITIL). Available from www.itil.co.uk; provides best practices for IT infrastructure management.

Resources for investment financial value calculation:

Bodie, Zvi, Alex Kane, and Alan J. Marcus, *Investments* (New York: McGraw-Hill/Irwin, January 1993).

Brealey, Richard A. and Stewart C. Myers, *Principles of Corporate Finance* (New York: McGraw-Hill, July 11, 2002).

Gardner, Christopher, *The Valuation of Information Technology: A Guide for Strategy Development, Valuation and Financial Planning* (John Wiley & Sons, 2000).

Moskowitz, K. and H. Kern, *Managing IT as an Investment: Partnering for Success* (Upper Saddle River, NJ: Prentice Hall, July 2002).

Remenyi, Dan, "IT Investment: Making a Business Case," *Digital Equipment* (December 1999).

Remenyi, Dan, Arthur Money, Michael Sherwood-Smith, Zahir Irani, and Alan Twite, *The Effective Measurement and Management of IT Costs and Benefits* (Boston: Butterworth-Heinemann, Computer Weekly Professional Series, August 2002).

Van Grembergen, Wim, *Information Technology Evaluation Methods and Management* (Idea Group Publishing, March 2001).

NOTES

1. Jay H. "Dizzy" Dean, "Biography—Dizzy Dean," Available from http://www.hickoksports.com/biograph/deandizz.shtml (Dececember 19, 2002).
2. Henry Ford, "Henry Ford Quotes," Available from http://www.quotationspage.com/quotes/Henry_Ford (December 19, 2002).
3. Dave L. Chapman and Barry Sheehy, *Smart Business* (Provo, UT: Executive Excellence, May 1, 2002). pp. 53–56.

8

Application Management

We sometimes get all the information, but we refuse to get the message.

—Cullen Hightower[1]

This chapter outlines major processes, key decisions, and approaches for managing business applications in the enterprise. It further covers best practices for organizing and managing applications, including support, enhancements and upgrades, direction setting, and portfolio analysis. Additionally, we discuss the importance of working with the business to set and manage service-level expectations and soliciting business input on direction setting. Understanding the evolution of applications over their lifetimes and the implications for application strategy and overall architecture is also covered.

This chapter is organized around the major components of application management: *Application architecture* covers the methodology for documenting the current landscape of your company applications, as well as the process to create the targeted optimal application architecture that will provide the company better integration, functional coverage, and lower cost of support. *Application strategy* covers determining when to retire current applications and determining the best replacement—based on custom development, best-of-breed package implementation, or an integrated package implementation. *Maintenance of existing applications* outlines the responsibilities of the applications maintenance group in managing the day-to-day operations of the application. Finally, the chapter covers *custom applications* and the *implementation of package systems*.

Why This Topic Is Important

The IT director and applications team are faced with a difficult balancing act, akin to trying to make progress in a leaky canoe. They must split their time between bailing (application help desk, bug-fixes), rowing (application enhancement and upgrades), and steering (high-level application strategy setting).

Of particular importance is *application strategy setting*. The IT department must understand how to best support the business, deciding between implementing new systems versus upgrading existing ones, selecting packages versus creating custom systems, picking comprehensive enterprise resource planning (ERP) systems versus cobbling together best-of-breed packages by area, and a host of other decisions. To make effective application strategy decisions, IT must not only engage the business, but also develop a deep understanding of the company's business.

Complicating matters further is the fact that even at a steady state, applications require significant effort to maintain. Continual changes to the environment in which the applications operate (interfaces to other applications that change; changes to hardware, software, and operating system environments; new data from users or imports) mean that even in a steady environment, a dedicated team of applications developers and specialists are required. The more typical environment involves user enhancement requests, required application software upgrades, customer- and supplier-driven changes, business acquisition integration, new system interface requirements, and other events that increase the complexity of managing the application environment.

Topics discussed in this chapter include:

- Documenting the current application portfolio and developing a target application architecture.
- Evaluating the existing applications and relative investment the company should make to enhance, upgrade, replace, or retire them.
- Defining major external factors that influence application life-cycle decisions.
- Determining key decision criteria and framework for whether applications should be purchased or custom developed.
- Determining key decision criteria and framework for making trade-offs between cost, functionality, and integration of packaged applications.
- Organizing the application support function to maintain applications and effectively support end users.
- Avoiding common pitfalls when developing custom applications and implementing package applications.

Architecture

Architecture: The art or practice of designing and building structures and especially habitable ones.
—*Webster's Dictionary*

The whole intent of developing an application architecture is to define a "habitable" set of applications that support the company now and into the foreseeable future. The architecture includes the manner in which the components of an application set are organized and integrated.

Exhibit 8.1 highlights four major components of IT architecture: business, information, application, and technical architecture. This chapter is focused on application architecture and its implications for application management. Brief descriptions of the four components follow:

- *Business architecture:* Major business activities, functions, and their supporting processes. It further translates the business processes into enterprise business requirements that can be organized into functional groupings. These requirements are supported by information flows and package and custom applications.
- *Information architecture:* Information flows, data entity relationships, and enabling tools that are dictated by the business processes and activities from the business architecture.

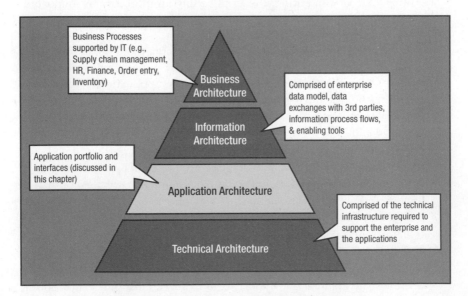

Exhibit 8.1   Enterprise Architecture Framework

- *Application architecture:* Software programs that automate and support business processes; the functions of the applications; articulates the platform where the applications reside; details the set of applications that will support the business in the future; and displays the linkages between both internal applications and the company's applications and those of its vendors, suppliers, and customers.
- *Technical architecture:* The computing infrastructure (i.e., systems software, hardware, network) that supports the information and application architectures.

The first step in managing business applications and determining application architecture strategy is to understand the current systems deployed.

Application Architecture

Application architecture is the description of all software applications and how they interface with each other. There will generally be two architecture models in an organization: the current deployment and one that represents the portfolio of applications that the company will migrate to over time (called the *target*). We use the name *target application architecture* synonymously with *application portfolio strategy*—or the optimal application portfolio for the company over some period of time in the future (typically two to five years).

Defining and documenting the application architecture is important because:

- It allows the application support team to organize applications on a companywide basis; without a well-defined application architecture and target, application enhancements and new applications will be completed without adhering to an overall plan for information sharing and coordination. The result is a hodgepodge of systems unable to share information and with duplicative functionality.
- It promotes information sharing across the organization by providing a road map to the information being captured in each application.
- It promotes information sharing and real-time data exchange with customers and suppliers by facilitating conversations with those partners on interapplication interface opportunities.
- It helps guide corporate information technology investment priorities and allows the assessment trade-offs quickly by more easily identifying capability gaps in the existing set of systems.
- It allows the application support team to serve customer needs better, faster, and more cost effectively by helping identify the implications

of any system change throughout a complex set of interdependent applications.

- It reduces systems development, applications generation, modernization time frames, and resource requirements by providing a clear view of application functions, interfaces, dependencies, and capabilities from which system management, enhancement, and replacement plans can be drawn.

The need for application strategy increases with the size of the business being supported by IT (e.g., the more complex the business or application portfolio, the greater the need for an application strategy). For example, in a medium-sized services company, the application environment may be fairly simple: an accounting package, one application dedicated to the major business activity (e.g., loan processing), a customer database, a business transaction Web site, and an electronic data exchange with suppliers. A simple architecture such as this does not take much effort to document.

In contrast, a Fortune 500 company can easily have hundreds of standalone and integrated applications managed on multiple platforms by a variety of support groups. In both cases, it is important to document what is in place currently, understand any capabilities gaps in the existing application portfolio, develop a consistent set of standards (as outlined in Chapter 6), and build a plan for delivering day-to-day service and additional application capabilities. It is easy to see both the value and complexity of an overall application architecture in the latter case.

Exhibit 8.2 outlines the application architecture definition process. It is important to note that the process is an ongoing effort; when the team has successfully migrated to the target architecture, changing business requirements and newly available technologies will most often dictate that a new target architecture be defined and the migration begin again.

Application Architecture—Baseline

Creating a strategy for application architecture begins with establishing a baseline documentation of the existing architecture. This baseline should depict the set of software applications in the current enterprise application landscape. The baseline should contain three key elements (1) an inventory of the applications by functional area that the applications support, (2) a view of how these applications communicate with other internal and external systems, and (3) a description of each application and its purpose. This is the "as-is" state of applications in the company.

To create the baseline, the team should first catalog and categorize all applications by functional area. This application inventory provides a

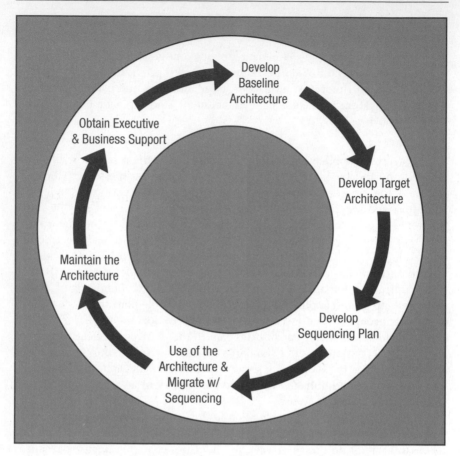

Exhibit 8.2   Application Architecture Definition Process

comprehensive view of the suite of applications currently used and supported by the enterprise.

Exhibit 8.3 shows an application architecture diagram for a representative company. In this case, the company has dozens of applications supporting the business. The applications have been categorized along two axes.
The first is by major functional area, such as finance, manufacturing, and
marketing. For most companies, the applications should be categorized into
fewer than a dozen business-unit or functional categories. The second axis
segments the systems by the three primary functions that the application
might provide:

1. *Planning and control:* Systems that aid in operational planning, configuration of business systems, and general control of the business.

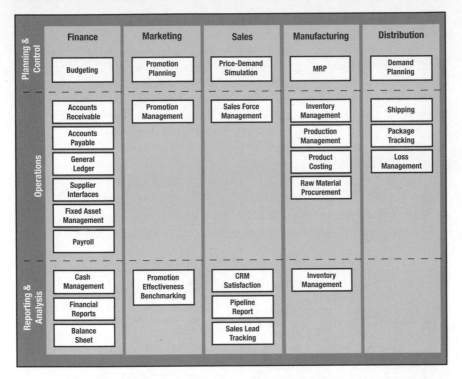

Exhibit 8.3   Example Application Portfolio

2. *Operations:* Transaction-driven business applications; for example, accounting, order entry, manufacturing planning, inventory control, warehouse management.

3. *Reporting and analysis:* Applications that primarily aggregate data from the planning and operations systems to produce reports and analysis, which are used to operate the business.

Segmentation is important because each application type requires different types of maintenance and support, as well as a defined level of investment. Furthermore, this portfolio analysis of existing (or target) application architecture may point out areas of weakness in the overall suite of applications (e.g., insufficient planning and control applications for marketing, overburden of reporting applications for HR).

In many cases, the corporate applications were designed and implemented without consideration for the overall application portfolio, but instead to optimize a specific function in the organization, such as order entry or inventory management. Unless the company has implemented an ERP application, there is likely an accumulation of individual applications that support the organization on multiple computing platforms for a diverse user base.

After the full inventory of applications is categorized, the team analyzes how the applications interface with each other and with external applications. This analysis includes understanding the business event or calendar which drives application interfaces, as well as the communication content, method, and protocol. An application architecture diagram that illustrates the current interfaces between the applications discovered in the application portfolio process is shown in Exhibit 8.4. Several key items are depicted, including:

- The application or application submodule and its primary functions.
- Interfaces between the applications or modules.
- Notation of the platform/third-party software that runs the application.

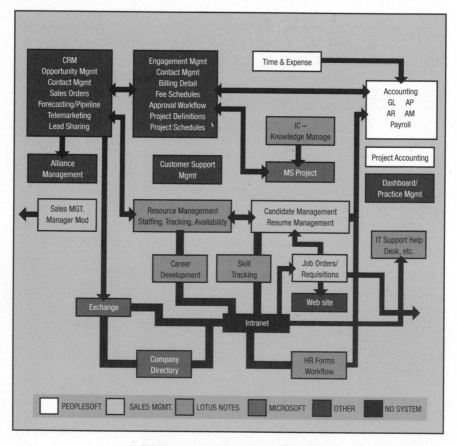

Exhibit 8.4   Application Architecture

An interesting outcome of this assessment is the identification of applications that run in a "silo" with little or no interface to other applications, and the identification of areas of duplicate data maintenance or opportunities to avoid manual data entry by implementing additional application interfaces. The assessment also shows the level of complication in the environment; that is, number of platforms being supported and complexity of the cross-application interfaces.

The final piece to the application architecture is a system inventory that describes the applications depicted in the application architecture diagram (Exhibit 8.5). The key information that should be collected for each application includes:

- *System:* The system name.
- *Name:* A description-based name for the application.
- *Functions:* The primary functions of the application.
- *Platform:* A description of the platform that runs the application, the level at which it runs (e.g., department, corporate, plant, warehouse).

After the application support team has finished the existing application architecture inventory, they should have a clear picture of the current environment supporting the business. The analysis should be presented to the IT steering committee, along with any findings from the assessment (e.g.,

SYSTEM	NAME	FUNCTIONS	PLATFORM
XYZ-360	Management Reporting	• Maintain product characteristic information • Maintain corporate product master files • Load inbound sales data • Print quarterly sales reports	Corporate VM/XA Mainframe
LL-720	End Customer	• Enter, maintain, and transmit inventory position files	Customer System
RPR-328	Product Management	• Sales clerk keys all transactions into system (invoices, orders, receiving, inventory, etc.	Sales Register at Local Store
PA-PM	Local Sales	• Processes local sales transactions • Generates forecast for local store • Communicates information to corporate forecasting system	In-Store Application

Key column information in the table is as follows:
- *System:* The system name
- *Name:* A description-based name for the application
- *Functions:* The primary function of the application
- *Platform:* The technical platform for the application and the level at which it runs (e.g., department, corporate, plant, warehouse, branch

Exhibit 8.5   Example Application Description Table

missing planning, operations, or reporting capabilities, additional application interface opportunities).

Target Application Architecture

The *target architecture* is the set of applications that the organization implements over time, that are planned to improve IT support for business functions. The target architecture is often referred to as the "to-be" architecture.

To begin defining the target application architecture, the application team should review the prioritized project list to understand what business initiatives will have an impact on the application portfolio—what new applications will be needed, what additional capabilities will be added to existing applications, what changes or enhancements to existing application interfaces will be required, and what additional application capacity will be demanded. The process for creating, defining, and prioritizing the list of projects is covered in detail in Chapter 15. Reviewing this set of projects will, in turn, dictate the application architecture over the mid-term (2- to 4-year time frame).

Further, the team should review the existing application architecture to determine the "sunset" on existing systems. This can include systems that will be decommissioned because they are no longer needed by the business; applications that will no longer be supported by the vendor and will be replaced; or applications that have been superceded by newer, more effective technology. The target architecture can then be defined based on the changes emanating from the project list and the systems life cycle for the application.

A critical variable in the target architecture is deciding the time frame the target will cover (i.e., what period of time must the plan cover, by what date must the target architecture be implemented). Typically, a two-year window in smaller companies is appropriate, while a three- to five-year window in larger organizations is more useful.

Document the desired end-state architecture (the three diagrams described earlier), the benefits, and the anticipated costs. The documentation can be done by defining differences from the current model or as a completely new set of diagrams.

Building the Target Application Architecture Migration Plan

The *path to target* or *sequencing plan* is a document that defines the strategy for migrating the enterprise from the current baseline to the target architecture. It defines and schedules the activities that evolve the architecture to the target. The plan should include required company resources, budgets, work tasks, sequencing, dependencies, and time constraints. In some cases, the migration plan may call for several intermediate steps before the target application architecture can be achieved.

In any case, the plans, costs, and benefits of the migration projects should be documented and then serve as input to the IT demand management process outlined in Chapter 15. The IT demand management process will ensure that architecture migration projects are prioritized along with the full suite of other possible IT projects.

Application Strategy

After the target application architecture has been defined, one of the most critical decisions required of the IT director is what strategy the company will undertake for delivering the capabilities required in each area. Exhibit 8.6 contains the basic decision tree required from the IT manager for each application. The remainder of this section outlines each of the critical

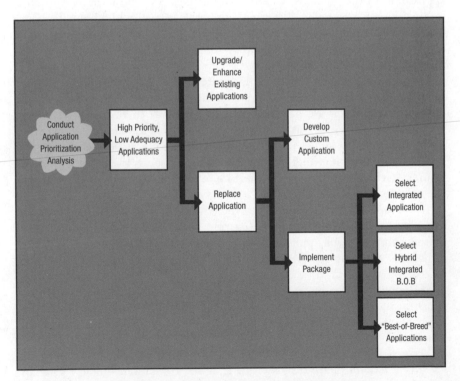

Exhibit 8.6   Application Assessment Decision Tree

decisions outlined and what factors should influence the IT director in making those decisions.

Application Priority Assessment

Determining when to retire an application is an important, yet often neglected, analysis in the IT department. Companies can generate considerable operational efficiencies and cost savings by rationalizing their application portfolio and retiring applications of little value, particularly those that use uncommon technologies and require excessive support and maintenance. The analysis that should be performed to make this determination is similar to the project prioritization analysis presented in Chapter 15. First, the team must assess the current system's adequacy. If no major modifications are made to the current application, how long can the business continue to use it? Develop a scale to assess system adequacy (e.g., 1 to 10) based on criteria set by the business community (e.g., Low = Next 3 to 6 months, Medium = Next 6 to 24 months, High = Next 2 to 4 years).

The second piece of the analysis is to determine the relative value of the application to the business. Chapter 15 outlines several methods for determining the business value of a project or application and highlights the variables that the team may want to consider. After the current system adequacy and potential business value of the system have been determined, the options can be plotted as depicted in Exhibit 8.7.

If the business importance of the application is low, then the application should receive little or no new funding or attention. All applications with low business importance are candidates for retirement. In the case where the system adequacy is low, the team should add projects to the project inventory that show the cost savings or other value generated by decommissioning the system. For low-value, high-system adequacy systems, the team should adjust service levels and resource focus to minimize new investment or effort in the system.

If the business value is high, then the course of action will be determined by current system adequacy. If the current system is adequate, a decision on new investment in the application can be deferred for 6 to 12 months. In the meantime, the team should ensure that adequate resources are maintaining the system.

If the business importance is high and the system adequacy is low, the application should be upgraded. You must then determine whether enhancing the current application or replacing it is more cost effective and better fulfills business needs.

Most of the information needed for this analysis is provided during the *package selection* phase discussed in Chapter 10. Enhancement to the application needs to be treated in the analysis similarly to purchasing a new application.

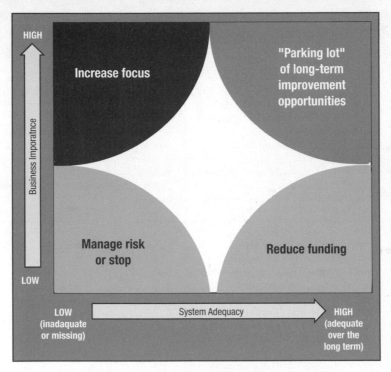

Exhibit 8.7   Application Prioritization Framework

Upgrade/Enhance Existing Applications versus Replacement

For each application that falls into the "increase focus" quadrant of the application priority analysis, the team should determine an application strategy. For each application, the team may choose to upgrade/enhance the existing application or replace the application entirely. This decision will be divided between two key criteria:

1. *Total cost of ownership (total costs over the life or remaining life of an application):* Analyze the total cost of each option over the life span of the application. For example, if one option is to upgrade the current order configuration custom application, then the total costs to code the enhancements, roll out the changes, train the users, and maintain the application must be estimated. A similar analysis needs to be done for the other alternative, which may be (a) developing a totally new application or (b) implementing a third-party packaged application.

2. *Functional fit:* As Chapter 10 details, the applications team should document the requirements of the system and assess the package

	EXISTING APPLICATION	REPLACEMENT APPLICATION
	DIRECT COSTS	
ONE-TIME COSTS	• Software—Total cost of developed or purchased enhancements to application. • Cost of additional support software. • Implementation costs for redeployment or conversion. • Training—Cost of training (personnel), expenses, capital. • Hardware—Cost of additional hardware required (include: expensed and depreciated, lease fees, upgrades, spares, supplies).	• Software—Total cost of selection, new application license, development. • Implementation costs for redeployment or conversion. • Training—Cost of Training (personnel), expenses, capital. • Hardware—Cost of additional hardware required (include: expensed and depreciated, lease fees, upgrades, spares, supplies).
ON-GOING COSTS	• Operations—Cost of continuing support and maintenance (include technical services, performance tuning, Tier 2 problem resolution, maintenance labor, operating system support, user administration, capacity planning, backup, service desk [Tier 1], DBA's, functional and technical application support, process and planning management, and maintenance contracts). • Administration—Cost of supervisory management, administrative assistance, asset management, auditing, purchasing, vendor management, IT course development and training, End user course development and training.	• Same as "Existing Application" plus:—Software maintenance fees.
INDIRECT COST	**INDIRECT COSTS**	
	• End-user operations—Cost of peer support, casual and formal learning, file or data management. • Downtime (end user or IT).	• Same as "Existing Application."
FUNCTIONAL COSTS	**FUNCTIONAL ANALYSIS**	
	• Assessment of functional fit across key business requirements (see vendor selection chapter).	• Assessment of functional fit across key business requirements (see vendor selection chapter).

Exhibit 8.8 Analysis Framework: Replace Existing Application versus Replaced with Package or Custom-Developed Application

alternatives that can fulfill the requirements. Add additional factors into the analysis as described in Chapter 10.

Exhibit 8.8 shows the decision between enhancing the existing application versus replacement. After completing this analysis, the team will be able to quantify cost trade-offs for each alternative and be able to judge whether the additional cost for one option is worth the additional functionality and ease, or whether that option poses more costs for less functionality.

Developing Custom Applications versus Implementing Package Applications

Once the decision has been made to replace an application, the next question is whether the company should purchase a package or custom develop software internally. Chapter 10 presents a detailed methodology for the assessment of package applications that provides a road map for determining the costs, benefits, and fit of the package.

In general, the team should work to determine if any package option exists. The benefits of packaged applications most often outweigh the potential functional give-ups. The significant development costs and high-support burden of custom-developed applications makes them an unattractive option for most companies. In previous decades, building business applications from scratch was the only option available due to lack of software for particular business areas. However, a host of application companies emerged to provide

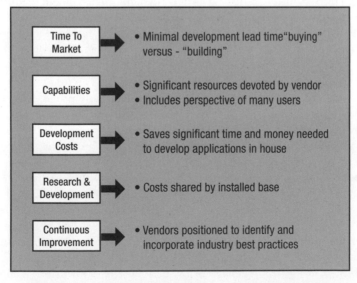

Exhibit 8.9   Package Application Approach Advantages

business applications to fill increasing demands to automate almost every business process. Today, there are few application areas with no offerings from third-party software companies. Exhibit 8.9 outlines the major advantages of package applications.

The final decision of whether to buy or build can be driven by the answers to the questions in Exhibit 8.10 which provides a clear indicator of whether a package is a viable option. As mentioned, the burden of proof should rest with the custom-development option. In only a few unusual cases will the custom-development option be the appropriate approach for an application replacement.

Integrated Applications versus "Best of Breed"

If the replacement decision has been made in favor of a package system, the team is now faced with a final choice: Whether to implement a best-of-breed package or an integrated ERP suite.

Best of breed is the process of selecting the best package or set of packages available that provide a narrow set of capabilities, but which are highly specialized and configurable for the specific function they cover (e.g., forecasting system for industries with highly variable demand, product design system for highly engineered product, or manufacturing planning system for custom garments). Best of breed is the process of selecting the solutions that provide the most robust feature sets in vertical functional needs, yet provide the openness to integrate as an enterprise solution with other best-of-breed packages or with an integrated ERP system horizontally across the enterprise.

Under this definition, a best-of-breed financial management solution provides a win-win solution with depth of financial management capabilities in the vertical functional domain and with the ability to scale and integrate with other best-of-breed vertical systems across the enterprise.

Enterprise resource planning (ERP) applications are an amalgamation of a company's information systems designed to bind more closely a variety of company functions and operations. These systems usually provide support for the entire internal company supply chain (forecasting, manufacturing planning, procurement, manufacturing management, shipping, distribution), as well as functional areas such as human resources, finance, and marketing. ERP software applications were initially created in the 1980s as a response to demand for more enterprise integration. Today, these packages incorporate internal integration across business operations and functions, as well as to external entities such as suppliers and customers. ERP software companies, such as SAP, Oracle, PeopleSoft, JD Edwards and many others, offer integrated ERP applications. Additionally, many of these vendors have specific configurations and package modules that are geared toward specific industries.

The best-of-breed approach generally delivers the closest fit to a company-specific business process by providing the richest functionality, the greatest flexibility, and the fastest time to market for new initiatives. The argument

DIMENSION	DESCRIPTION
Time to market	• How fast can solutions be deployed to operations?
System capabilities	• Robustness—How complete and rich is the functionality? • Quality—How free of problems/bugs the solution is likely to be? • Flexibility—How easy is it to adapt code to meet requirements?
Cost/Investment levels	• Development—Initial investment in building the solution. • Buying—Costs of purchasing the solution. • Deployment/Implementation—Costs related to rolling out the solution to the different operations. • On-going support/maintenance—Costs involved with troubleshooting/solving solutions technical problems. • Research and development—Investment required to keep the solution technically and functionally advanced. • Testing—Costs related to ensuring technical and functional quality. • Training—(See Total Cost of Ownership in previous section).
Continuous improvement	• Best practices—Including industry best practices put into the solution. • Advantaged capabilities—Incorporating leading edge functionality into the solution. • Technology renovation/update—Maintaining the solution in the most advantageous/economically sound technology platform.
Risks	• How prone is the solution to fall short of expectations (e.g., time, costs, functionality, technical soundness)? • What are the costs of failure? • How new are the technologies both provided by packaged vendors as well as the development environment if developed internally?

Exhibit 8.10   Key Decision Criteria for Buy versus Build Decisions

for a single, integrated approach is that it is much simpler, has cross application integration built-in, carries less vendor and implementation risk, and will likely have lower implementation and support cost.

Best-of-breed applications, on the other hand, pose a challenge to the integration front. Because of the complexity associated with integrating multiple applications in a best-of-breed scenario, many companies have chosen a hybrid approach that implements a core ERP system for basic functional areas and business areas that do not have unusual requirements. They then use a best-of-breed application in the one or two areas that have strategic advantages or are critical to the company.

Business and functional areas with strong best-of-breed applications include:

- Supply chain management.
- Product pricing and promotions.
- Inventory management.
- Forecasting and demand management.
- Warehousing and logistics.
- Delivery/route planning.
- Order management.
- Order configuration (for highly engineered products).
- Professional services management (client/hours tracking).
- Human resources/employee recruiting systems.
- E-business applications (e.g., content management, Web commerce).
- Customer relationship management (CRM) software.

Analysis of the three package-based options is required to determine if the trade-off of less integration makes sense given the functional fit, the objectives, the costs, and the overall application architecture plan. Exhibit 8.11 lists specific characteristics between best-of-breed and ERP. Exhibit 8.12 further compares and contrasts the focus of the two approaches. The final three sections of this chapter cover the application maintenance, development of custom systems and the implementation of package systems in further detail.

Maintaining Existing Applications

The Application Help Desk Concept

As outlined in Chapter 7, nearly all IT departments have a help desk function which manages inbound calls from end users. The application help desk is a similar function, but it is charged with supporting the application and resolving application-related issues. It is typically organized into teams dedicated to specific applications.

In support of the help desk, it is important to ensure that responsibilities in the IT organization are clearly divided between developing/enhancing applications and fixing applications. Too often, the development team is asked to meet critical deadlines for a new release of an application while, at the

BEST OF BREED CHARACTERISTICS

Best of Breed

- Built for optimization of a key business process.
- Must itegrate with other applications (poses challenge).
- Can better leverage a legacy environment.
- May deliver competitive advantage (assuming superior functionality—this is not always the case).
- Flexibility (provides options on future direction).
- Quicker implementation timeframe (assuming less modules).
- Greater dependency on internal staff for knowledge of application and integration with other applications.
- Must build complex interfaces to other application.
- Dependency on multiple, smaller vendors.

INTEGRATED ERP CHARACTERISTICS

Enterprise Application

- Core modules delivered for most functional areas.
- Uses best-of-breed applications or custom development for weak areas.
- Implementation could include full breadth of functionality.
- May have industry specific solutions.
- Leverages vendors scale, user base, and expertise in industry and building software.
- More standardization in environment (user interface, security, user administration, platform, database).
- High level of integration (data flows are built-in).
- Dependency on a single vendor.

Exhibit 8.11   Characteristics of Best of Breed versus ERP

same time, being barraged with urgent calls from end users for day-to-day maintenance issues. Because the team is faced with handling ongoing application support, while simultaneously attempting to add new application features, development falls behind, and the new release comes in late and over budget. When possible for large applications, the development team should be separated from the application support team.

Exhibit 8.13 depicts how the development process can be significantly longer if the application support and development teams are mixed. In this example, the team in the top row responsible for both development and support

ISSUES	BEST OF BREED	INTEGRATED ERP
Time to implement	6 to 12 months	18 to 48 months
Value	Focused on business process.	Company-wide
ROI	12-month payback	2 to 5 year payback
Integration with other applications	Build interfaces to other applications.	Built-in except for outlier applications.
Functional fit	High in business process area.	Depends on area and vendor.
Quality	Similar	Heavy spending by vendor in R&D.
Vendor risk	Many smaller vendors.	Few larger vendors.
Users	Small functional group.	Company-wide
Training	Focused	Focused for function but company-wide.

Exhibit 8.12   General Guidelines for Best of Breed versus ERP

expends 40 hours on the development effort and 24 hours on support. When separated into two teams, the development team still expends 40 hours, but the support takes only 16 hours. Two phenomena are occurring. First, when split into two teams, the development schedule is completed 37 percent earlier because the development team does not need to split its focus. The support is completed in fewer hours because the support team focuses strictly

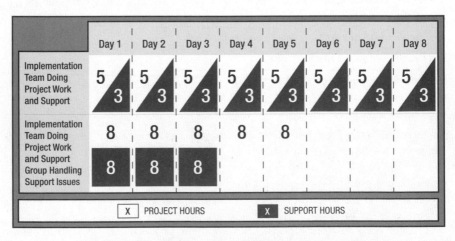

Exhibit 8.13   Separation of Application Development and Support Responsibilities

on support issues to which they are able to respond quickly, not having to wait for users, and where they can optimize the knowledge base.

To effectively manage the application help desk process, two processes should be put in place. First is the support process for trouble-ticket tracking and break/fix calls, as described in the Chapter 7.

The second process to put into place is the enhancement request process. *Enhancements* are generally defined as features/functions that were not designed in the original system specification. If the application is still in a developmental stage, the enhancement team may be the original development team. Enhancements should be prioritized with other development efforts and projects. Enhancement requests are usually delivered several ways:

- User requested fixes or changes.
- Through the business owner—usually in a monthly or quarterly meeting.
- Through the IT department—the help desk or enhancement team categorizes some set of recurring issues with the application and recommends a long-term enhancement solution.
- Through the IT Steering Committee.

Any type of enhancement should fall under the same scrutiny as development projects. A group of enhancements can be approved and batched into an interim "release" of the application. General communication flow should be as follows:

1. An electronic or paper form should be completed documenting the enhancement request.
2. The system designer and business users should meet to review the request, or a batch of requests, to understand the context, the business processes affected, and the objective of the request.
3. The technical team should estimate the effort required to complete the request, by detailing the requirement and designing the fix.
4. Final sign-off should be given to the business user after they review the "cost" of the enhancement to ensure it is worth the effort.

Setting Service Level Agreements

Just as with the operations support area, application service level parameters should be set for all key business applications. Doing so helps manage the support team, determine roles and responsibilities, establish resource requirements, as well as set mutual expectations between the IT group and the business users. Key parameters to consider include:

- Roles and responsibilities (between the application support team, technical support team, help desk, and business users).
- Support hours of operation.

- System request process (a process diagram showing how system requests are routed).
- Problem resolution procedures (how calls are handled, tracked, and closed).
- Severity levels (assign level of importance to each request; it is not the user's responsibility to assign severity; it is a joint determination).
- Priority levels (priority denotes a level of importance in a group of service requests of the same severity).
- Status codes (detail whether the tickets are open, closed, in-process, waiting for information from user, waiting for information from vendor).
- Escalation process (details the process by which calls are escalated up the organization in level of importance).
- Key metrics to track all application support performance:
  —Mean time to resolve tickets on first call.
  —Percent of tickets resolved on first call.
  —Mean time to resolve calls.
  —Time to complete enhancements as percent of total time.
  —Percent of tickets resolved correctly.
  —Average satisfaction score (1 to 5 scale) from customers with tickets.

Key Roles in Application Management

Roles that need to be fulfilled by members of the application management team include:

- Batch job scheduling.
- Application print management.
- Application startup/shutdown.
- Application data integrity.
- Application production status monitoring.
- Review of software patches, upgrades, bug fixes, and service packs (packaged software).
- Implementation of software changes, upgrades, and service packs.
- Configuration and customization management and documentation (packaged software).
- Coding modifications, unit and integration testing.
- Conduct user acceptance testing for enhancements and fixes.
- Application performance tuning.
- Application security management (if not responsibility of operations security group).

- Application service request management.
- Application change control.
- Application administrative functions (user ID requests, group changes, user-level configuration/profiles—if not handled by operations group).

Application Environments Management

To provide the application development/management team with the ability to develop and test changes prior to deployment into production, they should create several systems environments outside the production area in which the applications can run. These environments can be logical partitions on one server or, ideally, separate servers entirely. Optimally, the team will maintain three environments, one each for development, testing, and production. In some cases, teams will set up additional environments for specialized purposes, such as end-user or volume testing. The purpose of three environments is to:

- Keep the production environment stable and minimize production changes to fully-tested application enhancement installs.
- Develop enhancements in a separate development environment, which is free from production capacity issues or scheduling constraints.
- After code set is ready for testing, it can be frozen and moved into the testing environment. This reduces the number of moving parts (testing team won't think code is changing daily). Additionally, it allows the development team to continue work while the testing team is testing.

Application Life Cycle

Applications have a life cycle just as any other technology component. Although significant attention is usually given to the initial development effort, that effort tends to be a very minor portion of the overall corporate investment in the application over time—usually coming to 10 percent to 20 percent of the total investment. Although many "legacy" applications have seen decades of use, technology and business priority changes usually dictate a three- to five-year lifespan for the typical application. Exhibit 8.14 outlines a typical application life cycle.

Application Management Best Practices

A variety of best practices have emerged for documenting current architecture and are noted here:

- To minimize new investment and system disruption, new application strategy should be chosen according to the following order of priorities: re-use, buy, build (custom develop).

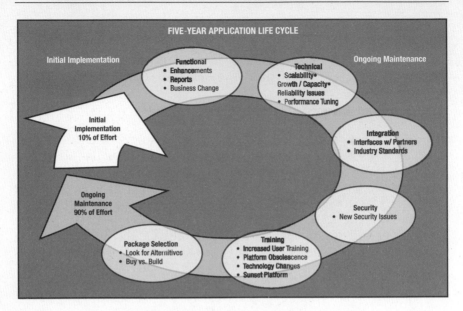

FIVE-YEAR APPLICATION LIFE CYCLE

Initial Implementation

Ongoing Maintenance

Functional
• Enhancements
• Reports
• Business Change

Technical
• Scalability•
Growth / Capacity•
Reliability Issues
• Performance Tuning

Initial
Implementation
10% of Effort

Integration
• Interfaces w/ Partners
• Industry Standards

Ongoing
Maintenance
90% of Effort

Security
• New Security Issues

Package Selection
• Look for Alternatives
• Buy vs. Build

Training
• Increased User Training
• Platform Obsolescence
• Technology Changes
• Sunset Platform

Exhibit 8.14   Application Life Cycle

- In general, business process redesign should precede system development, particularly in the case of new capabilities being supported by the application. The application requirements should emerge from the business process redesign effort.
- Third-party package software should comprise the majority of newly implemented systems.
- The application support team must aggressively limit package customizations to reduce the threat of an unsupported package that is highly customized and eliminates the upgrade path. Heavy (and undocumented) customizations eliminate the benefit of a packaged application and drive overly high maintenance costs.
- When implementing packaged software for noncritical business processes, attempt to modify the business process to match the package application where feasible to avoid excessive application customization and configuration efforts.
- If business process modification is not feasible, an alternative is limited use of bolt-on packages or self-contained, tightly-scoped, custom-developed applications for package gap areas.
- When selecting application platforms, select those that can operate on low-cost infrastructure and technologies that are less costly to support over the long term (labor and support costs).
- Integrate applications using a middleware messaging tool (enterprise application integration [EAI] tools). This allows replacement of systems

as needed into a messaging subsystem rather than modifying intersystem interfaces each time an application is changed in the portfolio.

Developing New Applications

Entire books have been written that cover in great detail the process for building custom-developed applications, from scoping and requirements gathering, through technical design and development to quality assurance and user acceptance testing, data conversion, and implementation. The body of knowledge available for this particular topic is extensive and is readily available for any systems professional, therefore, we briefly address only a few key management considerations in developing applications.

The major work steps that comprise an application development effort include:

- Planning and estimating.
- Requirements definition.
- System design.
- Detailed design.
- Testing.
- Implementation.
- Ongoing support.

Each of these steps should be planned in detail; the plans should be revised at the completion of each major step, particularly the requirements definition and system design tasks that may result in changed assumptions about the project timing, benefits, and costs.

The application team should give special consideration to estimating custom-development projects. Although there are multiple estimating methodologies, many times the estimating effort is neglected or ignored altogether. Often project estimating, when it is attempted at all, is done on a top-down basis, resulting in overly optimistic predictions for resources, timing, and completion dates. A preferable method determines the key drivers of effort for the project, such as number of functions, interfaces, tables, and screens in the application. Based on these, or other appropriate predictors of overall work effort, the team can build a credible estimate of the likely effort to complete the project.

Structuring Projects

For large development projects, the team requires resources for the following roles: graphical and user interface design, functional expertise and configuration, database design and management, data conversion, code development, and quality assurance testing and infrastructure configuration and engineering. Additionally, the team should have representation from at least one business user who will take ownership of the business requirements and help with application design. Exhibit 8.15 lists and describes the minimum deliverables that should be expected from the team.

Managing the Software Development Effort

Finally, application managers should become familiar with several control and quality issues associated with large systems development efforts, for example:

- *Software version control:* There are multiple tools available to help the team manage software versions and manage the code, objects, and executables during development.
- *Documentation:* Documentation covers business process, requirements, database schema, and software code. There are tools available that cover these categories as well. For smaller projects, the documentation effort can easily be accomplished with word-processing and spreadsheet programs.
- *Productivity measures:* There are a variety of methodologies for assessing and measuring both the quantity and quality of development resources. The development manager should become familiar with these and implement them where appropriate.
- *Milestones:*
  —Estimating and work steps to drive a project plan.
  —Adhering to the project plan and the major milestones is critical to instilling discipline in the team environment. Ignoring missed deadlines sends the message that deadlines do not matter. Even if a deadline is not critical to the project, a missed milestone should be treated seriously. Missed deadlines can often help highlight potential project issues, or identify poor productivity in individual team members.
- *Testing:* Testing serves to simulate real-world environments to make sure the software performs as designed and as needed. Developers and users should be involved with testing. In large projects, a dedicated quality assurance testing team may be necessary. There are generally four steps to the testing phase:
  —Create test plan.
  —Create unit and system test scripts.
  —Create performance test scripts.
  —Create user acceptance test.

PHASE	DELIVERABLES	DESCRIPTION
Planning and estimating	• Client business overview	• Overview of company—lines of business, operations profile/footprint, organization, key statistics on business.
	• Business situation/problem assessment	• Description of business issues that project should address.
	• Cost estimating	• Cost estimating.
	• Project goals and priorities	• Concise goals and priorities of project.
	• Key success factors	• Specific challenges or hurdles that exist for the project.
Requirements definition	• Audience analysis	• Overview of potential audiences for system (users, operators, administrators, etc.).
	• Comparable site application analysis	• Inventory of comparable sites. • Select for similarity of underlying business model, process, navigation, or design. • Critique of process or design elements. • Inventory of elements to be incorporated.
	• UI Site design	• Site colors, typefaces, look-and-feel. • Rationale for design, incorporating information from audience and comparable site analysis.
	• Screen templates	• Inventory of key user/administrator system interface screens. • Preliminary user interface designs. • Highlights key user selections, screen design elements (pick boxes, lists, radio buttons, etc.). • Data required to populate screens. • Triggers and data resulting from screens.
	• Information architecture	• "Road map" inventory of all pages on application with short description of content. • Parent-child relationships and preliminary navigation links.
	• Navigation design	• One-page template showing primary top-tab and side-link navigation approach.

continued

Exhibit 8.15 **Overview of Project Phases, Key Worksteps and Deliverables**

PHASE	DELIVERABLES	DESCRIPTION
System design phase	• Business process diagrams	• Inventory of key business events and their impact. • Organized to show people, processes, systems, and information used by the process. • With accompanying specifications sheets.
	• Context diagram	• Overview of key business components and their interactions. • Used to set context and terminology for the remainder of the visioning and systems designs documents. • All components should be linked back to the overall context diagram.
	• Functional requirements	• What the applications must "do."
	• Application architecture	• Inventory of applications. • Cut by business process and application type to show coverage of important areas. • Shown by function, interface, and platform to demonstrate key elements of application communication and functionality.
	• Data architecture	• Overview of tables, fields, data types, unique keys, foreign keys, and so on. • Organized by master files, lookup files, and transaction files. • Referential integrity requirements and approach.
	• Technical architecture	• Overview of technical platform to support deployment of the application. • Key elements include servers, clients, OS, system software, network, cross-application interfaces.

	• Workplans for construction phase	• Detailed workplan for entire construction phase.
		• Workplan elements should include:
		  –Key project phases.
		  –Tasks/subtasks, timeline.
		  –Resource assignments.
		  –Key milestones.
		  –Deliverables/description of deliverables.

Exhibit 8.15 *Continued*

PHASE	DELIVERABLES	DESCRIPTION
Design phase	• Report design	• Inventory of all reports to be produced by system: operational reports, system management reports. • By report: format, data required, trigger (on-line, batch), frequency.
	• Testing plan	• Overview of testing approach—should exercise every functional element of systems as well as cross-module interfaces and referential integrity. • Inventory of test cases.
	• Migration plan	• Migration workplan; timing requirements, data availability, and so on. • Should cover conversion of old systems (when shut off), approach to converting to new systems (by geography, division, etc.). • Workplans and checklists at the server, client, and application configuration level.
	• User documentation	• User-level documentation: FAQ's, training, and instruction manuals.
	• Technical documentation	• Technical documentation oriented toward technical systems support and application developers.

Exhibit 8.15 *Continued*

- *Maintenance:* The development team will likely move into the maintenance team when the software goes live.

Implementing Packaged Applications

Work steps for package implementation are similar to development projects except the development phase is generally replaced with application configuration. Common work steps for package implementation include:

- Package selection (covered in Chapter 10).
- Planning, estimating, and definition.
- Design.

- Configuration and customization.
- Testing.
- Deployment/implementation.

Estimating

As noted, there are many methods for estimating the total work effort and costs for implementing an application; most major vendors have their own method that is tailored to their application. While vendor-based estimating tools are useful, the application team should perform their own estimate as well.

The estimating process should identify the key drivers of effort for the customization, configuration, testing, implementation, conversion, and roll-out of the system. Typical drivers of effort in application package implementations include:

- Number of business events that trigger financial changes from inside or outside the company (e.g., purchase orders or invoices).
- Number of system functions—number of options that would appear on a main menu for the application.
- Level of customization required to provide the capability—usually a mix of configuration and customization.
- Number, size, and complexity of database tables.
- Number, size, and complexity of files.
- Number of user interfaces to be developed.
- Number of major inputs to the system and outputs generated by the system.
- Number of minor inputs to the system and outputs generated by the system (screens and reports).
- Number of sites to be rolled out.
- Number of people on the project.
- Number of technical alternatives (how many infrastructure alternatives are to be considered).
- Number of systems/modules being replaced.
- Number of test cycles to be completed.
- Number of user system tests.
- Number of new modules to be implemented.
- Number of training sessions to be completed.
- Average length of training sessions.
- Number of geographies/offices required for rollout.

With some thinking, the package implementation team can build a comprehensive list of the key drivers of effort for their specific effort, using the sample list as a starting point.

Managing Milestones

As with application development, milestone management is critical to the success of the package implementation effort. The implementation manager must request and receive proof of completion for each major task. If project schedule slippage forces the team to modify the due dates and push the milestones back, the manager should document the root causes and take any actions required to ensure that the team is productive.

Typical milestones for package implementations include the following:

- Requirements complete.
- Business process documents complete.
- Project plan complete.
- Gap analysis complete.
- Installation of hardware/software complete.
- Conference room pilot.
- Configuration/customization of software complete.
- Development of gaps and interfaces complete.
- Unit testing complete.
- Integration testing complete.
- Volume testing complete.
- Parallel testing complete.
- Go live—rollout and final data conversion.

To ensure that the application vendor's interests are aligned with the implementation team, the manager can tie vendor compensation or payment to the timely achievement of the key project milestones.

Conference Room Pilot

An often-overlooked critical step in the package implementation is performing a conference room pilot (CRP). This step allows the team and end-users to preview the system or selected subfunction of the system with company-specific data, executing a company-specific business process. Many applications vendors try to dissuade the IT director from completing this step because of the time commitments required from both parties. However, there is no better assurance that the system meets the business requirements than by viewing it in a more realistic environment than the canned demonstrations the vendors normally perform. The pilot should be conducted on the company site with a business process (end-to-end) tested for critical functions. Company data should be converted so that the software is processing easily recognizable information, and should involve business users for the specific functions tested. The success or failure of the conference room pilot is highly predictive of the overall success of the project.

Business Process Definition

Another often overlooked task is the definition of company business processes. Implementing a package is almost impossible without good documentation of business processes. Detailed documentation of existing business processes provides for detailed gap analyses that highlight areas where the application will require additional customization. Chapter 10 outlines the business process definition and gap analysis process in detail. This process should be an integral part of any package implementation.

Other key points that should be observed by the application team when implementing a package include:

- Keep data clean in the package. Do not assume the package will maintain data integrity appropriately. For mission-critical applications, the team should schedule periodic data checkups to make sure that data integrity is being maintained.

- Minimize package modifications. A highly customized package solution reduces the major benefits of package software.

- If modifications must be done to the package, ensure that they are well-documented and are constrained to as few package modules as possible. This will facilitate the later implementation of package upgrades and patches, which can be challenging to install in highly customized package environments.

- Ensure that the applications team, and not the vendor, is driving the agenda during and after the implementation. Chapter 11 addresses vendor management concepts.

- Find ways to influence the development and enhancement priorities of the application vendor so that new releases of the application will provide incremental features with value to the company.

- Do not assume that one major training program at the end of the implementation will suffice for the end user. There should also be retraining sessions every three to six months to ensure consistent usage of the application and to help achieve the planned benefits from the system.

Summary

Managing application decisions in a company is complex and requires significant forethought and planning. Applications should fit into an overall strategy and be tightly integrated where appropriate. The application portfolio should be analyzed periodically by the application management team to spot weaknesses where inadequate planning, operations, or reporting capabilities exist in a given business area. Periodically, all applications should be assessed based on business value and current adequacy. In cases where the applications should receive more focus (high business value, low adequacy), an additional assessment to determine enhancement or replacement strategy should be conducted. If the application is to be replaced, the application management team must develop a strategy based on custom development, best-of-breed package, ERP package implementation, or a hybrid approach.

In a steady state, the application management team will split their time between application support and development of enhancements and customizations to the existing systems. Ideally, these duties are split between individuals to facilitate the most rapid completion of the scheduled enhancements. The development portion of the application team may be responsible for the creation of new custom systems, as well as the implementation, configuration, and customization of package systems. In each case, the standard disciplines for effective project management apply and help the team to be successful in planning, building, and managing the application portfolio.

NOTE

1. Cullen Hightower, "Selections from Cullen Hightower." Available from http://www.conservativeforum.org.

9

IT Human Resource Practices

If you don't want to play in championship games and you don't want to achieve at the highest level, then I don't want you here, because that's what I'm trying to do. I am not trying to finish fourth.

I'm convinced that if you get people onto your team who share the same goals and the same passion, and if you push them to achieve at the highest level, you're going to come out on top.

—Bill Parcells, NFL Coach[1]

This chapter introduces the IT human resources (HR) life cycle for management of the IT-specific staff employment issues. The HR and employment issues that must be managed by an IT director can be unfamiliar territory for corporate HR departments; thus, the IT group must work in conjunction with HR to manage the staffing process within IT effectively. The IT HR *life cycle* covers major processes that are the responsibility of the IT director and managers, including resource planning, candidate sourcing, interviewing, hiring, and managing.

This chapter is organized around the *IT HR life cycle* that has five key steps:

Step 1: *Determine personnel needs:* Determining what type and quantity of human resources are required to deliver projects and maintain service levels.

Step 2: *Candidate sourcing strategy:* Determining best sources for candidates to hire, deciding if the position should be contract or permanent, and processes for prescreening candidates to reduce the interviewing workload.

Step 3: *Effective interviewing:* Best practices for interviewing and identifying star performers.

Step 4:   *Effective hiring:* Management of the process after the offer is made and before the team member comes on board.

Step 5:   *Managing the workforce:* Ongoing management of the IT team, including distinguishing performers, training and career development, staff retention strategies, and handling staff departures.

This chapter provides an overview of HR issues as they relate to information technology and IT departments. Most often, the staffing focus of the IT department is on interviewing candidates for open positions and on management of specific projects. This results in a lack of focus on other HR practices that are critical for the group, such as appropriate use of contract staff, training and development, and performance improvement. This chapter outlines the full life cycle of HR management issues faced by the IT manager and emphasizes the balance needed to run an effective IT unit.

Why This Topic Is Important

Labor costs are 30 percent to 40 percent of the average IT budget. Labor can be more than 50 percent of costs if outside contractors and consultants are included. Clearly, IT labor is a significant expense for companies and their IT departments. Furthermore, the quality of the personnel within the IT department has an enormous impact on the effectiveness of the IT function, end-user satisfaction, extraction of full value from the IT investment, and proactive use of technology. The right IT team can be a significant competitive advantage for a company; a poorly performing team can be devastating. Given the size of staff-related expenditures and the criticality of IT to corporate success, appropriate HR practices for managing staff are essential skills for IT management.

Regardless of the state of the overall economy, the market for highly proficient IT resources, skilled in the latest technologies, is still competitive. Talented technologists who keep their skills updated and can deliver on their promises are seldom without multiple employment opportunities. In spite of recent economic downturns and increases in overall unemployment, the supply of the best technical talent will likely be constrained for the next decade; hiring and retaining the best resources will continue to be a critical success factor for the IT director and the department.

Adding to the complexity of IT HR management is that, compared to the general pool of labor, IT professionals are most often highly skilled, well-educated individuals who have held a variety of positions in several companies. They typically have a diverse set of career aspirations, often putting factors such as interesting projects, access to training, and working on new technologies ahead of more typical career desires such as compensation, status, and advancement. This factor poses an additional management challenge for IT leadership.

Compounding the challenge is the fact that IT directors and managers are not particularly well trained, by experience or education, in managing human resources. Furthermore, they (rightly) see their main responsibilities as implementing systems, executing projects, monitoring networks and other technology-related efforts; therefore, those processes get the bulk of IT management attention.

Adhering to the processes discussed in this chapter can generate large benefits for the organization. Turnover costs are enormous and can be as much as 100 percent to 250 percent of the departing employee's salary. For example, in a mid-size IT department with 20 employees, if the attrition rate is 20 percent, four employees leave during the year at an average salary of $50,000. This firm may spend $200,000 to $500,000 in recruiting costs, lost team productivity, reset project deadlines, and other turnover costs. In large companies with hundreds of IT workers, the costs can be astounding. An effective IT life cycle can help reduce and control turnover and the associated expense.

Understanding how to optimize the department HR assets is critical to being successful and running a productive and cost-effective operation. This chapter discusses how IT managers and consultants can more effectively hire and manage their workforce to build a high performance team. Topics discussed include:

- How to build an overall resource planning model that helps clearly define roles and responsibilities of individuals on the IT team.
- How to determine the right mix of staff between permanent employees, contract staff, and consultants.
- How to determine the right number of positions that should be open for hiring purposes.
- How to recruit, interview, hire, and, when necessary, release staff.
- How to mentor, train, develop, and retain key staff.
- How to identify, counsel, and weed out the underperformers on the team.
- How to hold staff accountable for delivering against agreed-on work products.
- How to optimize IT's people investment.

Introduction to IT Human Resources

Managing the human resources in an IT department is a complex task consisting of finding, hiring, managing, evaluating, coaching, promoting, training, developing, and releasing staff. While these processes are similar in other departments in the organization, IT poses an especially difficult challenge because of the dynamics of the technology industry. Technology life spans are short; thus, the skills of workers can quickly become obsolete as technology platform changes and they have difficulty transitioning to newly required technologies and platforms. Evidence of this phenomenon was visible in the early 2000s, as demand for COBOL programmers dropped off rapidly after most year 2000 remediation work was completed. Many COBOL programmers had difficulty retooling in new technologies such as Java and found themselves out of work. This meant that hordes of COBOL programmers on staff would have similar difficulty being retrained in e-commerce applications, which was a focus of corporate IT spending and initiatives at that point. A similar trend occurred as the dot-com era ended and Java programmers became the next victims of a weak demand cycle. Companies are constantly having to balance and match in-house skills with new technologies being implemented in response to changing business imperatives. Compared to other functional departments such as finance, marketing, or HR, the pace of change for the base skill sets required is much more rapid. The skills required by any employee in a given company evolve over time, but most often at a much slower pace than within IT.

Many IT managers and directors have pursued career tracks that have given them little chance to build staff development and management skills. IT managers receive little training and less experience in HR policies, staff hiring, management, retention, and development. As observed in Chapters 2 and 5, the IT management team rarely has exposure to the nontechnical aspects of their jobs prior to promotion, leaving them weak in the very skills that will provide the most value to the department.

Likewise, HR departments in companies often have little experience with the unique development, training, and mentoring needs of the IT professional. The scarcity of IT professionals in emerging technologies, coupled with the training demands of the existing workforce and the rate of technology obsolescence, has created a training and career development challenge for IT managers and HR practitioners alike.

Finally, many large companies have implemented centralized procurement of contract and permanent staff in order to enjoy the discounts attendant with high-volume purchasing agreements. Unfortunately, this arrangement can insulate the hiring manager in IT from the vendor providing the contract technical professionals or the permanent employment candidates. The importance of IT department specific knowledge and high cost of recruiting and attrition makes IT involvement in the recruiting and candidate sourcing process even more critical.

This chapter examines policies, procedures, and tools for identifying, interviewing, recruiting, and retaining the best IT professionals and effectively managing this staff. We accomplish this by reviewing each step in the IT HR life cycle.

IT HR Life Cycle

The IT HR life cycle is the continuous loop of key HR processes in the IT department. It follows a logical progression of HR activity, beginning with identifying staffing needs, then hiring, training, and retaining the staff. The first step is determining the actual people/labor needs of the IT department. There are a variety of approaches for determining the answer, and we provide some examples in this chapter. After the full breadth of resource needs is understood, the second step is to put together a candidate sourcing strategy and begin identifying potential new employees. The third step is interviewing candidates for the positions that have been identified. The next step, the hiring process, has multiple substeps and is the area we have found to be most often undermanaged. We have highlighted the best practices in this step. The last and longest step in the process is actually managing resources. We focus on management as it specifically relates to HR issues. The IT HR life cycle process is repeated in scheduled intervals to make sure that the health of the IT HR organization is well protected. Exhibit 9.1 shows the steps in the IT HR life cycle. A brief outline of the steps follows:

IT HR Life Cycle Steps

Step 1:

> Determine personnel needs:
>
> —Use the organization chart.
>
> —Perform a swap analysis and identify personnel gaps.
>
> —Determine staffing strategy—contract, permanent, contract-to-hire (CTH).
>
> —Define roles and responsibilities.
>
> —Create final hiring plan.

Step 2:

> Candidate sourcing strategy:
>
> —Permanent and contract candidate sourcing.
>
> —Additional screening for permanent hires.
>
> —The recruiting funnel.
>
> —Working with agencies and technical recruiters.

Step 3:

> Effective interviewing:
>
> —Interviewing techniques.
>
> —The interview team.
>
> —Best practices for conducting interviews.
>
> —High-volume interviewing.
>
> —Interviewing contractors.

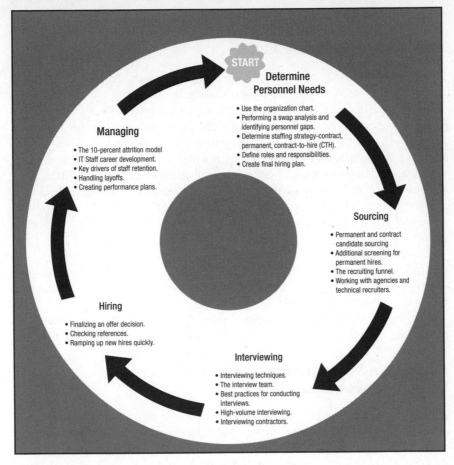

Exhibit 9.1   IT HR Life Cycle

Step 4:

> Effective hiring:
>
> —Finalizing an offer decision.
>
> —Checking references.
>
> —Ramping up new hires quickly.

Step 5:

> Managing the workforce:
>
> —The 10-percent attrition model.
>
> —IT staff career development.
>
> —Key drivers of staff retention.
>
> —Handling layoffs.
>
> —Creating performance plans.

Step 1: Determine Personnel Needs

Use the Organization Chart

It is the responsibility of the IT director to assemble the team that will give the company the best chance of succeeding in achieving the goals established for the IT department in conjunction with the IT steering committee. The current organization chart is the right place to begin determining the configuration of the required team. Creating a clear organization chart prior to hiring is essential and Chapter 4 outlines in detail the most effective organization structures as well as organizational roles and responsibilities. The required roles and responsibilities, as well as the organization chart that will best support the IT department's goals, should be compared to the existing team and organization to identify gaps or overlaps that will drive the hiring process.

Completing the exercises in Chapter 15 will help the IT manager determine the right resource levels. Because labor demand in IT departments is driven heavily by project work, the inventory of prioritized projects will dictate much of the overall hiring and staff capacity plans.

Finally, the committed service level areas (SLAs) in the operations and applications support areas will drive required staffing levels for those functions.

Perform a Swap Analysis and Identify Personnel Gaps

A swap analysis is a review of the existing resources, including their skills, and a mapping of this information against the skills needed to execute the current work in the department identified in the previous step (support, projects, service levels). If there is a mismatch between the capacity and technical skills available and what will be needed, the IT director must "swap" overlapping or no longer required resources for replacement resources with the skill set to achieve the desired end work product. The existing resource must be released from his or her current duties to open the spot for a new person to take over. In some cases, the existing resource may be released from the company, but the team member can sometimes be retrained for the new requirement, or moved to another area within IT or within the overall company.

The intent of the swap analysis is for the IT manager to objectively assess the organization needs versus the capabilities of the existing staff. As new business demands are made on the IT department and new technology capabilities become available, a mismatch between current staff skills and required skills emerges. The swap analysis highlights the mismatches and ensures that team members with skills that are no longer required can be identified rapidly so that their disposition can be determined. Swap analysis can be executed for a small group or for the entire department. We recommend that the swap analysis be completed quarterly or, for rapidly changing departments, even monthly. Creating a swap analysis the first time can be time consuming because of the detailed nature of the task; however, on an ongoing basis, the job is much smaller.

In a typical swap analysis, the IT manager might have a small application development group consisting of two individuals—one with a background in Cold Fusion and the other a Microsoft dot-net programmer. The IT manager will list their full suite of skills and review the upcoming six-month project schedule. In addition, the IT director has determined that the company will suspend any development on the Cold Fusion platform. Meanwhile, all development is scheduled to be Microsoft-based. The project plans call for two full-time employees (FTEs) for the next six months of application development. After executing the swap analysis, the manager determines that the Cold Fusion programmer needs to be transferred to either another development group in the company, sent to training to update skills, or released to another company that uses Cold Fusion, and the team needs to add another Microsoft developer. Although this example is simple, it can become complicated as the number of resources increases. The well-organized IT manager will, however, have the service level definitions, project plans, application, and technical architecture definitions built in advance, making the resource determination effort considerably easier.

Often the IT director is asked to execute cost-cutting measures in the department. In this case, the senior executive team may have requested a 20 percent reduction in IT staff costs. The IT director then executes the swap analysis, determines the team members that possess skill overlaps, selects the best resources and then plans to release the others.

Exhibit 9.2 depicts each step of the swap analysis process, for example:

- *Analyze required skills needed to support IT.* Exhibit 9.3 shows a form that can be used to inventory all key skills required to support IT operations and projects, along with the relative skill level of each IT professional in the department. Use information on current platforms and upcoming projects to develop this list.
- *Determine required number of FTEs by position.* This information should be calculated based on the SLAs and project schedule. If executing a cost-cutting initiative, this should be the minimum FTEs that could hold that position and still keep basic service.
- *Determine whether positions should be permanent, contract-to-hire, or contractors.* Choosing between contract and permanent staff is covered later in the chapter.
- *Analyze skills of current IT team members.* Map each current employee's skills versus the required skills for the upcoming year. Exhibit 9.3 shows a sample analysis. Employees' names are listed across the top row; skills

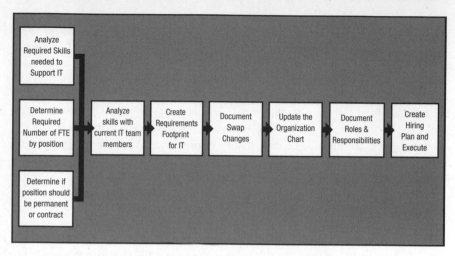

Exhibit 9.2   Swap Analysis Process

Operations	Team Member A	Team Member B	Team Member C	Team Member D	Team Member E	Team Member F	Team Member G	Team Member H	Team Member I	Team Member J	Team Member K	Team Member L
IT Team Members												
Interviewed?	X	X	X		X	X			X		X	
Firewall	◔	○	◑		●	◔			◕		○	
Printers	◑	◑	●		◑	●			●		○	
NT Admin	●	◔	◔		○	●			◕		○	
Exchange Admin	◕	○	◑		●	◑			◑		●	
Desktop Support (PC)	○	◑	●		●	◕			○		●	
Network (Cable, Hubs)	◕	●	●		◑	●			●		◑	
Cisco Switches	◕	○	●		◑	○			●		◕	

○ No experience   ◔ Limited experience   ◑ Some experience   ◕ Capable   ● Highly skilled

Exhibit 9.3   Skill Mapping and Assessment of Current Employees

required are listed vertically. For every technology required, the staff member should be assigned a rating: Blank = Not applicable, 0 = None or poor skills, 1 = Entry-level skills, 2 = Average skills, 3 = Above average skills, and 4 = excellent skills.

- *Create requirements footprint for IT.* Determine the positions and skills required for optimal staffing. This is the inventory of skills and the resource capacity required, by skill.
- *Document swap changes.* Document staff movement within the IT department, and staff being released from the IT department (anyone who does not fill a required spot in the new organization). When planning to release any staff from the company entirely, work with the HR and legal departments to ensure that the process is handled according to company policy.
- *Update the organization chart.* Reflect the swap changes created from previous analysis.
- *Document roles and responsibilities.* To support the IT department, roles and responsibilities should be listed for each position on the new organization chart. Chapter 4 outlines the typical roles and responsibilities within the IT department.
- *Create hiring plan.* Summarize new positions in a document that can be handed to the responsible managers and to HR and corporate recruiting. Each position should have a profile detailing the skills, experience and educational background required for the position, as well as an inventory of likely sources for ideal candidates.

When the swap analysis is complete, the IT director will have a new organization model and a finalized disposition determined for each staff member. The four possible dispositions include: keep in same role, move to new role, release to other company department, release from the company.

Determine Staffing Strategy

The IT director must next determine whether a position calls for contract, contract-to-hire, or permanent staff. There are four ways to satisfy IT demand and execute work:

1. *Permanent staff:* Hired as full-time employees of the company and form the core of the IT department staff. Best suited for positions that last with little change; for example, management positions, analyst positions, programming positions for applications that likely won't change, basic infrastructure positions, and in areas where the technologies are part of the long-term plan for the corporate technology architecture. Additional permanent staff is well suited for areas of

competitive advantage or information sensitivity to the business. The benefits of using permanent staff are:

- Permanent staff salaries and benefits combined can be 10 percent to 30 percent less expensive than using outside contractors.
- Maintain knowledge of systems in the company.
- Have industry and company specific idiosyncratic knowledge of systems and interfaces.
- Focused on their careers within the company and will be long-term participants in the team, driving decision making focused on the company's best interests.

2. *Contractors:* Temporary workers contracted for their specific skill set for a short period of time are *contractors.* Contractors are best used for areas that require a surge of work over a three- to nine-month period, after which the contractors depart the organization. Retaining contractors for this period eliminates the need to hire a full-time resource and dismiss them immediately after the work is completed if no additional work emerges. Contractors are also appropriate for use in areas that need highly specialized skills that may not be available internally. The benefits of using contract staff include:

- Help keep resource costs variable because contractors can come and go in very short time frames, with no HR implications.
- Pay for only the amount of work that is needed.
- No training is necessary.
- Hire the exact skill needed.

3. *Contract-to-hire:* The process of hiring a resource on contract for one to three months and then hiring that person full time if their performance is good and the resource need turns out to be permanent. This "try-before-you-buy" approach minimizes the risk usually associated with permanent hires that do not perform to expectations, as well as provides time to determine if the demand for the staff member's skills will continue in the long term. The company enters into a contract with the candidate that states that he or she will be evaluated at the end of the contract period for a full-time position. If the candidate was contracted through an agency or recruiting company, there will usually be a conversion fee at the end of the contract. For long-term contracts (greater than 6 to 9 months), the conversion fee may be waived by the contracting company.

One disadvantage of the contract-to-hire approach is that top candidates may prefer an immediate offer of full-time employment. If a bidding war erupts for their services, or if another company makes them a permanent offer during the contract term, the IT team runs the risk of losing them.

4. *Consultants:* Consultants are resources hired by firms who take responsibility for the delivery of an entire project or operation area. They are responsible for delivering to you an end product or service based on expected service levels. Consulting firms are best used for discrete projects for a period of three to six months with well-defined requirements, work plans, and deliverables. Additionally, they can be used to outsource infrastructure or application areas. The benefits of hiring a consulting firm are greatest when the expertise to complete the project is not in-house and is difficult to find, or the company trying to reduce costs by outsourcing. If a project is particularly risky or of critical business importance, hiring a consulting firm with experience in similar endeavors can help mitigate the risk and increase the likelihood of success.

Contract staff can make up from 10 percent to 50 percent of the IT staff in a company, depending on the rate of change, the variability of demand on the IT department, and the current project priorities within the company. As a rule of thumb, target about 25 percent contract staff and vary the ratio, depending on what works best for the IT department and company at a given time. If the company runs into economic difficulties, contract labor costs can be shed rapidly.

Typically, managers and analysts should be permanent staff, especially key leadership positions unless the function is outsourced. The IT director should annotate the organization chart showing which positions must be permanent and which positions may use permanent or contract resources.

The overall goal of a staffing mix is to maximize productivity of permanent staff, reduce turnover, increase throughput of the group, provide rapid access to specific skill sets, allow costs to be easily varied, and boost morale by allowing permanent staff to avoid some of the less desirable work in the department. Exhibit 9.4 outlines a framework for determining the staffing strategy by application type and employee risk.

Steps for analysis in this framework include:

- *Build an inventory of systems and applications:* This step involves pulling together the inventory of systems to be supported. The activities completed in Chapter 8 will have resulted in the application portfolio being readily available for this exercise. This inventory can be used to understand skill requirements, systems complexity, and risk.

- *Determine systems complexity/business risk by technology area:* For each system or area supported, measure the risk on a scale of 1 to 5 (least risk to most risk). Risk categories include system size and complexity, business value (e.g., Is the application revenue driving?), business criticality (e.g., Can the application sustain downtime?), number of system interfaces to other systems (complexity), and level of customization

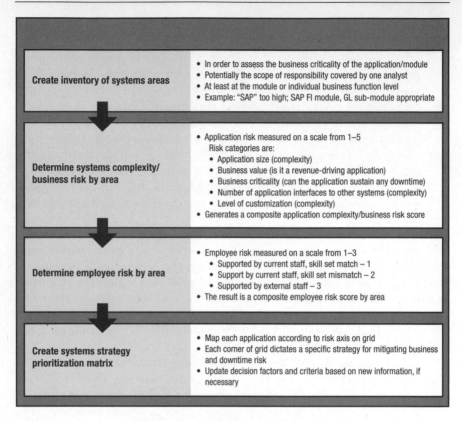

Exhibit 9.4 Staffing Strategy Overview

(complexity). The sum of these scores generates a system complexity/ business risk score for each system or area supported.

- *Determine employee risk and skill level required by area:* For each system, measure the employee turnover risk level and skill level required to manage and maintain the system. Low ratings should be assigned to systems with easy-to-find skills in the general IT labor pool and low likelihood of employee departures. High ratings should be given to areas in which employees will have highly demanded skills that command a premium in the market or high-pressure areas that result in increased staff burnout and turnover.

- *Creating the permanent versus contract staff matrix:* Each system should be plotted on the grid in Exhibit 9.5, according to the application and employee risks determined in the previous step.

The resulting mapping dictates a specific strategy for mitigating business and downtime risk as well as properly staffing the area:

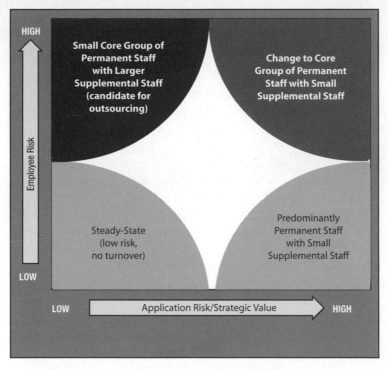

Exhibit 9.5   **Permanent versus Contract Staffing Strategy**

- The northwest quadrant suggests a small core group of permanent staff to manage and direct these systems supplemented with a larger contract staff. The business risk with these systems is low, therefore there is a low likelihood of trouble caused by system outages; however, the skills are in high demand, making a contract staffing model more appealing. An application or function in the northwest quadrant can also be a good candidate to test the outsourcing waters. At minimum, receiving bids from outside firms to maintain this system could provide benchmark data as to how current costs compare to the costs and benefits of outsourcing.

- The northeast quadrant also suggests a small core group of permanent staff with some supplementation through contract staff. The situation is similar to the northwest quadrant, except that the systems in this quadrant are of high strategic value to the company, meaning that a reliable core set of permanent employees should be overseeing these systems. The team should be supplemented with outside contractors or consultants who bring in the most recent, in-demand skills for these areas to help the permanent staff keep up with changes to the technology.

- The southeast quadrant suggests mostly permanent staff. For systems that are strategic in nature, where the internal skill set matches well to the skills required, and where, in general, employees like the work and are not likely to be enticed by outside opportunities, there is very little reason for the organization to outsource or use temporary staff in this area. A small number of contractors can be used to supplement the team on an as-needed basis and to manage peaks and valleys of project or seasonal demand.

- The southwest quadrant suggests no changes to the current staffing situation. It covers applications and systems with lower strategic importance to the business and where the existing permanent employee skill set is a good match. Systems in this category may also be scrutinized to determine if they are good candidates for outsourcing, which may lower overall support costs for the area and allow permanent employees to focus on the higher value systems.

Define Roles and Responsibilities

Whether new or existing, each position in the IT department should have a clearly documented skills, experience, and education profile, as well as a detailed job duties description completed and filed in IT and HR. This provides the IT team with very clear instructions on the IT director's expectations and their responsibilities. Additionally, the documents should outline the objective performance measures on which the position is evaluated. The following need to be known for each position:

- Position title.
- Role within the organization (position on the organization chart).
- Reporting relationships (direct reports supervised by this position, where does this position report).
- Job requirements: technology skills, educational background, work experience, company tenure.
- Documentation of day-to-day ongoing responsibilities.
- Priorities for responsibilities.
- Objective and subjective measurements of success in the role.
- Promotion criteria.
- Success criteria or objectives.

This information can also be used by internal or external recruiters as hiring specifications, as well as for evaluation criteria during the annual employee review process.

Create Final Hiring Plan

At this point in the life cycle, the IT director will have a list of key personnel actions, a list of new open-to-hire positions, and a determination of whether those hires are contract or permanent positions. The final stage of Step 1 is producing a hiring plan. A sample hiring plan worksheet is shown in Exhibit 9.6.

The hiring plan details the following information:

- Position title.
- Number of positions to be filled.
- Type of resource (permanent or contract).
- IT department manager responsible for hiring this position.
- Recruiter responsible for managing the recruiting process for this position.
- Yes/no flag indicating if a position description has been written up and is available.
- High-level summary of skills required for the position.
- Target offer and start dates for position.

The IT director should also work with the HR department to determine target salary rates for each position. This should be based on a combination of corporate standards for the role, market rates, and current compensation levels within the IT department.

The hiring plan neatly summarizes the current hiring needs of the organization. It is also a useful tool for facilitating communication between IT, the steering committee, HR, and internal and external recruiters.

Position Title	# of Positions	Permanent or Contract	Manager	Recruiter	Position Description	Skills	Target Offer Date	Target Start Date
Consultant – Peoplesoft	2	Contract	JD	TL	Y-Attached	Psft functional, Financials – AR/AP/GL. V8.0	1-Jul	15-Jul
Network Systems Engineer	6	Permanent	JM	TL	Y-Attached	Senior network, CCNA	1-Jul	15-Jul
Programmer Analyst	2	Permanent	JD	TL	Y-Attached	Visual C++, SQL Server	15-Jul	1-Aug
Technical Analyst	1	Contract	SG	TL	N-TBD	3 years technical support, NT, Windows 2000, MSCE	15-Jul	1-Aug

Exhibit 9.6   Example Hiring Plan Worksheet

Step 2: Candidate Sourcing Strategy

After the hiring plan is complete, determining approaches for identifying candidates from the at-large labor pool is called *sourcing*. The process will vary, depending on the urgency of the search, the position type (permanent, contract), the rarity of the skills required. The sourcing process is made up of the following steps:

- *Develop candidate profile:* Detailed job specification that shows the full requirements for the position. The internal or external recruiters use this information to screen candidates. This profile can be easily derived from the roles and responsibility document created for the position in the previous step.
- *Prescreen strategy:* Necessary to ensure eliminating low-potential candidates with a minimum of effort. Implement several filters for eliminating candidates. For example, one common filter is years of experience: "If candidate does not have three years of Peoplesoft functional experience, eliminate from consideration." Other typical prescreens include degree requirements, geographic location (local candidates only), and industry-specific experience (e.g., financial services, energy, telecommunications).
- *Importance of timing:* While the IT director should interview a sufficient number of candidates, they should also work to minimize the search time. The more rapidly they can carry candidates through the screening, interview, and offer process, the more likely the manager is to get an acceptance from the desired candidate. Candidates who move slowly through the pipeline are at great risk of either receiving another job offer during that time or being forgotten about, particularly in high-volume hiring situations. If more than three weeks elapse between the candidate's first interview and the decision to make an offer, then the process is moving too slowly and the timing issue is likely to lose appropriate candidates.
- *Technical testing:* Another useful screening (or prescreening) tool. Technical testing through one of the many online providers such as Brainbench or ProveIt provides third-party verification of the candidate's technical skill level. For management positions, the team should include other testing, such as IQ tests or tests of other nontechnical required skills.

Permanent and Contract Candidate Sourcing

There is a substantial difference between recruiting a permanent hire and a contractor because of the hiring cycle and nature of the individuals who are looking for the opportunities. Contractors are comfortable working on a temporary basis under highly uncertain conditions. Contractors are willing to accept and manage the risk of not working for one to six months until their next engagement comes through.

The hiring cycle is normally about five days for a contractor (the time between an interview and an offer). The hiring cycle for a permanent job position ranges from 20 to 30 days, because both the company and the candidate require additional time to gather information and perform a mutual assessment given the permanent nature of the hiring decision. Different strategies are appropriate for sourcing permanent hires. The best sources for hiring permanent technical candidates include:

- Other companies that use the same technologies or skill sets.
- Previous employers of current IT employees.
- Referrals from existing employees (this is the most productive source for most companies).
- Staffing agencies and recruiters that cater to permanent IT professionals. The Yellow Pages of your local phone directory lists pertinent companies under Permanent Placement Services, Computers—Technical Recruiting, or Recruiting and Placement Services.
- Internet job boards are a source for hires, but unfortunately, they cater to candidates who are actively looking for jobs and who may be frequent job hoppers. For permanent hires, many companies prefer the "passive candidates" that are best identified by using staffing agencies or internal recruiters. Some of the most prominent and well-trafficked sites are www.monster.com, www.hotjobs.com, and www.headhunter.net. With tens of millions of resumes on the Internet and similar numbers of job postings, the Internet is an important factor in technical recruiting.
- Universities, colleges, junior colleges, and technical training centers provide candidates through their placement offices.
- Technical associations and industry associations can be very helpful in finding technical candidates. The National Association of Computer Consulting Business (NACCB) and the Information Technology Association of America (ITAA) both cater to the technical market.

The following is a list of resources available to assist in hiring temporary technical candidates:

- Staffing agencies that cater to contract IT professionals. Your local phone directory Yellow Pages lists pertinent companies under Technology Consulting, Computers—Information Technology Consulting Services, Computers—Temporary Placement Services, or Computers—Technical Recruiting.

- The magazine *Electronic Recruiting News* (www.interbiznet.com/ern) tracks resources for contract and permanent recruiting resources.
- The *Airs Directory* is a premier directory of recruiting resources located at www.airsdirectory.com.
- Project managers and peers can provide referrals. Ask your project managers and other peers for a list of the firms they use to help hire contract resources.
- Technical associations and industry associations, such as NACCB and ITAA, can help with temporary resources.
- Contract staffing-focused Web sites such as Dice (www.dice.com) cater specifically to the contract-oriented candidate.

The other difference in sourcing the two types of candidates is the specificity of information. With contract resources, the position must be very specific, the pay rate set to a certain range, and the time frame for the project clearly communicated. This allows contract recruiters to cut through a huge candidate pool quickly.

Additional Screening for Permanent Hires

For permanent hires, the IT manager may choose to do additional screening. Some additional things to look for when reviewing resumes include a consistent history, a proven ability to stay employed for a material length of time (e.g., longer than 18 months), and a clear, consistent track record of logical career progression. There are a number of quality assurance checks you can add to the recruiting process to help diminish the likelihood of hiring a candidate who is a poor fit, including background testing and behavorial screening. Depending on corporate-level policy, a permanent hire may require the ability to gain a U.S. government security clearance or to pass a drug test. In any case, the IT team should work closely with the HR department in developing the appropriate set of screening criteria for permanent candidates.

The Recruiting Funnel

The recruiting funnel refers to the reduced number of candidates that are carried through each step of the recruiting process (i.e., out of 100 potential candidates, fewer make it through each successive screen, all the way through to the job being offered). For a given position, the manager should interview a minimum of three candidates in person, after they have been passed through all the prescreening and preliminary phone interviews. A high interview-to-job-offer ratio may indicate that the recruiters do not understand the specification, that the manager is being overly selective, that the requirements are too narrow or possibly all three.

Exhibit 9.7 shows one method for tracking the recruiting funnel. The exhibit shows activity against each of the key steps in the process (candidate identification, interview, offers, acceptances) by open position. The team should maintain an activity summary chart to provide tracking and status of progress against open positions.

Additionally, by position, someone (usually the recruiting department) tracks each candidate in the pipeline. The IT director should request a period report that shows status similar to the example in Exhibit 9.8.

Understanding the recruiting funnel helps the team monitor how well the hiring process is proceeding. Typical rules to follow:

- Recruiters searching for passive candidates make 75 to 100 calls to get one qualified resume.
- Referrals can greatly enhance the productivity of recruiters.
- Ten resumes screened result in one interview.
- Three to five interviews produce one hire.

Working with Agencies and Technical Recruiters

Working with technical recruiting companies can be a productive way to find candidates for open positions. Agencies can reduce the time and cost of identifying quality resources as well as locate candidates who may not have been found by the IT department or the internal recruiting department. Agencies have highly efficient recruiting and sourcing processes that are hard to match within a given company.

Position	Recruiter	Open Positions	Candidate Interviewed	Candidate Deselected	Sent to Mgr	Offers	Offer Declined	Offer Accepted
1	JP	7	58	35	14	9	3	6
2	JB	6	44	21	21	11	2	9
3	SW	1	52	28	7	17	8	9
4	JK	7	42	24	14	8	3	5
5	WQ	4	15	8	3	0	0	0
6	FD	0	0	0	0	0	0	0
Total		25	211	116	59	45	16	29

Exhibit 9.7   Recruiting Activity Summary

Candidate Name	Position	Source	Recruiter	Manager	Screen	Presented	1st Int.	2nd Int.	Offer	Accept	Start	Follow-up
Jones, Cheryl	Network Systems Eng	Referral	JM	JD	1/20/2004	1/20/2004	1/21/2004	1/22/2004	1/23/2004	1/24/2004	2/15/2004	
Smith, Chris	Programmer Analyst	Dice	JM	JD	1/20/2004	1/20/2004	1/22/2004	1/23/2004	1/24/2004			
Floyd, Terry	Consultant	Advert	JM	JD	1/20/2004	1/20/2004	1/24/2004					
Jones, Mary	Lead Technical Analyst	Referral	JM	JD	1/20/2004	1/20/2004						

Exhibit 9.8 Candidate Tracking Summary

The interface between the hiring firm and the agency is the agency sales-person. Referrals from other IT directors are a good way to identify potential agency sales professionals. If referrals do not produce good results, the IT director should call the agency and speak to the general manager of the of-fice. The general manager should provide a referral to the agencies top sales-person; this person should have at least five years of experience. It should be made clear to the agency that they should provide an experienced account manager, preferably with knowledge of the industry.

Other agency screening questions include:

- *Size:* Work with a firm that has a large database of candidates. An indi-cator of size is the number of full-time employees (sales, recruiting, and technical). A firm with 10 or more sales and recruiting personnel is the appropriate size. Other size metrics include annual revenues and num-ber of consultants or placements the firm makes annually. Because of the low barriers to entry in the staffing business, the industry is filled with small, undercapitalized players.

- *Fee arrangement:* For permanent hires, the placement fee will range from a low of 10 percent of the candidates starting salary to as much as 35 percent. When the agency is working on multiple positions, and particularly if the agency has exclusive rights to filling the position, it is easy to negotiate lower fees. On the other hand, a difficult-to-find, one-position specification generally commands 25 percent to 30 percent. Agencies will usually charge the end client the placement fee on the candidate start date. The agency will also usually provide a replacement guarantee for a certain period of time. The guarantee is that the agency will replace the candidate free of charge if the hired candidate does not work out or resigns during the guarantee period.

  Fees for contract consultants are handled differently. There are no separate fees associated with contract consultants. Instead, the agency will be quoted an hourly bill rate for each candidate presented. Bill rates are very negotiable and are driven by market demands for the skill and resource the team is attempting to hire, as well as committed contract length, geographic location, and type of work. The agency ap-plies a markup to the cost of the consultant that covers employment taxes, benefits, and a profit for the agency. The markup is usually be-tween 20 percent and 50 percent, depending on skill set, demand, contract length, and geography.

- *Retainer fees:* Firms should generally avoid paying a retainer fee for agency recruiting, except for searches targeting the most senior execu-tives. Another arrangement, similar to retainer-based recruiting is on-site recruiting. In this case, the firm can strike an agreement with the agency to have recruiters work on-site and recruit exclusively on the company open positions. This becomes economical if there are a substantial number of positions to hire and internal recruiting support is inadequate.

- *Years in business:* Ask how long the company has been in business. Staffing agencies operate in a very competitive environment and longevity of more than 5 to 10 years indicates an ability to please clients and adapt to changing markets.
- *Top five clients:* Ask the general manager who are the agency's top five customers. This provides an indication of the market the company caters to as well as the relative success of the company. Companies that have good relationships with blue-chip clients, particularly over long periods of time, usually have the best recruiting capabilities.
- *Size of database:* Ask how many technical candidate resumes are on file or in an online database. The larger the database, the faster the recruiting process will be and the stronger the agency's ability to provide the best-fit resource.
- *Number and location of recruiters:* The number of recruiters is an indication of agency size and ability to rapidly work on new requirements. The location of the recruiters is important as well. Recruiting is fundamentally a local process and recruiters in the geographies in which the search is taking place will have much more success identifying the right candidates. Also, the agency recruiting team should be dedicated to recruiting and not mix sales and recruiting responsibilities.
- *Top skills hired:* Understand the skills sets that comprise the firm's core competencies. For example, do not hire a firm for programming job openings if the firm specializes in recruiting network professionals. Determine competency by asking for a list of the skills placed over the past 6 to 12 months.
- *References:* Ask for recent references from the company and call at least one of them to determine if the agency is successful at producing positive client references.
- *Screening process:* The agency should provide its candidate prescreening methodology. The agency can also prescreen candidates using technology tests, background checks, reference checks, education verification, or other checks. The agency should provide a list of screens that it can complete as part of the recruiting process.
- *Candidate sourcing approach:* The agency should provide their candidate sourcing methodology as well as their primary source for candidate resumes. The best agencies are effective at using their internal proprietary database, finding passive candidates through aggressive phone calling and through referrals from existing contractors or candidates. Weaker agencies simply search job boards for candidates without expending the extra effort to delve into other sources.

While this list is helpful for identifying one or two agencies to work with, for high-volume, long-term hiring needs, the team may want to select vendors via the competitive bidding process outlined in Chapter 10. The previous list provides a starter set of requirements for the full-scale vendor selection process.

If the company has a central HR or procurement function, they will often have a vendor list of recruiters and temporary staffing firms that are approved to work with and are proven resources.

After signing up staffing agencies to assist with open positions, the company should also be sure to add an *off-limits clause* that states the recruiting company cannot recruit employees from the company. Usually these clauses are in effect for a full year after the start date of the last permanent or contract candidate hired from the agency.

Agencies can be particularly useful for positions that are difficult to fill. For lower end positions that are easy to fill or for positions that internal recruiters are successful at filling, agencies should not be used.

Step 3: Effective Interviewing

In this section, we discuss best practices in interviewing. The interview process should be focused on understanding how well the candidate fits the profile, as well as the corporate and IT team culture. The process should also provide some information to the candidates on the company, department, and position, although the primary focus is on identifying candidates that will receive offers. Once an offer has been made, the IT team can focus on providing information to the candidate. Specific approaches for successful interviewing include:

- *Compose an interview team for the position:* The manager responsible for the position, his or her direct superior, and one or two people from the team the new hire will be working with should provide the right balance between ensuring top quality and team dynamics. Each interviewer brings a slightly different focus to the interview (e.g., technical skills assessment, culture fit assessment, or understanding management experience).
- *Create a candidate scorecard:* The interviewing team should agree on and create a scorecard for assessing each candidate interviewed. This scorecard should be based on the candidate profile that has been created in Step 1 of the IT HR life cycle.
- *Prepare ahead of time:* One of the most common mistakes made by interviewers is failing to prepare for the interview. Managers and IT teams are busy and often have schedules booked right up to the interview time. Many times the interviewer is taking his first look at the candidate resume after the candidate arrives and the interview starts. Instead of listening to the candidate, the interviewer is scrambling to think about what questions he will ask. A more effective interview preparation approach is to read the resume at least 15 minutes prior,

circling each items of interest and making notations of specific questions to ask. Second, plan the interview and develop an interview script if you interview for this position repeatedly.

- *Conduct the interview in 10- to 15-minute time increments:* The interview should be 30 to 60 minutes and the time should be allocated into three equal components. First, have the candidate walk through his or her background. The candidate should be able to show a clear history of logical career progression and an explanation of why each successive career move was made. The interviewer should also ask the candidate why he left his previous job, or is considering changing positions. Next, the interviewer should give a brief overview of the objectives for the position, give the candidate an opportunity to show that he understand the position and can map these objectives to something in his past experience. Finally, the interviewer should see how well the candidate thinks on his feet by giving the candidate a short business case (see below), or asking appropriate technical questions. Allow the last 5 to 10 minutes to answer the candidate's questions and discuss next steps. To save time in the in-person interview, an advance phone screen is sometimes useful for getting resume background conversations out of the way. If the team is hiring for multiple positions or needs to talk to many candidates, the phone interview can help screen out some of the candidates without having to conduct a full-scale interview.

- *Allow the candidate do the talking:* The candidate should be talking 80 percent to 90 percent of the time. The interviewer should not make the mistake of consuming excessive time by talking about how great the position, group, or company is. There will be time for that conversation after the candidate has been made an offer.

- *Check off key criteria during the interview:* Culture fit, energy, leadership, technical skills required, history of achievement, or performance.

- *Focus candidate on individual accomplishments:* Interviewees often spend too much time discussing group accomplishments in an interview, without addressing their specific contributions to the accomplishment. Allowing the conversation to focus on group or team accomplishments can disguise shortcomings in the individual candidate's abilities. The interviewee should focus on his or her specific contributions to the team and prior company.

- *Write the interview assessment on a scorecard:* Develop a scorecard with criteria that is important to you. Give a scorecard to everyone in the interviewing process. Ask them to return the scorecard immediately after each interview so they can write what they think, versus listening to everyone else first and then developing their opinion biased by others' feedback. Writing down the assessment also helps document the interview in case the person reappears in the future.

- *Candidate testing:* Can provide some objective feedback on candidates, particularly for technical positions. The test results can also show how candidates for a specific position score relative to each other. Tests may include technical testing, IQ testing, or business function testing.

- *Behavioral testing:* Psychological behavioral tests have also been effective in determining the personal behavior traits of successful candidates. Behavioral tests work best when a pre-existing profile of successful candidates has been completed and new candidates are compared to that profile.

- *Business case interview:* Case interviewing provides another chance to test the thinking skills of the applicant. Cases are business problems that are presented to the candidate verbally, or in writing, to analyze. The candidate provides a recommendation on what actions they would take to solve the case issue. A typical case will pose a business problem to the interviewee, such as "how would you evaluate competing application vendors given a certain set of facts?" While for most case questions, there is no specific correct answer, the candidates response will provide insight into how well they can logically dissect a problem, ask for additional information, and construct an argument and set of recommendations.

- *Perform additional screening:* A variety of background screens can be helpful in determining candidates likelihood of success and distinguishing between candidates in a close race for the same position. The internal HR department, the recruiting agency or other third-party services can conduct drug tests, criminal background checks, reference checking, and education/degree verifications. The IT department should coordinate with the HR department before conducting any of these screens, to ensure compliance with company policy.

- *Assess candidates in an informal setting:* Spending time with candidates in more informal settings, such as lunch, dinner, or a sporting event, can help in further assessing their fit. This can be particularly helpful for differentiating between closely matched prospects. Characteristics revealed away from the office setting may be just as important as work skills.

High-Volume Interviewing

If the hiring needs analysis determined that the department needs to hire a large number of candidates (more than four or five at a time), the process differs from filling only one position. The short-cycle scheduling effort consumes considerable time, let alone conducting the interviews themselves. The best process is to set aside a block of hours and a conference room on the same days of each week to concentrate on interviewing. Recruiting companies also have space for interviews and they can arrange for the interview team to see candidates at the agency office, which will minimize the distractions that are a natural part of on-site interviewing. This process will facilitate making rapid hiring decisions based on the entire candidate pool; without setting aside time for structured interviews the complicated scheduling logistics and the passage of time will be an irritant to both interviewers and candidates. By handling all interviews for a specific position over a short period, the decisions can be made immediately and the candidates informed of the decision.

Interviewing Contractors

Interviewing contract staff entails a different process than permanent interviews. The time cycle, content, assessment, and the negotiations are differ from permanent hires. Questions and tips for contractor interviews include:

- *Assess contractor technical skills:* Usually companies will be willing to accept less exact fit for permanent employees, provided cultural fit and other experience is appropriate. For contractors, the technical fit should be exact, since they are usually being brought in to provide a specific set of expertise. The contractor should complete technical testing, as well as a technical interview with experienced team members to ensure proper knowledge.

- *Assure contractor reliability and quality:* Often contractors are brought in to provide a short-term surge of effort to push through a major project. In this case, if the contractor is unreliable or cannot provide quality service, the company incurs a high cost and loses crucial time. Referrals from the agency or previous contracts can be helpful in determining the contractor's ability to deliver quality work on time.

- *Establish a contractor day rate:* Unscrupulous contractors will occasionally charge excessive hours for unnecessary work, recognizing that the project is short-term and that they will soon move on to another project. Ask the contractor if they will provide a cap to their daily billings (8 to 10 hours) and require manager sign-off on additional hours is a way to help avoid this issue.

- *Understand contractor employment status:* Contractors may not be incorporated as a business and will have to be considered W-2 or 1099 contractors for tax and benefit purposes. These statuses each have specific implications for the company hiring the contractor and may imply certain benefit and tax liabilities. While contractors provided through an agency may be slightly more expensive than those hired direct, the agency deals with W-2, 1099 and contractor incorporation issues, providing a seamless interface and mitigating liabilities for their client. If contractors are hired directly by the IT department, the IT director or hiring manager should consult with the HR and legal departments to ensure that the contractor status is in line with corporate hiring policies.

- *Make clear final hiring intentions:* If the position has the potential to convert to a permanent position and the contractor will be considered for that role, he or she should know up front. This will prevent the contractor from prematurely looking for a new position when the contract is close to ending.

- *Make a rapid decision:* Once the interview is complete, the team should make a decision within one to three days. Contractors are accustomed to rapid turnaround in the decision-making process. Often the contractor will have several simultaneous opportunities and will generally take the first forthcoming offer. Once the interviewing team has identified the appropriate contract resource, they should move to rapidly make an offer.

Agency recruiters who are presenting a candidate can help with the assessment. If the contractor has been on previous engagements through the agency, the agency can provide references and feedback from the contractor's previous work.

Permanent hire interviews follow a more traditional process and time frame. Typically the process of determining the candidate profile, sourcing candidates, interviewing, offering, and closing the position can take up to 30 days. Permanent hires are making a major career decision, whereas contractors are simply making a commitment for the next two to six months. The permanent candidates require a more detailed scrutiny and need more information from the team on their career path, job stability, strategic direction of the company, training, culture, and team fit.

Step 4: Effective Hiring

The next step in the IT HR cycle, effective hiring, is often overlooked. The bulk of the attention is paid to sourcing, recruiting, and interviewing. After the hiring decision is made, the team's focus and activity level drops off. The recommendations in this section can help ensure that offers are accepted and can help make the difference between a successful hire and an unsuccessful one.

Finalizing an Offer

After receiving feedback from the other interviewers and everyone agrees that the candidate is a hire, make the decision without procrastinating. Procrastination only increases the chance that the candidate will go elsewhere.

One of the critical hiring errors interviewers make is the search for the mythical perfect candidate. After all the interviews and background checks, there is little likelihood of new information emerging that will change the decision. Once the decision is made, the offer should be extended to the candidate as soon as possible and followed up with a formal offer letter.

When the candidate is offered the job, the manager should be frank as to the expectations for the job—roles, responsibility, work hours, career mobility, and any policies or other issues that may affect his or her decision. The offer letter should be specific, spelling out the expectations that have been communicated verbally. In addition to describing the roles and responsibilities, the offer should also establish specific performance objectives and time frames for the role. For example, the offer might specify the following objectives: Candidate must complete five modules for the new billing system by the end of the third month after the start date. Candidate must complete requirement gathering for the asset-tracking database in the first 90 days of employment. Candidate must attend the following training classes in the first year of employment. This part of the offer is often included in an addendum to the formal offer letter. This approach helps both the new hire and the manager in ensuring the expectations have been clearly set and provide an objective, pre-agreed measure for assessing performance, allowing the manager to detect hiring errors as early as possible.

The first 45 days should be an evaluation period with a formal review cycle. The IT director or manager should schedule a meeting with the candidate 45 days after the start date to review performance to date against the preset performance metrics and objectives.

The candidate should sign the offer letter and the job expectations and performance metrics addendum, accepting the offer and acknowledging that he clearly understands the expectations; make sure a signature line is on the offer letter. This letter goes into the candidate's personnel file in HR as well as into the IT manager's files.

Checking References

Rarely does a reference not check out well, especially when checking the candidate provided references. A few rules of thumb to improve the quality of reference checking are:

- Check three references for each candidate and document the conversations and feedback.
- Check at least one reference that is not given by the candidate (e.g., a previous project manager) and ask that person for names of others who worked with the candidate who can be called as well.

- Ask pointed questions on reference calls. Would you work with this person again? What are his or her weaknesses? What does this person do well?

- Use care when interpreting the references. Seldom are references negative; generally they are either positive or neutral. Therefore, for a quality candidate, expect all the references to be highly favorable. If they are not, it may indicate that the manager has not had a good experience with the candidate, but is bound by company policy or other considerations to avoid revealing this.

Ramping up New Hires Quickly

The faster a new hire can become a successful part of the team, the more productive the IT department is going to be. Typically, people expect the first week on a new job to include background reading, meeting their coworkers, and learning more about the company. Many new hires expect to take several weeks to get to the actual work they were hired to accomplish. The IT team can avoid this expensive ramp-up period by laying the groundwork for a successful first week for the new team member:

- Have administrative staff establish workspace before the start date; for example, office, cubicle, computer/laptop, voice mail, and other administrative details.

- Have the employee meet with HR to take care of signing up for payroll and benefits prior to the first day on the job.

- Arrange a team breakfast or lunch the first day to have new hires meet team members.

- Give new hire or contractor material and background information to read prior to the start date.

- Have the first week of employment scripted in advance, with specific goals.

- After the first week, have the new-hire detail and document his or her work plan for the next 30 days and review it face-to-face.

- If the new-hire's main job or project is not ready to kick off immediately on the start date, have a secondary project lined up and ready to go or delay his start date until the main task can be started.

Step 5: Managing the Workforce

Managing the professionals in the IT department can be challenging. There are scores of management books and leadership books available, oriented toward both general management as well as specific approaches for leading IT teams. In this section, we cover some of the specific models we have employed in successfully managing IT staff.

The 10-Percent Attrition Model

The *10-percent attrition model* means that every year the IT director should release the bottom 10 percent of the workforce. This process ensures that the department is constantly upgrading the team. It also helps the workers falling in the bottom 10 percent. This model is applicable to most IT departments; after a few cycles, the IT team will be a stable, high-quality group and the attrition model may no longer apply. However, we have found this situation to be the exception. Also, although we have emphasized the high costs of turnover in the introduction to this chapter, the costs of an ineffective team far outweigh the impact of losing out the poor performers.

To accomplish this attrition, during each review cycle, the IT director should rank IT staff according to relative performance. One useful method is to adopt the A, B, C, D model, which equates A to the top 10 percent of performers, B to the middle 60 percent, C to next 20 percent, and D to the bottom 10 percent. Adhering to a 10-percent attrition model works, at least for a struggling IT department, because the cost of D players is significant. The obvious costs include the cost of compensating employees who are not producing value for the organization. However, this is only a small portion of the cost to the department. D players traditionally command too much management attention either because of personal issues or performance problems. The management attention could be used for driving projects forward and otherwise ensuring the department success. Further, management or teammates have to cover for the nonperformance of the D-ranked staff members. Finally, and most corrosive, D performers tend to drive away the A and B players, who ask "Why am I getting paid the same for producing twice as much work?" Management attention should be spent on caring for and developing A and B players and on reducing their attrition to zero. The forced-attrition model and the swap analysis are powerful tools for managing a world-class IT team.

IT Staff Career Development

Training and career development are the two most important aspects of a job for technical professionals. Besides having a good relationship with their direct supervisors, training and career development are top reasons technology professionals keep or change jobs.

Training is the number one benefit desired by technology employees. Technology employees value training because they enjoy the challenge of learning new skills and recognize that keeping current with rapidly changing technology ensures interesting future assignments and helps guarantee job security. To facilitate the delivery of this benefit, each position identified for the organization (Step 1 of the IT HR life cycle) should have a specific training regimen. This should include both recommended and required training for each level. Promotion should be made contingent, in part, on completing the required training. The HR department can work with IT in establishing a training program and can help with conducting training, tracking completion and certification, as well as identifying outside providers for delivery of the training. This should be done in conjunction with the IT staff, who can identify the training that would be both interesting and useful for the role. For example, network support employees who have achieved their Microsoft Certified Systems Engineer (MCSE) certification might want to follow up with Cisco training and achieve additional networking certification.

Because training invariably involves significant time and expense for the company, the IT manager should ensure that employees make a reciprocal commitment to the organization. In exchange for the training, staff should sign a training certificate. This certificate outlines the training program and the cost for each piece. The employee should sign an agreement stating that he will reimburse the company for training costs if he leaves the company voluntarily within 12 months after completing the course. This acknowledgement accomplishes two things: First, it shows the employee the actual dollar amounts invested by the department in his training. Second, it reduces the risk of investing in employees who depart the company as soon as he receives the training, lowering attrition in the IT department.

As employees receive training, their market value increases and they will likely graduate from one job to the next. To keep the staff interested and engaged, they must be provided opportunities to move ahead, use the new skills they have learned, and continue to learn new technology skills. If the company does not provide employees with these opportunities, the best employees will find an employer who will. Providing training, development, and a chance to use new skills generates loyalty and goodwill.

In some cases, the team member may be trained outside of the company. After completing a training regimen and improving his technology skills, the employee's value continues to increase. At some point, the organization may not be able to provide him the on-the-job responsibility that he would command in the open market, and he may elect to move on. This is a natural outcome of having qualified employees, and, while employee retention is critical, should not be cause for alarm. We have heard good IT managers characterize it thus: "The department should be more like a college than a prison. We miss our best team members when they elect to move on, but if we cannot provide them opportunities to grow, then they must seek them on the open market." Allowing employees to leave on good terms will also mean that they may return eventually.

Providing rigorous training and development opportunities entails some short-term expense for the IT department, but will be a crucial factor in the department's ability to retain the A players. IT organizations that fail to train, develop, and challenge their staff will only retain those who cannot find employment elsewhere.

Key Drivers of Staff Retention

A variety of studies have unearthed key drivers of retention and attrition in IT departments. Based on analysis of these studies, as well as first-hand experience, we list the following key drivers of retention in priority order:

- *Satisfaction with immediate supervisor:* Because of day-to-day contact, employees identify with the company through their immediate supervisors. If an employee does not have a good relationship with his immediate supervisor, that employee is at risk of leaving. Conversely, if that employee has a productive working relationship with his supervisor, risk of the employee's departure drops precipitously. To reduce the likelihood of uncontrolled attrition, IT directors must ensure that their managers are top performers whom people respect. HR can help the IT director track attrition by manager to determine if there are problems with a particular manager.
- *Opportunities for training:* As outlined above, investment in training is a major driver of IT employee satisfaction.
- *Satisfaction with team and coworkers:* Dysfunctional teams and coworkers drive out employees quickly. Additionally, when best practices of a particularly good team emerge, find out what these are and pollinate them across the other teams.
- *Opportunities for career growth and ability to move to different projects:* The IT director must create opportunities for staff to move through the organization. This can be accomplished through regular staff rotations, through promotion or lateral responsibility changes, and through project work. This provides the technical staff with challenges to satisfy their demand for learning.
- *Compensation:* Compensation, while the most obvious variable, is not the number one factor in the career decisions of technical workers, as long as the compensation is within 10 percent of the market rate. If an employee's compensation is far below market they will, of course, seek alternative employment (or possibly reduce their efforts). To avoid under-compensating staff, the IT director should benchmark department salaries against the market every three to six months. An annual schedule for compensation reviews, tied to performance appraisals, is usually sufficient. For certain high-demand skills, a six-month incremental check is

necessary to make sure the market has not changed significantly. Salary adjustments can work both ways (i.e., down as well as up). If the market has come down significantly, downward salary adjustments may be in order.

- *Opportunities for promotion:* Not all technical employees care about titles or moving up in the organization because of responsibilities that are concomitant with such positions. For the staff who have advancement ambitions, the IT director should be sure that there is a clear promotion ladder. The department should also ask individuals to perform at the level of skills the promotion requires before actually promoting the person. This ensures that employees do not fail because they could not handle increased skill level.

The retention program should incorporate these variables. The recent economic difficulties in the United States and elsewhere, teamed with the implosion of the dot-com companies, have created an employer's market, lowering attrition. However, there are still ample opportunities for top-echelon technical talent and when the economy starts to grow, the market will shift. An effective retention program now will avoid trouble later.

Handling Layoffs

Layoffs or reductions in force (RIFs) are unavoidable at times and the IT director may not have a choice if business conditions dictate cost reductions that are mandated by the board and senior management. If the workforce must be reduced because of budget cuts, these procedures can minimize the impact of the process. As with our previous recommendations, policies and process dictated by the corporate human resources or legal department should always take precedence.

1. Evaluate employees as described earlier in this chapter (A, B, C, and D ratings).
2. Build a preliminary list of potential staff members to lay off from the ranking, from the bottom up.
3. Prior to making a final determination, ensure that critical projects can be covered by the remaining staff. If cutting resources jeopardizes projects, the low priority projects may be deferred or eliminated. This can be determined in conjunction with the IT steering committee.
4. Provide the list to the HR department and review with senior management to ensure that the cuts provide the anticipated cost reduction benefit.
5. Decide on severance by employee level. Generally, this is set by the executive team or HR; however, if no rules are in place, the IT director

must determine the severance level. This is generally set by title level in the organization or years of service.

6. Develop separation letters for each individual. The separation letter should include anything the employee is to do in return for accepting severance; for example, noncompetition and nonsolicitation of employees and nondisclosure of company information. Most severance letters ask for a general release of liability from the employee in exchange for the severance amount. There are a variety of legal restrictions that impact companies conducting a layoff and the legal department or external counsel should advise every company contemplating large numbers of layoffs.

7. Determine a time, place to meet, and communicate the separation clearly and simply to the individuals affected. Give them the separation letters and ask them to sign and return by a specified date to receive their severance.

8. Keep communication short. Because the decision is final and is usually based on factors beyond the employees' control, there is little to be gained from a lengthy discussion.

9. Conduct the meeting quickly and professionally. Allowing staff to leave with dignity helps the company preserve a good reputation in the market even in the aftermath of layoffs.

10. Do not leave staff with the impression that there may be a reprieve from the decision. Inexperienced managers sometimes say, "We really want you to stay; however, my hands are tied and I'm being asked to let people go. I will talk to senior management to see if there is any other potential for you to stay. Let me get back to you." This creates a variety of problems and will improperly raise false hopes for the staff being laid off.

Creating Performance Plans

While a host of management books with advice and guidance on effectively managing the workforce are available, the management of employees can often be overcomplicated by the pundits. The IT director should pick a management philosophy that matches her personality and capabilities. In most cases creating a high-performance team boils down to four things:

1. Setting (and documenting) clear objectives and expectations of superior performance.

2. Developing a joint plan that lays out execution of those objectives and expectations over a period (usually quarterly or annually).

3. Measuring progress against those objectives and expectations monthly or quarterly and at annual review time.

4. Providing feedback to employees after analyzing the measures in Step 3. Feedback can occur in one of four ways, depending on the situation:

- *Positive feedback:* Give positive reinforcing feedback to individual.

- *Negative feedback, but employee has potential:* The IT director must assist the individual who has potential to get back on track. This may entail weekly meetings to help mentor the individual.

- *Repeated negative feedback:* After repeated attempts to help the person or after concluding the person is not capable, make the employee take responsibility by putting him or her on a performance improvement plan where he or she is accountable to achieve some short-term objectives in a short time (e.g., 45 days) or risk being terminated.

- *Negative feedback and employee has failed his or her performance improvement plan:* It is the IT director's responsibility to the company and the IT team to terminate the employee or move him into a position that requires fewer skills.

Summary

The IT HR life cycle is a continuum of management processes focused on hiring, training, managing, and retaining the best workforce available for the IT department. Because IT practitioners have a natural preference for technology management, these issues are often under-managed by the IT director, leading to poor overall performance of the department. The bottom line is that the IT department's success is contingent on identifying and retaining an effective IT workforce. Implementing the strategies in this chapter helps build that high-performance team and should be approached with as much rigor as the other disciplines outlined here, such as IT demand management or vendor selection.

By implementing the recommendations in this chapter effectively, the IT director improves odds of success in:

- Determining how to staff the organization and how many people are needed to accomplish the objectives set out in the strategic plan.

- Eliminating C and D players from the team and raising the overall performance of the entire team, resulting in more successful projects, lower budget variance, and a lower defect rate in implementations and applications.

- Hiring new employees with greater speed and success.

- Optimizing the mix of permanent employees and contract workers in the IT department.

Reference HR-Related Web Sites

Following is a list of Web sites that may be useful in determining the best way to hire and manage the IT workforce:

Recruiting-Related Information
- www.techrepublic.com
- www.airsdirectory.com
- www.recruitersonline.com

Online Job Boards
- www.monster.com
- www.hotjobs.com
- www.headhunter.net
- www.dice.com—specializes in contingent workforce
- www.flipdog.com

Technology Professional Salary Information
- www.salary.com
- www.airsdirectory.com/library/staycompetitive/salarysurveys

NOTE

1. Bill Parcells, "The Tough Work of Turning around a Team," *Harvard Business Review* (November/December 2000).

10

Vendor Selection

Thinking is the hardest work there is, which is probably why so few people engage in it.

—Henry Ford[1]

This chapter outlines the process for selection of major outside service and product providers and the subsequent management of the vendors. The list of external vendors used by even a small IT shop is often lengthy. Vendors provide products and services across a wide variety of categories—telecom, networking, consulting, software, and hardware. In a given category, often multiple vendors are used by the department.

This chapter is organized around the first of two major vendor-related tasks facing the IT manager: selecting vendor partners and products. The next chapter covers the management of the vendor relationship "after the sale." It provides a comprehensive methodology and approach for vendor selection. Most often, the major vendor selection activities of an IT manager are focused on the selection of software to support the business, with decisions on vendors for hardware, services, and supplementary systems emerging from the primary package decision; therefore, this chapter is primarily focused on the selection of package application software and accompanying products and services.

The selection approach defined here is intended to be a full-fledged, comprehensive methodology that results in the most rigorous, thorough (and painstaking) process for determining the "best" vendor. The steps described can, and should, be skipped or otherwise de-emphasized, depending on the specific situation facing the IT manager. As with all other frameworks described in this book, common sense should prevail and the applicable portions of the methodology applied to the specific situation at hand.

Why This Topic Is Important

The successful selection and management of vendors plays a large part in determining the overall success of the IT department and, as importantly, the ease with which the department achieves that success. Successful selections are also most often complex and lengthy processes that require the collection and analysis of large amounts of information. Vendor-supplied technologies are often the largest pieces of the IT picture that are most visible to the business and have the largest impact on end-user satisfaction. Well-thought-out vendor choices and solid vendors who behave as partners can ease the work of the IT manager considerably. Conversely, poor vendor selection can hamstring the organization with constant fire fighting, failed projects, and angry users.

Because the operations and applications in most IT departments rely heavily on outside vendors, the IT budget generally has a significant component allocated for third-party vendor spending (i.e., 30%–60% of budget). Because vendors are necessary suppliers of products and services, as well as significant sources of expenditure, the IT director cannot afford to ignore their proper selection and management.

Vendor interests and incentives, unfortunately, are not always precisely aligned with those of the IT director. While client satisfaction is part of the equation for vendors, so are other factors such as profitability, sales commission, quarterly revenue, and market penetration. A vendor salesperson's natural role is as an advocate for his or her product or service. This means that to be most productive for the IT department, the director must supervise and actively manage the delivery of services and products on an ongoing basis to ensure that the delivery and execution are consistent with the expectations and goals of the organization.

Picking the vendors on which to rely is a high-risk proposition. The selection and subsequent implementation of software or hardware can go awry, wasting millions of dollars, disrupting the business, and ending careers for IT staff. As outlined in Part I of this book, the IT landscape is littered with failed implementations. The fact that many of the failed projects were conducted inside successful companies and supervised by smart IT managers highlights the inherent risk of the process, even in the best of circumstances.

In spite of the criticality and risk associated with vendors, experience has shown that IT managers are at a significant disadvantage in the vendor process, particularly vendor selection. A technology professional may manage a vendor selection for package software a handful of times in his or her career, whereas his or her counterparts on the vendor side are generally senior-level sales professionals who close multiple deals each year. This puts the IT manager at a distinct disadvantage to the vendor, from an experience standpoint alone.

Compounding the issue is the fact that once a vendor selection is complete, it is generally difficult to undo. If it turns out that better, more appropriate vendors are available, often the sunk-cost and previously committed contractual obligations prevent them from being used. Because of the high investment in hardware, software, and services to deploy a vendor product, the opportunity to replace a vendor may appear only once every few years, at best. This means that vendor selection can be a one-way street with very few turning off points and that vendor selection and management are a critical part of the successful IT manager's toolkit.

Specific topics covered in this chapter include:

- How to plan and execute a comprehensive, rigorous vendor selection process.
- Approach for generating target vendor lists for systems replacement or renewal projects.
- How to conduct an effective request for proposal (RFP) process.
- Work required to complete due diligence on vendors and their products and services.
- How to produce meaningful feedback from vendor reference checks.
- How to perform a gap assessment on package systems and estimate costs of gap coverage.
- Specific considerations for selecting hardware and professional services vendors for package implementation.
- Vendor negotiation techniques that ensure best pricing and service.
- Creation of a complete economic plan for implementation of the vendor offering, including project-related investment and steady-state cost changes.
- How to partner with and manage vendors on an ongoing basis to produce the best results for both parties.
- Best ways to work with other vendor customers for information sharing.
- Actions to take when a vendor is experiencing difficulties.

Application Vendor Economics

The software selection process most often drives the vendor selection process for hardware and software. The economic rationale for the acquisition of package software applications, therefore, is important for IT teams to understand.

In general, companies purchase package software in the hopes that the combined pool of research and development (R&D) dollars from a large number of customers will produce greater aggregate benefit than the drawbacks created by the implementation of an off-the-shelf system. Software vendors plow a significant portion of new license and maintenance revenue back into their applications, providing enhanced features and a clear upgrade path for their customers. To compensate for the standard approach required by package applications (U.S. custom), vendors have worked hard over time to provide configuration options and customization points of entry to allow the most commonly varying features of the package to be most easily changed.

A package software customer also benefits from the scale benefits attendant with a large marketplace presence. Software packages with a large following create a set of standards that allows the emergence of a robust set of third-party options for add-on software and consulting. Standards created by packages for a variety of application characteristics—application interfaces, technical and data architectures, user interfaces, and so on—mean that follow-on customization and system integration become much easier and cost effective to execute.

Last, packages provide a level of standardization in the labor marketplace. A company running PeopleSoft can rely on recruiting additional PeopleSoft resources that can get up to speed in a reasonable time.

The marketplace has proven over time that the combined benefits of pooled R&D, sophisticated third-party service, and a ready pool of skilled labor more than outweigh the compromises created from the implementation of noncustom systems for supporting critical business functions.

Vendor Selection Methodology

Overview of Methodology

Exhibit 10.1 shows an overview of the vendor selection methodology covered in this section. The methodology is intended to provide a comprehensive, thorough approach to the vendor selection process.

The process begins with the definition of scope for the product (or service) being acquired and proceeds through the identification of a team to support the selection process, the identification of potential vendors, the issuance of an request for proposl (RFP), the selection of vendor finalists, due diligence on the finalists, selection of supplemental vendors (if needed), project planning, and final vendor pricing negotiations. Each of these steps is further detailed in the following section with a diagram highlighting the subtasks, required information, and outcome for each subtask.

Of critical importance throughout the selection process is to ensure that at all times the effort is being managed, organized, and driven by the IT manager in charge. Top vendor sales professionals did not reach that status through passivity. Vendors are well-practiced at the art of seducing the hapless IT manager and will take on as much of the work, and own or drive as much of the effort as the manager lets them, to remain in control of the process.

A second critical component to vendor selection is the evaluation team's discipline in creating, updating, and maintaining the documentation for the

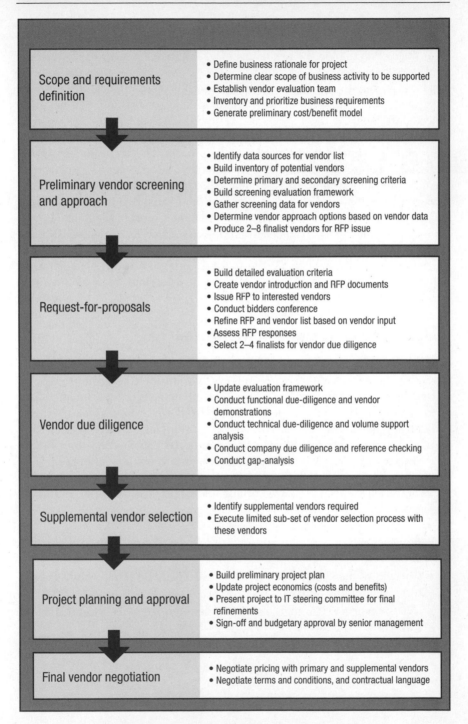

Scope and requirements definition
- Define business rationale for project
- Determine clear scope of business activity to be supported
- Establish vendor evaluation team
- Inventory and prioritize business requirements
- Generate preliminary cost/benefit model

Preliminary vendor screening and approach
- Identify data sources for vendor list
- Build inventory of potential vendors
- Determine primary and secondary screening criteria
- Build screening evaluation framework
- Gather screening data for vendors
- Determine vendor approach options based on vendor data
- Produce 2–8 finalist vendors for RFP issue

Request-for-proposals
- Build detailed evaluation criteria
- Create vendor introduction and RFP documents
- Issue RFP to interested vendors
- Conduct bidders conference
- Refine RFP and vendor list based on vendor input
- Assess RFP responses
- Select 2–4 finalists for vendor due diligence

Vendor due diligence
- Update evaluation framework
- Conduct functional due-diligence and vendor demonstrations
- Conduct technical due-diligence and volume support analysis
- Conduct company due diligence and reference checking
- Conduct gap-analysis

Supplemental vendor selection
- Identify supplemental vendors required
- Execute limited sub-set of vendor selection process with these vendors

Project planning and approval
- Build preliminary project plan
- Update project economics (costs and benefits)
- Present project to IT steering committee for final refinements
- Sign-off and budgetary approval by senior management

Final vendor negotiation
- Negotiate pricing with primary and supplemental vendors
- Negotiate terms and conditions, and contractual language

Exhibit 10.1   Vendor Selection Process Overview

analysis. Organizing a large amount of information being gathered from a variety of disparate sources is difficult for the most diligent team. Keeping clear documentation on the raw data, analysis, and outcome of each step covered in this chapter helps explain to outside observers how the decision was reached, serves as organizational memory, and, most importantly, ensures that no steps are skipped and that the analysis is completed in a rigorous, thorough fashion.

The third key to success is the detailed requirements analysis done by the team in preparation for the vendor analysis process. This step should be completed long before the first vendor is contacted. Vendors long ago perfected the courtship required to manage clients through the sales process, and if IT managers have not done their homework in the form of the up-front analysis and scope work, they will be at the mercy of a sales process they neither control nor fully understand. The necessary objective analysis becomes lost in the feel-good haze of endless vendor dinner outings, rounds of golf, and vendor-led conference calls and demos. The result is, at best, a distorted, suboptimal outcome. We have observed dozens of software selections and have seen success emerge from a vendor-driven process.

Scope and Requirements Definition

SET SCOPE FOR BUSINESS AREAS SUPPORTED. The IT manager should first seek to clearly understand the full range of business activities to be supported by the systems in question. The business, vendor, and technical requirements for the system flow entirely from this scope, making this a critical step in the overall analysis. The efforts during this step provide dividends later as vendor due diligence is executed. The evaluation team will be able to ask clear, concise questions of the vendors and understand the priorities for the business, based on scope.

To accomplish this, the manager must understand the business reasons for the systems initiative. Common reasons include:

- Replacement or renewal of end-of-life cycle or otherwise-obsolete systems.
- Changes to business model (new lines of business, acquisitions, divestitures, increased volumes).
- Cost recapture (through productivity improvement, substitution of capital for labor, etc.).
- Benefit capture (increased sales, market presence).
- Response to other systems changes (supplier or customer demands).
- Competitive parity (response to business initiatives or technology capability-based offerings from competitors).

The outcome of a vendor selection, like any other systems initiative, should help the company drive revenue, reduce costs, or gain control over the business. The scope of the system effort should be based on the business imperative, and the systems should have the capabilities required to support them. The scope covered should be wide enough to justify the selection of a vendor for support but constrained enough to be achievable within a single implementation.

The application scope is generally focused on a specific business function with clearly defined boundaries and interfaces to other business processes. Examples include purchasing, materials requirements planning (MRP), warehouse logistics, fixed assets, customer service, or purchasing.

The scope definition can also be achieved by defining what is not in scope. For example, the scope might be defined as "all purchasing activities, not including receiving, payables, and forecasting" or "all purchasing of products, not including office supplies." The scope definition should also draw clear distinctions between business processes or systems that are replaced or supported versus affected but not changed as part of the project.

A useful tool for understanding the scope is a context diagram that shows the business process area in relation to other areas that interact with it, demonstrating both what is in and out of scope (Exhibit 10.2).

In every case, a detailed document that defines the specific scope under consideration is the first step in the vendor selection process. The document should define the scope in as detailed a manner as necessary, with appropriate illustrative charts and diagrams.

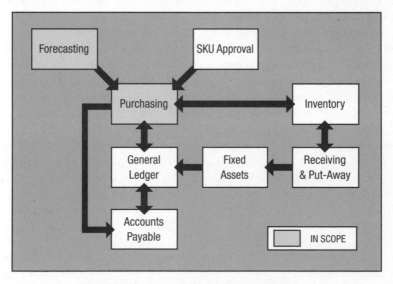

Exhibit 10.2 Example Context Diagram

The final scoping step is to get sign-off from the IT steering committee. Any final ambiguities or inconsistencies in the scoping should be clarified under the scrutiny of the committee. Getting final scope sign-off may take several iterations of presentations and questions and answers before the committee.

ESTABLISH EVALUATION TEAM. After the scope has been defined, the next task is to establish an evaluation team to provide expertise and effort to complete the selection process. The scope definition helps identify business and technical knowledge required for a successful assessment. Vendor selections, particularly if covering a large scope, are labor intensive and require a team of dedicated resources.

The team should include members from outside the IT department and have some representation from each business area affected (e.g., accounting, marketing, manufacturing). This ensures that both the technical expertise and the business unit- or business function-specific knowledge are incorporated into the requirements and evaluation process from the start. Further, early participation from business users facilitates the most rapid acceptance of the vendor selection outcome by the business. Finally, business users tend to catch potential issues that may be missed by IT or that IT is unaware of; for example, the length of time required to replace and train customer service representatives in a high turnover environment.

The overall team size varies by company size, scope of business functions under consideration, and the size of the investment being made. A small vendor selection team might consist of one full-time team member from IT, one from the business unit or function affected, and one part-time manager to drive the effort, along with ad hoc participation from IT and the business. A large-scale selection team, assessing, for example, a full-scale ERP implementation for a large organization might contain 15 to 25 full-time team members and as many as a dozen part-time members. The mix would likely be 50 percent to 70 percent IT team members and the balance from the business.

The most effective way of building team membership is through nominations from the IT steering committee. The list of potential team members should be interviewed by the IT manager and/or the committee to determine if they have the requisite skills, knowledge, interest, and ability. Exhibit 10.3 shows an example selection team structure.

Ideally, the team is co-located with dedicated office space to facilitate communication and maintain focus. Part-time team members should also have dedicated workspace in the team area, so that they can easily pick up their work where they left off and easily join the team on their own schedules.

Achieving the right skill mix, participation level, and environment for the team will have a strong impact on the overall effectiveness and results of the selection process. Even small-scope vendor selection efforts are

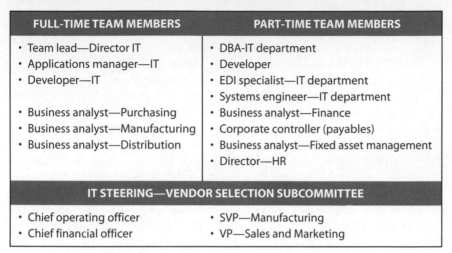

FULL-TIME TEAM MEMBERS	PART-TIME TEAM MEMBERS
• Team lead—Director IT • Applications manager—IT • Developer—IT • Business analyst—Purchasing • Business analyst—Manufacturing • Business analyst—Distribution	• DBA-IT department • Developer • EDI specialist—IT department • Systems engineer—IT department • Business analyst—Finance • Corporate controller (payables) • Business analyst—Fixed asset management • Director—HR

IT STEERING—VENDOR SELECTION SUBCOMMITTEE	
• Chief operating officer • Chief financial officer	• SVP—Manufacturing • VP—Sales and Marketing

Exhibit 10.3   Example Selection Team Structure

large undertakings and require considerable sustained effort on the part of the team.

INVENTORY BUSINESS REQUIREMENTS AND SET PRIORITY/WEIGHTING.
One of the toughest realities of vendor selection is that the only way to truly understand if a package (or other vendor product or service) is a good match (and where its weak points are) is to first understand the in-scope business processes at a painstaking level of detail. A complete understanding of the business processes, events, calendars, volumes, and policies governing the area under consideration allows the team to rapidly and accurately assess the systems being considered and determine the optimal approach for covering the gaps in the system.

Unfortunately, the work of blueprinting business processes and documenting requirements is unavoidably difficult and tedious. However, it is an *absolute prerequisite* of a successful vendor selection, and it forms the bedrock foundation of a successful implementation. Without understanding the business processes supported, the team cannot possibly judge the level of software fit, what the shortcomings are, how they are dealt with, the level of change required by the business, and the expense of configuration and customization to make the system work well. Superficial, weak understanding of business requirements and the inevitable weak analysis that follows are primary reasons for the failure of large systems implementation projects. Requirements gathering for vendor screening is similar to that for custom systems; the team should not neglect this effort simply because a product or package is being considered.

Because starting the "courtship" process with vendors is infinitely more enjoyable than nonstop internal team meetings where business processes are white-boarded at excruciating levels of detail, this step is also the most commonly skipped. The smart IT manager waits until the proper amount of homework has been done before making the first vendor contact.

There are literally dozens of methodologies for capturing business system requirements, and most are good. The important factor in capturing system requirements is ensuring that the appropriate level of detail has been captured and documented. The most common failing of any of the methodologies is a tendency by the team to gloss over the details by neglecting to document its efforts. The only true way to demonstrate a complete, satisfactory, and comprehensive understanding of a business process is to map and document it clearly. One of our favorite catch phrases during the business requirements definition process is "writing is thinking." The effective IT manager ensures that his or her team has done its homework by both understanding and documenting areas of responsibility. Exhibit 10.4 shows a sample business process flow diagram.

Most of the common system requirements gathering methodologies are focused on custom development but serve very well for software selection projects, as the information needed for package requirements is similar. The bibliography for this chapter refers to several books covering this topic.

Documentation should start at a high level of detail for setting scope and context and proceed through one or two descending levels of business process detail. The requirements should capture business events and the processes that handle them. The documentation should also capture not just what the systems do, but also what the people operating the systems are responsible for, what business policies or practices affect the process, and the information required and produced by each step. The documentation should also draw a distinction between the current business process and the planned or "to-be" processes. Iterative interviews with business managers and end users are an effective way to flesh out the document.

If the vendor under consideration replaces an existing product or service, the existing requirements, training material, process flows, or other documentation can serve as a baseline for the new requirements definition. This is particularly true in the case of package software selection. The working, existing systems are the most complete articulation of the business requirements, and the things the existing system does right make a great starting place for what the new system should do as well. In this case, if the existing system does not have documentation, the team should conduct baseline requirements gathering and documentation based on the current system capabilities. Further benefits of an existing system baseline include a clear understanding of interfaces or other systems being affected, a clear definition of the overall technical environment, and an early start on rollout, data conversion, and cutover planning.

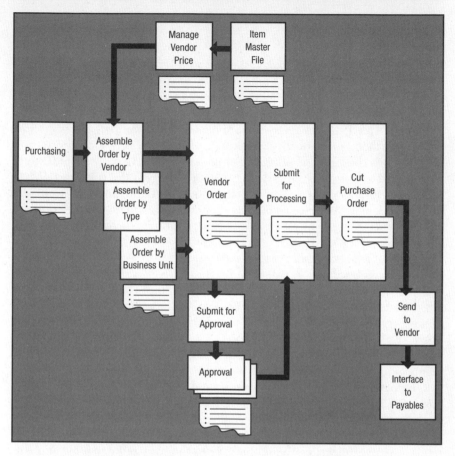

Exhibit 10.4   Example Business Process Flow Diagram

Typical deliverables emerging from the requirement phase for a package selection may include:

- Business process flows.
- Process descriptions showing required inputs, outputs, procedures, calculations, interfaces, and human intervention.
- Business event triggers (synchronous, asynchronous).
- Data content (entity, lookup, transaction) and format requirements.
- Processing calendar—daily, weekly, and monthly transactions; volumes, events, and reports.
- Processing volumes.
- Reporting requirements.

- User interface requirements.
- Security requirements.

When choosing a methodology, simpler is better—if the team spends time wrestling with a tool, it winds up with a second-rate analysis. Our favorite systems design tools are a whiteboard, a graphics package, a spreadsheet, and a word processor.

Once defined, the business requirements should be assigned a preliminary importance or criticality weighting so that as the vendor alternatives are assessed, the assessment team can understand early on the significance of potential give-ups in the system. Simplicity is again the rule, particularly for this preliminary rating. We suggest a "high, medium, and low" rating for each requirement, with a goal of 25 percent or fewer "high" priority requirements and 30 percent or more "low" priority ratings. Any weighting system can be used, but more than 10 grades of priority begins to lose meaning.

An example requirement prioritization might be: "Fill rate for Customer A must always be above 98.5 percent because of contractual obligations; system should warn for potential stock-outs in products ordered by Customer A—priority HIGH" or "Statistical forecast calculation should compensate for seasonality based on manually maintained adjusting factors for items flagged as *seasonal*—priority MEDIUM."

As with any requirements definition, the temptation is for all requirements to have a high priority; if they weren't requirements, they wouldn't be in the document, after all. The team should understand that every requirement will be assessed, and the priority ratings are for ranking the requirements relative to each other. The high priority requirements have a large impact on the selection process (vendors that can meet the requirements most easily, with least configuration rise to the top) and drive much of the focus work during the vendor due diligence. Therefore, it is important to take a hard line on which requirements are allowed a high priority stamp. Selections with a large number of "must-have" functional requirements often run into trouble later in the process during vendor due diligence. The team should also understand that at this point, only functional requirements are being prioritized—the technical and vendor requirements are prioritized as part of a later process.

Depending on project size, the team may want to engage outside help in completing the business process mapping and requirements definition. The primary reasons for this are the provision of extra capacity and the addition of knowledgeable resources that have conducted such an exercise previously. The IT manager should use outside help judiciously. Third parties involved in the selection can have agendas and motivations that are at variance with the organization, creating an agency problem. Also, by sidestepping the difficult work of the analysis, the vendor selection team loses the benefits of developing a complete mastery of the content and process. The best use of third parties is in an advisory role, helping guide the process and provide coaching for the vendor selection team. The best third parties for this role have extensive experience in vendor or package selection and are not necessarily candidates for an implementation partner.

Finally, invariably during a rigorous review of business processes such as this, business process improvement or reengineering opportunities are identified. Ideally, the team should document and inventory these and put them in a "parking lot" for later analysis by the business. The temptation to achieve business process improvements as part of the analysis (or later implementation) can be difficult to resist, but the team should not confuse knowing about an improvement opportunity with an obligation to implement it. Trying to achieve major business process change as an integral part of a system implementation has been the downfall of many projects and should be approached with great caution.

GENERATE PRELIMINARY COST/BENEFITS MODEL. With a business case created, clear scope defined, combined business/IT team built, and the systems requirements defined and prioritized, the final step in this phase is to generate a preliminary cost-benefit model and estimated project time line. Although this may seem premature given that a system has not been picked, it is important to create at least order-of-magnitude estimates of project costs and benefits at this point in the project. This accomplishes several things for the team. First, it helps start a paper trail of estimating models that can be revised as new information is added and provides a common set of assumptions that can be confirmed or disproved during the further process.

Second, having an early forecast of the potential costs and benefits gives the selection team (and company senior management team) numbers that provide context for the rest of the project. It also provides at least preliminary validation for moving forward with the project based on best estimates of return on investment (ROI). The process also gives the team a head start on finding ways to quantify some of the softer, more-difficult-to-estimate benefits of the project. Finally, it ensures that the team is focused early on the most important aspect of the effort: creation of benefits that outweigh the costs for the business. The chapters on project estimating, IT budgeting, and return on investment (Chpaters 13 and 15) cover the topic of cost-benefit estimating in more detail.

We have observed on many occasions a hesitance on the part of the IT team to complete a forecast of costs and benefits at this point in the project. The numbers, however difficult to determine, must be *something*. There is little harm in at least creating a starting point for costs and benefits, so that all the subsequent conversations can be around revisions of these baseline numbers. IT must overcome its reservations to "commit" to a number and, instead, be willing to put a stake in the ground. In the eyes of most corporate senior management teams, it is more acceptable to be wrong, with an explanation of what new information changed the estimate, than to obstinately refuse to generate even order-of-magnitude estimates around costs and benefits. Exhibit 10.5 is an example of a cost-benefit summary.

PROJECT COSTS		ONE-TIME BENEFITS	
Hardware	$50K	Inventory carrying	
Software	150K	Cost reduction	$450K
External resources	225K		
Internal resources	75K		
	$500K		$450K
Net one-time cost	$50K		

CHANGES TO STEADY STATE COSTS		ONGOING BENEFITS	
Additional IT FTE	$60K/yr	Reduce WHSE rent	$120K/yr
Additional processor usage	TBD	Improve fill rate	TBD
Ongoing SW maintenance fee	15K/yr	Reduce spoilage	25K/yr
	$75K/yr		$145K/yr
Net on-going benefits	$70K/yr		

Payback: Approximately nine months after successful implementation for on-going benefits to cover gap between one-time costs and one-time benefits.

Exhibit 10.5   Cost Benefit Analysis for Project Alpha

The final step in this phase is to present the results to the IT steering committee. This is an opportunity to show the committee the results of the requirements gathering, get final agreement on scope, and show preliminary results of the cost-benefit analysis. This is also a good time to present the parking lot of potential business process improvement opportunities for possible further action by the committee. In addition, it is also the right time to begin enlisting the aid of the senior management team in helping drive the benefits. In some cases, the committee may want to refine the scope or pose follow-up questions on the project economics; the selection team should plan two or three iterations in front of the committee before final sign-off.

As reiterated throughout this book, we are strong believers in a literal sign-off at major project milestones, and this process is no exception. The important psychological step of document signing forces ambiguities and disagreements to the forefront where they can be resolved. We highly recommend this step for *all* critical IT documentation. After the document has been revised and approved by the steering committee, it should also be signed off on by the selection team for the same reasons.

Preliminary Vendor Screening

The goal of the vendor-screening step is to quickly build a comprehensive list of potential vendors. These vendors form the pool from which to make the final choice. A successful preliminary screening lets the team quickly review a comprehensive set of vendors to ensure all options have been considered but then rapidly narrow the list down to a handful of vendors for full due diligence. Exhibit 10.6 shows an overview of this process, from data gathering through due-diligence vendor selection. The following sections cover the process in detail.

PRELIMINARY VENDOR IDENTIFICATION AND SCREENING. The first step of vendor screening is to identify a full set of potential vendors. The approach for this step is to conduct a sweep of the marketplace for vendors whose offering fits the scope of business processes defined in the previous step. If the scoping step was completed well, the vendor marketplace participants should be relatively easy to identify.

The team should employ a variety of sources for its vendor search:

- *Consultants:* Large-scale technology consulting firms often have entire practice areas specializing in the selection, implementation, and

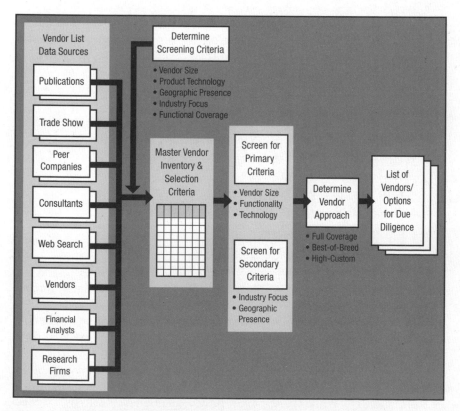

Exhibit 10.6   Preliminary Vendor Screening Process Overview

management of the technology in question; in these cases, they are often willing to provide free, up-front advice in exchange for an opportunity to be involved in the bidding for a later customization and deployment.

- *Technology and industry publications:* There are dozens of credible, independent publications focused on the technology industry that can provide vendor lists. *InformationWeek* and *CIO* magazine are among the many publications that address enterprise-level technology management. Publications focused on the industry in which the organization competes can also be a source of information related to technologies that apply specifically to the business. These are most useful for vendors that supply technology very specific to a particular type of business (e.g., insurance, financial services, manufacturing).

- *Industry and technology trade shows:* Many of the larger players in a particular technology field have a presence at technology trade shows. Vendors with industry-specific technology solutions also exhibit at industry-focused trade shows.

- *Peer companies:* Technology managers from firms in the same industry are an often-overlooked source of information, and they can be particularly valuable for their objectivity. Developing peer relationships with similar companies can provide insight into their decision-making processes and rationale as well as jump-start vendor data gathering. Peer managers who have recently been through a similar vendor selection exercise can be particularly helpful.

- *Focused Web search:* A Web search can turn up candidate vendors as well. The search should be focused on technology-specific Web sites, as opposed to generalized search engines; for example:

  —*CIO* magazine: www.cio.com.

  —*CMP Media:* www.techweb.com.

  —*Computer Business Review:* www.cbronline.com.

  —*E-Week:* www.eweek.com.

  —*Tech Republic:* www.techrepublic.com.

  —*Darwin* magazine: www.darwinmag.com.

  —*Analyst Views:* www.analystviews.com.

- *Vendors:* Although reading between the marketing obfuscation found in many vendor brochures and Web sites can be difficult, vendor-supplied information can be useful once a specific set of vendors has been identified.

- *Technology research firms:* There is a full-scale, mature industry of research firms dedicated to assisting companies in setting technology direction and helping companies understand in which technology standard they should invest. While these sources provide high-quality analysis, their expense can often make them prohibitive except for decisions involving large capital expenditures. Although this marketplace has dozens of players in it, some of the industry leaders include:

—Aberdeen Group

—AMR Research

—Forrester Research

—Gartner Group

—Giga Information Group

—International Data Corp (IDC)

—META Group

- *Financial analysts:* Most large investment banks have one or more full-time analysts covering the market in which a given vendor competes. The analysts can be an invaluable source of information about the vendor and overall marketplace, as well as a specific product. Analysts spend considerable time talking with end customers and can be an unbiased source of up-to-date information. If the company has a banking relationship already, that can be a good place to start. If not, the analysts can often be found lurking in various Internet forums for the product under consideration, soliciting user input.

The evaluation team should manage its search using each of these sources to ensure that a comprehensive list is built. The team should start with technology publications, reports from research companies, and trade show information and proceed to detailed data gathering from consultants, peer companies, and vendors. This research order provides early results for the team and context during later data gathering after a preliminary set of vendors has been identified. The team will be able to ask specific, targeted questions of consultants or managers based on their earlier research.

As the team reviews a variety of sources of data, the right list of vendors should emerge. Except for the most unique searches, the team should avoid feeling that it needs to "scour the earth" to identify the suite of potential vendors—vendors that are difficult to find after multiple searches across a variety of sources are not likely to be viable vendors. Good vendors should not be needles in a haystack—the location of an obscure vendor is not necessarily the harbinger of success. The best vendor names emerge repeatedly from the research.

The result of this step should be a list of vendors ranging from as few as four to as many as several dozen entries in length. Although vendors may be added as additional information is uncovered, this is probably the vendor list from which the winning candidate is drawn.

BUILD FIRST-SCREEN EVALUATION FRAMEWORK AND WEIGHTING. As vendors are added to the list, screening data should be gathered in a template to facilitate analysis. The specific information gathered depends on the vendor selection being completed, but it generally falls into a few categories. These categories are outlined next, along with potential information to gather in each category and how much weighting each category might be given.

Vendor Size

To consider: Vendor should be of adequate size to continue to invest in the product and continue to attract additional customers. Exception may be niche-product vendors providing highly specific products or services.

Potential information to gather:
- Vendor revenues.
- Vendor profitability.
- Acquisition history.
- Number of employees, developers, product specialists.
- Number of customers.
- Number of end users.

Product Technology

To consider: Does the selection of the vendor limit technology platform choices in a way that matters to the business or IT? Is the product compatible or consistent with existing or planned technical architecture?

Potential information to gather:
- Server technologies supported.
- Database technologies supported.
- Development technology.
- Technology supported under original product.
- Percent of user base on a particular server or database platform.

Geographic Presence

To consider: Does the vendor have the appropriate geographic focus and availability? Is the vendor sufficiently focused on the geographies that matter for the company (United States versus Europe versus Asia versus other geographies that impact how the technology works or support is delivered)?

Potential information to gather:
- Corporate headquarters location.
- Nearest branch office.
- Number of branch offices.
- Proximity of branch offices to company branch offices.
- Primary location of development team.

Industry Focus
To consider: Does the vendor have sufficient expertise in the specific industry to ensure development of the best solution? Does the vendor have a product or service line dedicated to the company industry? Is industry-specific expertise relevant for this evaluation?

Potential information to gather:
- Industry-specific additions/modifications to product.
- Industry implementations of product (number of implementations/users).
- Presence of leading industry customers.

Functional Coverage
To consider: Does package or product provide this broad functionality?

Potential information to gather:
- Proven ability for package or product to support business function in question.
- Presence of function-specific modules.

This type of information is relatively easy to gather and can be used to narrow the vendor list down rapidly. As the information is gathered, the team should begin building a spreadsheet to capture the information.

This process is the most rapid, least-effort method to review the largest number of vendors and quickly screen out the vendors that are not viable contenders for carrying through to due diligence. The preliminary screening forces out undercapitalized, unfocused, or otherwise inappropriate vendors, as well as allows the remaining vendors to be preliminarily ranked. The team should constantly ask the common-sense question: "Can you envision a scenario in which we would actually choose, implement, and rely on this vendor?"

The result is a comprehensive list of vendors participating in the marketplace, along with a clear, consistent rationale for the inclusion or discharge of each one. Exhibit 10.7 shows a sample rating sheet.

DETERMINE PRELIMINARY VENDOR APPROACH. The full vendor list review helps the team understand what marketplace components need to come together to provide a solution that covers the full scope in question. Generally, one of three vendor approaches emerges (particularly for package application searches):

- *Full coverage:* Functions covered by a single vendor with minimum customization.
- *Best-of-breed:* Majority of coverage by a single vendor, with one or more complementary vendors providing applications for specific, clearly defined functions (e.g., pricing) or functional areas (e.g., accounting).

Vendor	Package/System Name	Vendor Revenue ($ millions)	Corp. Headquarters	Nearest branch office	Total Vendor Staff	Developers on Staff	Product Age (months)	Notable Customers	Industries Served	Installed Base - customers	Databases Supported	Server Platform	Installed Base - users	Function A	Function B	Notes
Vendor A	System A	325	UK	local	599	150	72	ITT Cannon, Dunlop, Bic	All	250	Oracle/SQL Serv	NT	25k+	X		
Vendor B	System B	722	CA	local	1397	350	32	AMD, Boeing, Mercedes	Mfg.	400	Informix/Oracle/IBM	UNIX	45k+		X	
Vendor C	System C	125	OH	none	217	52	9	Alcatel, Ericsson, Siemens	Dist.	75+	SQL Serv Supra	NT	10k+	X		
Vendor D	System D	425	IL	local	922	190	49	Nike	All	550+	Oracle	NT	100k+	X	X	
Vendor D								Seiko			SQL Serv	UNIX	5k+		X	

Exhibit 10.7   Example Vendor Data Gathering Sheet

- *High custom:* Most functions covered by a single vendor with some specific custom-coded modules and product customizations.

The potential solution set may include one or more solutions in each of these categories. The team should go beyond a superficial analysis to be sure all of the possible combinations and potential solution platforms have been identified. Generally, full-coverage solutions are the most desirable because the system requires no integration, requires a single vendor, and has been proven to work in practice. However, in some cases, the specific functionality advantages created by the other two options are enough to overcome the inherent disadvantage and increased cost and risk of integration and multiple vendors. For the remainder of this chapter, the term *vendor* refers to a single vendor, or a best-of-breed combination of vendors.

Exhibit 10.8 shows an example set of "finalist" vendor solutions for a package selection. The result of the vendor screening process should be a list of as few as two but no more than six vendor approaches. A list of three or four vendors is ideal. More than six vendors makes the RFP effort too onerous, and only one vendor provides limited options and makes relative comparison impossible. A one-vendor approach also lowers the team's negotiating power with the single vendor during the pricing phase of the process.

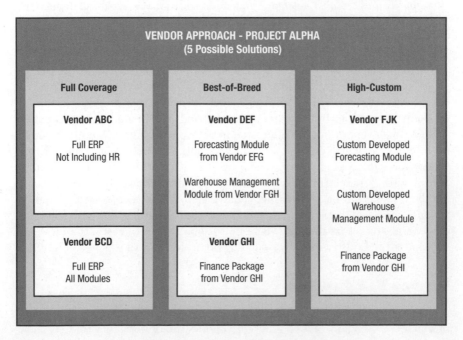

Exhibit 10.8   Example Vendor Approach Options

As with each of the major process steps for vendor selection, the IT steering committee should sign off on the results from this phase.

WHAT IF NO VENDOR OR SET OF VENDORS EMERGES FROM THE ANALYSIS? Occasionally, at the end of a preliminary vendor screening process, no viable vendor or combination of vendors emerges, or a vendor emerges but it feels like a tremendous stretch in terms of customization. In these cases, the team should go back through the analysis and look for these common missteps in the process described previously:

- *Scope set incorrectly:* Too narrow or too broad for a vendor solution to emerge.
- *Scope indistinct:* Difficult to assess vendor capabilities because of lack of clarity on scope.
- *Not enough vendors identified:* Not enough data sources searched to yield proper number of vendors; search of data sources too superficial.
- *Vendor data incorrect or missing:* Team did not gather enough vendor data, or vendor data is incorrect leading to vendors screened out improperly.
- *Primary or secondary screening criteria set too tight:* Criteria for vendor screen set too tight, forcing out viable vendors.
- *Additional criteria needed:* Team adds additional relevant criteria with higher weighting, allowing viable vendors to pass primary and secondary screening.

The team should analyze the process for these common mistakes, as well as other holes in the overall analysis. If the team concludes that the analysis has been completed correctly, the marketplace for the scope in question has no vendor participation. In this case, the team needs to pursue one of two paths. A close-finish vendor may be interested in developing the required functionality or enhancements to its package or product. The team can approach the vendor and work with its product management group to investigate the potential for adding the capabilities. Second, the team may have to consider a custom-built solution based on the requirements. The economics, benefits, planning, creation, implementation, and management of custom-built solutions are separate topics treated elsewhere in this book. In both cases, the IT steering committee is also a valuable sounding board for how to proceed.

Manage RFP Process

A *request for proposal* (RFP) is a time-honored method for choosing vendors, in which the company gives a group of vendors the opportunity to show their capabilities by responding to a specific set of requirements and information requests. These typically request a broad swath of information—product data, technical architecture, vendor company financials and structure, customer references, qualifications with similar work, training and support capabilities, and more.

Requiring interested vendors to respond to a well-thought-out RFP can be a highly effective approach for both gathering additional data without imposing incremental workload on the team and screening vendors for ability to produce quality work. There are a variety of good reasons to conduct an RFP:

- Distributes immense data gathering to multiple vendors instead of internal team.
- Allows vendors to withdraw if the RFP focus indicates they are not a good match.
- Introduces an element of natural selection to the process—vendors that cannot manage their way through an RFP process are not likely to be viable long-term partners.
- Gives a view of the vendor's capability for producing a "finished product" early on with little risk; if vendors cannot produce quality RFP responses (typos, clarity, answering the questions asked, organization), there may be similar issues with their products or service.
- Allows vendors to "self-team," working and proposing in concert on areas where a multivendor solution makes sense.
- Creates a level playing field for the vendors; all vendors see the same RFP request and provide the same response information; this has the double benefit of encouraging vendors to participate if they perceive a fair selection process and of forcing the internal evaluation team to consider each vendor equally, mitigating any potential biases.
- Multiple analyses of the requirements and information in the RFP by highly skilled vendor sales and delivery staff may point out shortcomings or inconsistencies in the previous analysis by the internal team.

Not every vendor selection is a good candidate for a full RFP. The team may elect to not conduct a full RFP for a variety of reasons. In these cases, the team may proceed straight to the vendor due-diligence process. Some examples include:

- The number of vendors identified during the previous screening is small enough to justify proceeding directly to due diligence.
- In a seller's market, the RFP may be considered too onerous by target vendors and discourage participation; they will opt to go after easier-to-win business.
- The preliminary vendor selection conducted in the previous step unearths enough information to satisfy the selection team.

- The final decision needs to be made rapidly and not enough additional time is available for a full RFP-response-analysis cycle.
- Vendor(s) being selected is minor or level of investment is minor enough and does not justify the effort of a full RFP.
- There is such a large separation between first- and second-place vendor, so first-place vendor takes the decision by default.

Creation of a high-quality RFP requires the team to have an in-depth, unambiguous command of the vendor and functional and technical requirements. If creating a good RFP is difficult for the team, it is likely that the scope and requirements were not clearly defined in the previous section or that the team has not fully delineated the priorities and weighting by which it will judge the target vendors. A good RFP not only reduces the effort for the team, but also ensures enthusiastic and full participation by target vendors.

Exhibit 10.9 provides an overview of the RFP process. The remainder of this section covers this process in detail.

CREATE RFP. A well-constructed RFP contains two primary sections: an overview of the project, which gives the responding vendor information on the company and project to help in its response; and a section for vendors to provide a detailed response to specific questions on company, capabilities, functionality, and other relevant considerations.

This section outlines how to lead the evaluation team through the creation of an effective RFP. In larger corporations, the team should also consult the corporate purchasing or procurement department to ensure compliance with corporate policies regarding vendor selection, as well as for advice and help

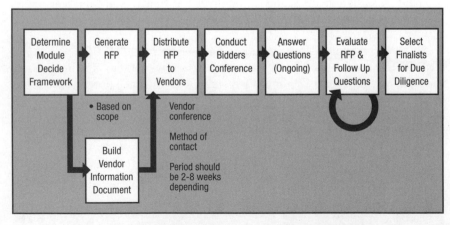

Exhibit 10.9 Vendor Request for Proposal Process Overview

in creating the RFP. The purchasing department can be particularly helpful with legal or process questions.

The project overview portion of the RFP should be detailed enough to answer most potential vendor questions and provide a full orientation. An effective project overview section minimizes the follow-on questions from vendors and ultimately saves considerable time for the evaluation team, particularly for selections involving a large number of vendors. The overview portion also helps create a level playing field for vendors by showing all the vendors the same information in the same format at the same time. It also encourages vendors to participate by demonstrating that the company intends to undertake a credible, serious approach to the selection process and that the lead is a quality opportunity with a reasonable probability of closing.

The project overview portion of the RFP contains three subsections—information on the company, the process, and decision-making criteria. Typically, each of the sections contains all or some of the following details:

Company Information
- History of company.
- Size of business—three- to five-year revenue history, number of employees.
- Geographies covered—headquarters, branch offices, and plant locations.
- Product or service line overview.
- Key customers or markets served.
- Current technical architecture.
- Key points that differentiate the company business operations (e.g., large number of geographically separate customers, highly engineered product, hard-to-forecast "fashion" product).
- Single point-of-contact e-mail address for all questions and responses.

Project Information
- Business rationale for project and anticipated results.
- Budget approval (Is a budget approved for the project, and if not, when will one be approved?).

Process Information
- RFP distribution method.
- Response required (number of copies, format).
- Who (decision makers) is on the evaluation team?
- Vendors invited to participate.
- Time line for response and review of RFP.
- Anticipated time line for project start and completion.

- Project scope.
- Criteria for selection and relative weighting (e.g., vendor size, functionality match, pricing, references).

The focus of the document should be on providing information helpful to the vendors, as well as answering the qualifying questions that most smart vendors ask before pursuing a lead:

- Is the scope under consideration a good match with my product or service?
- Is the playing field level?
- Is there a budget approved?
- Who will make the decision?
- How long will the evaluation take?
- Which of my competitors will take part?
- Does the client have a clear understanding of what they are doing and a good process for getting there?

Although clearly the buyer of products or services is in the driver's seat during an evaluation, going to the trouble of providing the right kind of information to the candidate vendors in this section ensures that the opportunity is attractive to successful, smart vendors—the exact kind that will be ideal partners.

Because the vendor orientation section of the RFP often contains company proprietary information, the team may want to consider having the vendor recipients sign nondisclosure agreements (NDA). The corporate legal team or retained counsel can put together a simple NDA to be completed by all participants prior to receipt of the RFP.

The second major section of the RFP should be focused on gathering the detailed data from the vendors; this helps determine which vendors should be carried forward through vendor due diligence. This information is similar to the data gathered for the preliminary vendor screening, but goes into considerable depth. Achieving this level of detail is possible because the individual vendors alone have the expertise to fully answer the questions and because the work is distributed across multiple vendors instead of the selection team.

The typical categories of information to be gathered in this section include:

- *Vendor:* Information concerning the vendor company—size, stability, and resources.
- *Functional coverage:* Coverage of the full scope of required functions or capabilities by the vendor application, product, or service.

- *Technical:* Information impacting the technical deployment of the product, including available hardware, operating system, and database platforms.
- *Customer qualifications:* Positive references from existing customers with similar requirements.
- *Project/implementation approach:* Preliminary information from vendor as to its approach for implementation and time lines.
- *Economics:* Vendor list pricing schedules; drivers for pricing (seats, servers, units, etc.).

Generating the full list of questions for this section is, after the scope and requirements definition, one of the most challenging tasks in the vendor selection. If the scope and requirements definition has been done properly, the functional coverage assessment should be fairly straightforward. However, to help vendors understand how they are evaluated (and to provide a guideline for the team after the RFPs have been returned), the team must weight each category appropriately, at the levels described previously, and within the levels.

This question generation and weighting process can be difficult because it requires the team to go beyond a superficial vendor selection based on functional fit and consider broader issues such as vendor strength, customer qualifications, and technical platform implications. Because the work must be completed eventually, however, the team should wrestle with this issue now to inform the participating vendors how the RFP will be evaluated.

The easiest approach for category weighting is to distribute 100 points among the five categories. Usually, the category receiving the bulk of the points is the functional coverage category. After all, if the product or service in question cannot provide the required capabilities, the other categories have little relevance. This primary weighting for the functional coverage category puts added pressure on the team to understand the relative importance of the functional requirements in the category. This prioritization of requirements (high, medium, and low) was completed in the previous step, and the RFP should provide the priority ratings along with the functionality requirement description to the vendors for response.

The remaining categories are weighted differently in each vendor selection, depending on what is important to the selection team. Vendor stability and customer qualifications are good candidates for second-place priority behind functional coverage. A stable vendor with a large customer base and the financial strength to provide support and improvements for a product over the long haul is a good choice for a partner in a critical role. Likewise, a vendor's ability to produce solid clients who can provide a reference for the client and who have solved similar business problems in similar environments provides empirical evidence of the vendor's ability to successfully achieve the results again.

Technical architecture and project/implementation approach tend to be the lowest-weighted categories. Most large vendors are at competitive parity concerning technologies supported—major vendors are able to support nearly any technology platform that might matter to the end client—therefore, this category offers little opportunity for them to differentiate themselves. Project implementation approach is also usually similar across vendors and may not offer a chance for differentiation. Occasionally, a vendor has a unique or proprietary approach in this category and should receive correspondingly high points relative to the competition.

Examples of the type of information that an RFP might include in each category, with a slant toward RFP questions for applications vendors follow:

Vendor

- Company overview, including history, services, core capabilities, office locations, management team, and organization structure.
- Contact information for this RFP—account manager, technical sales representative, senior manager in charge.
- Financials—three- to five-year revenue and profitability history for vendor.
- Financials—three- to five-year revenue and profitability history for the product or service in question.
- Overview of vendor product lines and revenue distribution among product lines.
- Total company employees.
- Number of developers or engineers working in product development and location.
- Account management approach (account representative organizational structure; are accounts managed by region, by industry, or other?).
- Customer input method—how it works (along with reference to client who has provided input to development process).
- Service levels—how does the vendor measure its delivery or product or services—measures might be quality, user satisfaction, support calls, or other; how does the information get reported internally, and how often; how does information get reported to the customer?
- Timing and results of last user satisfaction survey conducted by vendor or third party.
- Service levels available for the product under consideration and what they mean (usually gold, silver, platinum, or other tiered support structure).
- Training—number of professionals, class schedule (administrator, end user, etc.).
- What does vendor regard as its competitive advantage(s)?
- Is vendor qualified for disadvantaged business minority/women-owned-business preferences?

Functional Coverage

The RFP should contain an indexed list of each functional requirement identified early on in the vendor selection process:

- Vendor should provide a mapping of system modules or capabilities to functional requirements with particular emphasis on high-priority areas.
- Each requirement should be rated by the vendor as "works with no customization," "works with customization," or "not present."
- For each "works with . . ." rating, vendor should provide a brief explanation of where the functionality exists (screen or submodule reference).
- Brief overview of how configuration is accomplished in the product.
- Brief overview of how customization is accomplished in the product (usually associated programming-language based).

Technical

- Overview of technical architecture of the product—application, data, network, hardware, or other technology component.
- How does required or recommended technology work with current or planned technology platform in the client company?
- Technologies supported by product (operating systems, hardware, databases)—along with number of seats/customers/implementations in that architecture combination.
- Release and patch history for product (dates, summary of incremental functionality, and bug fixes/enhancements in each release and patch).
- Third-party products required to operate; inventory of the products and their roles.
- Demonstrated product scalability—volumes for key areas (in the lab and on real clients).
- Interface method—how interproduct interfaces are accomplished; variances between batch and asynchronous interfaces.
- Security—how it is managed at the user level; what levels of management it can handle; does it integrate with other security packages?

Customer Qualifications

Vendor should show customers with closest possible match to target environment across a variety of aspects; although it is difficult to find an exact match to the target, the vendor should be able to produce a variety of clients with at least a few similarities:

- Customers competing in the same industry or with the same business model.
- Customers using this specific product or service (and latest version).
- Customers with same technical platform (existing or planned).

- Customers with similar size (measured in revenues, number of users, totals staff, or other proxy).
- Customers with corresponding geographic footprint (number of locations, same states, countries, language requirements).
- Customers with similar business volumes or patterns (seasonality affect, orders, invoices, stock keeping units [SKUs], etc.).
- Customers who have interfaced same systems as the target environment requires (if applicable).
- Customers whose implementation of the product was similar in size/scope.

An ideal way to get relevant references from a vendor is to provide a matrix for marking which implementations have functional, industry, technical, or other relevance for the RFP. Exhibit 10.10 shows such a sample matrix as it would be completed by the RFP respondent.

The vendor should also include any relevant awards and third-party recognition for excellence, as well as any relevant industry certifications (ISO, SEI CMM, etc.).

	Same industry or same business model	Specific product or service	Same technical platform	Similar size	Corresponding geographic footprint	Similar business volumes or patterns	Interfaced same systems as target	Similar size/scope of product implementation	TOTAL
Customer A	X				X		X	X	4
Customer B			X				X		2
Customer C	X		X		X	X	X		5
Customer D		X		X	X	X	X		5
Customer E		X	X		X	X			4

Exhibit 10.10   Vendor Reference Matrix

Finally, the RFP should make clear that the vendor response is completely optional and in no way obligates the company to engage any vendor or to carry the project forward past the RFP process. This avoids any possible misunderstanding on the part of the vendors and creates an exit path should the RFP results prove unsatisfactory or the business mandate change during the process.

Project/Implementation Approach
- Implementation approach—outline of any specific or proprietary approach that will be required, how long the implementation is likely to take, and any unusual requirements for implementation.
- Does current or target technology and product platform (or other factors such as office locations, number of users, volume) dictate a certain implementation approach?
- Approximate effort to implement—hours, cost, or other.

Economics
- What are the main drivers of product acquisition pricing (number of seats, number of servers, number of units, or other driver)?
- List price or approximate total for installation.
- Maintenance pricing terms (percent of license fees or other basis).
- Other associated product license pricing (third-party software or other licenses required).
- Pricing and terms for training.
- Other professional services pricing and terms (hourly bill rates).

To facilitate later comparison and analysis, the RFP should provide a clear format and organization for responding to questions. The RFP should also specify the number of hard copies that the vendor must provide, as well as desired electronic formats. The responses should be standardized as much as possible; reading through a large number of responses inconsistent in format and organization adds considerable work to an already labor-intensive process.

ISSUE RFP. After the RFP has been created, it should be distributed to the target vendors. The best way to manage the issuance process is to send paper and electronic copies to the sales professionals who have been identified at each vendor. A team member should be designed to make a follow-up call to each vendor to ensure that the package has been received.

To gauge interest in the RFP and provide an equal-footing forum for vendor questions and answers, the evaluation team should conduct a bidders' pre-conference one to two weeks after the RFP is issued. This timing ensures that the vendors have had enough time to review the information and show up with good questions. The invitation should limit the number of attendees per vendor to three or fewer. Otherwise, vendors sometimes send a small army of sales and technical people, particularly for large proposals. More than one bidders' conference we have attended has been so oversubscribed that it had to be postponed or moved to a new location. Rare is the bidders' conference that is not standing room only. The conference is also an ideal time to distribute additional technical information to interested vendors in electronic or paper form.

The team should require each attendee to sign an attendance roster and enforce the sign-ups by allowing RFP responses only from vendors who send at least one representative to the conference. This list can then be published to all vendors. Vendors should be allowed to partner where appropriate (particularly for best-of-breed solution approaches), but they should make clear in their joint RFP response which capabilities are provided by each party.

The agenda for the conference should be simple. The team lead should introduce the selection team members and give a brief overview of the material in the vendor orientation portion of the RFP, with a particular focus on expected business benefits and evaluation process. A brief explanation of how the vendor invite list was created may be appropriate here as well. The bulk of the conference should be an open-ended question-and-answer session for the vendor representatives. A scribe should document the questions asked (and answers given). If vendors ask questions for which the team does not have a ready answer, the question should be documented and a response sent later. In some cases, the team may simply choose not to answer the question. The entire process should take between 60 and 90 minutes, depending on the RFP complexity and the number of vendors in attendance.

After the conference, the team will have some new information to process. First, the vendor attendance should indicate the level of overall interest that the RFP has generated. If a number of vendors do not attend, there may be several reasons, including a mismatch between the project scope and vendors' capabilities, a misread of the RFP by the vendor, or even a simple mistake. In any case, the team should contact the vendors who have opted out to solicit their feedback and possibly revise the scope, RFP, or process based on the information.

Second, based on the questions asked by the vendors, the team may find holes in the project scope, requirements gathering, RFP questions, or RFP process. In this case, the team should decide if any of the previous work should be revisited or refined and the corrective action, if any, to take. Unless the fault is particularly egregious, there should not be any disappointment in a few mistakes. Vendors are highly experienced in scouring and picking apart RFPs and have undoubtedly invested many hours in analysis before the conference.

Within a few days of the conference, the full transcript of questions answered during the session, as well as follow-up questions, should be e-mailed to all vendor representatives. As incremental questions are asked by vendors, they should be documented and the questions and answers should be sent to all vendors.

Often a host of uninvited firms show up at bidders' conferences. Interestingly, these firms are generally there to meet the sales and technical teams from the potential bidders, in hopes of forming a relationship and potentially subcontracting on a given bid. Depending on how open the team members are keeping the RFP process, they may choose to have attendees bring business cards or other proof of vendor association to gain entry to the conference.

Other possible forums for vendor data gathering that the team may want to provide during the RFP vendor analysis period include individual vendor site visits, allowing vendors to come on site and interview evaluation team members or other business or IT staff. If a large amount of information on technology infrastructure, application architecture, or other IT components is easily available, nonproprietary, and useful for the analysis, the team may elect to create a "data room" that vendors may visit to do additional research or data gathering. Access to the room should be strictly controlled, and the room should be available equally to all vendors.

During the RFP analysis process and the following vendor due diligence, the team should resist the urge to hold information too closely. While some information should not be revealed (for example, target project budget), most information should be shared as widely as possible. A common misconception is that keeping information concealed or responses ambiguous and nonspecific somehow improves the team's negotiating position or otherwise compromises the process. Quite the opposite is true—most vendors want to put their best foot forward and win a deal by having the superior product or solution for the client's needs. Sharing as much information as possible with the vendors facilitates the process and ensures a quality selection. Often, a selection team's hesitance to share information with the vendor is indicative of a lack of confidence on the part of the team.

Finally, during the RFP analysis period, the team may want to contact a few vendors to see if the amount of time allowed for the RFP response is adequate. While, invariably, every vendor wants more time, some probing questions can ascertain if the response period set by the team is inadequate. In these cases, the team should not hesitate to provide additional time for a quality vendor response.

RFP RESPONSE ASSESSMENT. The process should allow between one and four weeks for the vendors to formulate a response, depending on the complexity of product, level of investment in question, and depth of the RFP questions. Vendors should provide the requested hard copies and electronic versions of their responses by the date and time established in the RFP.

Vendors should also be asked to refrain from additional contact with the evaluation team during the evaluation period, with disqualification as a possible penalty. Without this threat, the most resourceful (or aggressive) vendors will pester the team (and anyone else in the company that may have influence) endlessly with follow-up questions, status checks, and offers to "provide additional information." By communicating clearly the evaluation process and setting hard deadlines for the decision, the team can satisfy the vendors' need for understanding the timing of the next steps.

In some cases, the team may have determined additional questions or data points to gather during the RFP response period or after reading the responses. In these cases, supplemental questions should be aggregated and distributed to the vendors via e-mail with a reasonable, but rapid, time frame for response.

The actual evaluation process should have the team reading each RFP in no particular order and scoring the vendor response based on the requirements and weighting determined before the RFP distribution. In some cases, the team may break out its evaluation by specific functional expertise (the representative from manufacturing scores manufacturing capabilities and the representative from finance scores finance capabilities). To the extent possible, the team members should conduct individual reviews of the RFP responses to avoid biasing one another. Team members can debate the merits of each RFP after all the individual scoring is complete.

After the RFP reviews are complete, the scores should be summarized, with a final score by vendor and category created from the mean of the team scores. Exhibit 10.11 outlines this process.

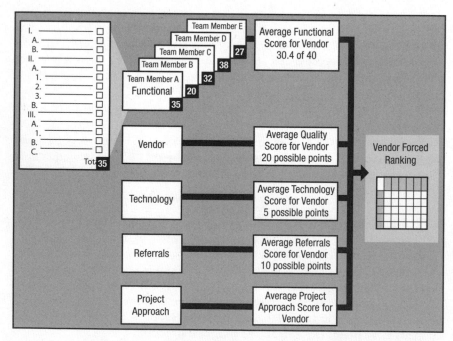

Exhibit 10.11   Final Vendor Scoring Roll Up Process

REFINE VENDOR LIST. After the vendors have been scored across each category and the mean score from the team members has been assigned by vendor, it is a straightforward exercise to force-rank the vendor options by total score (Exhibit 10.12).

The team should conduct a final round of debates to ensure that the outcome passes a "sanity check" and that everyone agrees with the results of the quantitative analysis. After any alterations to the score have been made and a final force-rank vendor list is complete, the team should decide which vendors to carry through to the due-diligence process. The team should make the cut at the first point in the force-ranking where there is a significant drop-off in score. This should usually be between two and four vendors, although a thorough due diligence on more than two vendors can be a challenging effort.

As with all previous major end-of-phase work products, the evaluation team should walk the IT steering committee through a summary of the process and outcome and get a sign-off from the committee and the evaluation team so that the evaluation can proceed to vendor due diligence.

After the results have been finalized, the team should inform each of the vendor participants of the outcome in writing. The notification should thank them for their participation and provide a contact if the vendor would like follow-up information. It is not necessary to inform the losing vendors of the scoring or disclose which vendors will be carried forward through due diligence. A

	Functional	Quality	Technology	Referrals	Project Approach	TOTAL
Vendor A	30.4	20	4	8.9	14.3	**77.6**
Vendor B	35	17.6	4	10	13	**79.6**
Vendor C	32.6	15	3.5	7	14.2	**72.3**
Vendor D	28.9	13.4	5	8.5	12	**67.8**
Vendor E	37.7	19	2	7.2	12.5	**78.4**

Exhibit 10.12   Vendor Forced Ranking

courteous, professional notification ensures the future participation of the vendors and provides a backup set of vendors if the due-diligence process produces unsatisfactory results. If time permits, the team should provide feedback to the losing parties. Most good sales professionals are interested in understanding how they can compete successfully in the future; they appreciate the feedback and will incorporate it into their next sales pursuit.

Vendor Due Diligence

The focus of this piece of the work is to prove to the satisfaction of the team the assertions made by the vendors in their RFP responses. The particular focus is on understanding the details of how the functional requirements are covered, how the system will operate from a technology standpoint, and talking with other vendor customers to understand how well the vendor has served them, as well as beginning to build relationships with them for future information exchange. The team accomplishes this primarily by working with the vendor sales team and taking the actual product through its paces.

Exhibit 10.13 shows an overview of the vendor due-diligence process. The remainder of this section covers each of the steps in detail.

UPDATE DUE-DILIGENCE EVALUATION FRAMEWORK. Because the RFP evaluation contains a detailed list of the required functions, technical capabilities, and vendor references, the framework for the due diligence simply mirrors the criteria from the previous phase—the *what* to assess has been created and refined by the team in the previous two phases. Focus of this portion of the work is on the proof of the vendor claims made in the RFP. Scoring

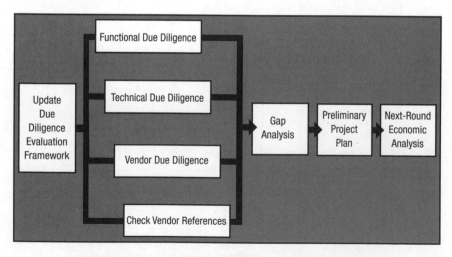

Exhibit 10.13   Vendor Due-Diligence Process Overview

sheets used by the team should be the same as those used in the RFP evaluation, with the same weightings and priority. A few minor adjustments emanating from the work in the RFP exercise may need to be made to the framework and assessment questions.

As the team proceeds through the due-diligence exercise, it should focus the majority of its attention on points of differentiation between the vendors, as it is on those points that the ultimate vendor decision is made. For example, if order entry is a required function and both vendors handle the order-entry process similarly and to the proven satisfaction of the team, the team should not spend time attempting to differentiate the vendors based on capabilities in this area. Similarly, if both vendors demonstrably support the latest release of Microsoft's SQL Server database with dozens of end-client installs, ability to support SQL Server is not a potential point of differentiation. Because vendors are often at competitive parity on many of the functions provided, adherence to this approach dramatically cuts down the breadth of analysis required for due diligence, as well as ensures that the ultimate selection is based on the factors that provide real differentiation between the competing alternatives. The focus on the key business areas helps the implementation team later avoid most surprises that so often plague a large project.

In vendor selections where investment is low, functionality is well understood, or a single vendor is the clear winner, the team may elect to de-emphasize certain portions of the due diligence. In these cases, minimum research by the team should include a focused vendor demo and a set of good reference checks.

CONDUCT FUNCTIONAL DUE DILIGENCE. The focus of the functional due diligence is to prove, to the satisfaction of the selection team, that the product or package can perform the required business functions in a way that is acceptable to the business. This portion of the due diligence is the most important because it is the element most difficult to evaluate and, therefore, the area with the potential for concealing the most surprises to be discovered during implementation.

The depth of business process knowledge required and level of detailed examination of the system can be daunting. The functional due-diligence process can be tedious, particularly if the vendor is having trouble understanding the business process. The team must steel its resolve to plow its way through multiple demos and to keep asking questions until it gets an answer that makes sense and is consistent with what it sees the system doing.

During one memorable selection we participated in, a vendor remarked that our selection team "was just too detail oriented." We took this as a compliment of the highest order. If the vendors participating in due diligence are not complaining about the level of detail orientation, the team is not chasing out the ambiguities. Vendor discomfort with detailed analysis is a sign that the effort is going well.

The principle vehicle for conducting functional due diligence is the vendor product demonstration. This is a familiar venue for vendors and customers alike, and it is one of the best ways for vendors to put their products through the appropriate paces.

We recommend that each vendor participating in the due-diligence process conduct two separate demonstrations. The first should be an unscripted, open demo in which vendors can demonstrate the product with any agenda they care to put together. The second demonstration is a highly scripted walk through of the top priority requirements using data and procedures assembled by the evaluation team.

Incredibly, vendor demos are the point at which we have observed many companies beginning the vendor selection process. Naturally, these superficial, vendor-driven, ill-fated projects were profitable for the vendors fortunate enough to be invited and ultimately led to failed implementations and massive budget overruns for the companies in question. In one particularly egregious example, we were asked by the senior management team of the company in question to help think through possible solutions after a three-year failed implementation resulted in an unusable system. When asked about their original selection and implementation process almost every worst case scenario we have described occurred including a poorly documented and vendor-led selection effort. In another example, a company spent two years evaluating two vendors, negotiating pricing, interviewing implementation partners yet could not get the final purchase approval from the board of directors because of the superficiality of analysis and a lack of understanding of the business requirements on the part of the selection team that let the vendors dictate the process and refused to document business processes and requirements.

The order of these demonstrations is important—all vendors, correctly or not, feel that they know the best way to show their products. Providing them with an open, anything-goes forum for doing so is the only way to satisfy them that they have had every chance necessary to show what they can do. It can be difficult for a team to let the vendor take the driver's seat during these demonstrations, but it is important to let vendors "get it out of their system." The second demonstration provides ample opportunity for the team to drive the agenda. The team provides a detailed list of the desired functions, along with sample data and outcomes they would like to see in the second demonstration, to the vendor at the conclusion of the first demo.

The content of the second demonstration is crucial. The team must understand not only how the product accomplishes each of the key requirements, but also how the function is configured and what level of customization is required to make it work. The answers to these questions can be difficult to pry out of the vendor, and many clients have been dazzled by a highly customized "smoke and mirrors" demo from the vendor. A running joke in most vendor demos is the repeated "It can do that," which, of course, is always true. The real question is how much has to change from the default installation to get there. Bearing in mind that heavy configuration and customization drives

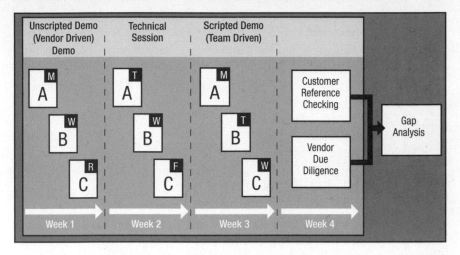

Exhibit 10.14 Due Diligence Vendor Calendar

considerable labor cost in the end implementation, the team should keep track of the approximate level required to meet each of the requirements being evaluated. The vendor should be asked for as many additional demos as it takes to satisfy the team members that they understand in detail how each of the functions will be accomplished.

In addition to the key functional requirements, the team may want to review some of the nontransaction-oriented portions of the system. This can include workflow, configuration tools, customization language, third-party integration tools, application programming interfaces, data extract tools, event scheduling, and reporting capabilities. Many of these are typically covered by the vendor in the first demonstration, but they can be areas to investigate further in the scripted demo if questions are still outstanding.

To best facilitate the rounds of vendor demonstrations, as well as the technical due diligence and customer review sessions, the team should establish a due-diligence calendar to be distributed to all participants—team and vendors alike. The team should set the first demos for each vendor during the first week and the second demos during the following week. Each demonstration session should be planned for an entire day. The one to two weeks afterward should be dedicated to customer references and additional vendor research. The team should have adequate time between demos to recover and document its findings, but the events should be scheduled close enough together to ensure a good comparison between vendors. A break of one day between demonstrations is a nice interval. Exhibit 10.14 shows a typical vendor calendar for a due diligence involving three vendors.

Key tips for having the best possible outcomes from a vendor demonstration include:

- Set vendor expectations clearly on the meeting agenda for the scripted and unscripted demos.
- Make sure all attendees are on time and pay attention; selection team members should take the demonstration seriously.
- Ensure that the evaluation team asks questions and stays engaged for the full session.
- Conduct the demonstrations on the vendor site—the vendor can give the best show there and won't have any excuse for not having the right technical pieces in place.
- Have the evaluation team set aside the entire day so that no other commitments interfere with attendance.

CONDUCT TECHNICAL DUE DILIGENCE. The technical due diligence is focused on ensuring that the full suite of required technical components are understood by the team and that any implications for the current or planned technical architecture are surfaced and dealt with. The technical due-diligence sessions are usually conducted with one or more technical sales staff from the vendor, evaluation team members, as well as select technical managers from the IT department. The agenda for the technical due diligence should concentrate on a few key areas, which are discussed in the following sections.

Technical Platform—Options and Requirements. The technical team should cover the technical options that are available for deployment of the system. For applications vendors, this should include operating systems supported, hardware supported, and databases. Large applications vendors support nearly all major platforms but may have more installs on certain platforms.

The team should ask for details on the target platform. If an application vendor selection has as a target technical platform Sun Solaris on Sun Servers with EMC DASD and an Oracle backend, the vendor should demonstrate that the product has worked in the target environment for a specific client. The client reference process, described in the following section, contains more details on how to conduct a technical reference check. The team should also examine the evolution of the product; if it was originally deployed on a specific technical platform, then migrated to others, it may operate more effectively on the original platform. If this is possibly the case, the team can look for vendor proof that the product has been completely migrated.

The team should also unearth the minimum standards, recommended standards, and probable requirements for all technical components. To minimize cost implications, application vendors sometimes focus attention on the minimum requirements. Probable requirements are the most important, as they are the primary driver of cost if new hardware, software, networking, or other equipment is required as part of the deployment.

The team may choose to investigate a variety of other technology areas during the due diligence. The most important outcome is a complete understanding of the likely cost picture from a technology standpoint so that the team can begin creating project budgets at the end of this phase. The potential questions are selection-specific—the technical staff and the evaluation team should decide in advance which technology questions will impact the overall decision and which have implications for overall cost. Examples of areas to investigate include:

- Preferred technical architecture: OS, servers, clients, DASD, network, database.
- Number and type of required servers.
- Integration tools and approaches (middleware, batch, API, object-level, or other).
- Third-party applications required to run the application (middleware, reporting, database applications).
- DASD requirements for application and operating system.
- Minimum client-side requirements (browser based or other).
- Bandwidth/network capacity required between servers and clients.
- Load-sharing capabilities (clustering, balancing).
- Backup requirements and approach.
- Failover and recovery capabilities.
- Startup and shutdown procedures.
- Recommended and probable requirements for failover, development, and test environments.
- Systems security and audit—user setup and administration; systems security capabilities.

An additional option that may be considered by an application selection team is hosting. Many application vendors and hardware vendors have teamed to offer hosting and data center services as part of a comprehensive package of offerings. Many vendors have also developed application service provider (ASP) options, which provide for offsite hosting of the entire application.

Outsourcing of hosting is a topic beyond the scope of this text. Like most other IT decisions, it should be investigated with a clear understanding of the costs and benefits involved, and it should generate a clear ROI for the company. The benefits and long-term implications of ASP relationships are still uncertain. However, a consensus appears to be emerging that ASP services can be valuable for noncore applications (e.g., salesforce contact management, HR/recruiting). The data-gathering section of this document points to Web resources where the latest thinking on the topics from industry leaders can be found.

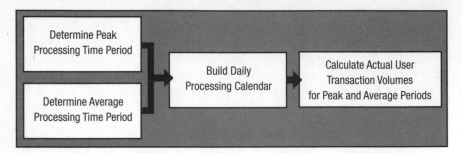

Exhibit 10.15   Process for Required Volume Support Calculation

Transaction Volume Support and Scalability.   The second key area of inquiry for the test team is to validate the system's ability to support peak transaction volumes and handle changes to future business. Scalability considerations for new hardware and software acquisitions are covered in detail in Chapter 6.

The technology due-diligence team should first ascertain the current peak batch transaction and online user volumes. This is a three-step process, which first determines the current peak processing day and time, then takes actual transaction volumes and user count from the point of peak processing. Exhibit 10.15 outlines the process.

As Exhibit 10.16 shows, the peak annual/monthly/weekly usage period should be determined first. This accounts for seasonality factors (for businesses with lumpy annual transaction volumes), as well as any monthly (e.g., month-end statement and financial processing) and weekly (e.g., end-of-week

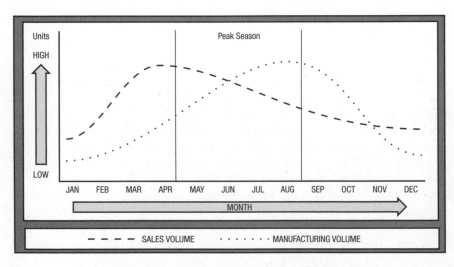

Exhibit 10.16   Company X Peak Period Analysis

order surges) effects. A variety of factors can be used as a proxy for volume, depending on the company. Exhibit 10.16 shows sales and manufacturing unit volume. The actual drivers, which need to be determined by the team, vary by industry, company type, customer concentration, business seasonality, and other factors.

After the highest volume day, week, month, and year are determined, the technical team should build a detailed daily processing calendar to determine which online and batch processes are running at a given hour of the day. Exhibit 10.17 shows a sample daily processing calendar, with the peak online usage and batch processing periods identified. Because designing the system for peak volumes can be cost prohibitive, the team should also identify an average, or typical, processing day.

With the peak day and interdaily processing hours identified, the team can estimate (or pull from system logs and transaction history) the number of online users and transaction volumes for the peak and average periods. This

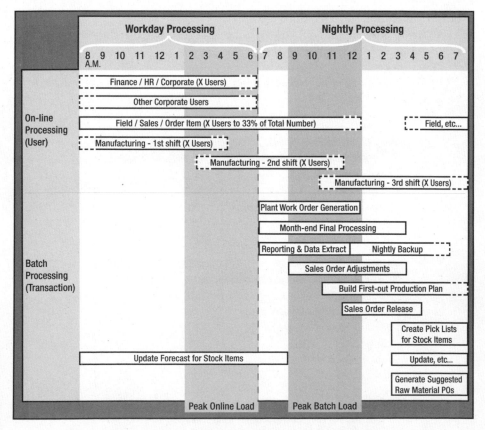

Exhibit 10.17   Company X Daily Processing Schedule

information should be summarized as input to the volume validation process. Exhibit 10.18 shows the volume summary from Exhibit 10.17.

Now that the peak and average volume requirements for users and transactions are documented, the team can compare them to the proven volumes supported by the systems under consideration.

Vendors usually have two types of proven volume capabilities. The first is created from lab-based "stress tests," which show the maximum system capabilities under a variety of technical environments and conditions. The second is empirical evidence created in actual customer implementations of the product. These can be particularly useful for the team, especially if the benchmark implementation is similar in terms of business processes and volume.

If the vendor supplies the benchmark information for clients, the team should follow up with a call to the client to validate the numbers and get the client's feedback on performance management and the system's handling of peak volumes. A detailed conversation with the end-client often produces relevant details not volunteered (or understood) by the vendor. The solicitation of this feedback can be incorporated into the customer reference calls described later in this chapter.

A host of possible benchmarks can be assessed, but the bottom line assessment should answer at least these two questions:

1. Will online users have reasonable response times from the system during peak usage?

BATCH/TRANSACTIONS	PEAK	AVERAGE
Invoice processing	50	35
Order release	45	25
Sales to work order conversion	100	50
Shipping label print	20	5
Production plan generation	125	100

ONLINE/USERS	PEAK	AVERAGE
Order entry	250	90
Manufacturing—Heavy usage	75	25
Manufacturing—Light usage	150	110
Corporate	25	20
Finance/accounting	100	80
Other	50	20
Total user estimate	650	345

**Exhibit 10.18   Company X Peak and Average Period
Transaction Volume and User Estimates**

2. Will the system be able to process all the work required within a reasonable period of time (ability to handle a day's work in a day's time)?

Development Environment/Approach. The technical due diligence should also allocate some time to understanding the development methodology and technologies used by the vendor for its system or product. These two factors have implications for the overall cost structure of the vendors. Vendors that have made an investment in implementing highly structured development methodologies (SDLC, CMM) for managing their development process or vendors with quality certifications such as ISO may have lower long-term cost structures. The technology due-diligence team can validate the actual adoption level of certifications and methodologies within the vendor by interviewing the team lead from the certification process, internal developers or researchers who use the methodology, or verifying the certification from the third party that grants it.

Similarly, vendors who use standardized development tools and technologies may ultimately have lower cost structures. The more common the toolset, the higher the availability of the skills in the workforce, and the lower the labor costs. By virtue of their widespread use and, therefore, constant refinement, common toolsets and technologies can also lower vendor costs by improving the productivity of the development team. The team can investigate the technologies and standards used by the vendor, as well as talk to the head of development or research to gather details. Again, the evaluation team can do some basic validation with the vendor; for example, ask the vendor to produce its development standards manual.

The technology due diligence is rarely an area in which vendors are able to separate themselves from the pack. Most application vendors are at competitive parity: They support the same technologies, use the same development tools, provide the same interfaces, and have support for volumes far in excess of expected or anticipated peaks.

With this in mind, the technical due diligence should be focused on understanding the potential costs involved with the system deployment from a hardware and infrastructure standpoint, as well as any surprises (particularly on scalability or platforms supported) that emerge from the analysis. The exercise also sheds light on the vendor's likely internal cost structures, which influence pricing, competitiveness, and viability over the long run. Further, the effort in understanding peak and average volumes will be used in the sizing exercise if the system deployment requires new or upgraded hardware.

CONDUCT COMPANY DUE DILIGENCE. The focus of the company due diligence is the verification of the RFP data provided by the vendor. Because most of this information is factual, this portion of the due diligence should be a fairly rapid "check the box" exercise. Information verifying the vendor's locations, revenue history, and relevant product lines should be readily available from a variety of sources on the Internet.

In addition to verifying the information supplied in the RFP, the team should do an analysis on the vendor-supplied revision and release history for the product in question. A product history with multiple service packs or bug fixes may indicate a product that was prematurely released with a large number of flaws. In these cases, the vendor should provide a detailed explanation behind the large number of service pack and patch releases.

Typically, applications vendors have a major release every 12 to 18 months. Vendors without a major release in more than 18 months, or who have unusually long release cycles, may be having issues pushing forward their product. Because software maintenance fees usually entitle the licensee to the benefits of product upgrades and patches, the customer may not receive full value of the maintenance fees paid to a vendor with difficulties in this area. In these cases, the team should get the committed vendor release plans for future releases, with highly specific details on planned functions and upgrades. Vendors should not be able to avoid this issue—after all, if the systems development team is working on it, there must be a set of requirements that can be shared. This also mitigates against another common strategy that application vendors employ—charging clients for a "new product" when the functionality and enhancements should have been included in a new release of the already-purchased application as part of normal maintenance and upgrades.

The vendor should also be able to give examples of how customer input is gathered for new release requirements and show an example of how the requirements were carried through into a new release. The client who participated in the process should be contacted by the evaluation team to get another perspective on how well the vendor listens and incorporates input from clients to the development prioritization process.

Finally, to gauge the level of support the vendor can provide, the team may want to conduct a few "mystery shopper" calls to the vendor's technical support line to see how quickly the phone is answered and how convoluted the integrated-voice-response menu system is. Additionally, the team may request access to the online product knowledge base and run a few scans for typical application questions.

CHECK VENDOR REFERENCES.   Vendor reference checking provides two important benefits. First, it provides independent verification and validation of a vendor's claims. Although the odds of discovering adverse information about the vendor are low, the effort expended is moderate, and the value of any adverse information is very high. The search, therefore, must focus on uncovering adverse or disconfirming evidence—any good management scientist knows that "the value of information is inversely proportional to its probability." The evaluation team would appear foolish and shortsighted indeed if a few phone calls would have turned up such critical information.

Our consulting practice was helping a client salvage a particularly rocky implementation, where a few reference checks might have changed the outcome of the vendor selection. The client CEO remarked to the evaluation team: "So, this was important enough to spend two million of my dollars on but not important enough to call a couple of people on the phone?"

Second, calling vendor references establishes a relationship with other IT departments, which can later facilitate best practices sharing, vendor information sharing, and other mutually beneficial exchanges. This can be particularly valuable as the project proceeds with a particular vendor—other customers can often help the implementation team avoid many of the missteps that they made. Over the long haul, having a relationship with other customers increases the company's ability to influence the vendor as well as provides additional information for negotiations.

Exhibit 10.19 provides an overview of the vendor reference process. There are two sources of customer references for a given vendor. First, as part of the RFP process, the vendor should have provided a list of clients according to similarity. The preceding section of this chapter on RFPs covers the list in detail. The client references should be ranked according to similarity to the company, size, technical platform, planned product, business volumes, or geographic footprint. The evaluation team should call on the references that have the most similarities to the project underway.

The second source of references is those customers of the vendor identified by the evaluation team without assistance from the vendor. This is an important step because by going off the pre-planned program devised by the vendor, the team improves considerably the odds of unearthing any adverse information. There are a variety of ways of identifying target vendor clients. Although vendor Web sites and technology trade-focused magazines can be helpful, we have found other methods to be the most effective:

- *Internet job board postings:* A scan of the top job boards reveals which companies are advertising for positions with a specific skill set; presumably, companies advertising technology positions for vendor skill sets have that technology in-house. The best boards for this purpose include TMP's Monster Board (www.monster.com), DICE (www.dice.com), ComputerJobs.com (www.computerjobs.com), Headhunter/Careerbuilder (www.headhunter.net), and Hot Jobs (www.hotjobs.com).
- *Internet job board resume search:* If the team has access to the searching capabilities on any of these boards, it can do a resume scan for the vendor in question. Individual resumes generally have the technology used listed, along with the employer. This rapidly identifies companies with the technology and has the added benefit of identifying their geography and type of business and size of the implementation.
- *Technology staff augmentation companies:* If the team does not have access to job board resume searching, it can turn to a local contract

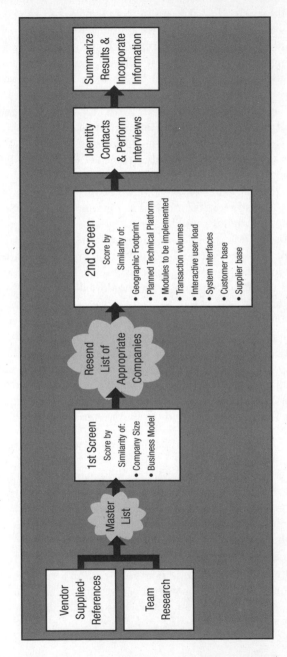

Exhibit 10.19 Vendor Reference Process

staffing company that specializes in technology resources. These firms are generally happy to conduct these searches for a small fee and, further, can usually easily identify every company in their service area that uses a specific vendor.

As with the vendor-supplied references, these potential references should be scored according to similarity for prioritization.

The vendor-supplied list and the team-constructed list form a master list of references to call. Depending on the size of investment being considered and the depth of the due-diligence effort, the team should plan to call between two and eight vendors from each of the lists. The vendor-supplied list provides contact information, and the vendor will likely prepare its customer contact for the call. In the case of the team-generated list, the team should identify the CIO or director of IT at each potential reference and send a letter or fax in advance of the call, outlining the reason for the call and providing a list of questions in advance. The team should then follow up with a phone call to perform the interview or determine whom the CIO would designate from his or her team to take the call. If possible, the team should conduct the interviews in person and make a site visit as part of the interview.

The list of questions that the team asks varies from project to project. The team should have a specific list of questions prepared in advance but should also leave time for open-ended responses from the reference. Many of the most interesting findings come from the unscripted portion of the interview. Focus is on determining how the vendor has performed for the client both before and after the sale, as well as getting a preview of any key lessons learned during the implementation.

Some of the questions that we have found effective in a vendor reference interview include:

- What products did you consider as part of your evaluation?
- What were your key decision criteria when making this decision?
- How did you complete the functional assessment, and what business functions were the most important?
- How did you weight the criteria (what was important to you)?
- How will you achieve a payback or return on investment from the system?
- What period did (will) it take to achieve a payback on the system?
- What were the benefits to the system (cost reduction, revenue enhancement)?
- When did you make your decision?
- How long did you take to complete your vendor evaluation?
- What modules or products did you purchase and implement?

- Did the technical architecture work as planned?
- How was the vendor service after the sale?
- Did you use an implementation partner to accomplish the implementation?
- Have you had input to the product development process?
- Have you had any technical/user support issues? How did the vendor respond? What was the escalation level required for resolution?
- How have the system and technical architecture scaled with volume changes?
- What were the surprises (good and bad)?
- What are the key lessons learned from the selection process and the subsequent implementation?
- Would you do it again?

CONDUCT GAP ANALYSIS. The gap analysis effort is intended to accomplish two objectives. First, the analysis should confirm that there is a satisfactory approach for handling each of the requirements, particularly the high-priority areas. Second, given the approach for each priority requirement, the team can estimate the effort required to cover the gap, which is usually one of the biggest components of the implementation costs.

Each requirement that the team has identified in the previous exercise may qualify as a gap, depending on how the system handles the function. A way of prioritizing the requirements for gap analysis is to assess each requirement according to its importance to the business and the level of fit the application has "out of the box." Exhibit 10.20 outlines the methodology for prioritizing requirements for the gap analysis.

After the requirements have been assessed along the two axes and mapped to the two-by-two framework in Exhibit 10.20, the gap analysis should be conducted on the requirements appearing in the northwest corner. The requirements in the other quadrants either have lower importance to the business (therefore, the business will accept cost-effective methods to cover the gap) or can be handled by the application with a minimum of change and are, therefore, adequately covered.

The next task in the gap analysis is to complete a detailed assessment of the method for covering each northwest quadrant requirement. For each one, the approach will be some mix of two options—reconfiguring or customizing the product or changing the associated business process and requirement. In most cases, the answer will be some mix of the two. For highest priority requirements for the most critical business processes, coverage may involve a solution that has no impact on the business process. Exhibit 10.21 shows a typical gap analysis spreadsheet. The key elements to be captured include priority; a description of the method to cover; estimated effort to cover; and a checklist for configuration, customization, or business process change for gap coverage.

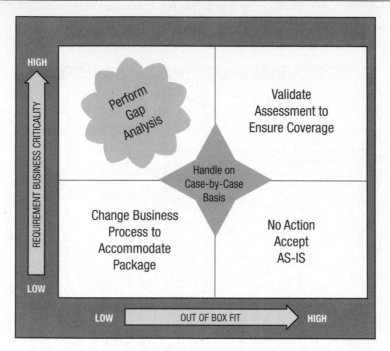

Exhibit 10.20   Requirement Prioritization Matrix for Gap Analysis

This analysis can and should be done in concert with the vendor, and it should be a principle outcome of the scripted demonstration, follow-up demos, and question-and-answer sessions. This is another main source of surprises during implementation and an area that drives much of the labor cost of implementation. Therefore, it is important for the evaluation team to put a thorough, exhaustive effort into the work—"measuring twice before cutting once." The team must also adhere to strict discipline in documenting the gaps and approach to cover. These documents facilitate later negotiations (and help resolve disputes) with the vendor. These sources of disputes in the implementation often center on the product's ability to cover the gaps as represented in the due diligence. Vendors are aware of this and sometimes resist the gap analysis. The evaluation team must keep asking tough questions until it is completely satisfied with the approach for key functions.

When the gap analysis is complete, it should be reviewed to understand what overall level of configuration and customization is required to make the system work well and satisfactorily cover all requirements. If the level of customization is particularly high (more than one-third of the modules have customizations or several modules have major customizations), the application begins to lose its appeal as a package. Because customization drives large costs in both implementation and steady-state maintenance, makes vendor

Gap #	Requirement Area	Req #	Gap Description	Method to Cover	Consultation	Customization	Price Change	Estimated Effort to Cover
2.09	Forecasting	7.32	• System must hold forecast for final market intelligence adjustment by territory managers	• Add consensus FC system and workflow step for manual incorporation and release	X	X		2 FTE days
2.10	Fixed Asset Management	5.09	• Cannot calculate dep for general ledger in weekly increments • Supports monthly only	• System will be configured and customized to work in weekly increments for GL drop	X	X		10 FTE days
2.11	Inventory Management	8.21	• System does not allow tracking of product variations by color below SKU level	• Will have to add custom code and make database changes to accommodate • Biz process change to support entry/maintenance of product color schemes		X	X	57 FTE days

Exhibit 10.21 Example Package Gap Prioritization Assessment Sheet

upgrades and enhancements difficult to install, and defeats the purpose of a packaged product, the team should take a step back and revisit the process for vendors who require heavy customization.

Supplemental Vendor Selection

In the case of a packaged application vendor selection or other product requiring additional hardware or professional services for implementation, the team may be faced with a subselection process to determine which supplemental vendors to use.

This subselection process should be managed as a subset of the activities covered in this chapter. The key sequence of scope definition, requirements gathering, vendor identification, vendor demonstrations, and reference checking can usually be completed rapidly. The front-runners for the primary vendor will have emerged, narrowing the scope for the supplemental selection considerably. In most cases, it is not necessary to go through the effort of a complete RFP process. Furthermore, the scope and requirements for the supplemental vendor selection should easily emerge from the previously completed work—for example, the volume processing calendars and technology footprint driving hardware selection, preliminary project plan, and resource estimates driving professional services vendor selection.

A starting point for the supplemental vendor selection list can come from the vendor reference calls completed as part of the due diligence. The managers will usually divulge which supplemental vendors they used for hardware, additional software, and professional services. After several references, the team usually sees the same names of supplemental vendors begin to turn up.

After supplemental vendors have been selected, the project plan and economic analysis can be updated based on new information.

HARDWARE VENDORS. If a supplemental selection is required for a hardware vendor, the selection team may want to evaluate the following hardware vendor specific considerations:

- *References:* Look for references with similar configuration and processing profiles (peak and average volumes); for hardware, the processing and configuration similarity matters more than business model similarities.
- *Versions:* Hardware vendors have rapid product cycles; reference accounts are usually on hardware a generation or two behind the hardware under consideration; in these cases, the vendor should provide a clear inventory of changes in the platform.
- *Reliability/service:* If the application being deployed is mission critical, the hardware should provide the appropriate reliability, including failover and subsystem redundancy; the vendor should have four-hour or faster component replacement as an available service.

- *Pricing:* The vendor should provide pricing for varying levels of capacity; often professional services and applications vendors have entered into agreements with hardware vendors as resellers and, therefore, have access to discount pricing that is not available to the one-time purchaser. In these cases, the application or services vendor will work with the hardware provider to provide pricing.

- *Upgrade path:* If the application scalability requirements entail ability to expand capacity at a later date, the hardware vendor should propose systems that have a clearly defined upgrade path that minimizes incremental cost and implementation disruption.

- *Existing environment:* If the hardware must fit into a pre-existing environment, it should be proven to interface with the existing equipment and systems; customer references can help surface any potential integration issues.

- *Sales model:* Hardware vendors often use an indirect sales channel; in this case, the hardware vendor can help identify a value-added reseller (VAR) that can provide pricing and service. Generally, the hardware vendor "co-sells" in conjunction with the VAR to ensure that all questions are answered to the prospect's satisfaction.

Chapter 6 provides a detailed model for ensuring that technology-purchasing decisions are made in a consistent, cost-effective fashion.

PROFESSIONAL SERVICES PROVIDERS. If a supplemental selection is required for a professional services vendor, the selection team may want to evaluate the following vendor-specific considerations:

- *Pricing:* Is the provider willing to enter into a fixed-pricing contract? If the evaluation team has completed the scoping and requirements definition phase at the appropriate level of detail, the vendor should be willing to fix-bid the project, as most of the details and gaps have already been documented and understood.

- *Performance guarantee:* Will the vendor tie its compensation to completion of specific project milestones and/or the achievement of the anticipated project benefits? Will the vendor enter into a "gain-sharing" agreement with bonuses and penalties tied to performance during the implementation?

- *Bench discounts:* Will the vendor provide discount rates for consultants on its "bench" who have a solid skill set but do not have experience with this specific type of implementation?

- *References and experience:* Has the vendor seen the full implementation of this project previously with a similar client (company size, industry, modules implemented, project budget, business model)?

- *Staffing:* Have the specific team members proposed for this engagement participated in a similar engagement with the vendor? Will the vendor provide proposed team member resumes in advance and allow client veto or approval power for team members? Will the vendor provide the hire dates of the proposed team? Will any of the team members be provided to the vendor from third parties?

- *Approach:* Does the vendor have a proprietary, client-proven approach for this type of engagement? Does it reduce risk or cost or otherwise improve the outcome? Has the vendor submitted a potential work plan that demonstrates a detailed understanding of the key challenges for the project? Has the vendor performed an implementation with a conversion from the system being replaced?

- *Location:* Will the proposed team work on-site? Where are the home offices of the team members? What is the vendor policy on travel costs and per-diems?

The team should be inclined to sharing information (e.g., requirements documentation, gap analysis) with vendors during all parts of the process, and the supplemental vendors are no exception. Often, vendor selection teams are hesitant to provide information to vendors. This reluctance usually slows down the process and results in a lack of clarity in communication with the vendors. Obviously, the team should not compromise proprietary information that might hurt the company, but reputable vendors are always willing to sign nondisclosure agreements in exchange for a clearer understanding of the process.

Finally, the evaluation team should investigate both a consulting and staff-augmentation approach to outside professional services help. Consultants are generally willing to assume responsibility for the project and will provide both doers and leaders. A staff-augmentation approach provides the implementation team with contractors for specific skill sets, but the responsibility for project delivery rests completely with the internal team. Both approaches have been proven successful, and the team should decide the appropriate use of outside resources based on cost, availability, references, level of internal expertise, project risk, and estimated return on investment.

Project Planning and Approval

BUILD PRELIMINARY PROJECT PLAN. The next task for the team is to create a preliminary project plan and revise the previous first-cut economic analysis. Labor effort to cover the gaps, particularly when provided by outside professional services firms, is one of the largest drivers of cost in an implementation. Therefore, after the gap analysis has been completed, much of the information that produces variability in the project economics is known, and a re-estimate can be completed.

As with requirements gathering and analysis, the creation of a quality project plan is a topic that justifies a separate book (or three). There are a wide variety of project planning methodologies available. Books covering a few approaches are listed at the end of the chapter. Chapter 15 of this book discusses the topic in more detail. A few key principles are outlined here. The project plan should include these elements:

- *Work tasks:* This inventory of tasks and subtasks required to complete the project should have 5 to 10 major tasks at the top level and each level of detail breaks down into an additional 5 to 10 subtasks for as many levels of detail as required.

- *Sequencing and dependencies:* Plan should account for the order in which tasks should be completed; the plan must highlight which tasks are required predecessors of following tasks and which provide a deliverable that feeds a following task.

- *Deliverables:* The plan should identify the document, function, submodule, or other clearly defined outcome of each task.

- *Milestones:* Identification and inventory of major points of completion and way-points in the plan facilitates later measurement of progress against the plan.

- *Task timing and duration:* The calendar date for the commencement of each major phase of the project should be identified, along with the duration of the tasks and subtasks.

- *Resources:* Includes level, skill set, and amount of resources required to complete the task (e.g., "Senior-level SQL Server DBA for four weeks"); the resource should be identified as an internal or external resource. These requirements will drive the overall labor cost for the project.

- *Rollout and cutover:* The rollout and cutover portion of the plan shows how the system will be deployed to the user base; the rollout plan may be organized around department, geographic region, plant location, or other bundling of users that facilitates training and minimizes business disruption.

- *Training:* The plan should show the number and type of end users that require training, along with an estimate of training hours required per user, and a plan for executing and managing the training process (vendor supplied, internal training, classroom based, etc.).

- *Lead times:* The plan should factor in vendor lead times required for shipping, receiving, installing, and configuring hardware, software, or other vendor-supplied components. The team should perform a "right-to-left" analysis so that the order date can be calculated based on the lead-time and date required.

- *Business calendar:* The development, implementation, and deployment schedule should be audited to ensure that no key events conflict with important events on the business calendar; this is particularly true for highly seasonal businesses (e.g., grocery stores at Thanksgiving, florists on Valentine's Day).

Because this plan is merely the first-cut, preliminary effort, the team should produce the plan in a top-down fashion and avoid overcomplicating the plan with excessive detail. For example, tasks measured in hours or even days are probably too much detail at this point. The plan should instead lay out in broad strokes what comprises the overall effort, at the level of major pieces of work measured in weeks.

Similarly, the team should avoid overcomplicating the preliminary plan with excessive use of project planning tools. A host of applications is available for project organization and management. Particularly for first-round plans, these tools complicate matters. The IT manager should be cautious of a desire from the team to delve into project planning tools (and the concomitant distraction of installing, training, and tweaking). The first draft is best done in a spreadsheet or word processing document. Over-reliance on a tool can often mask a lack of content. A good plan stands on its own, regardless of format.

PERFORM NEXT-ROUND ECONOMIC ANALYSIS.   After the preliminary plan is complete, the team can update the costs portion of the costs-benefit model. The new information to be incorporated comes from three fronts:

1. Preliminary project plan supplies updated estimate of internal and externally supplied labor, along with resource type, quantity, and estimated hourly cost.

2. Updated application or product costs—at a minimum, the vendor will have supplied list (or pre-negotiation) pricing for the product being selected, along with an understanding of the key drivers of pricing (servers, seats, processors, or other).

3. Preliminary estimate of hardware, supplemental software. The processing calendar and sizing performed as part of the technical due diligence will provide enough information to attain a preliminary estimate of any additional hardware or software required; as with software costs, these numbers will also be order-of-magnitude pre-negotiation estimates based on vendor input.

The team should produce the following components of a complete project economic analysis:

- *Project cost:* The total cost of original acquisition of all technology components and their complete configuration, customization, integration, implementation, training, and deployment, based on the preliminary project plan.

- *Vendor maintenance:* Estimated annual fees due to vendor as part of maintenance agreement for all technology components—hardware and software.
- *Steady-state cost model changes:* Any incremental costs (or savings) incurred in the organization, covering all portions of the IT budget. These costs are found across a variety of categories, including labor (additional staff, different salaries based on new technology), consumables, facilities, and capacity.
- *Accelerated depreciation:* Some projects will obsolete an existing system or set of systems. In these cases, depreciation of amounts capitalized from the previous implementation may be accelerated and taken as expense after the new system is deployed; the amounts and accounting issues around this topic should be addressed in conjunction with the finance department and the CFO.

As with the project plan, economic analysis should be simplified by taking a top-down approach and making assumptions and documenting them where information is missing or incomplete. The economic analysis should also be a spreadsheet-based exercise, which rolls project costs up into the traditional "hardware, software, people" categories and takes a stance on probable post-implementation changes to steady-state IT costs.

Often, evaluation teams (and very often vendors) are uncomfortable with beginning to assign numbers to the project. Each round of economic analysis should be positioned as a preliminary estimate only. At some point, the team will have to put a stake in the ground and begin talking about what the numbers are. Completing this exercise early allows key assumptions to be surfaced and examined and provides context for all of the cost-benefits discussions with senior management.

After the project and steady-state costs have been re-evaluated, the team can re-calculate the project return on investment, payback period, or other relevant cost-benefit measures. Any additional benefits identified during the RFP or due-diligence processes should be added to the model as well.

Finally, based on this analysis, the team may begin to see some separation between the vendors at this point because project economics are always a major factor in any vendor selection process. If a particular vendor is at a major cost advantage (or disadvantage), the team may elect to shift its focus to the front-runner.

PROJECT PRESENTATION/APPROVAL.   At this point, the evaluation team should present the results of the vendor due diligence, preliminary project plan, and economic analysis to the IT steering committee. Based on the vendor due diligence, vendor scoring, and economic analysis, the team should have identified the vendor of choice, as well as supplemental vendors. The package presented to the committee should have every element of the planned project identified, except the final pricing negotiations with the vendors.

This provides the committee a last chance for input to the process before final selection of a vendor and before the team invests significant effort in negotiations with the vendor. Because a thorough vendor selection can take several months, the committee will often have new information regarding business benefits and refined requirements.

As with all previous steps, the members of the evaluation team and the IT steering committee should sign off on the recommendation before proceeding to the next step.

Vendor Negotiation

After the IT steering committee has approved the project and vendor selection, the final vendor pricing negotiations can commence. It is important to wait until this point to maximize negotiating influence with the vendors. If vendors know the project and budget have been approved by senior management, they will know that the deal is imminent and will be prepared to rapidly get to their best pricing.

Vendor negotiation is a complex topic; IT managers generally find themselves at a disadvantage in negotiations. Vendor sales professionals participate in pricing negotiations every single week. The IT manager does not have the advantage of either practice or complete information. Because of this, IT managers often bring in consultants who are experienced in conducting vendor pricing negotiations. The best consultants are objective and not associated with a firm that implements or resells any vendor's products. They will also have conducted a negotiation with the specific vendor in question during the prior twelve months. The high cost of a large-scale vendor investment allows the client to recoup the negotiation specialist's consulting fees many times over.

Often, IT managers have an inherent hesitance to ask for discounting before closing a deal with a vendor. There are a variety of reasons for this, including inexperience negotiating pricing, not understanding vendor pricing drivers, or unwillingness to push back on the vendor sales reps. Unfortunately, this can be costly for the company and earn the IT manager a reputation for being a patsy. IT managers lose nothing by at least asking the question of vendors. We were asked to review a ready-to-be-signed contract for a new client as a "formality." We called the sales manager and asked if this was the best pricing available. The manager remarked that no one had asked for a discount, but that he would provide a 10 percent discount for an immediate execution of the contract. One phone call, five minutes, $20,000 in savings generated.

Because of the large number of different factors involved in a large technology purchase—licensing, maintenance, training, professional services, terms and conditions, and more—the IT manager must proceed cautiously. Often, vendors will turn a loss on one portion of the negotiation into a major win on another piece. Therefore, the IT manager must understand and negotiate each variable (license, support, financing, peripherals, etc.) with a specific strategy and lock down agreed upon items in the process. In buying a car, if you negotiate a trade-in on your used car, the price of the new car, and the financing separately you are much more likely to receive the best possible deal on each versus negotiating all together to get to a desired monthly payment. The same is true for vendor negotiations in technology. Negotiations can be lengthy, but time is on the side of the buyer. The manager should tightly control both the agenda and, most importantly, the pace of the negotiation. This allows the manager to keep the upper hand and achieve the best pricing and terms.

We have collected a few practices from participating in a host of software, hardware, and services vendors' negotiations. Key points are provided in the following listing. However, we highly recommend the engagement of a negotiation expert for large-expenditure items, or at a minimum, self-study with the negotiation texts mentioned in the bibliography for this chapter:

- *Negotiate each point separately.* Vendors are experienced in achieving a higher total price by bundling and shifting prices of individual components throughout the negotiation process. The opportunity of vendors to obfuscate the true pricing is high if licenses, maintenance, hardware, financing, professional services, training, future discounts, and a dozen other terms are negotiated simultaneously. Instead, the buyer should carefully and separately negotiate each point, starting with the points that drive the largest amount of cost first. Often, the vendors will give up ground on this piece, hoping to gain back lost ground on the subsequent pieces.

- *Keep at least two vendors in the mix.* Keep a second option open until there is ink on the final contract; if the vendor senses that it is the only option, the manager's negotiating power declines significantly. As soon as a vendor thinks a final selection has been made—whether the winner or not—negotiating will become more rigid. Further, it is possible that the negotiations would produce pricing concessions from the second-place vendor that would move it into first place.

- *Don't single-source the negotiation.* Because many vendors offer a full suite of services in addition to their application, they often have a natural advantage in proposing consulting or training portions of a project. The team should still consider competing services to ascertain which vendor can deliver a better price or better service. The outcome of the negotiations may very well be a single-source approach for implementation, but driving to this solution early lowers the client negotiating power.

- *Timing is everything.* Like any other company, software, hardware, and professional services vendors are under pressure to achieve monthly, quarterly, and annual goals. A little research should reveal the fiscal calendar for the vendor in question. The maximum negotiating power is at a quarter or fiscal year end, as the vendor works to achieve its financial targets.

- *Keep talking to current and prospective customers.* Current data from other prospective customers as well as the installed base can give you insight into areas where the vendor might be more willing to offer concessions. With the right relationship built, IT managers from peer companies will be willing to share costing and negotiation information about a specific vendor.

- *Don't compare apples to oranges.* Because of the large number of pieces involved in a complex negotiation, it can often be difficult to compare individual elements of the pricing to adequately compare vendors. The team should continue to ask questions and deconstruct vendor-pricing proposals until they can be compared side-by-side on an element-by-element basis.

- *Nominate a "bad cop" for your team in advance.* The team may occasionally need someone to take a tough line with the vendor. If a "bad cop" is needed during the negotiations, the company CFO is often happy to fill that role.

- *Ensure that the vendor* must *close the deal.* Ensure that throughout the process, vendor invests considerable amount of time in the deal; the vendor sales team then often engages in "sunk cost fallacy" and believes that it must complete the deal because of the high level of investment so far. This has the effect of swinging the balance of power considerably.

- *Employ "bogeys" to force reciprocal concessions.* This is a common negotiating tactic to put forward points that are not actually material considerations ("bogeys"), then quickly capitulate on the point to force reciprocal concessions from the vendor on other points. This can be an effective strategy, but should be used with caution; they can quickly produce the reverse effect in the event that the vendor agrees to the nonmaterial concession early.

- *Check the contract for liability limitations.* Vendors generally try to contractually limit their liabilities to the total of their fees or to the limits of their insurance coverage. These liability limits often do not begin to approach the actual damages experienced by a business if an implementation goes wrong (see Chapter 1). The team should push for liability limitations that acknowledge the risk for the customer, not the vendor. For high profile, large-investment projects, the vendor should also carry "malpractice" or errors and omissions (E&O) insurance from an insurance carrier with a rating of A or better.

- *Never prepay maintenance.* Occasionally, vendors offer discounts for prepaid maintenance or other items. The IT manager gives up significant future influence over the vendor's behavior by prepaying these

NEGOTIATION POINT	COMMENTS	TERMS
License (server, seats)	• In addition to getting the overall price as low as possible, the timing of payment should be delayed as long as possible. • Typical discount should range from 10% to 30%. • Influencing factors include maintenance load, how close it is to quarter end, and whether purchase is done direct with the vendor or through a VAR.	• Typical to pay 50% of cost at signing. • Attempt to delay payment of remaining balance as long as possible—at least 90 days after satisfactory installation, to be defined by customer.
Future license discounts	• The time of the initial purchase is when the buyer has the most leverage. • Therefore, discount rates on potential future purchases should be negotiated at that time. • Being "optimistic" when estimating future needs gives the vendor more incentive to be generous.	• Rate—the current license discount or better should apply. • Duration—the negotiated rate should be in effect for at least one year after initial purchase. • Payment Timing—agree to longer terms on future purchases.
Service level/Help desk support	• Usually hierarchy of "silver," "gold," "platinum." • Depending on internal support plan, often not a high priority.	• Try to get free upgrade to next highest service level.
Consulting/ Professional services	• Vendor typically pushes for some professional services to be included to ensure "proper installation." • Depending on the implementation partner, professional services may not be needed. • Keep commitment low in first agreement—it can always be increased later.	• Typical fees range from $150/hour to $300/hour with an average of $225–$250/hour. • Need to prearrange costs while negotiating power is high; the price should be documented in the contract.

Exhibit 10.22   Key Negotiating Points for Package Application Pricing

NEGOTIATION POINT	COMMENTS	TERMS
Training	• Vendor typically has a price per person, not including travel and expenses. • Vendors try to link training discounts to the number of participants. • "Training the trainer" is an effective way to manage costs.	• As part of bundled negotiation, training prices can sometimes be reduced to zero. • If it is not feasible to get training for free, vendor should be able to discount by at least 10%. • Achieve volume discount by applying leverage as number of trainees increases.
Future training	• Negotiate the discount rate for any future training at the time of initial purchase.	• Rate—the current discount or better should apply. • Duration—the negotiated rate should be in effect for at least one year after the initial purchase.
Maintenance fees—First year	• Because of its recurring nature, this component can have a significant impact on ownership costs. • Pay an annual fee to receive upgrades until a specified future release. • Usually a hierarchy ("gold," "platinum," etc.).	• Usually ~8–30% of price. • Negotiate to have price based on discounted pricing—not list pricing. • Can also negotiate payment timing—try for date after last license payment.
On-going maintenance fees	• The key is determining if the basis for annual maintenance fees after the first year is software net price or list.	• Rate—the original discount or better should apply. • Duration—the negotiated rate should be in effect for as long as you are eligible for maintenance. • Payment Timing—agree to longer terms for future annual payments.
Additional required software	• Depending on package, this can include database, integration tools (SDK), or third-party bolt-on packages.	• Negotiate same as points for licensing. • High costs for these additional items may give a buyer more leverage on the license price.

Exhibit 10.22 *Continued*

charges. We have seen clients with several years of prepaid maintenance credit that is worthless because the vendor has gone out of business. However sharp the discount, the risk associated with prepaying is
too high.

- *Know when to disappear.* If the sides are at an impasse, the IT manager
  can "go dark" and avoid responding to vendor e-mail and voice mail;
  time is on the side of the buyer and the dearth of information will put
  increased pressure on the vendor if the vendor's negotiators perceive
  that the deal is slipping away.

- *Know when to say when.* When the negotiation is close to complete
  on all pricing, terms, and conditions, the manager should have at least
  one final concession at the ready; the vendor usually gives this
  final concession on the promise that the manager will sign the contract immediately.

- *Watch the licensing terms.* The team should carefully examine the licensing assignment rights in the contract. Often, applications vendors
  do not allow reassignment of the license. This can become a problem in
  the event the manager decides to outsource some or all of the application maintenance to a third party. The vendor may charge any third parties that the manager brings in to work on the system or even refuse to
  allow the third party to work on the system. Often, vendor contracts
  provide provisions revoking the license if maintenance fees are not
  paid. In those cases, the manager loses the ability to withhold maintenance dollars if he or she feels the dollars are not being allocated properly to development or if the vendor is not being responsive.

A variety of the key negotiating points that should be addressed in the vendor pricing conversations for application software is provided in Exhibit 10.22.

Vendor negotiations can be a daunting, difficult, and exhausting experience. However, it is also an unavoidable part of a system selection process
and has to be managed carefully to ensure the best pricing and terms. As a
CIO acquaintance of ours once remarked, "Every customer gets the system
they deserve."

RESOURCES

Requirements methodologies:

Derek J. Hatley, Peter Hruschka, and Imtiaz A. Pirbhai, *Process for System Architecture and Requirements Engineering* (New York: Dorset House, 2000).

David C. Hay and Barbara Von Halle, *Requirements Analysis: From Business Views
to Architecture* (Upper Saddle River, NJ: Prentice Hall, 2002).

Ian Sommerville, Pete Sawyer (Contributor), and Aan Sommerville, *Requirements
Engineering: A Good Practice Guide* (New York: John Wiley & Son, 2000).

Project management:

Jason Charvat, *Project Management Nation: Goals for the New and Practicing IT Project Manager—Guidance, Tools, Templates, and Techniques That Work!* (New York: John Wiley & Sons, 2002).

Richard Murch, *Project Management: Best Practices for IT Professionals* (Upper Saddle River, NJ: Prentice Hall, 2000).

Joseph Phillips, *IT Project Management: On Track from Start to Finish* (New York: McGraw-Hill Osborne Media, 2002).

The Project Management Institute. Available from www.pmi.org.

Negotiating:

Robert B. Cialdini, *Influence: The Psychology of Persuasion* (New York: William Morrow/Quill, 1993).

Roger Fisher and William Ury, *Getting to Yes* (New York: Penguin, 1991).

J. Edward Russo and Paul J. H. Schoemaker, *Decision Traps: Ten Barriers to Brilliant Decision-Making and How to Overcome Them* (New York: Fireside, 1990).

NOTE

1. Henry Ford, attributed.

11

Vendor Management

People who work together will win, whether it be against complex football defenses, or the problems of modern society.

—Vince Lombardi[1]

If, after the first twenty minutes, you don't know who the sucker at the table is, it's you.

—Unknown

This chapter outlines management practices for ensuring that the IT department manages outside vendors in a manner that delivers the most value to the company in exchange for considerations paid to the vendors, all the while working in a partnership with the vendor to further the aims of both the company and the vendor. The chapter emphasizes the high importance of properly managing vendors and provides techniques for monitoring and assessing vendors' performance. The chapter also covers the vendor management role within the IT department, how to take control of vendor relationships especially those inherited, how and when to recompete vendor contracts and provides guidance to the IT director on managing vendors in turmoil or financial trouble. The chapter is a companion to Chapter 10, which also contains a variety of critical vendor management concepts.

Why This Topic Is Important

Almost without exception, IT departments are highly reliant on a wide variety of vendors. Outside vendors provide the hardware, system software, application systems, networks, and peripherals that power most of the IT functions. Because IT managers get little training in managing outside partners, including measuring service levels, selecting service providers, and negotiating pricing and terms, many IT departments fall short in vendor management. This can be highly damaging to any IT department not only because of the reliance on vendors to provide mission-critical hardware, software, and services but also because of the high expenditures on outside vendors. Outside providers generally comprise between 20 percent and 40 percent of the typical IT budget. Failure to manage this expenditure suitably can be devastating.

A cooperative and amicable relationship is necessary to extract the most value out of vendor relationships, while applying good management practices that ensure that the vendor is performing up to expectations and meeting committed service levels. This can be challenging. A wide variety of vendors must be managed. Often, IT departments cover shortfalls in vendor performance by adding staff or other expenditures rather than confronting nonperforming vendors and instituting standard vendor management processes and procedures. IT directors and staff must work to hold nonperformers accountable.

Vendors, like most companies, also pay the most attention to the customers who provide their largest revenue stream or the customers who are most vocal. This means that smaller companies must learn to aggressively communicate their needs to vendors and to band with other small customers to influence vendor policies and priorities. It also means that larger companies with significant vendor spending should ensure that the vendor is reflecting their needs appropriately in product or service development priorities, rather than submitting to a vocal minority.

Topics discussed in this chapter include:

- The importance of establishing the vendor management function.
- How to work effectively with vendors to ensure that full value of technology investments can be achieved.
- How to build a mutually beneficial partnership with a vendor.
- How to take control of vendor relationships.
- The distinction between types of vendor contracts.
- Important steps in establishing new vendor relationships.
- Methods for establishing and managing vendor performance and service levels.
- Gaining value by working with the vendor's other customers.
- When and how to recompete vendor contracts.
- Approaches for managing vendors experiencing business difficulties.

Vendors as Partners

The most effective vendor relationships are the ones in which the vendor and customer build a close partnership. However, this relationship can be difficult to achieve. Vendors have a different set of incentives and priorities than the IT manager, and finding ways to work to mutual benefit takes effort and willingness on both sides to accomplish. Although we do not repeat them in this chapter, many of the techniques and approaches outlined in Chapter 10 on vendor selection are relevant to the ongoing management of vendors.

There are a host of ways for IT departments and vendors to work in partnership to mutual benefit. To illustrate the value and effect of a partnership, we take the example of a partnership with a packaged software provider. In a partnership, the vendor can provide a wide range of benefits to the customer, including:

- New features customized for the customer by the development team and included in the next release.
- Free minor application updates in advance of release.
- Access to alpha and beta tests for new applications or new functions in existing applications.
- Telegraphing major company announcements in advance of official notification.
- Concessions on license pricing for future purchases.
- Discounts on maintenance packages.
- Dedicated 24/7 emergency technical support representatives.
- Information on undocumented application features and application programming interfaces (APIs).
- Access to source code for customization or deeper understanding of application architecture.
- Introductions to other clients with similar technology platforms.

In return, the customer might provide:

- Acceptance of minor service level agreement (SLA) violations by the vendor.
- Continued business without any unnecessary recompetes.
- Detailed bug reports and product functionality and enhancement feedback.
- Press releases and references for vendor sales prospects.
- Specific letters of recommendation for vendor's sales calls.
- Contacts for vendors with companies in same industry or contacts from other professional relationships.

Most of these items are provided to the opposite party on a best-efforts basis. As shown in the previous list, items proffered in a partnership are of relatively low cost to either party, but they can be of tremendous value. This relationship could significantly increase the value of the contract without requiring arm's-length contract addendums whose cost and difficulty of enforcement may destroy much of the potential value.

The longer the relationship exists, the higher the potential benefits for both parties. For the vendor, sales costs are virtually eliminated and over time the cost-to-serve generally declines which results in long-term gross margin improvement. For the customer, the vendor's cost reductions are typically shared with the customer via pricing discounts. The customer's cost to manage the vendor also declines and "learning curve" costs from new vendor entrants are eliminated. Finally, the customer benefits from a vendor whose staff understands the business in intimate detail and can provide customer-specific solutions.

One of the most significant benefits of participating in a close relationship with a vendor is the opportunity to influence the vendor's product development process. This is particularly true for package applications but can apply to hardware and services vendors as well. Successful vendors have immense resources at their disposal for investment in current and future products. Software vendors have an income stream emanating from maintenance contracts to invest in enhancements and new system features. By partnering closely with vendors and providing input to the prioritization process for new feature or capability development, the client company can leverage vendor R&D investment amounts far in excess of the amounts it could dedicate to internal development. The client steers the product direction to its ultimate benefit.

One software vendor invited its top 25 customers to its corporate headquarters twice a year for product development and demonstration sessions. The product manager created a log of all enhancement requests, interface suggestions, and functionality recommendations from the biannual two-day affair and worked with the development staff to incorporate as many of the ideas as possible and appropriate. Although the software vendor had thousands of clients and an annual users' conference, these 25 clients drove a disproportionate amount of software enhancements and greatly benefited from partnering with the vendor.

An important fact to consider in building a partnership is that some vendors may wish to partner initially; however, the partnership can rapidly turn negative if problems arise. A variety of events can cause the partnership to go awry with the vendor, including turnover of key personnel, a merger/acquisition for the vendor or client, a strategic focus change for the vendor or client, financial difficulties for either party, or even another customer who is providing much greater benefits and monopolizing the vendor's attention and resources. In these cases, it is best to reevaluate the value of the partnership to ensure that the client organization continues to receive the expected partnership benefits.

In the final analysis, the customer is paying for the product and/or services. This should naturally put the customer in the position of most influence and provide final control of the terms of the relationship. When money has changed hands, vendors have a fiduciary obligation to discharge their contractual responsibilities. Vendors may try to take advantage of the relationship if the customer is unaware, too busy, or inexperienced in dealing with vendors. Savvy customers know that they are, ultimately, the "boss" in any vendor relationship. Given a choice between a partnership and an adversarial relationship, all parties prefer the former. However, if a partnership is difficult to achieve, the IT director should be certain that his or her company's needs are met by the vendor even if aggressive, confrontational action is required.

Vendor Management Role

The vendor management function in the IT department is vital to capture the benefits of vendor partnerships as discussed in the chapter. The IT director and direct reports should be intimately involved in building relationships with vendors. Other functions of the vendor management role should be delegated to an administrative resource. Tasks performed by the vendor management function include:

- Maintenance of all contracts.
- Assistance to IT managers in processing new contracts.
- Provide reports on vendor performance and contract status to management.
- Coordinate activities between internal IT teams and vendors.
- Define and enforce processes and procedures for vendor management.
- Assist with RFP and vendor selection administrative process.
- Develop standard approach to deal with each type of vendor.
- Summarize service level requirements by vendor.
- Execute vendor quality surveys.
- Track and report upcoming vendor milestone dates.
- Maintain deliverable signoff records.
- Report progress on fixed bid contracts (e.g., qualitative progress, percent complete versus percent billed).
- Analyze vendor pricing compared to industry average.
- Collect and distribute service level reports from vendors.

The tendency in most IT departments is to ignore the vendor management function and by default decentralize all vendor activities. However, the organization can benefit through reduced costs, reduced risk, and more effective communication between the company and its vendors by centralizing the function. The vendor management role helps ensure the company drives the relationship versus being driven.

Taking Control of Vendor Management

A defined process exists for taking control of vendor management. Most IT directors at some point will likely inherit a variety of disparate vendor relationships in various stages of health and efficacy. Without gaining control of these relationships, service problems can quickly arise from vendors in poor partnerships who are looking to take advantage of the chaos or changes in IT management at customer organizations or from benign vendors who are simply paying attention to the customers working hardest to manage their relationship. Without careful management, inattentive vendors can wreak havoc on IT departments; an IT management transition period or weak management of the function is a time when the vendor and client agendas can diverge, and the relationships deserve special attention and tight performance management during these times. Exhibit 11.1 depicts the vendor audit/cleanup process.

The first task is to assign the vendor management role to someone on the staff. This person will be responsible for the tasks previously described. This person will also be integral to the audit/cleanup process. The second task is to identify all current vendor relationships. These may exist in various sections of the IT department, business unit, functional units, and geographies. For every vendor relationship identified, all related legal, financial, and operational documentation should be collected in a single repository. The IT director should read each contract and make notes about service level commitments, prices, maintenance contracts, and evaluation/reporting procedures.

It can be difficult to locate the actual contracts for all service vendors in an IT shop. Particularly for long-standing relationships, the contracts may have been signed by an IT manager who has long departed and the original documentation lost. A contract may be filed in the purchasing department, legal department, or human resources department; it can be copied for use by

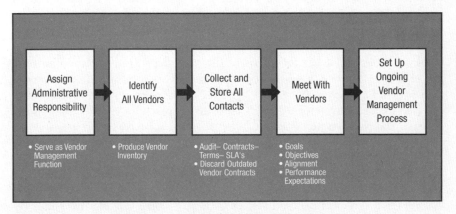

Exhibit 11.1   Vendor Audit/Cleanup Process

the IT department. Failing the location of an internal copy, the IT director can request a contract copy from the vendor. As a last resort, the IT director and vendor can renegotiate a contract to govern the ongoing relationship without necessarily changing the original terms. Often, long-standing contracts will have expired without renewal, while continuing use of the service or product. These situations create an ideal opportunity for the IT director to renegotiate the terms of the agreement.

As a next step, the IT director should meet individually with each vendor (if possible, depending on the number of vendors; otherwise select a vendor audit team) to gain a deeper understanding about the vendor, its organization, products and services, history of the vendor-client relationship, contractual obligations, recent events, and any outstanding issues. This vendor checkup provides a clear view on which vendors are true partners with the IT department and which vendors simply have arms-length relationships for specified products/services.

Finally, the IT director should rapidly install vendor performance management to manage the vendor relationships based on the self-reporting and audit cycles described in this chapter. This drives out underperforming vendors and ensures that money paid to vendors is providing the company the maximum possible return.

Beginning New Vendor Relationships

Getting off to a positive start with new vendors is critical to the success of projects and to the overall productivity of the IT department. Put processes in place to ensure that the organization is ready to work with the vendor on the agreed to install/start date. One process we have seen work well is a "readiness" check performed by the vendor manager. The "readiness" checklist is performed one week prior to the vendor coming onsite and is signed-off by all involved internal parties. It ensures that the internal team is free and ready to begin work with the vendor on the agreed date, the dependent hardware and software is ready to go, the work space is ready, the contract is signed and filed, and the vendor has reconfirmed the start date. If any of the items are not checked, the date is postponed. This process will ensure that no vendor shows up before the company is "ready." This saves critical down time for both internal teams and vendor teams. It helps to keep vendor costs down—in the spirit of the partnership hopefully benefiting the company in the long-term.

Vendor Contracts

A solid legal agreement should always form the foundation of any vendor relationship. While contract negotiations can be painful, contracts can often outlive the tenure of the individuals negotiating the terms on either side.

We have seen many contract negotiations fall short of the proper due diligence because the individuals involved had personal relationships or ample reason to trust one another. After these individuals left their respective firms, their successors are left to interpret what may have been agreed on but not documented.

In every case, the contract should explicitly set forth the terms that govern the relationship and define each party's responsibilities to the other in unambiguous detail. Further, the contracts for many vendor relationships, such as application software, are most often turgid, impenetrable, and complex. For purchases of any material significance, we recommend engaging attorneys or company legal counsel with experience negotiating contractual terms for technology assets or services. These professionals have seen the outcomes from poorly negotiated contracts and know which terms matter long-term, and they can identify the sometimes hidden, but significant, clauses in a contract.

The outcome of poor contract negotiations is often detrimental to the client company, who is generally the loser in interpreting ambiguities in the contract. In one case, an applications vendor found enough room for interpretation to ensure that the new functionality in its product be considered a "new product" and required new licenses to be purchased by the end clients. The functionality should have been included in a standard upgrade release and, therefore, provided free to all clients paying maintenance fees.

Negotiating the best terms for a vendor contract requires understanding the potential organization requirements not only today, but also in the future. In one case, we assisted a mid-size manufacturing company in the spin-off of a subsidiary unit. Fortunately, some forward-thinking person had negotiated terms that allowed the licenses for the ERP system used to run the business to be split between entities and reassigned in the case of such a transaction. This point was at variance to the standard vendor contract and would have likely resulted in significant new license cost from the vendor had it not been negotiated in advance.

In another case, a client decided to outsource its technology operations to a third party. The primary application vendor, also in the business of outsourcing, protested vigorously against a third party operating its system, arguing an invasion of their intellectual capital rights and asserting that their licenses could not be reassigned to third parties. Again, a prescient negotiator for the client had included the irrevocable perpetual right to assign the application license to any third-party vendor chosen as an outsourcing partner. Certainly, there was no consideration of outsourcing the technology department at the time of the contract signing, but the negotiation team made sure that all options were covered.

Below we define several important contract negotiating terms for services, software, and hardware contracts:

- *Insurance:* In many cases, clients taking on significant business risk require the vendor to maintain malpractice insurance (often called *errors and omissions* coverage [E&O]). In any case, critical vendors should be required to provide proof of general and professional liability coverage. Additionally, the client should be specifically named as an additional insured under the vendor policy.

- *Acceptance testing and deliverable sign-off:* Acceptance of services or delivery of software or hardware is probably the most important negotiating point. This is typically the point where payment is required. The risk is that the product does not perform as promised or the services are not completed as promised. To reduce the risk that the company will be obligated to pay regardless of performance, specific acceptance criteria should be constructed. For services, detail the specific deliverables required for satisfactory performance of the contract, the requirements for the deliverable, quality metrics for acceptance, and required delivery dates and milestones.

- *Assignment rights:* Software and hardware vendors generally like to restrict the assignment privileges of the customer. However, this is not in the customer's best interest. To allow for company reorganizations and potential merger and acquisition activity, the customer should include a provision to assign rights and transfer the contract in the event of ownership changes, reorganizations, and to subsidiaries and minority interest affiliates.

- *License and maintenance fees:* The best case in purchasing licenses is to obtain a perpetual, fully paid-up license that requires no annual license or maintenance fee. However, most software companies charge maintenance fees and aren't willing to support or provide upgrades unless an annual maintenance fee is paid. Set the future maintenance fees in advance otherwise the vendor will gain tremendous leverage during future negotiations of fees. Fees should begin only when the product passes the acceptance tests not when actually delivered.

- *Non-solicitaton clauses:* It is in the interest of both the client and the vendor to specify that neither party may solicit to hire each other's employees or solicit each other's customers both during the contract and for some period, usually 24 months after the termination of the contract. This avoids both staff poaching, as well as potential agency problems.

- *Description of products or services:* Ensure that the description of the product or service to be provided is unambiguous. In the case of software, specify the current version number of the application, include future versions, and potential major upgrades as "inclusive" of the definition of the product. This helps reduce the risk that the vendor will rename the product at the next major upgrade cycle and require additional license fees from customers in order to upgrade.

- *Right to withhold payment:* Ensure the right to withhold fees if vendor services are not properly delivered or product upgrades are not delivered as promised.

- *Disaster recovery:* Occasionally software provider licenses restrict the number of CPU's software may run on. Ensure that the contract provides the company the ability for mirroring, hot swapping, dual processing, and backup/recovery. With services, indicate who is responsible for backup/recovery of the development environment and the production application.

- *Dispute resolution:* Consider required mediation and arbitration alternatives that can reduce the cost of disputes and require negotiation prior to legal action. Also require notification in advance in writing for potential disputes.

- *Future pricing:* The vendor obtains significant leverage in the future if future pricing for products and services are not detailed in the contract. At a minimum, specify that future product pricing will be no more than the then current list less the current customer discount percentage. Ideally, the prices are specifically fixed.

- *Indemnification:* Vendors attempt to limit liability to the total sum of fees paid.

- *Liability:* Liability should be mutual with fair allocation of risk.

- *Outsourcing:* Provide the right for customer to transfer license to outsourcing partner without licensors consent and without fees. This enables the company to outsource a function without approval from the vendor.

- *Payment terms:* Payment terms specify the cash payments to be paid. Net 30 days is typical for service vendors. Allow for suspension of payments if vendor is not performing as agreed. Negotiate discounts for early payment.

- *Source code/working documents:* Most software contracts should allow for escrowing the source code of the application with a third-party escrow provider. This protects the company should the vendor fail; the escrow can be activated and the customer would receive the source code to the application. The fees for escrowing are very reasonable.

- *Warranty:* Require the vendor to warrant that the vendor has the right to license the software or provide the services. Warrant for Year 2000 compliance. Require disclosure of trojan horses or disabling devices built into software.

- *Training:* Negotiate free training with software products and specify in the contract.

- *Services discounts:* Pre-arrange volume discounts and specify in the pricing section of the contract.

The number of high-profile lawsuits involving hardware manufacturers, application providers, and professional services firms confirms that contract negotiation and tight management of the vendor relationship is crucial to

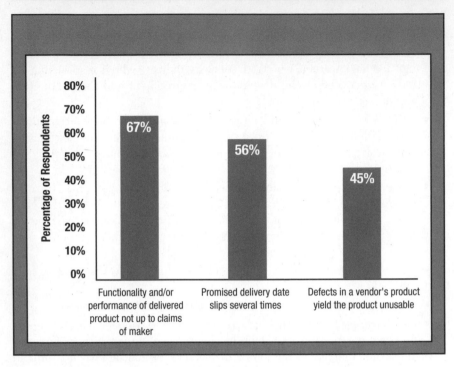

Exhibit 11.2   Primary Causes for Litigation in Technology Lawsuits

avoid business disruption and litigation, which can follow. In a study of technology vendor litigation, Cutter Consortium found that the top three causes for litigation include missing functionality or performance in the product, missed delivery or promise dates, and defects in the product, yielding it unusable.[2] Exhibit 11.2 shows the percentage of grounds claimed in the technology lawsuits researched by Cutter. A solid contract helps build a strong relationship by clearly articulating key provisions and avoiding ambiguous and off-the-record statements that lead to future disputes.

Managing Vendor Performance

A key piece of managing vendor relationships is mutually understanding expectations of the partnership and ensuring that the vendor fulfills those expectations. Often, the success or failure of the vendor in the IT department hinges on clearly setting performance metrics to be achieved and following through on those metrics. Ineffective IT departments rarely get past the first step of setting the metrics, and when they do, they do not follow up with periodic measurement of the vendor's performance.

The process is basic. For each vendor, define expected performance (may or may not be explicit in contract), track and monitor the performance, periodically report performance, take action to improve performance, or remove poor performing vendors. The designated vendor manager works in close connection with the IT director to manage vendor performance.

Because of the large number of vendors found in even small IT shops, determining measures and monitoring them can be a resource-intensive and, therefore, cost-prohibitive process. The most effective way to determine how to measure and evaluate vendors where the contract does not have specific deliverables (e.g., contract staffing vendors) is to ask them to provide metrics they believe are the most important determinants of their success with clients. Vendors know the most about their particular services and should be able to quickly articulate the top three to five metrics on which they should be evaluated. If they cannot identify how they should be evaluated, they are probably not a vendor that the IT department should be working with. The best vendors most often have internal benchmarks by which they measure their own performance, and they are usually happy to share those with customers who ask.

By having some vendors design their own performance metrics, incorporating them into contractual guarantees, and then having vendors self-monitor, the bulk of the effort to monitor and measure performance is absorbed by the vendor. To ensure that vendors are behaving honestly, the vendor manager should periodically and randomly audit one or two of the vendor-supplied, vendor-reported measures. If the vendor falls short, the potential of a random audit, coupled with contractual penalties, is generally enough to eliminate or at least minimize any dishonesty.

For the most mission-critical vendors, in addition to the vendor-driven approach outlined previously, the vendor manager and IT team should generate their own set of two to three key measures and perform the vendor assessments on a regular schedule. The IT director cannot afford to find out that a key vendor is falling short of agreed-on goals too late to mitigate the failure. The vendor manager should combine the key measures provided by the vendor with any other desired performance metrics to create a performance report card. This should be regularly completed and reviewed with the vendor to monitor ongoing performance and adherence to contractually established service level agreements (SLAs). If any SLAs have been violated, the customer can demand remediation in accordance with the contract specifications. Alternatively, in the spirit of partnership, the customer could make concessions in exchange for other benefits that could be provided without a monetary exchange, as illustrated in the previous section. In every case, the client should be rigorous in establishing and adhering to the regular reviews. Without these reviews, vendor relationships can go unmonitored for long periods, and significant problems can go unnoticed and unresolved.

In addition to vendor performance reviews, the vendor manager should periodically review all vendor contracts. This ensures that all service levels promised in the contract are being enforced or at least that goodwill is being built by not enforcing an agreed-on standard. Further, a review of the contract will ensure that any changes to terms or conditions based on changing business imperatives can be managed early on. We recommend re-examining every vendor contract annually at a minimum. For vendors on which the company has significant reliance, these reviews should be done on a quarterly basis.

Often, this periodic contract review is neglected by IT departments. A Cutter Consortium survey estimates that 7 percent of IT departments never review contracts, and fewer than half review contracts at greater intervals than annually.[3] Exhibit 11.3 shows research results in this area.

In all cases, the client should ensure that it can withhold any fees (maintenance or otherwise) becaue of the vendor in the case of contract breaches on the part of the vendor. One of the most rapid methods for getting the attention of a vendor experiencing performance problems is to withhold approval on accounts payable.

The speed with which vendors respond from the highest levels once a steady flow of receivables dries up can be remarkable. While this approach should be a last resort, it is generally successful. When it is not successful, the IT department has at least avoided continuing to fund a vendor that will not be part of the long-term picture and has saved money to invest in a relationship with a replacement vendor.

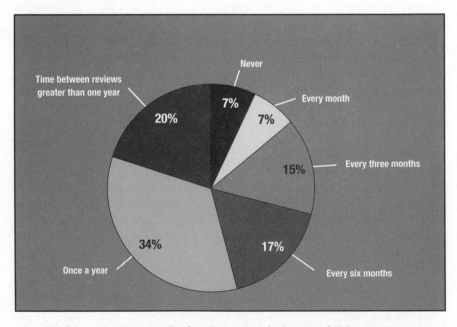

Exhibit 11.3   Contract Review Frequency in Surveyed IT Departments

Working with Vendors' Other Customers

One of the most important resources in managing vendors is information sharing with their other customers. There are usually well-established user groups for almost every product on the market with a reasonably sized client base. These groups typically communicate in online forums and Web sites. For some of the major products, regional or national user group meetings or conferences can help facilitate communication among users. These groups provide a wealth of information, such as:

- Latest news about the vendors and their affiliated service or product provider partner networks.
- Features, functions, and enhancements planned for future patches and releases.
- Best practices for using current software versions.
- Bug fixes and workarounds for common (or obscure) problems.
- Common maintenance contract terms and SLAs.
- Useful add-ins, bolt-ons, or third-party services.
- Informal answers to common questions.
- Direct response and ideas for addressing specific problems.
- General pricing and contract terms information.
- Shared metrics for vendor performance measurement.

While most IT departments usually pay attention to the "official" vendor-sponsored special interest groups, an often-overlooked and powerful tool for influencing vendors and driving pricing discounts is informal work with other customers in the same geographic region or industry. More direct interaction with other customers can provide deeper and more candid insights than are likely to be shared in a vendor-sponsored, public forum. Coordination with other vendor customers may reveal specific pricing information, specific service level agreements or vendor metrics, legal problems or issues with the vendor, and other information useful in negotiating with and managing the vendor. The best customer partners are those using the same vendor, located in the same locale, but in a different industry. While working with other vendor customers in the same industry can provide highly valuable information on specific applications of the vendor's products or services, the competitive dynamic usually minimizes the information that each party is willing to share. The IT director may want to consider coordinating informal periodic meetings between managers and directors to get together and exchange information as a small group. The information exchanged, particularly on pricing or input to product development, can be used to win some concessions from a vendor or to significantly influence the research and development process. This is particularly true for smaller customers of a given vendor. As noted in the opening to this chapter, small customers often find it difficult to manipulate vendor agendas. By banding together with several other small customers, they multiply their leverage considerably. Small customers should take the advice of Ben Franklin in working with other small customers: "Yes, we must, indeed, all hang together, or most assuredly we shall all hang separately."[4]

Other sources of information can include analysts, consultants, publications, and even the vendor's competitors. A detailed list of these information sources is included in Chapters 6 and 10, which cover information gathering as part of the initial vendor selection or standardization process. These information sources (research analysts, Internet sites, consultants, and others) continue to be highly valuable sources of information on the vendor.

A frequently underused source of information for IT directors is technology industry analysts working in investment banks. These professionals are typically charged with having a complete understanding of how the company is expected to perform in the future. One of the most important ingredients for their research is the current opinions and experiences of customers. For this reason, analysts are usually enormously interested in talking with a vendor's customers about their experiences, and they may even collect informal surveys to quantify user opinions. These analysts can become a nerve center of information about particular vendors, providing insight into the health of the vendor, marketplace changes, and competitive outlook. In exchange for customer viewpoints and opinions, they are usually willing to share not only their objective third-party opinions concerning vendor direction and performance, but also their published periodic research reports. Further, the analysts are often willing to facilitate the introduction of the IT director to other customers for the formation of the informal information-sharing groups discussed previously.

In summary, the wide variety of information available on vendors with a minimum of research and effort should not be overlooked as a critical component of managing vendors, setting metrics, and ensuring best pricing.

Vendor Recompetes

If the vendor selection process is done correctly and the vendor relationship is properly managed as a mutually beneficial partnership, the need to recompete business should be infrequent. However, it is important to periodically retest the market for enhanced products, services, and pricing. A recompete may not result in a new vendor choice, but it can be the springboard to introducing new thinking to an existing vendor relationship or to an IT department. As a long-term client once remarked to a services provider, "We like you a lot and value the partnership; you just don't necessarily have the market cornered on good ideas." Times to consider a recompete include:

- The end of a lengthy (5+ years) contract. Products and services will have evolved considerably over the duration of a contract; retesting the market for pricing, product, and service changes is appropriate at the culmination of a long-term contract.
- Major changes in the marketplace in terms of pricing or service quality. Newer technologies or technologies in rapidly changing markets often improve in reliability and diminish in cost rapidly as the marketplace matures.
- Emergence of additional service providers offering better and/or more cost-effective products and services.
- Discontinuous changes in the technology, necessitating a new product or service.
- Any severe performance problems with the vendor resulting in damage or potential damage to the customer's business.
- Significant structural changes at the vendor or client (e.g., merger, acquisition, divestiture).
- Material financial problems at the vendor or client.
- Mandate from the IT steering committee to investigate additional vendor options.
- Overreliance on a single vendor, resulting in business continuity exposure.

When any of these events occur, a recompete should be considered, but a full vendor selection as outlined in Chapter 10 should not necessarily be completed. Exhibit 11.4 shows a decision tree for deciding whether or not to recompete. The first step should be an economic analysis to determine the expected value to be created by recompeting the contract. The benefits to be gained should include:

- The difference between the present value of all the expected expenditures from a new vendor and the present value of all the expected expenditures from the current vendor.
- Other decreased internal costs (e.g., maintenance, management, training).
- Increased revenue.
- Improved control over the business (reduced risk).

In many cases, there are significant switching costs associated with changing a vendor. The costs should include all costs involved with switching

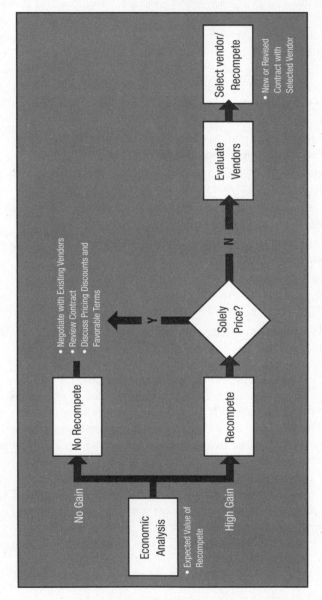

Exhibit 11.4   Vendor Recompete Decision Tree

between the original vendor and a new vendor. Examples of these costs should include, but are not limited to:

- Time and resources to be expended in a new vendor selection processes.
- Any mandatory close-out costs dictated in the current contract.
- Initial upfront costs that must be incurred with the new vendor, such as additional hardware, software, documentation, training, and maintenance contracts.
- Internal resources lost to managing and implementing the transition.
- Any potential system downtime during the transition.
- Accelerated depreciation on assets whose lifetime is reduced by the vendor switch.
- Additional operating costs that must be incurred while learning the new system (e.g., management time, training).

Even with significant gains from switching vendors, the costs can often heavily outweigh the benefits. Vendors are very aware of these switching costs, and these costs are precisely the reason they are often able to increase prices for current customers while offering "great deals" to new customers. This switching cost only further emphasizes contractual obligations and vendor measurement issues, as discussed previously in this chapter. The IT director should understand vendor decisions that entail high switching costs (e.g., ERP systems, high-dollar hardware) and those relatively easy to switch (e.g., telecommunications services, contract staffing providers) and aggressively manage the inclusion of tight performance metrics in the contracts of the vendors with the highest switching costs.

If the economic analysis shows that the benefits still greatly outweigh the costs, a recompete should proceed to the next step. If the reason for the recompete is purely price, a simplified form of the analysis shown to the vendor usually results in a price concession. If the reason for the analysis is more than price or the current vendor will not budge on price, the recompete should proceed using the standard rigorous vendor selection process detailed in Chapter 10, which has been organized to facilitate limited-effort vendor selection processes where necessary.

The length of the contract up for recompete should be based on the potential discounts available from vendors in exchange for a guaranteed term. For technologies that are rapidly changing and are rapidly coming down the cost curve (e.g., telecommunications services), the contracts should be no longer than a year. The savings of a new contract usually more than compensate for the lost term discounts on the original contract. For vendors that are difficult or unlikely to be changed out often by the department (e.g., ERP package), longer term contracts with heavy discounting are more appropriate.

Managing Troubled Vendors

Because of the wide variety of vendors used by a given IT department, inevitably, one or more of the vendors will experience financial difficulties. The forward-looking IT director usually has ample warning of these troubles, particularly if he or she is participating in the informal forums and alternative information gathering discussed in this chapter. In these cases, it is crucial for the IT manager to aggressively protect the company's interests by ensuring that adequate coverage for the vendor product or service is available and that the company's financial exposure to the vendor is minimized.

For well-established, competitive vendor marketplaces, ensuring adequate coverage in the case of vendor failure should be a relatively straightforward process of assessing competitive offerings and estimating the associated switching costs. For vendors providing highly specialized niche products or services, the IT manager may have to conduct additional research to find alternative products, approaches, or workarounds. Often, the effort of conducting this research can be shared among several customers who coordinate through the informal information-sharing groups.

The financial exposure to a vendor can come from a variety of sources. Prepaid or partially paid orders for equipment, prepaid or currently due maintenance fees, or other contractually obligated sums are common instances. We have seen many companies victimized by vendors that file bankruptcy while significant receivables have been paid by customers in advance of product delivery. Not only is delivery of the product delayed, but the monies spent to acquire the product are usually lost forever. The IT director should work with the CFO or finance department to minimize the risks of lost capital and work with the vendor to ensure that contractually obligated amounts due result in actual services received by the client. In extreme cases, the company must halt payment to the vendor and file a law suit to line-up for restitution when the vendor refuses to refund for services not performed. Many times the filing of the law suit will provide leverage—the vendor cannot usually raise money until the suit is settled, which provides motivation for the vendor to come to the negotiating table.

In one client situation, a worried IT director consulted us about the quarterly maintenance fee requested by a software vendor. While not concerned with the stability of the package, which was installed and operating properly, the director was worried that additional money invested in maintenance fees would be lost if the vendor continued to struggle. Careful research indicated that the vendor was indeed in serious trouble, and the client delayed the $100,000 maintenance payment based on various vendor contract breaches. One month later, the vendor filed Chapter 7 bankruptcy, leaving no hope of additional software development or application support.

The impact of $100,000 spent for services that would never be delivered would have been devastating for the IT budget of this client.

In every case, the IT director should ensure that the IT steering committee is fully informed of the company's operational risk and financial exposure because of troubled vendors. The IT steering committee can be instrumental in helping reduce the risk and can help the director manage the advance planning and alternative brainstorming needed to minimize the potential risks.

Summary

As emphasized throughout this chapter, well-executed vendor management is one of the keys to success for the IT director. Because the expense outlays are so large and the dependence on outside vendors so high, vendor management is an area that the IT director cannot afford to ignore. The most experienced IT directors find ways to share the burden of vendor management by instituting self-monitoring programs, which force vendors to report their own metrics and results and agree to be subject to periodic random audits of the scoring and performance. Further, they carefully allocate their attention in proportion to the vendor's overall importance to the business. These IT directors approach vendor relationships with a keen appreciation of the value of a partnership but also ensure that the vendors are delivering the value promised. Finally, the directors ensure that they receive a steady supply of information concerning critical vendors from objective third-party sources, including other customers and industry research analysts.

NOTES

1. Vince Lombardi, "Vince Lombardi's Quotes about Teamwork," Available from http://www.vincelombardi.com/quotes/teamwork.html (December 19, 2002).
2. "78% of IT Organizations Have Litigated," *The Cutter Edge* (Cutter Consortium, April 9, 2002).
3. See note 2.
4. Benjamin Franklin at the signing of the Declaration of Independence (July 4, 1776), *Bartlett's Familiar Quotations*, 17th ed. (New York: Little, Brown, November 2002).

PART III

Senior Executive IT Management

12

Working with the Business

The play was a great success, but the audience was a disaster.

—Oscar Wilde[1]

They said come skating;
They said it's so nice.
They said come skating;
I'd done it twice.
They said come skating;
It sounded nice. . . .
I wore roller—
They meant ice.

—Shel Silverstein[2]

This chapter addresses the frequent failures in the day-to-day working relationship between the IT department and business users. This failure to work well together occurs at all levels of organizations—from IT management to IT staffers and from senior business managers to systems users.

Why This Topic Is Important

A key cause of IT ineffectiveness is the inability of IT personnel to work well with the business side of the organization. Sometimes IT leadership and staff fail to communicate clearly (or at all) with the business leaders and users and make little or no attempt to understand what is important to the business. The business leaders begin to ignore the IT department and make key decisions impacting IT without input from the IT department.

Failure to resolve these issues results in a variety of negative outcomes for both the IT department and the business units. The IT organization usually becomes more insular and internally focused, withdrawing even further from an effective relationship with the business. The business and other functional units, in the meantime, reduce their reliance on IT by hiring their own IT personnel and creating their own internal IT departments to compensate for the shortfall in service.

This is usually the beginning of a downward spiral in the relationship between IT and the business. IT staff complain that they are often brought in after the fact on key business decisions and are bypassed by the business on new projects, which are then later turned over to IT to support or, worse, "save." Applications and hardware that do not adhere to standards or architecture cause major irritation and skyrocket support costs. The business maintains that IT neither understands nor attempts to understand business priorities and uses failings in IT to further distance itself from any attempts at reconciliation. The result is an IT department struggling to remain relevant, and business units making one-off suboptimal decisions on IT matters that do not fall within their knowledge or specialty area. This scenario is one of the principle ways that companies wind up with the heterogeneous environments described in Chapter 6, and the symptoms described in Chapter 2.

Topics discussed in this chapter include:

- Why communication breakdowns so frequently occur between IT and the business.
- Specific actions IT managers and staff can take to help bridge the communication gap.
- The importance of personal relationships between IT and business users.
- How personal relationships between the IT director and the senior management team can positively influence IT.
- How to avoid the "tragedy of the commons" and the associated high costs in IT.
- What the senior management team can do to help IT improve decision making.
- How the IT department can ensure that it achieves proper "mindshare" from key decision makers throughout the organization.

Benefits of Improving the IT/Business Relationship

A solid relationship between the IT department and the rest of the corporation is critical for both IT personnel and IT unit success. It is also imperative in order to transform IT from an under-used, unappreciated cost center to a proactive, highly regarded business enabler. The most notable benefits include:

- Ability to engage at the senior management level on both IT and business issues.

- Improved ability for department to endure difficult times.
- Ability to sell technology initiatives to the business.
- Greater IT employee satisfaction, alignment, and productivity.
- Increased ability to attract and retain talented IT people.
- Increased success of technology initiatives.
- Increased use of corporate IT department.

A good relationship enables most of the abilities that are required to run a successful IT department, thus, improving and managing the IT/business relationship is a necessary condition for success.

The relationship can actually be measured using specific factors that influence the strength/weakness of the relationship. These factors include:

- *Reliability:* The degree to which the business believes that products and services are delivered with reliability (activities and services run when they are supposed to).
- *Quality:* The degree to which the business believes that the products and services are delivered with quality (requirements met, professionally engineered, etc.).
- *Appeal:* IT personnel are generally liked from a cultural and intelligence standpoint.
- *Leadership:* Degree to which the IT leadership provides vision, business value, and builds a high-performance team.
- *Management:* Level to which people respect the IT management team and their ability to manage processes, procedures, and personnel.
- *Customer focus:* IT cares about users and results, not technology; strong commitment to deadlines.
- *Employee quality:* The level of overall talent of the IT employees, their fit culturally with the rest of the company, and communication skills and performance.
- *Financial performance:* Ability to manage budget, limit or eliminate project cost overruns, and deliver IT portion of ROI promises.
- *Satisfaction:* The overall level of satisfaction with IT performance experienced by the business.

Without acknowledging that the above factors influence the overall relationship between the IT department and the business units, it is difficult to develop specific improvement initiatives. The first step in improving the relationship is an audit of these factors. Grade each factor and set the baseline. Then develop goals to improve the weak factors. We discuss specific items that can dramatically improve the relationship by driving these factors.

How to Improve the Relationship between IT and the Business

In a March 2002 article titled "IT's Rodney Dangerfield Complex," Tischelle George highlighted the difficulties that many IT departments experience in working with the business. The author quotes the recently promoted CIO of a major corporation, who perceives as one of his biggest challenges overcoming the fact that the IT department "gets no respect" from the business. In fact, the article continues, "IT was left out of business-process or technology-related discussions."[3]

Set Goals for Each Level of the IT Organization

For each level of the IT organization, set goals and activities required for the next performance cycle. Divide the organization into levels appropriate for the unit. For example, one might segment the unit into four levels as follows: (1) the CIO/IT director; (2) the direct reports/senior managers; (3) the project managers; and, finally, (4) the analyst, operator, programmer, and DBA level. For each of the four levels, specific "business relationship" goals would be set. Taking the CIO as the first level, set goals around the factors that the CIO can affect. These include leadership, management, customer focus, and financial management. The CIO has the greatest influence in improving these factors, so specific targets should be determined. Additionally, activities that strengthen the IT/business ties should be detailed. Some examples include: The CIO will meet every two weeks with each business unit leader individually; meet every month with the IT steering committee; will tour one plant, five customers, two suppliers, and one functional department each quarter; will sponsor the IT newsletter; and so on. The CIO's direct reports have the most influence over management, quality of employees hired, and project reviews—goals around these factors are appropriate. Example goals for this group might include: executing the customer (end-user) satisfaction survey in January and June, meeting monthly with at least one business unit leader, ensuring 100 percent of project reviews are completed at project completion, and so on. Other levels in the organization should have business communication and activity goals as well.

Improve Social Interaction with the Business

One of the major causes of communication disconnects between the business and IT is a lack of personal relationships between IT team members and business users. When the personal relationships are absent, the number of interactions and flow of communication is much lower. A lack of personal relationships makes IT an easy target when business users become frustrated.

This is particularly true when the IT department is geographically distant, or otherwise physically separated, from the rest of the business.

A highly effective way of promoting relationships between the parties is to facilitate informal interactions. A typical way that we have seen work includes the implementation of lunch-and-learn sessions led by IT or the business. In these informal lunches, a member of the business or IT team presents a topic of mutual interest, usually related to his or her job function.

Another very effective method for improving communication is starting an IT business "seat rotation" where IT team members, particularly those team members from the applications development and support areas, spend one to two days per week sitting with the business users. Although the team must sometimes solve a few technical issues to make this happen (e.g., acquiring laptops for team members or otherwise enabling them to work outside their normal seating area), the benefits of improved communication and personal relationships at the staff level far outweigh the costs.

The relationships must be improved at the management level as well. The IT director must work to create and improve his or her personal relationships with the senior management team in particular. The IT steering committee is the ideal vehicle for accomplishing this and provides a formal venue for frequent get-togethers with the senior management team. The IT director should seek informal get-togethers with the senior management team as well.

One of our clients had a particularly unproductive IT business relationship. We asked the IT director to set a personal quota of at least two lunches with business managers per week and one dinner per month. Gradually, over a period of a few weeks, some of the seemingly intractable tensions between IT and the business began to relax as the flow of communication and relationships improved.

The IT director should keep a mental count of the frequency of informal interactions between IT and the business, particularly for geographically distant groups of users. Time can pass more rapidly than the manager realizes, and the users can become increasingly disaffected. In one instance, our client had a manufacturing plant located several hours drive from the corporate headquarters, which housed the IT department. During a plant visit, we asked the senior managers when someone from IT last visited. The business team couldn't remember, but was certain it had been more than a year. They had hired their own IT support staff in the meantime. If necessary, a monthly calendar with joint business-IT events can facilitate the process.

Improve Verbal and Written Communication Skills

IT staffers often suffer from a reputation—deserved or not—for an inability to engage in effective verbal communication. Whether this is true or not, it is certainly an area in which almost anyone can benefit from an improvement in skills. Furthermore, a crucial part of the IT staff role is to negotiate with vendors, persuade business managers, and interview business users, all of which require better-than-average verbal communication abilities.

Richard Shell, a professor of legal studies and management at the Wharton School of the University of Pennsylvania, made a study of the communications skills of technical executives. In a March 2002 article in *CIO Magazine,* he provides feedback on how technical managers should approach communication with business users:

> I have done work with more technically oriented people and they have this problem . . . they think the goal is to sit down and craft out the right answer. They don't give any thought to the fact that it matters who makes the proposal. Or that there's going to need to be a compromise because the other person needs to feel like he or she has had a hand in the solution. Even if the compromise is less optimal than the technically oriented person would like, it's better to have a nonoptimal decision that the other guy really implements than it is to have an optimal decision that everybody resists. This notion of being persuasive and getting a commitment—not just being right—is really hard to learn.[4]

The best IT directors spend much of their time communicating both internally and externally. IT departments are notoriously bad at written communications. While generally very structured thinkers, IT team members are often too rushed or harried to construct appropriately clear, well-written e-mails or memorandums.

One of the best examples of this phenomenon is an e-mail received from a manager in the IT department in response to a relatively straightforward request from a business unit manager. This e-mail, while a particularly egregious example, is not necessarily a major departure from the norm for e-mail communications emanating from the IT department.

In the copy of the e-mail that follows, the names have been disguised to protect the guilty, but the formatting, grammar, spelling, punctuation, and content remain unaltered.

- - - - -Original Message- - - - -

From: <Phil Smith—SVP>
Sent: Thursday, June 20, 2002 10:47 A.M.
To: <John Doe—IT manager>
Subject: Need help; please explain priorities

John—

The Accounting conversion team is telling me that you did not get the desktops in Colorado converted on Friday per your previous commitment and that some of the Utah desktops are still not converted.
What happened?

- - - - -Response- - - - -

"Yes the part that the machines did not get converted on Friday is correct. The original commitment I made was that when the machines from the 4 people in accounting where done being used on Friday or early Monday they would then bring there machines into IT and we would convert them. I spoke with Jane and they we not using it that day. On Tuesday at 12:05 I began the conversation of all 4 machine and they were all up on the new version by 12:35 P.M. (TUESDAY). I understand that there are problems with the software in Utah that Jill is aware of and Chicago was receiving the same error they were receiving in Utah. I just spoke to Jill about 10 minutes ago and she said she has a call into Jane for a different problem with a candidate that says he is assigned on a project and she removed him but it still says he is on a project (or something to that affect) as I am unfamiliar with how they use the accounting system and so forth. Since we only have 4 staff in Colorado what machines am I missing? Jane's desktop is up and running and she turned in her laptop to be rebuilt? Is that what the complaint is? As of what day is this information that you were given? I realize today is Thursday but I am unaware of any more machines that need to be converted. If there are more that need the software on them please have someone contact the IT helpdesk and let us know who's machines still need to be converted updated or installed on. We will gladly install the software as needed. I showed a few other people in IT how it installed and we are ready to install it whenever and wherever it needs to be put. Also to let you know the T1 sprint cloud in New York was upgraded on Friday from a 256k to 768k and the feedback I am getting back from Stan is the speed increase since that is great.

A relatively straightforward question was asked, and the response is literally impossible to decipher. Not only is the content impossible to understand, but also, the author has avoided even the slightest attempt at formatting or punctuation that might have at least improved the readability of the response. Sadly, this type of written communication often emanates from an IT department. Because the original request came from a member of the senior management team, we can also reasonably assume that this represents the highest standard that the respondent can achieve.

Because IT team members must often send global e-mails or e-mails to large numbers of corporate users simultaneously, they should be trained in how to construct the ideal communication. E-mail communications should provide a bottom-line message as the very first item in the communication. This ensures that those who tend to ignore communications with IT will get the most important part of the message and avoids the common complaint that IT is not clear in its communication. The e-mail should also include some additional information to avoid the common complaint that IT is too abrupt in its communications. An example of a better e-mail follows:

> To: All corporate users
> Subject: E-mail access will be down tomorrow, June 25, for 2 hours from 9 to 11 P.M.
>
> Corporate users—
>
> The e-mail system will be upgraded tomorrow, June 25, from 9 P.M. until 11 P.M. Users will be unable to access or send e-mail during that time.
>
> Questions may be directed to the IT team.
>
> Why are we doing this? The e-mail system is being upgraded to a new operating system and server. This should noticeably improve performance for all users and provide more reliable access. The upgrade tasks will include the installation of a new server, the archiving of old e-mail data, and the migration of e-mail accounts to the new machines. We will be taking a full backup of the system in advance to guard against any loss of e-mail. No special preparation on the part of the user is required. We will send a global voice mail to all corporate users as soon as the procedure is complete.

Finally, the IT team should not just improve the content of its communication, but also the frequency and reason. IT is often accused of not informing users of status frequently enough during emergencies or of not providing ample warning of system maintenance or planned outages. An improved awareness within IT of how its actions may affect business users and a commitment to communicate those actions clearly, in advance where possible, will vastly improve the IT-business relationship.

The IT team should also work to determine the best medium—verbal or written—for a given communication. The choice of channel can dramatically affect how well the communication is received. "Written communications are lousy at changing people's minds," claims Steven Kerr, a vice president at General Electric. "Writing is such a seductive medium . . . it's cheap, you can get the message to everyone at the same time, and you go home thinking you've done your job. But you have no way of knowing whether your audience gets it until it's too late."[5]

The IT team should pre-communicate sensitive issues or items requiring persuasion verbally and in person. Kerr continues, "[In person] you can immediately gauge whether your message is confusing people or causing more controversy than you expected because you can see their faces as they are receiving your message." Written communications documenting the previous meetings can then follow.[6]

Hold the Business Units Accountable

As counterintuitive as it might seem, holding the business unit personnel accountable for their responsibilities, both on projects and in relationship building with IT personnel, will actually improve and strengthen the IT-business relationship and respect for IT. Clear responsibilities for business unit personnel should be detailed in project charters and plans. Business unit employees must be held accountable for the activities and deliverables they are responsible for. In many cases, IT cannot get the help from a business unit it needs to complete a project. Yet, when the project deadline slips, the failure is typically blamed on the IT project team.

Since business unit personnel don't report to the CIO, grievance and issues with business personnel typically follow the appropriate chain of command. Ultimately, the CIO can discuss problems with the head of the business unit in extreme cases. Regardless of the discussion, it is important for IT to let the business unit know when they are failing to provide the necessary resources. These discussions should be documented and discussed in front of the IT steering committee. Projects with insufficient business unit resources should either be postponed or re-prioritized in the scheme of activities the business unit is involved in, so business unit personnel can re-prioritize their time to the necessary level and correct projects. In the case of performance problems with a business unit resource, that resource should be replaced as soon as possible to eliminate project risk.

Ultimately, most people like to be held accountable for their commitments. It reinforces the fact that their work is important and valued. In the long run, holding business unit resources accountable will enable IT to successfully complete more projects in less time. Ultimately, the business unit will be pleased with the quality, rigor, and timeliness of projects executed under this management philosophy. IT customer satisfaction levels and respect will increase. From time to time, the approach causes discomfort and conflict, but in the long run, it ensures the success of the relationship.

Build Communication and Relationship Attributes into Personnel Reviews

What gets measured gets managed as the popular saying goes. This is true of relationship building and communication. The personnel review forms for each level of the IT organization should include a section for assessing both relationship building with the business as well as the communication (written and verbal) skills of the individual. First, this has the benefit of assessing individual team members on a very important success criteria. Second, it reaffirms the importance in the mind of the individual employee that those are two skills necessary for excellent performance in their job.

Further, if those two attributes are missing from review forms, it has the double negative effect of reinforcing their unimportance.

Recruit Staff from the Business Side

One way to cross fertilize IT and business units is to hire business unit staff for appropriate IT roles. This is a double win for the IT department. First, they get a known quantity based on prior working relationships. Second, they get a person who has already built strong relationships in the business unit and can use those to further the mission of the IT department. Before looking for outside candidates, attempt to "recruit" star performers from the business units when there is skill fit. The most likely position to be filled by a business unit employee is the business analyst role, which can typically be filled by business unit analysts and super users. Additionally, administrative assistants, testers, functional experts (e.g., accounting), and managers are good positions to fill via business unit employees. Obviously, IT shouldn't "steal" employees from business units, so clear and proper communication and reciprocal agreements with business unit leaders are required.

Promote IT

Promoting the accomplishments, objectives, and priorities of the IT department is critical to improving communication among the various stakeholders in the company. Do not assume that everyone in the company knows the IT department's priorities or its promised service levels and performance against those. Most corporate employees outside IT probably don't even know what service levels mean or the rationale for setting them.

Communicate to the business via multiple methods including marketing material, e-mail, newsletters, and the Intranet. These should be targeted to the distinct "customers" of the IT department. First, define the customers, then determine effective mediums for communicating to them and, finally, execute and deliver appropriate content using the determined mediums. Many IT departments we work with publish newsletters to the entire company. The most common mistake is to make the newsletters "technology" focused and not customer or business focused. Explain how IT is helping the company accomplish its goals (e.g., building revenue or reducing costs). Report on the performance of IT and its track record of delivering business-critical projects and SLAs. Make sure to periodically explain the rationale for the SLA metrics.

Communicating mandates and priorities determined by the IT steering committee is also important. Employees may not understand why the IT department is implementing a financial accounting software package instead of a warehouse management system, for example. Disgruntled workers on the warehouse floor might be saying, "Why do they keep tinkering with the accounting software when we can't even ship out multiple orders in one shipment. It makes no sense." Reporting in a newsletter that the corporate strategy entails tightening up financial accounting processes and thus IT is implementing new account software can bridge the unknown and raise the perception of IT accomplishments. Finally, relentlessly self-promote IT accomplishments like third-party industry awards received by the department. These will go a long way in positively shaping outside perception.

Build Online Communication Mechanisms

A corporate Intranet is a great medium to both deliver news and provide service to internal customers. IT can be the lead department if the company does not already have an Intranet. Building an IT page with features such as news, announcements, personnel directory, project statuses, and team work spaces can serve as both a communication and a productivity enhancement. One goal of the IT director is to make doing business with the IT department as easy and simple as possible. Developing a one-stop location to request office moves, phone extension changes, service requests, new employee notifications, project request forms, methodologies, online training, and so on will greatly help the effort, drive customer satisfaction, and improve IT's relationship with the business.

Make the Changes Permanent

It can be difficult to change the communication skills of the IT department and even harder to begin to build personal relationships where none previously existed. The best way to ensure that the IT team members adopt an open, communicative approach with the business is for the IT director to lead by example. An IT director whose verbal and written communications are clear and concise and who maintains close professional and personal relationships with corporate managers outside the IT department serves as a compelling example to his or her team.

The IT director should also implement formal and informal non-technical training and development programs that help the staff learn and practice the requisite communications skills.

Informal methods, such as books and self-study courses in communication, are an easily executed approach. More formal training can be provided by a wide variety of vendors, such as non-credit courses at local colleges. Further, the IT director should encourage the team's participation in outside, nontechnical speaking groups, such as Toastmasters.

Achieving major cultural change in the IT department can be challenging. To encourage compliance, as well as to send a clear signal to the organization that these are important issues, the IT director should make improving verbal and written communications an integral part of the staff appraisal process. Excellent communications skills should be a prerequisite for promotion within the department.

NOTES

1. Oscar Wilde, "Humorous Quotes of Oscar Wilde." Available from http://www .workinghumor.com/quotes/oscar_wilde.shtml (December 20, 2002).

2. Shel Silverstein, "Come Skating," *Light in the Attic* (New York: Harper & Row, 1981).

3. "IT's Rodney Dangerfield Complex," *Information Week* (March 28, 2002). All Rights Reserved. Reprinted with permission.

4. Danielle Dunne, "Q&A with Richard Shell, How to Communicate What's on Your Mind," *CIO Magazine* (March 1, 2002). Copyright © 2002 CXO Media, Inc. Reprinted with permission.

5. Christopher Koch, "The Way You Say It," *CIO Magazine* (November 15, 1996). Copyright © 2002 CXO Media, Inc. Reprinted with permission.

6. See note 5.

13

IT Budgeting and
Cost Management

Economy does not lie in sparing money, but in spending it wisely.
—Thomas Henry Huxley (1825–1895), British biologist and educator[1]

I will veto again and again until spending is brought under control.
—Ronald Reagan, 40th U.S. President, on vetoing a bill that
would have extended $2 billion in federal loan guarantees to farmers.[2]

This chapter presents a practical overview of IT budgeting and cost containment practices for the IT director. In creating the department budget, the IT director must analyze a large number of variables and balance multiple competing priorities, while devising the most cost-effective approach for delivering mission critical services. Because of the impact the budget has on the IT manager's ability to run an effective department, budget creation is one of the most important jobs an IT manager has.

The chapter is organized in four key sections:

1. *Budget components:* Key components of the IT budget and the typical ratios of spending in each component.
2. *Budget process:* Two processes for completing the annual budgets.
3. *IT cost drivers:* An overview of key cost drivers in the budget and strategies for reducing costs.
4. *Additional IT budget considerations:* Managing capital expenditures, cost audit practices, contingencies planning, managing the budget, chargeback mechanisms, lease/buy decisions, and handling out-of-budget business unit requests.

The first section describes key components of the IT budget, such as software, hardware, labor, and what ratios between the components the IT director should expect to see. The process section presents two methods for creating the budget and compares their merits. The cost drivers section covers key items that drive IT costs that affect the year-to-year change in the operating and capital budgets. Next, the chapter presents a number of strategies for minimizing IT costs, especially infrastructure and capital expenditures. Finally, the chapter presents a number of key management considerations for the IT manager to contemplate, such as lease versus buy decisions, audits, chargeback mechanisms, and so on.

Why This Topic Is Important

At a basic level, the IT director is judged on the department's output versus operating and capital input required. The lower the capital input required for the same high output, the better the ratio, and the actual effectiveness of the IT manager is judged to have increased. Effective management of capital is of prime concern to both senior executives and the IT manager; thus, it is a topic of high importance.

Successful management of the IT department depends on the IT director's ability to operate a fiscally sound unit. It also entails the IT director making good decisions about spending priorities and ensuring that these spending priorities are aligned with the direction of the business. A good IT director also ensures that the bulk of discretionary spending is focused on fulfilling the demands of business units and in support of projects and initiatives focused on revenue-generating activities.

IT directors may not have formal training or education in the business and budget management processes, and thus learn via on-the-job training. This makes the responsibility a challenge, especially in difficult economic environments or when the company is in cost-cutting mode.

Compounding the issue, IT directors face unabated requests for technology, a rapidly shifting technology environment, and constantly changing vendor landscape, which all combine to confuse the IT economic analysis and spending decisions.

Chapter 3 addresses how to develop a benchmark range for IT spending. The IT director should use this as a general guide to double-check the IT budget.

A failed budget process, budget decisions, or poor management of fiscal responsibilities during the year, resulting in high budget variances has serious implications for the IT directors career. The corporate senior management team, CEO, CFO, lenders, and shareholders expect companies to plan well, and accomplish their tasks within the plan. Because the company projected income, cash flow requirements, and capital requirements are based on budgets, the need for precise budget forecasting and aggressive ongoing management of the budget is critical. Going back to the CFO to ask for an additional unplanned budget to complete an ERP implementation when it wasn't in the original plan is often a career-ending move. The IT department is not in a position to ask to be trusted to wisely spend additional scarce capital when the original budgeted amounts have been poorly forecast and mismanaged. When the amount of budget or capital expense variance begins to attract the attention of shareholders or lenders, the IT department should prepare for unpleasant scrutiny.

Topics discussed in this chapter include:

- Key components of IT spending.
- Typical budget component ratios.
- How to budget effectively.
- Using zero-based and run-rate processes in creating budgets.
- Key drivers of year-to-year budget variances.
- Managing capital expenditures.
- Cost and budget variance containment.
- IT budget chargeback mechanisms.
- Managing out-of-budget business requests.

Introduction to the Budgeting Process

For an IT manager, particularly the newly promoted manager, the budgeting process can be a harrowing experience. IT managers are expected to forecast events, projects, and emergencies up to 12 months in advance, often with minimal guidance from the business about priorities or initiatives impacting the IT budget.

This chapter provides guidance for the IT manager to help with successfully navigating the IT budgeting process. We introduce key drivers of cost in an IT department, such as required service levels, booked projects, hiring/attrition targets, equipment turnover, as well as expected budget components such as people, hardware, software, and outside services. The chapter also outlines ways to work with the business in creating the budget to avoid surprises and budget overruns during the year.

The Corporate Budgeting Process

Budgets are created to promote fiscal management and generate clarity around expected spending so that financial targets can be communicated to shareholders, lenders, and other stakeholders. The budget is part of the annual business planning cycle. A corporate budget, produced by the CFO, is a projection of the organization's income statement for the next fiscal year. The IT budget is a subset of the overall corporate budget, and the CFO and other officers are relying on the IT director to contribute his or her part. The IT budget includes estimates of operating and capital expenditures for IT. Other information is frequently included as part of the budget, such as key assumptions (e.g., no major acquisitions, business volume remains the same, headcount growth or decline).

Corporate and department budgets are necessary for a variety of reasons:

- Budgets provide the overall company and each manager of a department, function, or business unit with a target and a basis for decision making on competing spending demands. The alternative is fiscal anarchy.
- Budgets provide control over expenses during the course of the year. Management compares actual results with budgeted forecasts and then accounts for any significant variances. Large budget variances may indicate the presence of problems in the operations or with management, or simply that the assumptions made in creating the budgets have changed. In any case, budget variances are cause for investigation.
- Budgets provide contingency plans for potential problems that may develop during the budget year.
- The budget process requires coordination throughout the organization. Each department or unit in the organization is responsible for preparing its part of the budget, which is then coordinated with the overall company budget. The units must also coordinate in cases where projects or initiatives they have planned will affect the budget in other areas.
- Responsibility is assigned to management in each organizational unit. Management is responsible for the development of the budget and its department's subsequent performance against its budget.
- Budgeting is an integral part of the planning process. Successful companies plan for their futures through the discipline of preparing an annual business plan, stipulating their financial and qualitative goals and strategies. The budget is an integral part of that plan.
- Budgeting is used by the corporate finance and senior management to put together a company-wide forecast:
  —To communicate to investors.
  —To understand how much cash/capital the company needs over the period.
  —To manage expenses in support of a given revenue target that is committed to by the sales groups.

The corporate office uses the budget to create the corporate pro-forma income statement for the next fiscal year and to project cash flow. Separate from the budget for operating expenses is the capital expenditure budget that contains expenditures for fixed assets or projects whose costs will be depreciated over time. In sum, many corporate decisions and planning are based on projections in a budget. Further, the compensation of the senior management team, as well as business unit and functional managers, is often tied to budget performance. Budgeting is, therefore, a serious topic even in small companies.

Understanding the Difference between Enterprise IT Spending and the IT Department Budget

Enterprise IT spending includes:

- *Operational expenses:* Amounts spent on day-to-day IT operations within any corporate budget.
- *Capital expenses:* Costs for acquisition of new fixed assets and long-term projects.
- *IT services and outsourcing:* Expenses for external technology services (IT consulting, research services, hosting, etc.).
- *R&D:* Technology-creation functions (new product incubation, experimentation).
- *New products and technology:* Post-R&D costs for the implementation of new products and technology.
- *Salaries and benefits:* For IT staff.
- *Applications:* Cost of implementing and enhancing application systems that support existing business systems.
- *Maintenance and administration:* Cost of IT staff functions plus baseline costs of running and maintaining systems.

By contrast, the IT department operational budget includes:

- IT operational expenses *including* depreciation that falls within the IT budget. It does not include IT spending funded by the other business units (e.g., the sales team hires a Visual Basic and Access database programmer to develop a customer database application to track sales leads).
- Implementation costs for new applications and technology (as long as they are being implemented by the IT department).
- IT department expenses (e.g., personnel salaries and benefits, packaged software, outside services).
- Application support such as the cost of enhancing application systems and supporting them.
- Maintenance and administration costs of IT staff functions plus baseline costs of running and maintaining infrastructure systems.

The IT department capital expenditure budget (subject to the rules and regulations set forth by the accounting department) includes:

- R&D costs.
- Application software development and purchases of large-scale packaged software.
- Costs related to projects whose benefits will be realized over a long period of time.
- Hardware purchases.

The main difference between enterprise IT spending and the IT budget is total enterprise IT spending comprises all IT spending in the company whether managed or the responsibility of the IT department, and the IT budget comprises only the operational and capital budgets managed directly by the IT director.

Key Components of the IT Budget

The IT budget is composed of six key components, as outlined in Exhibit 13.1. The following sections describe each component.

Hardware

Purchases of computers and systems hardware are generally considered a capital expenditure (cap-ex) and affect the cap-ex budget. These assets are typically depreciated over three to five years, depending on the accounting principles and procedures adopted by the finance and accounting department allowing the appropriate portion of the cost of the item to be part of the subsequent annual operating expenses. In some cases, minor hardware purchases will not be capitalized. Assets with short life spans or low costs may not be eligible for capitalization, or may not be worth the effort to capitalize. A discussion with the company CFO can provide instructions for capital expenditures and the associated depreciation schedule to use.

The operational budget includes depreciation expense for prior hardware purchases in previous years. The expense line item for depreciation of hardware is calculated by the accounting department based on actual prior years' spending on capital assets. This will be a non-negotiable amount, as the actual decisions that impact the depreciation expense will have been made in previous years. In some cases, accounting rules may accelerate the depreciation of an asset, or extend it, depending on new knowledge of the assets likely life span. An important calculation to be made when assessing project costs is accelerated depreciation by obsoleting current systems or hardware because of implementation of the new project. Failing to perform this analysis can result in a "surprise" depreciation amount on the IT budget.

BUDGET COMPONENT	DESCRIPTION
Hardware	• Category includes all non-capital spending on hardware. • Includes depreciation of hardware capital assets. • Examples: Cables, peripherals, network cards.
Software	• Category includes all non-capital spending on software. • Includes depreciation of software capital assets. • Examples: Utility software, off-the-shelf packaged application software for one-off use.
Labor (internal personnel)	• Includes salaries and benefits of all IT department personnel not included in capital budget (e.g., capitalized software development efforts).
External service providers	• Includes all costs for outside service providers. • Examples: Consulting fees, security audit fees, contractors.
Data and communications	• Includes cost for network infrastructure services, WAN connections, LAN management, T-1 access, ATM connections, cell phones, and pagers for IT staff, and so on. • Depending on company, this may or may not include the cost of voice communications.
Other	• All other miscellaneous spending is included in this category. • Examples: Training, recruiting fees, legal services, corporate allocations for space, and so on.

Exhibit 13.1   IT Budget Components

Items that go on the hardware expense budget include hardware upgrades, repairs and maintenance, short-life equipment, lease/rental expenses, and miscellaneous peripherals when not packaged with a computer system (for example, one-off purchase of mouse, keyboards, disk drives, and other small hardware items).

Software

Investments in significant software development and applications packages go on the cap-ex budget and depreciate over three to five years, depending on the accounting principles and procedures adopted by the finance and accounting department. As noted above, the CFO can provide specific company policies.

The operational budget includes depreciation expense for previously capitalized software. The expense line item for depreciation of software is calculated by the accounting department based on actual prior years' spending on capital software assets.

Items that go on the expense budget include new software, such as utilities (e.g., backup utility), non-capitalized off-the-shelf packaged applications (e.g., development tools), software upgrades, software maintenance and support fees, non-capitalized upgrades to new versions of software, and one-year license renewal fees.

Labor

All internal personnel costs are part of this category. Examples of these costs are salaries, benefits (e.g., health, vacation), bonuses, and overtime. Some companies include recruiting and training costs in this category, while some put those costs into the "other" category.

External Service Providers

This category includes all costs for outside consultants and contractors. Their services are typically billed on a time-and-materials basis; therefore, when the invoice is received, the expense is allocated to this category. There may be some cases where outside consulting company fees can be capitalized as part of a large project (e.g., ERP system implementation); the accounting department can provide specific circumstances and company policies.

Other services such as backup and recovery, off-site storage, and shredding and disposal services from third parties will also be included here.

Data Communications

The data communications category includes costs for items such as:

- Dial-up lines.
- Leased data lines.
- ISP/WAN services.
- Wide area network.
- Remote dial-in support.

Generally, this category does not include voice communications.

Other

This category is the catch-all for expenses that do not fit in the previous categories. These expenses include items such as:

- Travel and entertainment.
- Supplies.
- Physical plant (data center, furniture).

- Legal fees.
- Allocations for other corporate overhead expenses, such as rent, utilities, and corporate functional budgets. These are usually outside the control of the IT director and are therefore amounts provided from the finance department that will be included in the IT budget.

The template the IT manager receives from the finance department contains a multitude of line items, which may not be bucketed into these components. However, it is useful to create a summary sheet and map the line items back to these component categories. This facilitates comparison of spending to industry and peer groups, which in turn helps identify any budget components that require further investigation.

Estimating Hardware Requirements

As part of the budgeting process, the IT manager will be asked to estimate hardware purchasing requirements for the next fiscal year. These estimates should include servers, desktops, laptops, and peripherals (e.g., printers). This area is often over- or under-budgeted because of poor planning and assumptions.

One of our clients had acquired a new subsidiary. Six months after the transaction closed, the CIO of the subsidiary submitted a cap-ex form for 300 new desktop computers and application software for nearly $500,000. The CFO of the acquirer was stunned to receive the capital expenditure request for 300 computers. During the purchase due-diligence process, he had assumed that the investment would be over 18 months away and, furthermore, could be phased in over time. The CFO discovered that the existing computers had insufficient processing power (they were about five years old at the time). Additionally, the subsidiary was out of compliance on software licenses and thus had to purchase a significant number of desktop operating system licenses increasing the price tag on each computer additionally. Clearly, this outcome was unpleasant for everyone involved (save the hardware vendor), and could have been avoided by better capital expenditure planning (and due diligence on the IT platform).

A recommended approach to estimating hardware requirements to minimize the potential of surprises follows:

1. Review the inventory of total assets deployed today. Most automated help-desk packages will maintain a list of all deployed desktop assets, which are the hardest to inventory (corporate server assets are easier to locate and inventory). If a good inventory listing is not available, a variety of utilities can be used to prowl the network and automatically inventory hardware assets. If the company has an effective fixed asset system, or a centralized procurement department, then the finance or

purchasing departments may be able to provide an inventory of all assets. In any case, the work should concentrate on desktops, printers, and laptops, as they will comprise the bulk of the assets.

2. Determine information about the current inventory:
   - How old are the assets?
   - Are the assets purchased or leased?
   - If leased, obtain the lease information—for example, payments and lease end date, terms and conditions for return.
   - Where is the equipment located?
   - Who is using the equipment?

3. Determine the hardware refresh life cycle. Develop a standard time frame to keep IT assets (especially desktops/laptops) to be proactive about replacing them. If an anticipated cycle is not adopted, the computer assets will begin to deteriorate as they age (either physically breaking down, or logically by becoming underpowered for running new applications). Support costs increase dramatically as the age of the assets increases. Depending on the business and IT strategy, a few rules of thumb may apply here:
   - *Minimize IT/utility strategy:* If the company is in cash conservation mode, make the refresh cycle as long as possible. Adopting a five-year replacement cycle is the outer limit of reasonable life expectation of a desktop, laptop, or printer.
   - *Late adopter/low calculation intensive environment:* Companies that have low-processing requirements and a late adopter philosophy should adopt a three-to-five-year replacement cycle if sufficient.
   - *Average IT spender with significant numbers of knowledge workers:* Adopt a three-year replacement cycle.
   - *Professional services with professionals that rely on laptops:* Adopt a two-year or greater replacement cycle.

4. Obtain the corporate assumptions on net employee growth or decline for the coming year. The employee growth assumptions are available from the finance department and should be an outcome of the other departments budgeting process. Use this number to determine the net addition or subtraction of employees who require computers and the timing of those additions or subtractions.

5. Calculate equipment turnover:
   - Calculate the number of new computers for net employee growth. For example, if the employment base (for employees who need computers) grows by 50 headcount next year, 50 new computers are needed to support that growth. Conversely, if the employee base is expected to decline, no net new PCs are needed for new employees.

- Calculate the number of computers that need to be refreshed in the coming fiscal year. Take the current age of computers and map that to the adopted refresh cycle. For example, if adopted refresh cycle is three years, any computer that will be over three years old next year should be replaced. This should also account for net employee declines. If the company employment base is expected to decline next year, the department may not need to refresh any computers. For example, if the calculation determines that 25 desktops should be retired and purchased next year, but the corporation is expecting a net decline of employment by 25, existing computers can be retired and there is no need to repurchase.

- While desktops, laptops, and printers make up the bulk of the hardware to be purchased, the team should also estimate the end-of-life on servers, workgroup printers, network hardware, and all other centrally maintained equipment. This exercise should be relatively easy compared to the desktop equipment analysis.

- The numbers obtained in this step are used for the hardware capital budget. Take the computer count and calculate the replacement cost. The total is used for the capital budget.

6. Review maintenance contracts as a final step.

- Catalog hardware maintenance contracts.

- How much is maintenance spending, for what assets? Is the asset still being used?

- Can any of the maintenance contracts be eliminated or renegotiated?

- What is the risk of self-insuring and not renewing the maintenance contract? Provide senior management with options on self-insuring and avoiding the maintenance contract expenditure.

These steps should also be taken for all hardware that can be identified by the team as a result of support records, fixed asset systems, purchasing records, and network scans, which combine to build a reasonably accurate picture of the total corporate hardware in place.

Estimating Software Requirements

As part of the budgeting process, the IT manager will be asked to estimate software purchasing requirements for the next fiscal year. These estimates should include packaged applications, software development projects, utility software, business application software licenses, and miscellaneous software used by the business.

There are two difficult areas to analyze in the software budgeting process. The first is software licensing. Depending on how computers are purchased (with or without operating system licenses and office productivity software), the company may or may not need to purchase software licenses for major operating systems and applications during the coming year. However, if IT does not maintain good control over business unit software usage, they will find tens, if not hundreds, of users who are running non-licensed software. Loading a single copy of an application on multiple computers is, unfortunately, a common corporate practice. In recent years, vendors have become more aggressive in policing software license usage by corporations. We recommend staying current with software license purchases and using automated desktop scanning applications to periodically inventory applications that business users are loading on their computers.

The other difficult area to estimate is software development and system implementation work effort. The CIO of one of our clients, a mid-sized manufacturing company, submitted a budget request of $500,000 to develop a new order entry application. Three months later, the CIO submitted a second unexpected request for another $500,000 to complete the same application. Although the project was eventually completed, clearly the mis-estimation of the costs caused enormous budget chaos in the short term. Unfortunately, this is a fairly common occurrence.

A recommended approach to estimating software requirements to minimize the potential of surprises follows:

- Look at total software licenses deployed today for company standard software.
  - Get accurate number of current licenses by software product.
  - Get accurate number of current users.
  - Use the recommendations under the Hardware section to determine the number of new employees and new software licenses that should be purchased.
- Answer these questions about software upgrading:
  - What software applications may need to be upgraded during the next year?
  - What are the business benefits of upgrading (e.g., lowers support costs, eliminates a project, new functionality that will lower processing costs, new revenue opportunities)?
  - What are the consequences of not upgrading (e.g., will the vendor still provide emergency support, or will the IT team provide it)?
  - What is the cost to upgrade?
  - What will the cost be next year if the upgrade is deferred (i.e., does the cost change next year; will it be more expensive next year)?
  - Can we lower the cost of the upgrade by buying from a new vendor or negotiating the current discount?

- Review the top software maintenance contracts:
    - —Catalog software maintenance contracts—especially the top two or three.
    - —How much is software maintenance costing?
    - —What software is covered?
    - —When is the renewal date?
    - —Can any contracts be eliminated or renegotiated?
    - —What is the risk of self-insuring and not renewing the maintenance contract? Give senior management and the IT steering committee options on self-insuring.

Finally, determine if business unit software requests will be charged directly to the unit's budget or hit the IT department's budget. If they will be on the IT department P&L, schedule specific discussions to forecast business unit software requirements and review the current approved projects. Make sure the software requirements and capital requests are added to the capital budget. If the initiatives are approved already, the finance department may have included them in the cap-ex budget forecast. Chapters 10 and 15 have additional information on estimating project costs and project impacts on IT budgets.

Estimating Internal and External Labor Costs

To estimate labor requirements, start with a baseline of whom it will take to run the basic infrastructure, operations, systems administration, and help desk. This becomes the *baseline* labor.

To analyze your current baseline labor critically, answer the following questions:

- Can the department be run at the same service levels with less labor?
- Are there any staff redundancies?
- What will change during the year that might affect the current staff configuration?
    - —Changes to operating environment (e.g., new operating system).
    - —Growth or decline in employees in the company. Set a support ratio that the business is comfortable with, and use this metric against employee headcount to determine needs. For example, a low-cost, minimal service level might be one IT support person per 250 employees. Average would be one IT support staff per 120 employees. High cost, high service would be one IT support staff per 75 employees. What is the difference in service and cost? Present these options to senior management.

- After a support ratio is set, use employee headcount to determine IT staffing requirements for the next year. The same exercise can be done for application support areas.

Estimating development and project resources is driven by project backlog. This is covered in depth in Chapter 15. Complete the steps in Chapter 15 to understand the resource requirements from your projects. Chapter 9 contains details on assessing staffing resource needs through the completion of a swap analysis. These resources can then either be transcribed to the IT budget for software if expensed or to the capital budget if the project is to be capitalized.

Typical Breakout of Spending

After the first draft budget is complete, the IT director can use some benchmarks to understand if the spending matches industry practices. Exhibits 13.2 and 13.3 list sample spending ratios by category and by industry that are useful for guidance. There may be valid reasons that anticipated spending by category does not match the industry averages. However, compare and then analyze any differences to make sure any obvious errors in the budgeting process have been avoided, and that major variances to industry standards can be explained.

Assumptions

Assumptions are necessary to detail the rationale behind a particular line item estimation in the budget. For example, if the IT department assumes that company staff growth will result in a net addition of 250 employees in the coming year, it should be documented so that the CFO, controller and IT steering committee understand the assumption. In many cases, the senior

	ACTUAL 1994 (%)	ACTUAL 1996 (%)	ESTIMATE 2000 (%)	FORECAST 2003 (%)
Hardware	26	22	18	13
Software	8	14	13	15
Internal personnel	37	34	38	40
External services providers	10	16	11	19
Data communications	8	8	6	7
Other	11	6	14	6
IS budget	100	100	100	100

Note: For voice communication, add 10 percent to 15 percent to the IS budget.

Exhibit 13.2 IS Budget Distribution: Resource Category Comparison

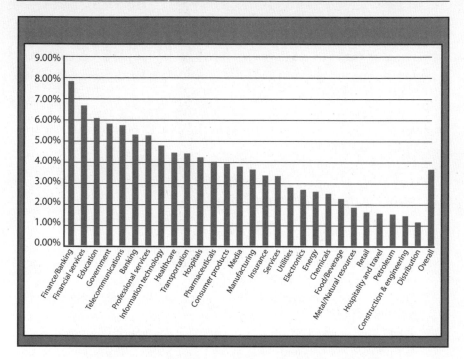

Exhibit 13.3   IT Spending as a Percent of Revenue by Industry

management team can help validate (or invalidate) the assumptions and refine the resulting budgets. The benefits of documenting assumptions include:

- Provides open disclosure and facilitates refinement of the budget.
- Sets expectations and communicates the basis for projections.
- Forms the basis of any explanations for variances later in the fiscal year.

If, during the year, support costs are not tracking to the budget, one issue could be that the underlying assumptions were incorrect, and the resulting discrepancies in the budget can be explained. If the assumptions are not documented, the IT director may be over budget and have trouble explaining the variance.

How to Budget

The Basics

To prepare for budgeting, collect in advance the following types of information to help streamline and improve accuracy of the budget:

- Actual operating, capital, and budget variance figures from the previous year.
- Initial statistics on employment growth or decline at the company.
- Initial statistics on profit and sales expectations for the company for the coming fiscal year.
- Any changes to company operating policies.
- Any changes to major applications in the past 12 months affecting support or development.
- Current approved IT project inventory and prioritization.
- Estimation of current peer spending (see Chapter 3).
- Payroll statistics for the IT department.

Following is an overview of the process:

- The budgeting effort is typically kicked off by the finance department in preparation for the next fiscal year.
- Most often the IT manager will be given the following information to get started:
  —Detailed accounting reports of the prior 12-month IT spending.
  —Template spreadsheet with budget categories already included and calculation complete.
  —Estimation of overhead line items to be allocated to the IT department.
- Complete a first draft—there are two different approaches to building the budget:
  —Zero-based budgeting (recommended, but more difficult).
  —Run-rate budgeting.

These methods are outlined later in this chapter. The first draft should incorporate all known information on service level agreements and anticipated projects (see Chapters 7 and 15).

- Review draft with CFO or other direct reporting relationship.
- Produce and present second draft.
- Incorporate input and produce final draft.
- Final draft goes through approval with IT steering committee and senior management.
- Once approved, final draft is sent to the accounting department as the "final new fiscal year" budget for IT.
- All actions for the subsequent 12 months will be judged against this final budget.
- At times there will be a quarterly and/or mid-year budget review sessions to adjust the budget to account for new known information.

Timing

The budget cycle usually kicks off between September and November, or one to four months before the end of the company fiscal year. The budget, in most cases, needs to be finalized in the last month of the fiscal year.

Budget Creation Methods

ZERO-BASED BUDGETING. Zero-based budgeting is the method used to prepare a budget that starts with a "clean sheet" and builds from the ground up based on assumptions, required service levels, and projects. In a zero-based budget, each activity or line item to be funded must be justified each year on the current merits for spending money on it. This method, while time-consuming, ensures that the annual budgets do not carry forward any poor assumptions from the previous budget, and that the underlying assumptions are reconsidered each year. Zero-based budgeting works particularly well in companies that are experiencing rapid rates of change (business growth, major initiatives, acquisitions or divestitures). The steps in zero-based budgeting are:

1. Determine components of the budget that are fixed (e.g., facilities, infrastructure, application maintenance, data communications) and those that are variable (e.g., hardware purchases, staff labor, training, software upgrades, enhancements).

2. Justify each fixed expense in the department. Is the expense reasonable given current market conditions? Can, and should, the expense be altered? Document assumptions and any actions that would contribute to cost reduction. Because these are fixed expenses, some creativity is necessary. For example, if IT leases its own office space, can the director go back to the realtor and negotiate a longer lease for a discount today? Does the expense change for any reason (step-up in vendor contract, annual increase in rate in contract, automatic fees tied to maintenance contracts)?

3. Total all fixed items. This total of fixed costs is called the *baseline* budget.

4. Document any potential cost reductions, and the associated reduction in service levels or project capabilities, and keep for presentation during the final budget review with the IT steering committee.

5. Build up the budget for variable cost line items (e.g., outside contractors, new software licenses) by performing an item-by-item analysis. Understand the key drivers of cost in the variability (e.g., number of projects, employees, and transactions). Make assumptions for each line item and calculate the variable budget. Once again, document assumptions, as you will use them in the budget presentation and need them to answer budget questions.

6. Clean up and prepare first draft.

METHOD 2: RUN-RATE BUDGETING. Run-rate budgeting is used to prepare a budget based on the current year and current time frame expenditures. For example, if rent is currently $25,000 per month, it is likely to run $25,000 next month. Run-rate budgeting starts from the current average monthly rate of expenditure (the run-rate) and is then refined from that baseline based on new assumptions (e.g., new project assumptions, new usage assumptions, service level changes). Each budget line item starts at its current level of spending and is adjusted upward or downward based on new or current information. Run-rate budgeting can be completed relatively rapidly, because the list of current line-items is readily available. The process also incorporates the best thinking on what the budget will be, as it is based on actual current amounts. Run-rate budgeting works best in environments where there is relatively little business change expected year-to-year.

Steps for run-rate budgeting:

1. Populate budget template with current run-rate spending or the last 12-month actual spending. Accounting can provide this information.

2. Review each line item in the budget and document assumptions for why the spending should be at or near the current run rate, or will change. Modify the subsequent months based on assumptions. Add any new budget line items for known new categories of expense, along with amounts and assumptions.

3. Prepare first draft budgets based on the current run-rate and assumptions on any changes.

A final note about budgeting process: Give the senior management team (CFO, CEO) options for key budget decisions. For example, produce two budgets—one based on current level of service and one based on a reduced level of service. This allows senior management to assess the price of any cost cutting they would like to execute (e.g., lower level of service means one-day turnaround on help desk trouble tickets versus four hours). Another variable that can be adjusted is the number of projects that can be executed, providing options for executing the top 10 projects versus executing only the top 5 projects. Management can then make tradeoffs of spending versus service. Even if management elects not to take advantage of these potential cost reductions, the IT team will enhance their reputation for thriftiness with the senior management team and IT steering committee.

Key Cost Drivers

Chapter 3 outlines a comprehensive list of IT cost drivers. This section lists some key factors that may affect the budget from year to year and some that are key considerations during the budgeting process (see Exhibit 13.4).

DRIVER	DESCRIPTION
• Complexity of infrastructure environment	• Infrastructure complexity increases support costs dramatically; it also drives unexpected costs due to the difficulty in controlling the environment. • Characteristics include multiple disparate platforms (e.g., AS/400, Unix, NT, Mainframe). • Build in a risk factor into your budget and dollars to rationalize the environment.
• Revenue growth	• Revenue growth drives increased costs to support the business including additionally capacity in servers, added support costs for end users, new applications to support customer and sales initiatives. • The higher the revenue growth the greater the demands on IT. Companies growing by 10 percent or more will see 10 plus percent increase in IT spending proportionate to the growth.
• Growth or decline in employee base (e.g., professional, clerical, users of PCs)	• Growth or decline in the number of end-users will have a tremendous affect on the IT budget. • Employee growth drives demand for capital expenditure in PC hardware as well as corresponding capacity on file and print servers and potentially end user software licenses. • Employee attrition will reduce demand by a corresponding amount.
• Downturn in business economic climate	• Depending on the sector in which the company competes, the organization will likely feel the affect of a recession in lower sales growth or even sales decline. • In a recession, CIOs should be prepared for budget and spending cuts. Preparing ahead of time by prioritizing discretionary spending and being proactive in making adjustments is recommended.
• Acquisitions	• Acquisitions drive a tremendous amount of IT integration if the acquisition will be integrated in to the main business. • Acquisitions are likely to drive integration costs of IT systems, end user licenses, and standardization of operating platforms.

Exhibit 13.4   Key Cost Drivers

Efficiency and high productivity are important goals for the IT department. Every IT director should attempt to build the most efficient infrastructure, application deployment, and IT organization possible. Recommendations for keeping costs low and attempting to run an efficient operation include:

- Develop baseline infrastructure costs as outlined previously. Attempt to reduce this baseline on a continual basis. For each baseline budget line item ask, "Will reducing this number cause any change to business service?" If the answer is no, the cost should probably be cut. A large driver of cost reduction is standardization of the environment. Chapter 6 lays out a framework for standardizing the environment. Standardization can reduce IT baseline spending considerably. Every effort should be made to attain it. The average company spends 70 percent of IT dollars on baseline and maintenance, creating significant opportunity for identifying potential reductions.

- Work only on the projects that the department can complete on time. Working on more projects than the department has capacity to execute causes whipsawing and makes the entire department less productive. Make sure no projects are started without proper business justification and ownership from one of the business units (except infrastructure projects). Chapter 15 contains an approach for ensuring that IT projects can be successfully concluded.

- Develop a review process to critically assess current projects. Each project should receive a status flag of green (going well), yellow (warning signs), or red (behind schedule or over budget). See Chapter 16 on IT metrics for a discussion on the project dashboard. The review will ensure that overbudget projects are dealt with before they greatly impact the budget.

- Periodically renegotiate vendor contracts to obtain savings from company size. If the company is growing, the department can often save IT dollars by aggregating spending into fewer vendors and demanding volume discounts in return. Chapters 10 and 11 cover vendor negotiation and management.

- Re-examine service levels. Make sure the service levels that the department is delivering to the business are actually what the business wants. Often service levels are actually overspecified—meaning the business could actually do with lower service levels, which would allow lower costs to deliver.

- Tighten asset management. Implement a sound process for managing IT assets, including their inventory and physical tracking. Critically assess requests for assets, and make sure that the assets are actually being used for high priority activities. Redeploy assets from low-return areas to highest return projects.

Managing Capital Expenditures

The capital budget is used for financing long-term outlays for assets that will be used by the company over a long period of time, such as hardware and large-scale software applications. Accounting rules provide for these assets to be expensed over their lifetime so that an appropriate portion of the expense for the item occurs in each year that the asset is in use. Capital budget items affect cash and the balance sheet, as the actual cash outlay for the item occurs in a short time period relative to the asset lifetime. Over time, the capital items are depreciated, and affect the income statement (and operating budget). A *capital expenditure* is any expenditure contributing value to the property and equipment of a business—expenditure toward capital assets rather than to cover operating expenses or purchase investments unrelated to the business. Accounting rules provide for the total cost (including labor) of some long-term projects to be treated as a capital asset. In many cases, accounting rules also provide guidance on the expected lifetime of the asset that will dictate how much of the asset's value will be expensed in each year's budget.

Capital budgeting is the process by which a company selects alternative capital asset investments. In making decisions on which capital investments to make, companies usually use a combination of formal financial criteria, including net present value (NPV), internal rate of return (IRR), return on investment (ROI), and payback period. Potential investments are also evaluated with respect to strategic consistency and risk. The capital budgeting process is designed to maximize company value by undertaking investments whose returns are equal to or greater than the average cost of capital.

An entity's capital budget and budgeting process are usually distinct from its operating budget and budgeting process. The two kinds of budgets represent different expenditures, are planned through different processes, use different criteria, and may even involve different managers. For a specific expenditure to be funded from a capital budget, its sponsors may have to justify it with a formal business case analysis, including estimates of NPV, IRR, ROI, payback period, and other financial criteria. If the company has limited funds for capital spending, moreover, the potential capital expenditure may have to enter a competitive capital review process, where all requested expenditures are compared on the same financial criteria and only the most favorable receive funding.

Computer and system asset components are generally capitalized as one unit (e.g., CPU, monitor, mouse, keyboard, software); however, if small components (e.g., a mouse or keyboard) are purchased separately from the system, they are expensed. Generally, assets above a few thousand dollars are capitalized. Hardware assets are generally capitalized over a three- to five-year period, while software and select application development initiatives are capitalized over three years. However, each company's accounting department has its own policies based on generally accepted accounting principles (GAAP); the finance or accounting department will dictate appropriate usage.

Minimizing Capital Expenditures

Suggestions for minimizing capital expenditures include:

- Make sure all computer and software capital expenditures follow the company standard capital expenditure process, including approval by the IT director and steering committee. This process ensures that only legitimate capital expenditures take place, those that have significant business value for the company.
- Require that all capital requests have a related business case justification completed and signed off by either the IT director (for infrastructure requests) or by both the IT director and the business unit general manager if other requests.
- Hold all requests in a batch and present them the IT steering committee periodically to discuss in aggregate.
- When completing the cost side of the capital request, ensure that personnel have used standard vendors and previously negotiated discounts.
- Have requestors provide one or two alternative options to the recommended request. For example, if the department is requesting 25 computers, the options are simply to approve or decline the request. However, if the team presents two options, purchase 25 computers as plan A or purchase 15 computers and reuse 10 older computers with pros and cons of each, management can make a better decision by weighing the tradeoffs.
- Ensure that the IT department is finding the root cause of problems before requesting capital for hardware such as storage, CPUs, memory, and so on. Chapter 7 contains details on operations root cause analysis. Capital requests that appear legitimate are often rejected after analysis. For example, a capital request for a new backup system resulted instead in new policies for e-mail storage quotas, resulting in avoidance of the expenditure.

Lease versus Buy Decisions

Lease versus buy decisions should be made principally by the finance department. The CFO and the finance team will have an overall capital strategy for the company. This analysis affects every large capital purchase that can be either purchased with cash or leased from the vendor or through a third-party leasing company. The CFO will make the decision based on the company's balance sheet, lender covenants, current cash on hand, budget forecasts, and financial performance. The IT team should work closely with the finance department prior to committing the company to any large capital expenditure or long-term lease.

Buying Equipment

When purchasing equipment, the buyer can usually negotiate the lowest overall price for the asset. Additionally, the purchase approach may provide access to a greater variety of vendors since not all of them offer lease options. Buying assets that can be capitalized will consume the capital budget and the asset will be fully owned by the company and can be used for any purpose intended. Disposing of the asset will also be at the discretion of the company.

Leasing Equipment

Most major hardware (and, recently, software) purchases can also be leased from the vendor or third party; this is a common industry practice and large vendors have well-articulated finance and leasing programs. Leases usually have the same affect on the expense budget as a purchase, but very different impact on company cash and balance sheets. Additionally, vendors will usually offer capital leases, which affect the capital budget instead of the operating budget.

In leasing, the company is essentially renting the asset from a third party. As such, a number of rules come attached to the equipment, which may limit the flexibility in using and disposing of it. For example, by contract, the company may not return the asset prematurely without paying an early termination penalty. Furthermore, financing instruments such as leasing come with financing costs. The IT director and finance department must evaluate the total picture of asset cost, asset life, financing cost, and other variables to determine which option (lease versus buy) is a better financial decision for the company. The IT director should focus on developing the potential options and let the accounting department determine the better value and make the lease or purchase decision.

Auditing the IT Department

An important part of IT cost containment is close management of the details. Thousands of small expenditures add up to big dollar expenditures for the IT department. A typical example of this build-up is data communication lines. Each data line may be only $40 per month; however, if the department maintains 100 data lines and potential long distance dial-in charges, the amount can reach hundreds of thousands of dollars on an annual basis. Computer purchases are another example. Even though each desktop computer may cost only a few thousand dollars, the aggregate spending at the end of the year can be enormous.

The IT director has responsibility for ensuring that vendor invoices and staff expense receipts are audited. One or more designated managers to perform this function; the designees should recommend to the IT manager ways to reduce either the expenses or vendor billing errors. Some common areas of billing errors and overspending include:

- *Data communications:* Line and long distance connections: As a company expands or contracts, adjustments to the original service are required. Otherwise, the department monthly invoice will contain charges for items not being used. If a company is growing, the team should ensure that they are receiving proper volume discounts.
- *Cell phones:* Cell phone plans, cell phones, pagers, and wireless handhelds for personnel in the IT department—any regular recurring billing should be reviewed periodically to rationalize disposed of assets and unused telecom plans. Volume purchasing discounts should be considered here as well.
- *Software and hardware maintenance contracts:* Many companies are paying maintenance on applications that are no longer in use. Inventory all maintenance contracts and make sure all the software is still in production, and that it justifies a maintenance contract.

Perform an audit once a year. Have an auditor from the accounting department review all spending, contracts, and services to ensure they are still justified and are applicable to supporting the current business.

Contingency Planning

Risk is inherent in any assumption-driven analysis. The over- and under-risk of the budget and plan should be assessed accordingly. Understanding how the key assumptions will affect the budget, which assumption changes will have the highest impact, and the likelihood of the assumptions changing can be combined to perform a budget sensitivity analysis. This helps identify the key risk areas, which have the highest chance of causing budget variance.

Budget planners sometimes try to pad their budgets with extra costs, anticipating budget reductions during negotiations. While tempting, this is an inadvisable practice that sows distrust between the IT department and finance and senior management. One IT director we worked with needed to have capital approval for 25 new laptop computers. The IT director was overheard remarking: "Let's submit the request for an extra 7 laptops for 32 total. We need to add a little accountant bait in here, so they can feel that they have accomplished something when they talk us down to 25." Clearly, this manager had trouble establishing a trusted working relationship with the CFO and the IT steering committee.

Managing the Budget

The company, its officers, its employees, and its shareholders are relying on the IT manager to meet the budget. If the department overspends the budget, both the company and its employees may be adversely affected. The corporate budgeting process and its subsequent success is dependent on all budget managers managing their share of the overall corporate budget and performing according to plan.

There are a variety of approaches the IT manager can take to help manage the budget on an ongoing basis:

- Schedule a regular monthly meeting with the CFO, controller, or finance analyst to review actual versus budget numbers. During this session, variances should be investigated, and the IT director should develop a list of key actions to improve any negative variance. After the meeting, the director should delegate the action items and get them completed quickly to experience the benefits in the subsequent month.
- Give senior direct reports (usually operations and applications managers) budget responsibility for their areas and hold them accountable for hitting the numbers.
- When large variances occur, take fast action, as it takes time for changes to be reflected in the numbers. For example, if a vendor agreement is modified, it may take 30 days to finalize the agreement and another 30 days for the changes to take effect.
- Dithering and delaying decisions and ignoring high variances is a recipe for disaster. The IT director has a fiduciary responsibility for the department and must make the necessary corrections to perform as promised to the rest of the management team. Delay may lead to senior management or the IT steering committee making unilateral decisions without the involvement of IT.
- When anticipating a large negative variance in the budget, enlist the CFO as soon as possible to work to help correct the situation and explain it to senior management and the IT steering committee.

Handling Out-of-Budget
Business Unit Requests

After the operating budget is set, business unit requests that might impact the operating budget need to be discussed in the face of other investment decisions the company is trying to make. While meeting the committed budget is important, over the course of the year, budget assumptions may change and some common sense and flexibility are necessary.

Business units often request projects that were not on their agendas when the budget was completed. As outlined in Chapter 15, projects should be evaluated on a business case basis and, if approved, executed. Large projects will likely hit the capital budget if approved and not affect the operating budget. Business unit project requests should be documented, along with a business case, and sent to the IT steering committee for review and approval. Every new request must be considered in relation to the current operating budget and the capital budget. Possible outcomes include:

- Project is covered by the current capital budget and approved.
- Project is not covered by the current capital budget but is higher priority than another project. Downgrade the priority of the second project on the list of backlog projects and replace with the newly approved project.
- Project is not covered by the current capital budget. It is a high priority. There are no other projects to displace. New funding for the IT group is needed. The business case is sound, so additional funds are approved to complete the project, and the ongoing negative capital budget variance is approved (i.e., the capital budget is increased or some other non-technology investment is displaced).
- Project is not a priority and has a substandard business case; therefore, it is not funded and further consideration is not necessary.

Chargebacks

Chargebacks are budget methods that charge the business units and functional departments for their use of IT by allocating IT costs to each unit. IT chargebacks are often considered when the business units would like more direct accountability from IT, and the senior management team wants to ensure that IT costs are being justified by the business.

In general, we do not advocate elaborate IT budget chargebacks for several reasons. First, they divert attention from the primary focus of the business, which is generating revenue and satisfying customers. Second, they take substantial effort from accounting. Third, companies with IT chargebacks often under-invest in common infrastructure projects; each business unit will only be interested in and approve projects that are of direct benefit. Finally, chargebacks effectively force the IT director to report to multiple department heads and business unit managers. This can create management chaos and an ineffective IT department.

In cases where IT chargebacks are appropriate, there are two options for infrastructure costs:

1. *Unallocated infrastructure:* Costs for the baseline IT budget are considered a corporate expense and are not allocated to the business units.
2. *Allocated cost center:* Costs for the baseline IT budget are allocated to business units based on some factor as a proxy for usage. Usage proxies can include the business unit's percent of revenue, number of employees, percent of profits, computer CPU cycles used, disk storage used, and so on.

Large companies with multiple divisions and a central IT department may be forced to use allocated cost center concepts.

In addition to infrastructure cost allocations, the company will need a mechanism for charging out IT systems development, package implementation and integration, and application maintenance different from those of the IT infrastructure. Several options exist:

1. Business units contract with the IT department on each project, agreeing to a cost including software licenses, time and material estimates, deadlines, and scope of project. Business units also contract with IT department on maintenance and support. Actual hours for supporting the business unit are tracked in a time reporting system and actual hours are billed. Service levels are defined and the IT department is responsible for achieving service levels guaranteed.
2. *Business unit-owned project budgets:* In this case, the business units actually own the budgets for IT projects and the IT department is used to support and execute the projects in those budgets.

Chargeback mechanisms are successful only if the chargeback drivers are fair and easily tracked, and the business has the ability to influence their usage of IT in order to contain costs. Otherwise, the chargebacks can cause under-investment in critical infrastructure components, as well as cause significant internal dysfunctional behavior, putting significant burden on the accounting department.

Summary

IT budgeting and cost containment practices are critical skills for the IT manager to master. Developing a sound budget, which provides a road map for managing the department, and which can withstand business changes and economic changes, is a challenge. Additionally, anticipating, understanding, and forecasting the known variables about the business distinguish an average IT director from a star performer. The average performer is reactive to the environment while the top performer has assessed the reliability of key assumptions and the associated risks, and planned contingencies accordingly.

Concepts presented in the chapter, such as prioritizing discretionary spending areas and keeping this prioritized list handy, encourage the IT manager to act quickly and decisively to negative budget variances. Finally, ensuring that IT assets are deployed against revenue generating and customer-facing activities help ensure that budget dollars are flowing to the highest value activities. Companies whose IT managers routinely ensure this, as well as the business value of IT investments, see much higher productivity and profitability from IT investments.

RESOURCES

Paul Strassman, *The Squandered Computer* (New Canaan, CT: Information Economics Press, 1997).

NOTES

1. Thomas Henry Huxley, *Aphorisms and Reflections*, ed. Henrietta A. Huxley (London: Macmillan, 1907).
2. Amy Wilentz, "I Will Veto Again and Again," *Time* (March 18, 1985).

14

Effective Decision Making and Risk Management

Take calculated risks. That is quite different from being rash.
— George S. Patton, letter written on June 6, 1944[1]

A foolish consistency is the hobgoblin of little minds.
— Ralph Waldo Emerson[2]

Quit building me a space shuttle, when all I want is a trip to the grocery store.
— Client CEO to IT department managers

This chapter outlines and illustrates the pitfalls of incentives inherent for IT managers that lower the priority on cost containment and increase the priority for minimizing risk, often at great expense. Many IT decision makers view risk as a binary decision—accept the risk or mitigate the risk. In the effort to eliminate risk, these same decision makers often show little understanding or appreciation for the high incremental cost required to mitigate all risk.

We examine key areas in which IT managers consistently overmitigate risks with excess spending or resource allocation. IT managers too often submit additional capital and labor requests without investigation into other alternatives. In addition, these requests demonstrate the limited knowledge most IT organizations have about the underlying business and its economics. We illustrate the phenomenon with multiple examples from client engagements.

The chapter is intended to raise awareness of the key failure points in IT-related decision making. Responsibilities exist for both the IT manager and the senior executive participating in the IT steering committee or approving IT budgets and expenditures. IT managers must help the steering committee understand the spectrum of options, including costs and risks. While the steering committee must ask questions that ensure that due diligence has been performed and that the business impact, whether for growth or risk mitigation, justifies the expenditure.

This chapter does not address other risk management-related topics such as redundancy planning, uptime management, disaster recovery, failover methodologies, systems recovery, systems security, and privacy issues. The technologies and approaches for these topics are covered in detail in a host of books, magazine articles, and online publications. The key theme in this chapter is that effective decision making and intelligent assessment of cost versus risk should be applied to all of these areas.

Why This Topic Is Important

Poor decision making concerning risk is one of the primary drivers of IT ineffectiveness and, more specifically, IT overspending. The responsibility for this decision making is shared equally by IT managers and the senior management team. IT managers typically fail to present any but the most costly (and risk-free) options for a given decision to senior management. Senior management, in turn, fails to ask the penetrating questions, which may reveal creative options for accomplishing the dual objectives of risk and cost minimization. Instead, one of two undesirable results occurs; either the senior management approves the request at high cost or rejects the request. Rejecting the request results in nothing being done to mitigate the potential risk, and the company is exposed indefinitely. The IT manager then holds leverage if the potential failure occurs by blaming the senior management for declining the capital expenditure request.

IT managers experience difficulty in helping the business understand the cost trade-offs they are making in setting service levels and expectations inside IT. If business management thinks of the cost of a failover server in terms of incremental sales, would they be just as happy to save the cost of the server and endure a potential four-hour downtime while tapes are restored? These risk-management questions often go unasked and unexamined in the IT decision-making process. This chapter introduces the key areas of decision making often affected and covers specific examples from IT departments in a variety of industries.

IT departments are paid to serve the business units and often have trouble quantifying and explaining to the business the actual costs of the service. Many IT departments tend to overinsure by overspending on both labor and capital, which provides higher levels of service to the business but is often not the best deployment of resources for the company overall.

Furthermore, IT is commonly a nonallocated cost, which results in two undesirable effects: agency issues and the "tragedy of the commons." Agency issues manifest in IT as unlimited service requests pour in from all segments of the business, and the "tragedy of the commons" effect occurs because there is no incentive for the individual business departments to help IT save money or effort, yet the entire company suffers from overspending.

Specific topics discussed in this chapter include:

- Relationship between risk and cost in IT decision making.
- How IT decision making suboptimizes in four specific areas: capital expenditures (cap-ex), IT emergencies, service level setting, and capacity setting.
- How creative approaches can identify options for minimizing both risk and cost.
- How to avoid the "all-or-nothing" thinking that characterizes many IT decisions, replacing it with "just right" approaches.
- How to avoid the "tragedy of the commons" and the associated high costs in IT.
- What the senior management team can do to help IT improve decision making.

Relationship between Risk and Cost

In one of our most memorable client engagements, we were asked to fix a particularly distressed IT department. One of the first decisions implemented was to hold all capital and vendor expenditures until the larger issues impeding IT performance were sorted out. After six weeks of hard work, we were ready to review the requests from the IT department. The first request was for the renewal of a maintenance contract for three-year-old corporate file-and-print servers. The request was for more than $50,000 for annual maintenance. Given what we knew about server prices and the low number of users on this particular system, we asked what justified such a large expenditure relative to the replacement cost of the servers. "Well, if they go down, we can't print or access network files in the sales department" came back the answer. "But, given the configuration of fairly old equipment, couldn't the machines be replaced for less than one-third of the annual maintenance contract?" we argued. "That may be true, and we could even create a backup machine to be deployed in case of failure, but that would mean the possibility of as much as four hours of downtime," was the reply.

Fortunately, this debate took place in the context of an IT steering committee, and, at this juncture, one of the business unit managers weighed in with some common sense. "To save $40,000, I am willing to put up with a little bit of potential downtime. It costs me $400,000 in sales to cover a gap of $40,000." Further probing revealed a few other pertinent facts: The existing servers had never gone down in the past and had a three-year track record of flawless performance. Backup servers were actually already available and could be configured and deployed in less than eight hours after a failure of one of the main servers.

This anecdote illustrates several of the decision-making and agency problems that assert themselves in IT decision making. First, there is a fundamental agency problem with decision making in many IT departments, and it is the responsibility of both IT management and the senior management team. The incentives of IT managers are usually not oriented toward the most cost-effective management of risk, and the senior management team fails to ask the right questions to understand how much risk reduction they are purchasing with their IT dollars.

Secondly, many IT managers do not seem to understand the relationship between risk and cost, instead assessing risk as a binary outcome. For example, IT managers view a given hardware decision or IT staffing level as either risky or safe with no gradations between. By seeing only two possible alternatives, the IT decision-making process becomes one sided—either implement the safe solution or put the business at risk. IT departments are notoriously bad at explaining consequences and alternatives. They frame requests as all or nothing, with only one option presented to the business, instead of a variety of options with varying costs and risks. IT requests and decisions are often made without soliciting input from the business and helping them understand the trade-offs for optimal decision making. The request is typically presented in a way that leads IT steering committees and senior executives to choose the safe solution, despite a high cost, to avoid appearing irresponsible by putting the business at risk.

Frank conversations on these topics often yield surprises on both sides. IT managers are surprised at how much risk the business is willing to absorb to achieve cost savings, and senior management is surprised at the high cost of the reduced risk and high service levels they are purchasing. The primary cause of these issues is a lack of clear communication between the IT department and the business on issues of risk and service levels.

A fundamental agency problem is present in IT decision making as well. IT departments achieve by pleasing the business. The primary incentive for IT managers is to ensure that systems are operational and performing well. A common saying in IT departments is "You know you are doing a good job when everything runs so smoothly that no one from the business knows you are there." IT operations managers receive the most vociferously negative feedback when key systems, such as e-mail, experience outages. If they overengineer a solution to ensure e-mail uptime, they are triply rewarded—the e-mail system stays up reducing their support work, they avoid negative feedback from the business, and, furthermore, by consuming budget dollars, they are assured a similar budget for next year's expenditures. The normal cost-saving motivation that applies to a business unit manager in charge of a P&L statement are not present. When IT departments spend more money, in general, their lives get easier; therefore, the normal incentives do not apply.

This agency problem, while troubling, is overshadowed by the inability of IT managers to effectively trade risk and cost to achieve an optimal mix. Exhibit 14.1 shows the well-understood normal relationship between risk and cost. This general relationship between risk and cost is applicable to IT decisions concerning investment and capacity. The exhibit highlights an enormously high level of incremental cost required to achieve the last few percentage points of risk reduction.

IT managers often do not acknowledge this relationship between risk and cost in their decision making. Instead, they see the decision as a binary choice between *no risk* and *risk.* This most often leads to high levels of service, low levels of risk, and, most troubling, high levels of cost in IT departments. Exhibit 14.2 outlines the decision-making behavior of many IT managers.

As shown in the exhibit, instead of viewing risk as a continuum, with ever-increasing marginal costs associated with marginal reductions in risk, IT managers tend to assess decisions more simplistically, with two outcomes: risky or not risky and costly or not costly. This mode of framing decisions, naturally, tends to favor outcomes that produce the minimum risk and the maximum cost.

While IT management deserves its share of the responsibility for such poor and uninventive decision making, the senior management team and the business are equally culpable for not asking the hard questions. When presented with requests from IT, the business fails to delve down to a meaningful level of

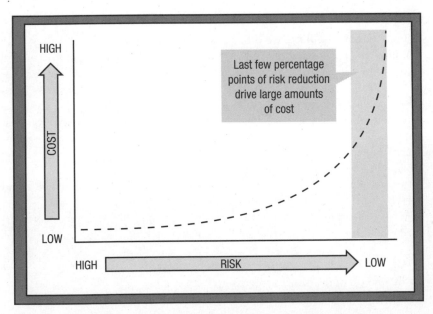

Exhibit 14.1   Typical Relationship between Risk and Cost

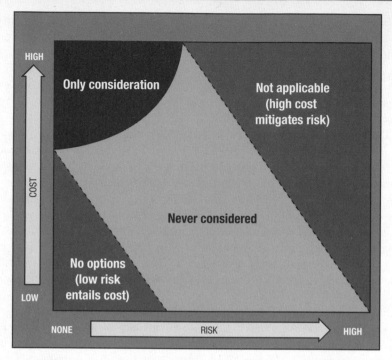

Exhibit 14.2   IT Approach to Risk Analysis and Decision Making

questioning that would expose other potential options. Push back is limited to a one-level deep question of "Why?' " Only through Socratic, multiple-level questioning with adequate technical intelligence and push back do other possible options emerge from the brainstorming that ensues. When business management takes IT recommendations at face value, without signaling the level of risk tolerance they are willing to accept, they usually get a solution that minimizes risk and maximizes cost. As decision making improves, senior management must also work with IT to improve confidence that IT will not be solely liable for downtime or outages that were preventable, but not avoided, to achieve cost savings. The decisions about acceptable risks should be made and owned by both IT and senior management.

We have observed this tendency to overinsure and overmitigate risk manifest itself in four specific areas of IT decision making:

- Capital expenditure or other spending requests.
- IT emergencies/disaster recovery.
- Setting and maintaining service levels.
- Setting staff and technology capacity levels.

We cover these scenarios in turn, illuminating each with specific client examples.

Capital Expenditures and IT Spending

IT spending and, in particular, IT capital expenditures are common areas where poor decisions are made. In their zeal to substitute capital for labor, IT teams have a particularly poor reputation because of the frequent over-purchasing of "toys." While it is true that part of the attraction of a career in technology for many people is the opportunity to work with an ever-changing variety of new technology, it has also led to a suspicion on the part of business managers that the IT team is purchasing more or better than is necessary. Compounding the issue is the fact that business managers are often rated on revenue, gross margin, expenses, or earnings before interest, taxes, depreciation and amortization (EBITDA); therefore, additional capital expenditure will have less effect on their incentives.

Recognition of these shortcomings enables IT departments and IT steering committees to analyze scenarios and ask questions, which either validate the business need for the IT expenditure or uncover other alternatives. With one of our clients, we were able to produce significant savings while at the same time keeping risk at very acceptable levels by participating in the IT budgeting and capital expenditure approval process. The IT team made an unplanned, mid-year request for virus-scanning software to be deployed to every single corporate desktop. The catalyst was a recent unexplained virus attack. This unanticipated expense would not only cause a significant budget variance for IT in the coming month, but also entail a significant software rollout project for the operations department and require additional ongoing support to monitor virus file updates. The position of the IT team was "either purchase this software, or we will be constantly at risk of viruses." Although senior management was sufficiently alarmed by the notion of viruses running rampant through the company to sign off on the request immediately, we asked to extend the debate. After much discussion, it was determined that viruses could only enter the corporate systems from one of three sources: inbound e-mail, diskettes brought from outside the company, and files downloaded from the Internet. Inbound e-mail was cleaned of viruses by a highly robust system, which was installed and operating on the corporate mail server and, therefore, could be discounted as a source. We asked the IT team to perform a quick analysis on the source of virus attacks for the past year. Their analysis concluded that less than 5 percent of the virus attacks had come from diskettes, and none of the attacks had come from downloaded files. Given this low level of probability, we suggested the alternate approach of disconnecting the floppy drives of most desktop computers, which were rarely used for business purposes anyway. The result was a highly acceptable level of risk and a response that was cheap, easy to implement, and commensurate with the actual threat posed.

A subsequent request from the team was for a highly sophisticated and expensive server, which would serve as failover capacity for an existing financial systems server. We first asked the IT team for more research: How often had the existing financial systems computer failed in the past year, where a failover machine would be necessitated? The answer was, interestingly, zero. In fact, the machine had failed only once in three years. On that occasion, it was quickly fixed with the installation of a new memory module. However, we were certainly willing to contemplate the notion that a complete, difficult-to-fix failure was possible. What was in question, however, was the best response to the failure. Working with the CFO, we ascertained that the four-hour downtime required to restore the server from tape in the event of a failure was an acceptable price to pay in the unlikely event of a failure, particularly given the high cost of ensuring 100 percent uptime and reliability.

In another purchasing audit, we were asked to analyze a request for an automated, high-speed, high-capacity tape backup system for the corporate systems. The business rationale for the purchase was that a complete backup of the system could not be completed within a 24-hour window, and corporate standards mandated that a full backup be taken of corporate data each day. Before signing off on this request, we asked the operations manager what seemed to be causing the trouble. "Most of the data is from our e-mail server," he replied. After conducting a detailed analysis of the e-mail system, we found that more than 70 percent of the backup data volume was from the e-mail system, and more than 50 percent of that data volume was associated with 20 percent of the users. Those 20 percent were storing enormous music, video, and other large files in their network e-mail folders. The CFO said it best: "You mean we are buying a tape jukebox so these people can watch movies over the network while they are at work?" Needless to say, the jukebox purchase was declined and e-mail storage policies and procedures were implemented.

Our favorite example of creative thinking that produced simple, cheap approaches is from a client working on its disaster recovery plan. The client had established a well-thought-out plan for ensuring availability of backup tapes and servers, as well as alternate (nonwater-based) fire suppression. The only remaining issue was the presence of water-based fire suppression equipment in the machine room. They were concerned that sustained flooding in the room would ruin the expensive hardware located there. For a variety of technical reasons, the disabling and removal of this equipment was going to be difficult, disruptive, and expensive. Elaborate plans were hatched, including architects, building contractors, and blueprint redesigns for the machine room. At one of the final sign-off meetings, a junior analyst from the IT department finally piped up: "Well, I hate to try to stop a moving train, but I noticed on the blueprints a water cutoff valve for the pipes that feed the machine room is located in the plant closet. The closet happens to be right behind the security post, which is staffed 24 hours a day, year around. Could we just create a procedure for the security guards that, if there is a fire, the first thing they do is turn the valve off?"

Occasionally, the decisions take a turn down a trail that is at best deceitful and, at worst, outright fraudulent. In a client engagement, we were assessing a particularly disorganized and ill-managed IT department. We found ourselves reviewing the training and development records for the IT team for the past year. We noticed that several members of the IT team had attended lengthy and expensive Oracle database training during the past year. What struck us as peculiar was the fact that at no time had the company employed Oracle database technology nor was it currently under consideration. When we quizzed the managers and team members who had attended the training on the rationale behind the training, they were frank enough to admit the truth: "We went to the training so we could build the skills for our resumes."

IT Outages and Recovery

A peculiar blind spot we have often observed in IT departments is found in their reaction to emergencies. The disconnect seems to be both the order of actions taken and in the level of urgency exhibited by the IT department when outages of key systems occur. First, the occurrence of an emergency in most departments does not invoke standard procedures as would be the case in companies with robust business continuity plans. Instead, a set of random acts result in random outcomes based on the on-call team. Second, we have seen particular insensitivity to what drives revenues and profits in the business. Few staff members in IT departments understand the impact when a key system is unavailable to business users. Unfortunately, we have witnessed this lack of IT understanding regularly demonstrated across many businesses. We provide three examples of actual client situations.

We happened to be on-site with a client in the inbound call center support business when the phone system, supported by IT, crashed. This idled hundreds of agents and sent the managers into a panicked search for the IT operations support team. After half an hour of downtime, we finally asked the IT team for the estimated fix time. The response from the team was, "We can restore service any time. Right now, we are trying to see if we can investigate what happened for our records." The IT team had little understanding of the thousands of dollars per minute costs of a phone system outage in the call center.

We witnessed a similar insensitivity to business mission criticality in work we were managing for a company that is highly reliant on its on-line presence. The particular company Web site supported about three million unique customer transactions a month. In one instance when the Web site went down, the technical professionals in charge attacked the problem with vigor, spending sleepless 24-hour shifts diagnosing the source of database trouble. When asked for an update and ETA, the team lead replied, "We could bring the site up in about 4 hours by restoring a backup, but I'd prefer to continue diagnosing the cause which could take 24 to 48 hours." Again, an IT manager was having difficulty comprehending the business urgency behind the system's outage. If they truly understood the business impact, the team would have quickly eliminated the second option, immediately restored the backup, then attempted to diagnose the root cause. Better yet, the IT team and senior business leaders would have already had the discussion months ago to agree on specific procedures to take in the event of this particular disaster.

A final anecdote occurred with a client where we were providing temporary IT leadership. A virus had managed to make its way into the corporate e-mail system, causing IT to pull the plug on the system. Like most businesses, this client was highly reliant on access to e-mail for communications with suppliers and customers. Like the thorough, deliberate professionals they were, the IT operations team began an exhaustive virus scan and removal on the entire e-mail database. "Should be up in just about six hours," came the diagnosis. In this case, the virus propagated only if a recipient *opened* the affected e-mail. "Couldn't we bring the system back up and notify everyone via e-mail and public address system not to open the particular e-mail?" we proposed. "After all, in the worst case, if someone opens the virus-laden e-mail again, we can simply shut the system down again. Best case, everyone can continue using e-mail while you can continue to scan and remove in the background. This way we don't lose an entire day of productivity." The IT team resisted, but ultimately the logic prevailed, and the system ran without further incident for the remainder of the day, while the virus scan and removal process worked diligently in the background.

Explaining the costs of system outages to the IT team and ensuring that the team behaves with sensitivity to those costs is the dual responsibility of IT management and the senior management team. There should be no ambiguity about the priorities for returning the systems to service as quickly as possible. This priority is rarely completely conveyed throughout the IT organization, resulting in slow-to-return service and fiddling with problems by IT before the system is placed back in operation.

Setting Service Levels

Another common failing in the decision-making area is related to setting service levels to the business. Most IT departments have been repeatedly informed that the business is their "customer." However, the level of customer service has been left to IT to determine, often without the normal cost and profitability constraints that dictate the setting of service levels in a normal company-customer relationship. In these cases, the service levels across a variety of business support areas are often treated as a single unit, without acknowledging potential differences in service level that may be appropriate (e.g., level of response to a desktop computer outage is treated the same as for a major server outage). Service levels are not only treated monolithically but also often set artificially high.

One of our clients was experiencing out-of-control IT costs. We were asked to investigate opportunities to reduce costs. In our interview with the IT operations professionals, they proudly claimed: "We can move any phone extension in the company from one desktop to another inside an hour." While this level of customer service was certainly appreciated by the business, it was not clear that the business benefits of rapid office moves supported the associated cost of service.

One of the difficulties with setting service levels in IT departments that most companies struggle with is the phenomenon of the "tragedy of the commons." Because inordinately high service levels in the IT department do not carry any associated *cost,* business users are perfectly content to keep the service levels artificially high. The incremental cost is absorbed by the company overall as part of its general and administrative (G&A) budget, but no business unit manager is forced to make good economic choices on his or her own budget. This phenomenon, combined with the natural instinct to please the business customer on the part of IT, leads to insupportably high and expensive service levels across the board.

Often, companies attempt to circumvent this problem by allocating IT costs to the business units they support. Doing this accurately can be exceedingly difficult and can force the IT team and the business to spend countless hours devising the perfect allocation mechanism, all the while pushing neither IT nor business initiatives forward. In clients where we have seen allocation methodologies implemented, individual business units naturally want to take control to manage their IT costs. The result is effectively the creation of an IT company within the parent company. The cost of IT may actually increase in the mid-term because of additional overhead required to negotiate service level agreements (SLAs), measure performance against the negotiated levels, prepare detailed explanations of the costs being allocated, and report to the individual business units. As P&L managers demand cost reductions in IT, IT costs may decline in the long term.

Although we do not recommend business-unit allocation of IT costs, the threat of allocation can serve a useful purpose. In the client mentioned, many of the cost savings we proposed were predicated on selective lowering of service levels on specific non-business-critical items. This was, naturally, met with considerable resistance on the part of the business. Because IT costs were so high, we offered two options: Keep service levels the same and allocate IT costs to business units proportional to their revenue, or lower service levels and continue to incorporate IT costs into G&A. The business unit managers were unanimous in their vote to lower service levels to reasonable levels.

Setting Capacity Levels

The final area in which we have observed decision-making difficulties is in setting capacity levels. In making decisions about staff and computing capacity, again the incentives of IT to ensure complete, failure-proof coverage without the associated cost pressures asserts itself.

IT teams tend to allocate capacity at the maximum level of potential demand instead of the overall average demand for a given function. This is particularly true in the operations area where shortfalls in capacity are rapidly noticeable to the business users; e-mail outages, downed application servers, and desktop computers or phones not working get the immediate attention of the business. Exhibit 14.3 shows the variability of demand in a typical operations support department. While systems are running smoothly, demand is relatively low. An emergency, a transient business problem, or a periodic surge because of business cycles increases demand on the staff temporarily.

Because of the incentive issues noted throughout the chapter, the IT department tends to create capacity at the maximum requirement, rather than find creative ways to staff at the average levels and still provide adequate service. In the exhibit, it is easy to see the cost of staffing to the *surge* compared to staffing to the *average* capacity requirement.

There are a variety of ways to combat these staffing surge issues. Typically, IT departments are organized along two main lines—applications and operations (see Chapter 4, "The IT Organization"). One strategy for handling surges in capacity needed in the operations area, without resorting to overstaffing, is to cross-train developers in the required skills to provide surge capacity to the operations team. While this might not be a wildly popular strategy with the

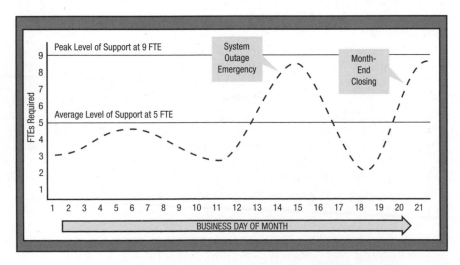

Exhibit 14.3 Monthly Demand for Operations Staffing Capacity

development team, generally, developers have the requisite technical skills to substitute in an emergency, thereby allowing companies to staff at the 60 percent to 75 percent of surge level, instead of 100 percent. Further, the IT department can find creative ways to selectively lower service levels by delaying baseline support tasks during emergency surges in demand.

Another creative way of ensuring that emergency capacity is available is to provide reciprocal tech-support capacity in nearby companies with similar technical environments. Locating these companies and having the operations teams spend an afternoon together once a month is a low-cost way of ensuring that a friendly army of extra technical consultants is available inexpensively and fast.

This setting of capacity to the maximum required level and, therefore, the maximum possible cost, is not limited to staffing. It is often found in the specification and purchasing of corporate systems as well. From the IT perspective, the desire is to provide the customer with the best possible service because the customer *sees* the service level and *feels* none of the cost directly. Therefore, it is easy to eliminate the risk of slow system complaints from business users by purchasing capacity equal to the maximum required level. Exhibit 14.4 shows a typical batch-processing calendar with system demand mapped against time of day.

Although the superficial answer is to request additional processing capacity or an entirely new system, again, the team can likely find creative ways to address the issues. In this specific case, an analysis of the batch job streams revealed nonurgent, noncritical path batch jobs that were competing with batch jobs submitted by online users during peak processing times. The team found ways to ensure that nonurgent batches are deferred automatically by the system until processing capacity becomes available.

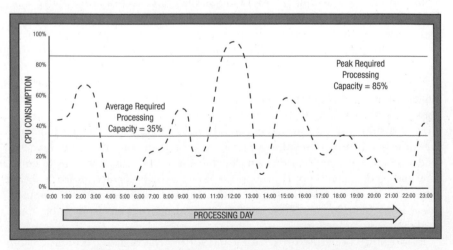

Exhibit 14.4   Batch Processing Capacity Requirements

IT steering committees must carefully weigh the costs of additional capacity decisions against other alternatives. When additional capacity is required, good IT organizations make every effort to design scalable solutions to provide a spectrum of options that enable the business to initially purchase the minimum requirement instead of the maximum. Scalability allows the business to expand capacity as needed, resulting in a step function of costs instead of a binary cost function.

Summary

As shown in the previous examples, even IT departments with the best of intentions can spin wildly out of budgetary control. Indeed, it is the IT departments with the highest commitment to service that so often exhibit this behavior. As shown in the previous anecdotes, asking probing questions, assessing the *real* risk, and using common sense and creative thinking can help the IT department and senior management work together to minimize both risk and cost.

Intelligent risk management should be an exercise in common sense for the IT team and the senior management team. We do not suggest a "band-aid-and-bubblegum" approach to the maintenance of corporate systems. The mammoth cost of being wrong in this area almost always dwarfs the cost of insurance. What we are suggesting is that a monolithic approach to risk without even the most cursory investigation of potential options is a primary driver of overspending in an IT department.

A tremendous amount of value can be created by senior management by ensuring that the incentives for IT are geared toward intelligent risk management and decision making. Most IT departments have the philosophy "Systems should work at all costs." Senior management should lead a change in that philosophy to "Systems should work at reasonable costs, and here is where we are willing to accept some shortcomings to ensure that those costs stay reasonable."

One practical approach to facilitating the decision-making process is the implementation of standard operating procedures and checklists. The Operations area is not the only area where standard operating procedures can improve decision-making and process standardization. Other areas here include capital expenditure approval, operating expense approval, hiring, and capacity decisions. The specific items on the checklists vary from company to company and by decision type. However, the tool can be useful to ensure that the proper questions have been asked and that the risk has been set at the appropriate level. See Chapter 7 for an example and instructions to develop standard operating procedures.

By working cooperatively with IT and setting reasonable expectations on service levels, the organization can reap the benefits of getting capacity, service levels, emergency response, and spending "just right." An illustration of this comes from a recent client engagement. The senior management team of a manufacturing company asked us to validate its IT capital budgets for the coming year. The previous material might lead you to believe that the focus of the engagement was the minimization of capital expenditures. In fact, the engagement mandate was to understand the real requirements for technology capital expenditure, regardless of outcome. Whether this meant spending more or less mattered less to the senior management team than ensuring that they were spending the right amount on IT, minimizing risk, and not overinsuring. The theme of the engagement was finding the *truth* as opposed to any particular cost target.

RESOURCES

Decision-making science is a complex and well-researched topic of study. A variety of leading thinkers on the topic have produced highly approachable, practical guides to improving the decision-making process. A few books we recommend for IT and senior management decision makers are listed here.

John S. Hammond, Ralph L. Keeney, and Howard Raiffa, *Smart Choices: A Practical Guide to Making Better Decisions* (Boston: Harvard Business School Press, September 1998).

James G. March and Chip Heath, *A Primer on Decision Making: How Decisions Happen* (New York: Free Press, May 1994).

Jeffrey Pfeffer and Robert I. Sutton, *The Knowing-Doing Gap: How Smart Companies Turn Knowledge into Action* (Boston: Harvard Business School Press, January 15, 2000).

J. Edward Russo and Paul J. H. Schoemaker, *Decision Traps: Ten Barriers to Brilliant Decision-Making and How to Overcome Them* (New York: Fireside, 1990).

J. Edward Russo, Paul J. H. Schoemaker, and Margo Hittleman, *Winning Decisions: Getting It Right the First Time* (New York: Doubleday, 2001).

NOTES

1. George S. Patton, *Letter to Cadet George S. Patton IV* (June 6, 1944).
2. Ralph Waldo Emerson, *Self-Reliance and Other Essays* (Mineola, NY: Dover Publications, November 1993).

15

IT Demand Management and Project Prioritization

The heavens themselves, the planets, and this center
Observe degree, priority, and place,
Insisture, course, proportion, season, form,
Office, and custom, in all line of order.

—William Shakespeare[1]

This chapter identifies and outlines an approach for managing the demand for projects of all types in the IT department. We define *IT demand management* as a metaproject that determines which IT projects should be commissioned and executed by the IT department by calculating their financial value and prioritizing the projects based on that value and other factors, particularly IT department capacity and overall organization capacity. IT demand management includes the process of identifying and inventorying all ongoing and planned projects, estimating effort to complete, determining costs and benefits, other project dependencies, ease of completion, risks, technical implications, and adequacy of current systems. The result is a properly prioritized inventory of projects and a corporate decision on how many simultaneous projects are feasible.

Demand management is a distinct and separate consideration from project management and is often a neglected topic in IT. IT project management concerns itself with clearly defining project scope, requirements, tasks, time lines, milestones, internal and external resources, costs, technical, application and data architectures, and business impacts for a given project. This discipline usually begins after a project or set of projects has been commissioned. IT demand management is concerned with which projects are commissioned before any projects begin. There is a comprehensive body of work on the topic of IT project management, and the tenets of successful project

400

management have been documented in dozens of books and articles, making it well-understood territory. Given this in-depth previous coverage, we do not attempt to address project management in detail but instead focus on overall IT project prioritization.

In spite of a host of well-defined, proven approaches for managing projects, as observed in Chapter 1, IT projects often fail, many times spectacularly. Our experience has shown that this often results as much from poor demand management and prioritization as much as from badly executed project management. Companies that do not allocate project demand on the IT department based on sound prioritization methodologies are plagued with dozens of competing projects with hazy objectives and often conflicting goals. The resulting project gridlock can often be perplexing to the hapless project managers, who find themselves failing in spite of their best efforts to adhere to accepted project management methodologies. Companies' inability to properly throttle project demand in the IT department is one of the top contributing factors in inefficient IT departments. Certainly, poorly prioritized and poorly run projects never stand a chance, but improper IT demand management is a common cause for the failure of otherwise well-run projects. Correctly managing the project demand on the IT department ensures that only "good" projects are commissioned and that only the appropriate number of projects is allowed to run simultaneously, giving well-managed projects a fighting chance.

Although the primary focus of this chapter is IT demand management, at the chapter conclusion, we offer some of the key success factors we have observed in the field of project management.

This chapter describes the concept of demand management and the issues associated with poor demand management. The prescriptive portion of the chapter is organized around a multistep process for project prioritization based on proven IT demand management principles.

As with the other chapters in this book, the ideas described are general best practices, and all or some of the concepts and ideas described may be applicable to each unique situation. In every case, common sense application of the prioritization frameworks should always prevail.

Why This Topic Is Important

A most visible, and often cited, measure of the success of the IT department is the business success of the projects undertaken and the completion of those projects in a timely, cost-effective manner. Therefore, the successful selection, prioritization, and execution of IT projects play a large part in determining the overall success of the IT department. Selecting which, and how many projects are allowed on the IT department schedule is a critical determinant of the overall success of those projects.

Project prioritization is a complex process that involves identification of the different projects and assessment of the projects based on factors such as strategic value, financial value, risk, existing system adequacy, time to completion, as well as organizational capacity and technical complexity. These assessments are made to differentiate the *high-priority* projects on a project list based on relevant factors, particularly financial value. They are used to accurately reflect the priority of IT projects in supporting the business unit priorities—not IT's self-mandated priorities. The chapter outlines our methodology for this process.

Issues covered in this chapter include:

- Concept of IT demand management.
- Distinction between IT demand management and project management.
- Organization challenges posed by improper IT demand management.
- Costs to companies from poor demand management and project prioritization.
- Symptoms of poor demand management, prioritization, and project financial impact assessment.
- Top causes of project failure not related to project management.
- Methodology for building project inventories and assessing project priorities.
- Key drivers for project prioritization, including financial value, ease of completion, strategic value, current system adequacy, and project risk.
- Approaches for calculating financial value of projects, including ROI, NPV, and payback period.
- Assessment of IT organization capacity for projects.
- Assessment of project manager capacity.
- Determination of overall company capacity to complete and absorb projects.

The Impact of IT Demand Management on Project Performance

The success rate of IT projects is abysmal. The Standish Group statistics quoted in Chapter 1 show that fewer than 16 percent of IT projects reach successful completion.[2]

A major contributor to corporate dissatisfaction with the IT department is IT's inability to complete projects on time, within budget, and to business users' satisfaction and expectations. Paradoxically, almost all IT departments are staffed with hard-working, technically skilled professionals who have the best intentions and want most of all to move their company forward and to be successful at their work. Nevertheless, the IT department is perpetually "staying incredibly busy," but no actual results are achieved, projects completed, or benefits realized.

Typically, a struggling IT department has dozens, even hundreds, of projects underway simultaneously. This is a common phenomenon that we have observed in organizations, regardless of size. The overall project inventory, if one exists, is littered with dozens of ill-defined, partially completed projects of indeterminate origin, benefits, goals, and status. Compounding the issue is that the projects are scoped at wildly varying levels of complexity, size, and business impact, producing absurd results such as "fix Martha's laptop" at the same level as "implement CRM." Further, the project list has multiple dependencies (some identified, some not), internal inconsistencies, conflicting time lines, and unclear ownership on the part of both the business and the IT department.

In most cases, each of these projects is partially completed and in a perpetual state of being slowly shepherded to a fuzzy, indistinct, and elusive finish line by the IT department, with little real hope of solid completion. Indeed, most IT departments have dozens, if not hundreds, of simultaneous projects, each being pushed forward infinitesimally each week. Because IT is attempting to work on multiple competing objectives, in many cases, the original rationale for the project has become obscured by the passage of time, personnel changes, and changes in the business, often rendering the project irrelevant. Xeno's paradox, which states that if you can achieve half the distance to the goal with each step, you will never arrive, comes to mind. The most troubling result of this common dilemma is the damage done to companies who fail to complete, or even identify, the high-value, high-priority technology projects.

The Price of Project Failure

Poor execution and noncompletion of IT projects are a material waste of corporate resources. The Standish Group research cited in Chapter 1 shows that the vast majority of technology projects have missed deadlines and overrun budgets. In addition to the direct costs of failed projects, companies suffer from missed opportunities to reduce costs, drive revenues, or improve operations that the failed projects were intended to deliver. IT project failure can be at best a hindrance and, at times, fatal to a company. In every case, working on the right projects ineffectively or working on the wrong projects is a drain on precious corporate resources. A co-worker's performance review once read, "You're working on the wrong things, and, worse, you're doing them poorly." Unfortunately, this is the case in many IT departments today.

A variety of other costs are associated with poor IT demand and project management that erode the IT department effectiveness as well:

- Resources are allocated equally to low- and high-priority projects, implying that high-priority projects may go understaffed or not be commissioned at all.

- IT department managers overhire to provide staffing levels that support low- and high-priority projects equally.

- The large number of simultaneous projects makes individual projects difficult to monitor; therefore, significant rework efforts, missed deadlines, and budget overruns may go unnoticed, and individual project accountability is difficult to track.

- Multiple disconnected projects create a heterogeneous IT environment, driving additional complexity and, therefore, cost into the baseline support required. Chapter 6 outlines the perils of non-standard environments in detail.

- Superficial and costly answers are adopted prematurely because the resources that can provide a long-lasting solution are tied up (e.g., additional hardware is thrown at an application performance problem as a quick fix, increasing capital expenditures).

- Deadlines are missed for key customer-required new business capabilities (e.g., EDI-based inventory position exchanges, mandatory online catalog, and product order access).

- Business units spend their own budgets on decentralized IT projects (in larger corporations, business units may fund the creation of their own IT group) because the centralized IT department is unable to adequately execute on priority projects.

- Hiring process emphasizes skills required for low-priority projects instead of, or as well as, high-priority projects, resulting in an IT staff with the wrong or weak set of technical skills to address the top business issues. To remediate, the organization will be forced to lay off and rehire or invest in expensive, time-consuming training.

- Dearth of IT successes results in low morale and high turnover in IT staff, driving up training, recruiting, and turnover costs, compounding the issues by driving out the top performers in IT.

These hidden costs can show up across the board in corporate spending as increases in capital expenditures, IT wage dollars, business unit budgets, increased baseline support costs, and extra external vendor spend.

Why Good Project Management Is Not Enough

A host of reasons explain why organizations manage individual projects well but fare poorly in project completion overall. The previously described symptoms and costs are associated with a set of common causes, which we have cataloged here.

Too Many Projects

IT staff tends to be "pleasers" by nature; the managers and developers fundamentally want to help the business and are usually excited about the benefits and solutions technology can bring to a given business problem. Unfortunately, this tendency often leads IT departments to have trouble saying no (or at least "get in line") to new project requests when they should. In the absence of a clear methodology for managing a project backlog, prioritizing the backlog, and chartering new projects, the IT department invariably takes on more than it should. The outcome is usually a pleased business user today and an angry one three months later when the promised results cannot be delivered.

IT professionals spend effort worrying over scope creep in a project but not enough time worrying about project creep at a macro level. A secondary, related issue is spending time talking about projects instead of doing them. When the IT department has a full set of projects underway, with completion of any of them in the distance, little value is added by discussing the backlog of non-chartered projects. New project ideas should be duly noted and added to the backlog for consideration when project capacity becomes available through the completion of an existing project. Discussing projects not currently underway can be particularly seductive because it closely resembles actual work. This is not to say that high-value projects should not be considered, but it would be a high-value project indeed that could convince the IT department and business sponsors to halt an existing project or to take on more project capacity and, therefore, a project that obviously merits additional consideration. The methodology detailed later in this chapter calls for a reprioritization of the existing backlog at each project completion to ensure that the current chartered projects always consist of the highest value known projects.

No Project Gatekeepers

If projects are allowed to commence without a clear justification, soon the in-process and backlog project inventory becomes cluttered with a morass of ill-defined projects. A good IT demand management process implements stringent requirements for adding projects to the project inventory. The process for adding new projects is documented later in this chapter, but, in short, it should involve a detailed understanding of the costs, business benefits, and scope of the project, as well as a defined business owner and preliminary effort/time line estimate. The project gatekeeping duties should fall to the IT steering committee, which should be both approving projects for the backlog and prioritizing backlogged projects as capacity becomes available.

In many organizations where we have helped institute IT demand management disciplines, the issue of how difficult it is to get a project started comes up. Most often, the senior management team is worried that we have erected too many barriers to justify new projects. In these cases, we know the methodology is working. Indeed, one of the key ways of keeping a clean project inventory is ensuring that the process has the effect of killing weak projects that have little return and no one in the organization passionate enough about them to fight for their existence. Institution of this form of "project Darwinism" creates a natural selection process that ensures that only the highest value projects survive and that the prioritization process is performed only on good projects. In fact, truly great projects are impossible to keep down and, based on their obvious benefits, rapidly make their way through any approval process.

Too Many Simultaneous Projects

It is hard for anyone to disagree that there is an upper limit on the number of simultaneous projects. Even in large IT departments and corporations, there are a finite number of projects that should be allowed to coexist. As the number of simultaneous projects increases, so does the likelihood of unintended consequences, difficulties of system integration, introduction of heterogeneous technology, and simple distraction for the IT organization. Further, and most practically, a given business unit or function can absorb only so much change over a period. Depending on company size, IT department size, and overall project size, the number of simultaneous projects allowed can be as low as three or four or as high as a dozen. We have seen project success rates fall dramatically when IT departments try to sustain several large projects and multiple small projects.

Moving the Goalposts

Business users are well known for changing the goals of the projects that they are sponsoring. This is a primary contributor to the perception that IT cannot generate clear successes. The whipsawing that occurs from changing the project charter or goals midstream can be damaging to the project, IT morale, and business users' confidence. IT managers have equal culpability here because they are all too often willing accomplices in changing project goals and scope midstream, and they wind up paying the price in the end as the project careens off course. One method for ensuring that the IT department can generate a clear track record of success, while providing flexibility over time, is to commission short-cycle projects (less than three months) with near-term, less ambitious goals. This technique ensures that IT can succeed in short cycles, yet refine the longer term goals at each project completion interval.

Too Much Elapsed Time

Particularly lengthy projects often fail because too much time elapses during their completion. During this time, a host of factors such as changes in the business climate, technology advances, staff attrition, and corporate senior management changes may impact the viability and value of the project. Breaking projects into smaller subprojects helps ensure that if conditions do change, clearly defined pieces of the project will be complete, maximizing their potential salvage value.

Overambitious Goals

Ambitious, large-scale projects suffer naturally from several of the woes outlined here. The length of time, functional and technical complexity, labor complexities, and tough-to-quantify benefits of large projects make them particularly difficult for even the best IT teams to complete. Breaking larger projects into smaller distinct phases provides a better probability for a successful completion.

Indistinct Goals

Projects with unclear goals usually fail spectacularly. If neither the business nor IT defines in advance what success entails, there is little chance of achieving it. While this is one of the more obvious causes of project failure, it happens with surprising frequency. IT professionals tend to have a bias for action over planning that often results in murky project goal setting.

Unclear Benefits

A project can have clear goals and still suffer from indistinct or difficult-to-measure benefits. Key projects, if chartered correctly, generate clearly defined benefits once the goals have been achieved. These usually take the form of cost savings, additional revenue opportunities, or additional control over the business. Good IT demand management discipline ensures that both goals and benefits are well defined before a project is allowed on the approved list.

Heterogeneous Technology

As we have documented in previous chapters, a heterogeneous technology environment can drive up project costs and complexity by an order of magnitude. Existing (or planned) chaotic, difficult-to-interface technical, application, and data architectures can doom an otherwise well-run project.

Overconfidence Bias

New or inexperienced managers often plan overaggressive projects with grand goals and tight time lines. Because of overconfidence, they are not able to anticipate the pitfalls of improper demand management outlined here. The result can be many of the other causes outlined in this section—overambitious projects, hazy end-goals, lengthy projects, too many simultaneous projects, and third-party interference.

Outsiders Drive the Agenda

While certainly the IT landscape is populated with a host of well-meaning hardware, software, and service providers, their agendas are not always perfectly aligned with those of the end client. Through simple misunderstanding, a narrow point of view, their own inexperience, or outright negligence, third parties can damage a project. The risk is highest when outside parties are allowed too much control over the project and are being allowed to drive the overall agenda. Allowing vendors to manage large pieces of the project and to make key decisions can be tempting for the IT manager, and most successful vendors aggressively work for as much power as the client allows. The successful IT manager finds productive ways to use vendor expertise while maintaining control of the overall program. The proper role of vendors of all types as partners in helping projects succeed is covered in the vendor selection and vendor management chapters of this book.

No Individual Accountability

Not surprisingly, clearly defined accountability for project results is often absent in ineffective IT departments. For example, one of our clients had particularly weak project completion, and nearly every in-process project had three project managers from IT, none of whom was held strictly accountable for the results. When each project was assigned a single responsible individual who was required to report weekly status to the IT steering committee, project completion rates skyrocketed. There is no substitute for individual accountability and frequent project progress scrutiny.

Project Size

The larger the project, the more difficult it is to ensure that it can be completed. As outlined here, smaller projects with short cycle times, easy-to-define goals, and minimized complexity always have a higher chance of success than do large, unwieldy, complex projects. While large projects are not always avoidable, breaking them down into smaller components and executing them serially can mitigate the costs of complexity.

Too Many Moving Parts

Even projects that do not appear to be overambitious can suffer from over-complexity. Systems projects are by their nature highly intricate endeavors with many subtleties. Even seemingly simple projects can become rapidly complicated and frequently produce multiple unintended consequences. If a given project spans too many vendors, technologies, business processes, interfaces, locations, or other "moving parts," its complexity goes up significantly, and odds of success go down proportionally. This phenomenon holds true for all types of systems projects—applications, databases, and infrastructure implementations. Again, the proper approach is to break projects into more palatable chunks, increasing the likelihood of near-term success and reducing the time to completion.

Poor Communication

Too often in challenged IT departments a project is tossed over the wall to IT, with little or no communication between the business sponsor and the IT department during the project. The project end product, naturally, is then inconsistent with the intent of the end user, whether through indistinct definition or translation problems at the outset or changes in the business during the course of the project. At a minimum, project managers should be in contact weekly with the sponsor and final consumers of the project.

   While each of these causes implies its own solution, the common theme is ensuring that only the proper number and type of clearly defined, prioritized projects are ever chartered. Proper IT demand management can mitigate the impacts of these causes on IT department project performance by ensuring that only the right number of high-value, properly defined projects is allowed to go forward. Good project management, in turn, ensures that those projects are successfully completed and deliver the planned value.

A Methodology for IT Demand Management

Our work with IT departments of all sizes in a variety of industries has resulted in a field-proven methodology for avoiding the perils of poor IT demand management. The remainder of the chapter outlines the methodology and covers our prescription for optimizing demand management.

   A multistep, analysis-intensive, complex process such as this that must be completed before a project can even commence can put off even the most disciplined of IT departments. However, the benefits of improved project execution and completion, which are the natural outcome of adhering to a rigorous, analytical process for IT demand management, far outweigh the upfront costs of documentation and planning that we suggest here. Exhibit 15.1 provides an overview of the process. The following sections describe each step in detail.

Inventory All Potential Projects

The first step in the demand management process is to create the inventory of all potential projects to be undertaken by the IT department. This is most often a lengthy list that requires considerable effort to assemble. Typically, the projects emanate from a wide variety of disparate sources scattered throughout the IT department and the company.

A good starting point in the search is the IT department project roster. Most IT departments have one or more lists of projects currently being worked or being considered. Interviews with business unit managers, functional department heads, senior managers, and business users will uncover other projects. Any current enhancement or upgrade lists from vendors or service providers should be obtained and consolidated into one overall project inventory.

After the full list of potential projects has been created, it should be rationalized by removing duplicate projects, as well as combining related small projects into a single effort, or breaking large projects into stand-alone components. This project rationalization (known more popularly as the "project rodeo") starts by creating a full inventory of all projects and then removing duplicates and overlaps, combining items to ensure that the work is defined at the same level. This work generally reduces the project list by 60 percent to 70 percent.

Most project inventory efforts also include projects that no longer have business sponsors or are no longer relevant for the company. These relics should be cut from the list. A key tenet of effective IT demand management is that good projects naturally assert themselves because of their self-evident return. It is common for IT departments, in an attempt to be conscientious

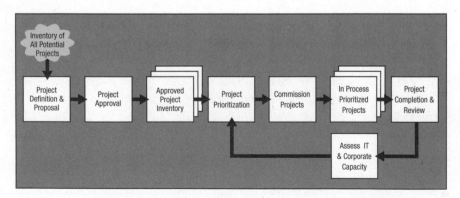

Exhibit 15.1   IT Demand Management Process Overview

and thorough, to keep projects on lists even if no one remembers how they got there. Managers should rest easy on this point—truly valuable projects find their way back onto the list, even if they are inadvertently removed. Bad projects that clutter the list, however, cannot usually sustain real scrutiny and do not survive this exercise.

The result of this process is an inventory of all potential projects, with a short description of each project. The team should avoid overcomplicating the exercise at this point with high-powered project management tools. A simple list of each project name, a brief description, the business and IT sponsor recorded in a spreadsheet or word processing document usually suffices. The content and comprehensiveness of the list are the focus, as opposed to fancy tools or excessive formatting. The projects will receive adequate attention in later steps to ensure that they are properly documented before being commissioned.

Project Definition and Proposal

The next step in the process is to clearly define the project's goals at a level that allows the IT steering committee to provide preliminary approval for the project to be considered for prioritization. This includes the objective of the project and preliminary estimates for the project effort, time line, costs, and benefits. These pieces of information quickly identify and help to provide a first-round estimate of the project's relative value.

Typically, the IT department creates a one-page form, which succinctly captures the critical information needed for the IT steering committee to understand and evaluate the project. The form should include:

- Project name.
- Brief project description.
- Requestor.
- Estimated duration.
- Estimated work effort.
- Current status or progress (if already underway).
- Estimated benefit to the business (reduced costs, increased revenues, better control of the business).
- Business unit sponsor.
- IT sponsor.
- Preliminary estimate of IT resource to be assigned.

Project Approval

Each of the projects, having been defined at the appropriate level of detail, should be presented by the business and IT sponsor to the IT steering committee for a disposition. The IT steering committee approves the project, rejects it, or sends it back for further clarification and definition. Project approval by the committee does not imply that the project will proceed immediately, merely that it is eligible for detailed analysis and participation in the project prioritization process that follows.

The approval is an important step in the process because each approved project will be part of the detailed project prioritization effort. The number of projects evaluated is a major driver of the effort in the prioritization process, so project approvals should be rigorous and serious enough to ensure that only legitimate projects make it through to the next steps. Any projects that are not clearly defined or are of questionable value can be re-evaluated for approval at subsequent IT steering committee meetings.

The outcome of the process is an inventory of projects that have been reviewed by the IT steering committee and approved for prioritization. Again, sophisticated management tools are overkill for this process—a simple binder with one-page descriptions of the projects, the date of approval, and the signoff from the IT steering committee usually suffices.

As a point of process, it should be noted that the IT steering committee can at any time add projects to the approved list because new projects are not started until the prioritization process is executed. The prioritization process is triggered when new IT project capacity becomes available because a previous project has completed or because the IT department has added new team members.

Project Prioritization

Project prioritization is the process whereby the IT department determines, in conjunction with the business users and IT steering committee, which projects will generate the highest value for the company and how many can go on simultaneously, given the organization and capacity within IT.

The prioritization process generates four key benefits for the IT department and the overall organization:

- The IT department will always be spending effort on the highest value projects—resources naturally flow to their best use.
- The process ensures that IT and business consensus on project value and priority are built in advance of the project start.
- The IT department capacity analysis ensures that the number of simultaneous projects allowed will be manageable for both the capacity of the IT department and the organization's ability to absorb change.
- The process ensures that project goals and scope are clearly defined in advance and individual accountability for project success is assigned.

The project prioritization process is the heart of effective IT demand management, and it gives the IT department more than a fighting chance to avoid many of the pitfalls described earlier in the chapter. It is imperative that the business users have adequate representation on the steering committee because their input is critical to proper prioritization. Correctly assembling the steering committee and its membership can make or break the process. Chapter 17 covers this process in detail.

After a preliminary project prioritization is complete, the prioritization process takes place under three circumstances:

1. When an existing project is completed and IT project capacity becomes available.
2. When new IT capacity is added (or reduced), changing the total number of possible simultaneous projects.
3. The prioritization may be reassessed if high-priority projects that should be prioritized over existing efforts are identified. This instance is a rare occurrence because of the high cost of an IT project changeover, but it may happen in some instances (e.g., key customer demands new capabilities, government regulation, or new technology that improves revenue or reduces costs).

Prioritization of approved projects is, therefore, not just a one-time effort but, instead, an ongoing process. While we outline here a quantitative approach for assessing the projects and prioritizing them, it is important to add a healthy dose of common sense to project prioritization. The methodology provides ample room for tilting the table for projects whose benefits it does not adequately incorporate. Exhibit 15.2 outlines the overall approach for project prioritization.

The prioritization process incorporates the best thinking of the IT and business leaders across the key project metrics that should drive project priorities: financial value, risk, strategic value, current system adequacy, and IT capacity. The analysis portion of the prioritization exercise should be completed by the IT department and business users and results presented to the IT steering committee for approval and signoff. In most cases, the process

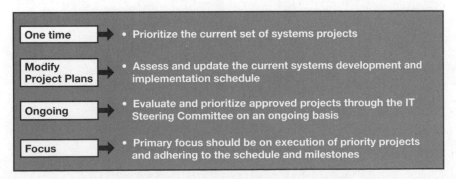

Exhibit 15.2   Key Components to the Prioritization Process

consumes several iterations of analysis after the first presentation to the IT steering committee, as additional information needs are uncovered through questions.

Key Components of the Prioritization Process

The analytic portion of the project prioritization process can be decomposed into seven discrete subtasks. The overall approach is shown in Exhibit 15.3 and is described in more detail in the following sections.

DETERMINE PROJECT FINANCIAL VALUE. Generally, the single best measure of the value of the project is its financial value to the company. In simplest terms, the financial value is measured as the benefit stream that a project delivers compared to the cost to generate those benefits. Exhibit 15.4 shows an overall framework for evaluating project value based on the associated financial value.

There are many methods for calculating the financial value of a given project, including return on investment, value on investment, project payback period, net present value, and internal rate of return. All specific methods for measuring project return have in common the inputs needed to understand project value: costs and benefits. Project costs usually come in

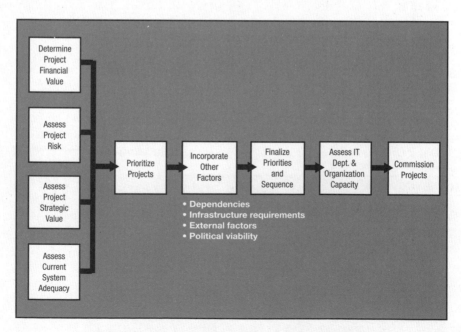

Exhibit 15.3 Overall Project Prioritization Process

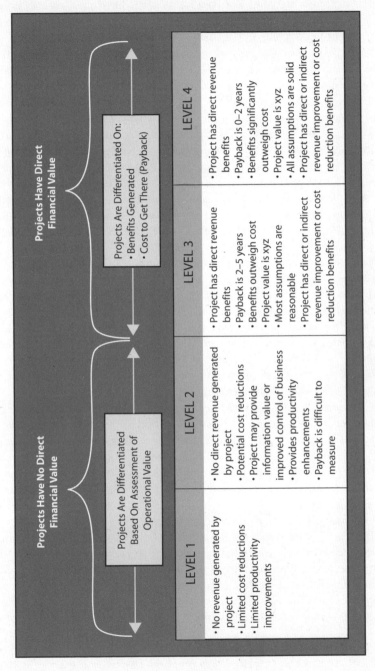

Projects Have No Direct Financial Value

Projects Have Direct Financial Value

Projects Are Differentiated Based On Assessment of Operational Value

Projects Are Differentiated On:
- Benefits Generated
- Cost to Get There (Payback)

LEVEL 1
- No revenue generated by project
- Limited cost reductions
- Limited productivity improvements

LEVEL 2
- No direct revenue generated by project
- Potential cost reductions
- Project may provide information value or improved control of business
- Provides productivity enhancements
- Payback is difficult to measure

LEVEL 3
- Project has direct revenue benefits
- Payback is 2–5 years
- Benefits outweigh cost
- Project value is xyz
- Most assumptions are reasonable
- Project has direct or indirect revenue improvement or cost reduction benefits

LEVEL 4
- Project has direct revenue benefits
- Payback is 0–2 years
- Benefits significantly outweigh cost
- Project value is xyz
- All assumptions are solid
- Project has direct or indirect revenue improvement or cost reduction benefits

Exhibit 15.4   Project Financial Value Scorecard

two forms: one-time project costs and steady-state cost changes (i.e., changes to the underlying operating model). Likewise, benefits have one-time and ongoing components. Usually, the majority of the costs occur in the one-time category, while benefits tend to come in the form of recurring savings or revenues.

Depending on the company requirements or IT steering committee's preferences, models of widely varying sophistication can be used to measure the financial value of the project. Our preference for project value measurement is a simple measure of the costs and benefits and clear documentation of the major cost drivers and assumptions for benefit generation. The analysis time saved by keeping the model simple can be spent on further validating the cost and benefit assumptions, thereby greatly improving the accuracy of the estimate. An estimate generated by a sophisticated calculation based on poor or incomplete assumptions is useless in helping guide investment decisions. Exhibit 15.5 presents our basic model for calculating project return. Because the model is simplified, particular attention should be paid to the timing of benefits. Speculative benefits in the distant future are of considerably lower value, especially when compared to real costs today. The assumptions behind the model should outline the stream of recurring benefits and their timing. Chapter 10 also addresses approaches for estimating project costs and benefits. An example of a simple project financial value calculation is shown in Exhibit 15.6.

It is also important to note that the financial value estimate should be done on a cash-flow basis. While accounting rules allow project, hardware, and software investments to be capitalized and the expense recognized over time, the project should demonstrate clear value on a cash flow basis, regardless of its final accounting treatment.

The CFO and business unit owners also generally want to understand how the project will affect the current fiscal year budget, so they can prepare for any variances that develop as part of the project. In cases where the project costs can be capitalized, the impact on current year budgets should be minimal. The CFO also wants to understand the timing of cash outlays for the project to effectively manage corporate cash reserves. Understanding timing of project expenses ensures that cash is available when needed for the project external resources, hardware, and software.

Finally, the IT steering committee can be helpful guiding the IT team in evaluating the return on technology-related projects compared to other projects throughout the company. In most cases, the senior management team wants corporate investment dollars to be spent on the highest-return project corporatewide, and the IT steering committee can provide context for the IT department on competing nontechnology projects that have been proposed.

ASSESS PROJECT RISK. Assessing risk impact on company priorities is the next critical step in the prioritization process. The overall project delivery risk has a large impact on the organization's ability to realize the project

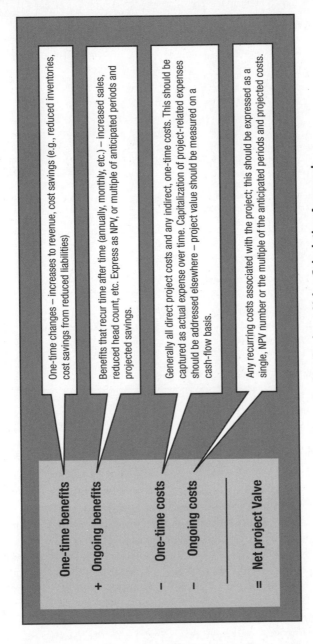

One-time benefits — One-time changes – increases to revenue, cost savings (e.g., reduced inventories, cost savings from reduced liabilities)

+ Ongoing benefits — Benefits that recur time after time (annually, monthly, etc.) – increased sales, reduced head count, etc. Express as NPV, or multiple of anticipated periods and projected savings.

– One-time costs — Generally all direct project costs and any indirect, one-time costs. This should be captured as actual expense over time. Capitalization of project-related expenses should be addressed elsewhere – project value should be measured on a cash-flow basis.

– Ongoing costs — Any recurring costs associated with the project; this should be expressed as a single, NPV number or the multiple of the anticipated periods and projected costs.

= Net project Valve

Exhibit 15.5   Project Business Value Calculation Approach

417

PROJECT VALUE FOR WEB SITE PROMOTION

	ASSUMPTION	CALCULATION
Estimated unique visitors per day	1,000	
Member points		
Visitors that become members (points)	15%	150
Members that earn coupons	75%	113
Number of Members earning coupons that visit store	50%	56
Revenue per day from Members earning coupons		$56
Contests and surveys		
Members that participate in contests	33%	50
Number of times visiting store for contest	20	
Store visits due to contests		990
Revenue per day from store contests		$2,267
Instant coupons		
Visitors that win instant discount coupons	5%	50
Number of people earning coupons that visit the store	65%	33
Revenue per day from instant coupons		$53
Incremental store visits		
Incremental visits per unique visitor per year	2	
Total participating visitors per day		183
Revenue per day from incremental store visits		$836
Total revenue per day		$3,213
Total revenue per year		$1,143,708
Gross margin on product revenue	90%	$1,029,337
Estimated cost of site		$245,000
Months to payback		2.86
Average price for product	$1.29	
Average price of uplift from product	$1.00	

Exhibit 15.6   Example Project Financial Value Calculation

benefits. Some categories of IT project risks include project complexity, user readiness, and technology to be used. The scorecard in Exhibit 15.7 shows other risk factors to evaluate when determining the value of a project. Depending on the specific project under consideration, other factors may be deemed appropriate by the evaluation team for evaluating project risk. In any case, the project should be assigned a risk rating relative to the other approved projects in the inventory, ranging from low to high.

ASSESS PROJECT STRATEGIC VALUE.   *Project strategic value* is defined as the impact a project will have on external entities, particularly customers and suppliers. The strategic value of the project gives a better idea of how the project gives the company new capabilities that improve the company's

LOW ← RISK LEVEL → HIGH

	Level 4	Level 3	Level 2	Level 1
Project Complexity	• Requirements well understood and documented • Scope well defined	• Good understanding of requirements • Limited potential impact of regional or customer differences	• Application supports new business practices not well understood • Limited experience with business function	• Major functionality blocks not clearly defined • Unclear understanding of IT requirements • Many outstanding issues
User Readiness	• Key resources have availability and capacity • Clear ownership and accountability • Specific and measurable targets	• Resources available • Shared ownership and accountability • Key issues tracked with impact understood	• Unclear or limited ownership • Broad accountability across several areas • Issues not tracked – no understanding of impact	• Key resources spread across many projects • No ownership of project or benefits • Limited accountability • Many outstanding issues
Technology	• Application built on stable platform in which IT has significant experience • Limited impact on operations	• Adequate time to test changes to technical environment and train appropriate staff • Release strategy easily understood and controlled	• Significant restructuring of technical environment with limited time for testing or training • Release strategy results in two or more versions of production code	• Application one of first delivered on new technical platform • Spans multiple technical platforms • Technology has unproven performance

Exhibit 15.7 Project Risk Assessment Scorecard

ability to work with customers or suppliers of the project to the company and how easily competitors can duplicate the new capability. The strategic value should be estimated though business unit user input as well as the executive management viewpoints. Exhibit 15.8 shows the scorecard used to evaluate the strategic value a project will have on a business. The result of the analysis should be a rating of the project's strategic value relative to competing projects, from low to high.

ASSESS CURRENT SYSTEM ADEQUACY. The adequacy of the current systems is also a critical factor to consider when determining the value of a project. In cases where systems already exist, they may provide adequate capabilities for the organization, minimizing, or at least reducing, the benefits from incremental investment and effort. We have observed a tendency in IT teams to look for incremental improvements in existing systems instead of tackling new initiatives, which may have higher value (and potentially higher risk or effort). The adequacy of the current system is, therefore, an appropriate metric for understanding overall project priorities. Overall capabilities can be measured in two categories—from both a systems technology standpoint and because of the process and procedures that are in place to support the system.

Exhibit 15.9 shows a system/process scorecard for varying levels of adequacy, which can be used to judge the level of coverage from the current systems capabilities.

PRIORITIZE PROJECTS. Now that the four key project assessments—financial value, risk, strategic value, and system adequacy—for the project values have been made, an overall project prioritization based on those evaluations can be done by plotting the approved projects on two-by-two grids according to the values assigned in the previous exercise.

The first evaluation is a comparison based on strategic and financial value of a project. Strategic versus financial value comparisons showcase the "worthy" projects, namely projects that provide the most benefit to the organization. Exhibit 15.10 on page 423 shows the various classifications of projects, based on their strategic and financial values. The projects with lowest relative financial and strategic value are in the lower left-hand corner of the quadrant. These projects will probably not be considered for the highest-priority project list, and possibly their addition to the approved projects list will be revisited.

After screening out all the low-financial/low-strategic value (lower left-hand quadrant projects), the remaining projects should be evaluated based on current system adequacy. Exhibit 15.11 on page 424 shows the two-by-two matrix for assessing projects based on financial value and system adequacy. In each case, the quadrants into which the projects fall suggest a course of action for the project. Projects that fall into the upper left-hand quadrant are high-value projects that have inadequate supporting systems

STRATEGIC VALUE

LOW ← → HIGH

LEVEL 1	LEVEL 2	LEVEL 3	LEVEL 4
• Little or no strategic impact • No external impact on customers or suppliers • Competitors will easily duplicate capabilities	• Supports keeping up with the market or provides competitive response • Sustains marketplace credibility • Provides better information – Drives sales growth – Supports better customer service – Reduces costs • Competitors duplicate capabilities in less than one year	• Significantly improves customer and/or supplier relationships by creating measurable value • Creates temporary competitive advantage or positioning • Competitive parity will lag by one to two years	• Establishes industry leadership position/delivers sustainable increases in market share • Helps solidify long term relationships with customers or suppliers • Creates sustainable, hard-to-copy competitive position • Competitive parity is difficult to match

Exhibit 15.8   Project Strategic Value Scorecard

	Level 1	Level 2	Level 3	Level 4
System	• No system currently handling the function proposed by the project • Current system handling function is unstable or not delivering necessary functionality	• System handling current function is adequate for next 0–6 months	• System handling current function is adequate for next 7–12 months	• System handling current function is adequate for next 1–2 years
Process	• No process currently handling the function proposed by the project • Current process handling function is unstable or not delivering necessary functionality	• Process handling current function is adequate for next 0–6 months	• Process handling current function is adequate for next 7–12 months	• Process handling current function is adequate for next 1–2 years

LOW ← SYSTEM ADEQUACY → HIGH

Exhibit 15.9   Current System Adequacy Scorecard

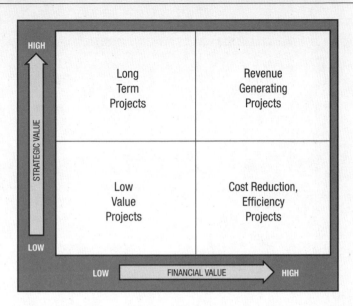

HIGH

STRATEGIC VALUE

Long
Term
Projects

Revenue
Generating
Projects

Low
Value
Projects

Cost Reduction,
Efficiency
Projects

LOW

LOW   FINANCIAL VALUE   HIGH

Exhibit 15.10   Project Strategic Value versus Financial Value Assessment

capabilities. These projects become the high-priority projects that will receive organizational focus. Exhibit 15.11 also shows a typical sampling of actual projects and how they may fall on the prioritization grid.

Finally, projects from the upper left-hand quadrant, *increase focus* projects, should be further evaluated and ranked based on "doability" (cost, speed, risk) versus financial value. Exhibit 15.12 on page 425 shows this analysis. The purpose of this ranking is to ensure that the projects that combine high value and ease of completion receive the highest ranking. This ensures that the benefits of the projects can be enjoyed by the company as rapidly as possible. Projects that fall into the upper right-hand quadrant are *gems,* which are easy to do and provide high financial value. This quadrant is where the top projects fall and is composed of the projects that the IT department should make first priority. Most of the projects that have made it to this phase of the analysis are likely to be valuable projects; this final prioritization simply helps force-rank the projects.

In every instance, the outcome of the prioritization should pass a "sanity" check. If the analysis produces skewed, or nonsensical results, and a careful check of the assumptions yields no changes in outcome, common sense should always prevail over methodology-generated priorities.

After each of the projects has been evaluated based on strategic, financial, risk, and system adequacy values, the scores for each variable should be recorded on the project prioritization analysis shown in Exhibit 15.13. Based on the scorecards discussed, a numerical score can be recorded (typically 1 to 4) for each variable, depending on the project evaluation. The approved

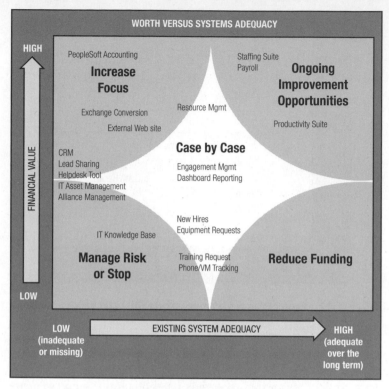

WORTH VERSUS SYSTEMS ADEQUACY

HIGH

FINANCIAL VALUE

Increase Focus
PeopleSoft Accounting
Exchange Conversion
External Web site

CRM
Lead Sharing
Helpdesk Tool
IT Asset Management
Alliance Management

Resource Mgmt

Case by Case
Engagement Mgmt
Dashboard Reporting

Ongoing Improvement Opportunities
Staffing Suite
Payroll
Productivity Suite

New Hires
Equipment Requests

Manage Risk or Stop
IT Knowledge Base

Training Request
Phone/VM Tracking

Reduce Funding

LOW

LOW
(inadequate
or missing)

EXISTING SYSTEM ADEQUACY

HIGH
(adequate
over the
long term)

**Exhibit 15.11 Example Project System Adequacy
versus Financial Value Assessment**

project inventory should be updated with the results of each piece of analysis. An example of the project prioritization is shown in Exhibit 15.13. The total score for each project can then be calculated and sorted in priority order from highest scores to lowest. The list and the priority rankings are periodically added to and reevaluated as new projects are added or projects are completed.

INCORPORATE OTHER FACTORS.   Assessment of other factors is the next step in the project prioritization process. A variety of factors may be considered by the team that may change the overall project priorities, including:

- *Dependencies that the project has on other projects or that other projects have on the identified project:* In these cases, the project dependencies may force serial sequencing of equally high-priority projects.
- *Infrastructure investment needed to complete the project:* Some projects may depend on infrastructure or facilities capacity that is not currently available and, therefore, must be deferred.

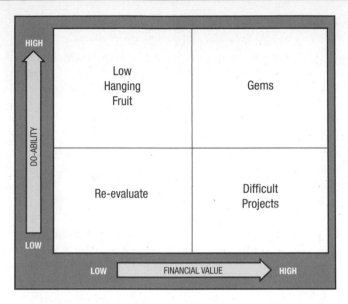

Exhibit 15.12   Do-ability versus Financial Value Assessment

- *Project timing:* External factors may dictate when a project is appropriate to begin or complete. For instance, implementing a new order system is a poor idea during the peak season in a highly seasonal business. Likewise, going live with new financial systems during year-end close is similarly poor timing. These externalities should be taken into account as part of the final prioritization.
- *Political viability:* End users and business decision makers must have a full understanding of the purpose of the project and the quantified benefits that can be achieved because of the project. Projects, regardless of

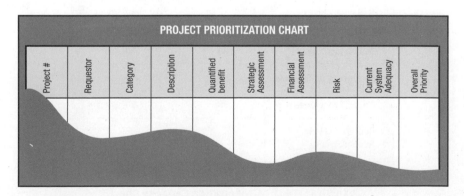

Exhibit 15.13   Sample Project Prioritization Data Gathering Template

high value, sometimes must be sold to the organization over time and, therefore, must be deferred until they are politically viable.

- *Technical or systems dependencies:* System upgrades such as file expansion, code standardization, or software patches may need to be executed before new software can be implemented. These dependencies should be taken into account.

FINALIZE PRIORITIES AND SEQUENCE PROJECTS. After all of these factors have been taken into account, the projects can be force-ranked, producing an inventory of the projects in the order that they are to be worked. The next step determines how many of these projects can be worked simultaneously and will, therefore, be commissioned.

ASSESS IT DEPARTMENT AND ORGANIZATION CAPACITY. After the projects have been prioritized, the team must determine how many of the projects can be worked simultaneously. This number is dependent on two factors: the resource capacity within the IT department (or external capacity justified by the project benefits) and the overall capacity of the company to absorb new projects.

The capacity of the IT department depends on a variety of factors, including the number of project managers available, the allocation of staff time between baseline support and project capacity, and the specific technical and functional skill sets required for the project. Each project must have a project manager and a team with the requisite skill sets. The project schedule is dictated by the aggregate number of available hours for project work from the team.

An example of a capacity chart for determining how many hours can be dedicated to project work is shown in Exhibit 15.14.

	IT Programmer	Network Support Personnel
Total Hours/Week	40	40
Emergency Work/Week	5	5
Project Work/Week	30	30
Operations/Base Support/Week	5	5

Exhibit 15.14   IT Organization Capacity Chart

	DEPLOYMENT			
Project Functional Area	Remaining Development Effort (FTE Hours)	Remaining Roll out Effort (FTE Hours)5020	Total Remaining Effort (FTE Hours)	Current BU and IT Resources Available (FTE Hours)
Sales	300	50	350	200 BU, 100 IT
Marketing	50	20	70	10 BU, 30 IT

Exhibit 15.15   Functional Organization Capacity Chart

Reviewing the number of hours required to complete projects, categorized into various functional areas, is also helpful. Exhibit 15.15 shows number of hours of project work needed versus number of resources available.

Project management capacity, in addition to IT capacity, must be taken into consideration when developing project schedules. Overall, on average, project managers can handle only a handful of projects at a time. The size and complexity of the projects need to be considered. Larger projects should be broken down into smaller projects, with three-month phases. On average, a project manager can complete four three-month phase projects over one year. In addition, if the project manager handles two projects simultaneously, he or she can complete eight smaller projects. Project manager capacity and capability relative to the project importance should be carefully weighed when trying to determine how many projects can be completed, as well as size of each project. Exhibit 15.16 shows an assessment between the adequacy of current project manager versus project business value.

Finally, the overall organization or company ability to sustain multiple, simultaneous projects should be evaluated. This number varies from company to company, based on factors such as company size, culture, geographic distribution, and business cycle. While the number varies, no company can absorb the change and disruption associated with large-scale projects. For our mid-size clients ($100 million to $500 million revenues), we recommend no more than two major projects and no more than four to seven simultaneous projects in total. For our Fortune 1000 clients, we recommend no more than one major program and five major projects. The subprojects underneath these majors vary widely but typically number from one to five.

The result of this step is a determination of how far down the project prioritization list the team can go and a decision on which projects are allowed to start.

Commission Projects

After the projects have been prioritized and IT capacity estimated, it is possible to commission a specific set of projects. The total project work estimates can be compared to the available resource estimates, and the process

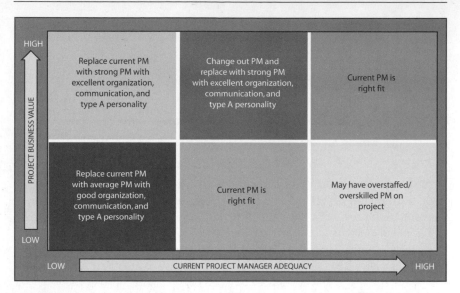

Exhibit 15.16   Current Project Manager Adequacy versus Project Business Value

of working down the project inventory begins. A threshold is set at the point where available project resources are exhausted. No additional projects can be commissioned past this threshold until (a) a project is completed, (b) a project is cancelled, or (c) the budget is increased to add IT internal or external resources.

The majority of the work of IT demand management is complete at this point, and the standard, well-documented disciplines of IT project management, including scope definition, requirements gathering, work-planning, and final estimating begin. For the top identified projects, each sponsor should sign off on a project initiation form to kick off the requirements, design, and development of the project. Most importantly, the business owner and the IT team should ensure that they have a clear definition of how project success and completion will be measured.

In-Process Projects

When projects are underway, the normal project management disciplines aimed at ensuring the proper planning, execution, reporting, and management of the effort apply. From an IT demand management standpoint, it is important that changes in the assumptions that led to the project's taking priority be rapidly communicated. Material changes in anticipated costs or benefits, risk, strategic value, or other prioritization factors may result in a reevaluation of the project priority.

Project Completion and Review

As projects are completed, the event should be confirmed by both the business users and the IT steering committee through a formal sign-off. A final analysis of the project costs and a renewed look at the project benefits should be completed. This is also a good time to record lessons learned and conduct team personnel reviews.

After a project has been completed, the next project on the priority list can be commissioned by the IT department. If, since the previous prioritization, new projects have been added to the approved list, they must be added to the prioritization analysis so that they can be considered for commissioning. Further, if any assumptions concerning financial value, strategic value, existing system adequacy, and risk for previously prioritized projects have changed, those changes should be taken into account.

Key Success Factors for Project Management

Having outlined our methodology for IT demand management, the remainder of the chapter briefly covers a few helpful practices for IT project management. As we have observed, there are a wide variety of well-defined, highly effective methodologies for IT project management. While a comprehensive look at the components of good project management cannot be covered in this chapter, we highlight a few of the critical components for successful project management.

Good project management is a necessary complement to effective IT demand management; the overall management of the project dictates the success or failure of the project, even if it has been properly prioritized.

Two key components of these key tools to managing a project are the project initiation document and the project plan. The project initiation document identifies the project sponsor, a business user sponsor, a project manager from IT, internal and external resources, scope, goals, financial returns expected, anticipated resource, hardware and software costs, and executive level sign-off on the project.

The project plan should incorporate the following:

- Defining 5 to 10 high-level tasks to complete the project (e.g., assess functionality, analyze economics/ROI, check references).
- Identifying dependencies between tasks so that task priorities, timing, and sequencing can be optimized and opportunities for concurrent execution of tasks can be leveraged.
- Defining specific outcomes/deliverables that must be achieved for a task to be deemed complete.

- Defining tasks at a high level of detail to make clear the actions that must be taken and the effort that the work step requires.
- Identifying a single owner who is responsible for completion of each task. Other members of the team who will participate in the task can then be defined.
- Promoting project discipline by diligently achieving key milestones and updating the plan to reflect current status.
- Using the deadlines as leverage to get vendors to perform according to the project timetable.
- Having formal discussions with business sponsors and the IT steering committee when deadlines are missed so that reasons for shortfall are clearly communicated and new expectations can be set.

Managing Resources Effectively

One of the key project management success factors is to be able to manage project resources effectively.

When starting a project, one of the first things is to set the tone of the project. This involves reviewing the project objectives and putting aside other agendas for the duration of the project. Setting the tone also involves ensuring that reporting relationships and accountability within the teams are clearly defined. The project manager has responsibility for delivering the project and, therefore, must be the ultimate decision maker.

When starting a project, milestone review dates should be announced and clearly documented. All team members should be aware of the key milestones, schedule, and criticality of meeting the dates. The project manager should delegate tasks and sub-projects to team members and make sure that they understand what they are responsible for.

Over the life of the project, project managers should take care to reward and recognize deserving personnel when milestones are achieved and celebrate significant team accomplishments. On the other hand, if time lines and milestones are not being met or performance issues arise, the project manager should move to rapidly address the deficiencies with the team. Many project managers have a tendency in these situations to ignore the underperformers and hope that the issues will resolve on their own. This type of approach is detrimental to not only the person with the issue but also the whole team, sending a signal that poor performance and missed deadlines will be tolerated.

In this situation, the project manager should work with the team member to remediate the problems with specific, actionable recommendations for changes in behavior. The manager should also make clear the consequences of further failures. The conversation with the team member should be documented in a letter with specific milestones and dates, and both project manager and team member should sign the document to ensure complete clarity. A subsequent performance evaluation with the team member should be made at a short interval, usually 30 days. Standard periodic reviews scheduled with each individual team member are an easy way to catch these issues early and provide a venue for ensuring that they are addressed.

RESOURCES

Project financial value calculation:

Zvi Bodie, Alex Kane, and Alan J. Marcus, *Investments* (New York: McGraw-Hill/Irwin).

Richard A. Brealey and Stewart C. Myers, *Principles of Corporate Finance* (New York: McGraw-Hill).

Christopher Gardner, *The Valuation of Information Technology: A Guide for Strategy Development, Valuation and Financial Planning* (New York: John Wiley & Sons, 2000).

D. Remenyi, Arthur Money, Michael Sherwood-Smith, Zahir Irani, and Alan Twite, *The Effective Measurement and Management of It Costs and Benefits* (Boston: Butterworth-Heinemann, Computer Weekly Professional Series).

Project planning:

Frederick P. Brooks, *The Mythical Man-Month* (Boston: Addison-Wesley, 1995).

Anita Cassidy, *A Practical Guide to Information Systems Strategic Planning* (Boca Raton, FL: CRC Press, 1998).

Project management:

Jason Charvat, *Project Management Nation: Goals for the New and Practicing IT Project Manager—Guidance, Tools, Templates and Techniques That Work!* (New York: John Wiley & Sons).

Richard Murch, *Project Management: Best Practices for IT Professionals* (Englewood Cliffs, NJ: Prentice Hall).

Joseph Phillips, *IT Project Management: On Track from Start to Finish* (New York: McGraw-Hill Osborne Media).

The Project Management Institute. Available from www.pmi.org.

Team leadership:

Bill Parcells, "The Tough Work of Turning around a Team." *Harvard Business Review* (November/December 2000).

NOTES

1. William Shakespeare, "Troilus and Cressida." Act I, Scene iii, p. 1602.
2. The Standish Group. *The Chaos Report* (Massachusetts: The Standish Group International Inc., 1994). Available from http://www.standishgroup.com/sample_research/chaos_1994_1.php.

16

IT Performance Measurement

If you can't measure it, you can't manage it.
—Tom Peters[1]

This chapter outlines a method of measuring overall IT performance. It distills the most practical measures of performance and discusses approaches for implementing an IT performance measurement program in the organization. The chapter covers the following key topics:

- The value of performance measurement.
- Developing and managing an IT measurement program.
  —Defining the IT dashboard.
  —Conducting a baseline survey.
  —Developing management, analysis, and reporting processes.
  —Managing the measurement program.
  —Reassessing the program.
- IT metrics.
- Commissioning and managing a corporate IT health check.

This chapter presents a pragmatic viewpoint to implementing an IT performance-reporting program.

Why This Topic Is Important

Today's senior IT director is confronted with an unending growth of new responsibilities. This book discusses many of them: strategic planning, infrastructure planning, operations management, personnel, and many others.

In addition, managers are regularly confronted with urgent and critical situations that must receive focused attention immediately. Unfortunately, at the bottom of the priority list is a performance management program. As the daily urgent matters monopolize the available time, the need to perform is much greater than the need to track performance; thus, this tracking gets perpetually delayed. Implementing performance management and process control can increase the performance and productivity of the unit dramatically. However, suspending some activities temporarily to establish a program is challenging.

Measurement, if executed well, can help the IT organization align work to key business objectives and help the organization gain credibility with business unit leaders through performance improvement and objective measurement reporting. To communicate effectively to the rest of senior management, the IT director must implement objective measures defining a common language that explains excellent versus poor performance. Without this language, business leaders have difficulty establishing performance targets and understanding actual IT performance levels. They also have a high degree of distrust for any subjective measures that then must be used to describe performance. Almost all other business units and functions in a company have defined targets and measures that must be achieved (e.g., inventory levels, sales quotas, day sales outstanding). Why IT organizations are not often held to this level of rigorous measurement is perplexing. This is especially confounding because the CFO, the typical owner of the IT function, is generally the strictest proponent of measurement systems in a company. Usually CFOs and other senior management don't have the training, experience, or technical education to construct meaningful measurements of IT performance and "generally accepted" metrics are not readily available for reference.

Implementing a standard, repeatable system for measuring and tracking performance enables the IT director to establish a common framework to use in his or her communications with the lines of business. Consistent use of this system allows the IT director to build trust and gain credibility across the organization. A performance management and reporting system can help the CEO and CFO track the return on technology-invested capital. Understanding and disclosure replaces ambiguity and unanswered questions.

Many IT/senior management communication programs are a result of the lack of standard measures. While executives would not ask a factory manager to cut costs or increase productivity without asking for common ratios such as units produced per day, they frequently ask IT to do the same without any knowledge of internal IT processes or operations. While most manufacturing and financial functions are controlled and measured by time-tested metrics, IT has relatively few measures that are useful for tying its operations to the business. IT measurement helps address this problem by providing a consistent framework that directly links IT to business unit objectives.

The benefits of implementing process control and performance measurement can be dramatic. The Software Engineering Institute's Capability Maturity Model, a software process management certification, is being increasingly adopted by organizations with software development groups. More than 10 years of data from companies that have implemented the process improvement tool has proven that process discipline has returned on average a minimum of $5 for every $1 invested. According to *Computer-World,* by implementing a project measurement system, "Merrill Lynch has saved between $25 million and $30 million over the past year by slowing down or stopping planned initiatives and redirecting project funding faster and more effectively than it used to."[2]

In another case, Belk, Inc., a national retailer, was "forced to adopt productivity metrics as a means of staving off devastating system failures." In 1997, the company was spending $1.1 million out of a $30-million IT budget on unplanned maintenance. "Belk's batch systems went down an astounding 800 times a month." A year later, after implementing performance measurements, system failures declined to 480 per month and maintenance expenses were reduced by $800,000.[3]

Finally, the importance of implementing a performance measurement program is critical to the success of the IT director. Managing the performance of the unit is obviously the responsibility of the IT director. Not having a program in place is a reflection on the IT director's level of understanding of business management and skills. The performance of the unit will ultimately suffer as will the perceived performance of the IT director.

Value of Measurement

Value from measurement is gained by analyzing the data, taking action, and then improving the operations. Improving the operations of the unit, increases productivity and the return on capital invested in IT. Because cost of implementing a measurement system is not trivial but is typically small compared to the benefits, measurement systems are usually a high return on investment proposition. Information technology investments and operations should not be measured unless the expected benefit of measurement exceeds the costs of data collection, analysis, management, and reporting. In other words, do not measure for the sake of measurement itself; expect a return.

The expected value of measurement is the difference between the expected benefits (both direct and indirect) and the expected costs. The value is derived primarily from the direct benefits that can be obtained from regularly measuring and managing the IT department. These benefits include better allocation of resources, improved system performance, reduction of risks, and improved customer service. Additionally, there are some "hidden" or indirect benefits that include the development of a performance culture, enhanced alignment of IT with the business, and increased transparency of the value of IT throughout the organization.

A critical mistake commonly made during the implementation of IT measurement programs is overcomplicating the program and tracking hundreds of complicated metrics. The error is in tracking every conceivable metric and not differentiating between metrics that are important versus ones that *might* be important. The result is a behemoth report of irrelevant information and untimely data. This approach is both costly and cumbersome. Return on the program is low, it generally dies a slow and painful death, and the effort to maintain the program is greater than the actual use of the data; therefore, benefits are minimal.

As illustrated in Exhibit 16.1, if the measurement program is constructed properly, the value of the program should be considerable.

Benefits of IT Measurement

The key benefits of IT measurement result from *actions* taken in response to its output; they include:

- Improved customer service.
- More efficient allocation of resources.
- Improved system performance and uptime.
- Reduction in risk and unplanned activities.
- Increase in staff productivity (development and support).
- Seeds planted for high performance culture.

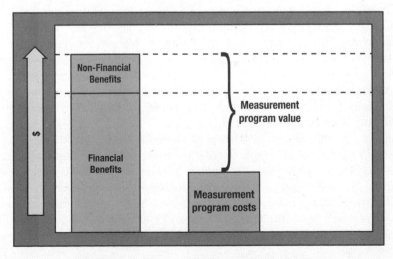

Exhibit 16.1   Value of IT Measurement Program

IMPROVED CUSTOMER SERVICE.   Improved customer service is a result of mutual agreement on service levels and then the meeting or exceeding of those levels. Many of the benefits are interrelated. For example, decreasing unplanned system outages reduces staff work and improves customer service. Increasing staff productivity allows projects to be completed faster, which again increases customer satisfaction.

Typically, there is a disconnect between the true costs of providing IT services to enterprise customers and the price of any actually paid by the customer for the services. Furthermore, there is often no correlation between a business unit's desired service level, the service level received, and what it actually pays for the specific services. Business units do not recognize this directly because they are usually charged for services via ad-hoc overhead allocation rules, instead of paying for differentiated levels of services. This lack of market discipline leads to high costs and potentially over-specified service levels. For example, business unit A may not need desktop support response within 30 minutes. Four hours would potentially suffice. Yet, IT makes an arbitrary decision to have a 30-minute response time, which means more people and more costs.

Prior to 1984, the only company that sold or leased telephones was AT&T. The telephones made were overengineered. They were rugged—made of heavy plastic—and rarely broke. However, they were very expensive; an average phone could cost well over $100. After the market was deregulated, new telephone equipment manufacturers began selling $20 disposable phones. They quickly became popular, and soon everyone was purchasing disposable phones made of cheap plastic that lasted for a year or two. Soon, a huge industry grew to satisfy consumer demand for designer phones. AT&T assumed that everyone needed the same phone at the same price—an incorrect assumption.

The same is true for the uneducated IT department; IT continually makes uninformed assumptions regarding user's desired service levels. The IT department typically sets its level of service to the highest common denominator. However, not every business unit or function requires the highest level of service. Most IT organizations can make tremendous improvements in their effectiveness simply by providing differential services for units willing to pay more for higher levels of service and providing low-cost options for those who do not require premium service.

Benefits accrue through utilization of customer feedback of their expectations and judgment of the department's relative performance across a variety of service areas. The knowledge highlights areas where IT has overinvested resources, as well as areas where additional resources are needed. This inevitably improves customer service as well as utilization of capital and operating expenditures. Since the program enables IT to track and analyze customer service levels, it facilitates genuine discussion of appropriate levels of service and performance.

MORE EFFICIENT ALLOCATION OF RESOURCES. Metrics allow the IT director to move staff to areas in need of improved service levels and divert staff from areas that already exceed service levels. Additionally, project-tracking metrics allow allocation of resources to appropriate projects.

IMPROVED SYSTEM PERFORMANCE AND UPTIME. Another clear benefit to measurement is improved system performance. This performance can be measured in many ways, including capacity utilization, system availability, and speed. Tracking of various system performance metrics can help managers quickly isolate problems before they become serious. Just as warning gauges on a car help the driver maintain the vehicle in high performance, system metrics help a manager keep systems running at peak performance.

REDUCTION IN RISK AND UNPLANNED ACTIVITIES. A benefit that is often hidden from typical analysis is the reduction of risk. Without any tracking or measurement, it is difficult for managers to understand trends in system usage and anticipate potential problems or upgrades required in the future. This can result in major problems creeping up on managers at the most inopportune times. For instance, at one client firm, a large server crashed unexpectedly not because of faulty hardware or a virus, but because a large group of acquired employees had recently started and drove usage that exceeded the system's processing capacity. Instead of methodically planning the system's upgrade in the most cost-effective manner, the IT department was forced to call the vendor to have new hardware shipped overnight. This resulted in additional costs that were both unexpected and exorbitant. In the end, the department still had to pay for the regular systematic upgrade in addition to the "quick patch" costs that were incurred on the day of the damage. This expense does not even include the costs for the firm being without the system for 9 hours. There were opportunity costs of lost business, lost goodwill, delayed shipments, and a host of other problems that cascaded from this unexpected event. If the team had been analyzing system metrics over time and planned for the additional employees, they would have known that the system was reaching capacity and could have avoided the large unexpected expense and effort.

INCREASE IN STAFF PRODUCTIVITY (DEVELOPMENT AND SUPPORT). Developing a process and tracking metrics allows the IT director to benchmark personnel. It will establish a baseline of "good" performance for personnel that can then be used in performance reviews. For example, if the total help desk tickets closed per day by employee is tracked, then all help desk personnel can be judged on their performance based on the number of tickets they close each day. Underperforming employees can be spotlighted and counseled for improvement.

HIGH PERFORMANCE CULTURE. Finally, implementing metrics will cultivate a performance-oriented culture. While this affect cannot be directly measured, it can be an important side-affect of instituting a measurement program. Even without necessarily tying incentive compensation to metrics, instituting a measurement program can often motivate employees and help them develop creative plans for ongoing job performance improvement. Competitive and goal-oriented employees excel in an environment that provides them specific goals and continuous feedback. They tend to succeed in such environments and deliver outstanding results. With an ongoing program of efficient and effective measurement, organizations can develop a performance culture that strives for continuous improvement. Over time, this can improve employee satisfaction and reduce undesired turnover.

The Costs of IT Measurement

While some of the benefits can be relatively difficult to measure, the costs of a program are relatively simple and straightforward. The costs fall into four major categories: planning, measurement, analysis, and management. With the exception of the planning phase, an efficient measurement program should not take significant time to manage, and should be integrated in regular IT processes, just like regular system maintenance.

The planning costs are usually the most significant in an IT measurement program, because they are critical for ensuring that the program is both effective and efficient. The planning costs entail some time of the senior manager (CIO) and one to three full-time employees for a few weeks. These resources are used to establish the goals, estimate the potential benefits of the program, select evaluation metrics, develop measurement processes, set organizational roles, and estimate the overall value of the program.

Measurement costs should be minimal, as the metrics selected should be fairly easy to observe and require minimal resources to capture. The majority of these costs are likely to result from the administration and management. Subjective measurement techniques such as user surveys can't be automated, and thus take the most resources to create and administer.

The analysis costs are high in the early stage of establishing the program, but fall over time with repetition and potential automation of more common analysis tasks. Analysis includes all the tasks needed to translate measured data into useful information that can help in decision-making. While some of the raw data may be interesting, it is useless for decision-making without framing it within a particular context that provides insight to the IT director. For example, overall IT spending per employee is not useful to a manager by itself, but it can provide some insight into the department's relative efficiency when compared with historical performance and industry benchmarks.

The management costs involve time spent by senior IT management interpreting the information so they can formulate recommended actions.

Without any action taken, the measurement program will be of no value, so when considering the costs of a measurement program, these costs must be taken into account.

Developing an IT Measurement Program

Successfully implementing a measurement program is not simple. Almost 80 percent of all IT measurement programs fail. Avoid the common pitfalls such as overcomplicating the system, tracking too many metrics, requiring significant manual recording from workers, and tracking meaningless metrics. All these pitfalls discredit the IT director, lengthen implementation time, and undermine the true objective.

Successful measurement programs have several characteristics in common:

- Recognize that 20 percent of the metrics provide 80 percent of the relevant information needed. Prior to implementing measurement programs, most of the client companies we have assisted collected network statistics, server performance data, and help desk statistics, but found little use in the pages of meaningless data.
- Are broad enough to capture more than just system/IT metrics, for example, capture customer satisfaction.
- Require little effort to track and produce.
- Results are communicated to staff and executives on a standard schedule.

The IT Dashboard

A successful approach we recommend is the *IT dashboard*. This is a practical and simplified snapshot of IT performance. It is similar in concept to the *Balanced Scorecard* developed by Robert S. Kaplan and David Norton, but not as rigorous or strenuous to implement.

The dashboard concept was developed using the metaphor of an automobile dashboard. The gauges describe in real time all the valuable information a driver must know to operate the vehicle safely. The IT dashboard serves the same purpose.

The IT dashboard provides an easy-to-understand framework for measuring and tracking metrics that reveal IT performance. The dashboard provides a nontechnical foundation to share departmental objectives and performance results across the organization and is a significant step toward developing credibility and respect across the business. This framework allows everyone in the organization to understand how IT is measured.

The dashboard is a single page subdivided into sections or gauges. These gauges, composed of three to five key performance indicators (KPIs), can be used to quickly assess IT performance on a regular basis. The KPIs are driven by one or more metrics (objective and/or subjective) and are normalized using a system that is easy to understand. An effective method of reporting KPIs is to represent conditions in green, yellow, and red for respective satisfactory, caution, and needs attention states. An example of an IT dashboard is shown in Exhibit 16.2.

The major areas or gauges of the IT dashboard include the following:

- IT investment; for example, IT spending, capital invested.
- Investment return.
- Infrastructure and operations.
- Project delivery.
- Customer satisfaction.
- People development.

To develop an effective and efficient IT measurement program, an IT director should follow these steps:

- Evaluate and define metrics that are important to the business.
- Define the IT dashboard by area, and map the associated metrics to each area.
- Define the target performance for each metric.
- Develop a summary IT dashboard as shown in Exhibit 16.2.
- Conduct a baseline survey and modify targets.
- Develop processes for data collection, analysis, synthesis, and reporting.
- Regularly reassess the program's value and adjust goals, metrics, and processes as necessary.

The overall process is outlined in Exhibit 16.3.

Evaluate Metrics

The most critical factor of success in this process is selecting a small set of valuable metrics to track. A framework for selecting those metrics entails the following:

- Review critical business measures. Understand key metrics tracked by business units and functions, and then translate those metrics into IT metrics that can impact their performance. For example, if sales are measured by new orders sold, determine IT factors that can contribute to the success or failure of the sales process. Gather key metrics from around the company, and begin to analyze the impact that IT can have on those metrics.

IT INVESTMENT

Cost per seat	H
Cost % of revenue	OK
Cost % of SG&A	H

INVESTMENT RETURN

Benefit Capture	L
ROI	L

INFRASTRUCTURE & OPS

Desktops	OK
Data Center	OK
Midrange	OK
Telecom/Network	OK

PROJECT DELIVERY

Number Completed	OK
Project Quality	L
Value Added	L
Delays	H

CUSTOMER SATISFACTION

Overall Satisfaction	OK
Support	L
Applications	L

PEOPLE DEVELOPMENT

Number of Layers	OK
Average Tenure	OK
Skills Availability	L

H = High   L = Low   OK = Average

Exhibit 16.2   Example IT Dashboard

441

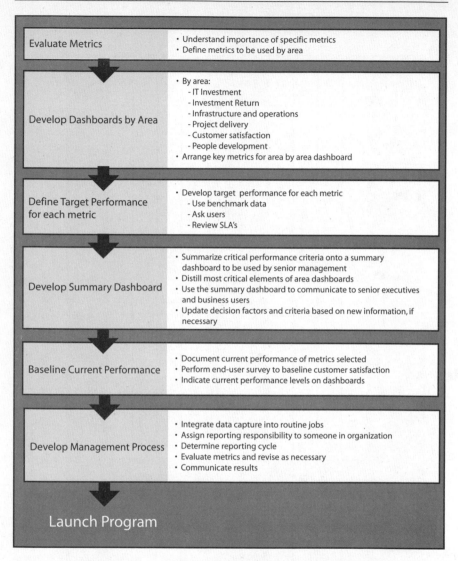

Evaluate Metrics	• Understand importance of specific metrics • Define metrics to be used by area

Develop Dashboards by Area	• By area:
	    - IT Investment
	    - Investment Return
	    - Infrastructure and operations
	    - Project delivery
	    - Customer satisfaction
	    - People development
	• Arrange key metrics for area by area dashboard

Define Target Performance for each metric	• Develop target performance for each metric
	    - Use benchmark data
	    - Ask users
	    - Review SLA's

Develop Summary Dashboard	• Summarize critical performance criteria onto a summary dashboard to be used by senior management • Distill most critical elements of area dashboards • Use the summary dashboard to communicate to senior executives and business users • Update decision factors and criteria based on new information, if necessary
Baseline Current Performance	• Document current performance of metrics selected • Perform end-user survey to baseline customer satisfaction • Indicate current performance levels on dashboards
Develop Management Process	• Integrate data capture into routine jobs • Assign reporting responsibility to someone in organization • Determine reporting cycle • Evaluate metrics and revise as necessary • Communicate results

Launch Program

Exhibit 16.3   IT Measurement Program Development

• Take each IT area in turn and develop a *sub-dashboard* for that area. This enables the creation of specific metrics, development of summary dashboard, and managemeant of the subareas on a daily basis.

The following is an explanation of key dashboard areas:

• *IT investment:* Metrics that describe how the IT organization is performing against budget. For example, the three most important measures might include: (1) performance against budget, (2) spending as a percent of revenue, and (3) spending as a percent of company gross margin. Other measures of IT investment are listed in the next section.

- *Investment return:* Summarizes results of captured business benefits from projects and system investments. For each business case, track the actual benefits versus the stated benefits, and report the results in this section of the dashboard. For example, track dollars returned versus dollars expected. Other examples include percent of end users adopting standards, percent of users adopting application, amount of green bar paper used (indicator of online reporting adoption), and revenue generated from new online ordering system.

- *Infrastructure and operations:* Critical measures in infrastructure include system and network reliability, support, security, virus protection, and others. Select the critical business measures and translate those measures into IT metrics. System availability may only be critical to business units that manage significant work processes through IT applications. Other measures of infrastructure and operations are listed in the next section.

- *Project delivery:* Summary of execution on projects. Projects should be segmented by size. Every IT project should be rated on four criteria: risk, client satisfaction, time performance, and budget. Risk is a measure of the level of uncertainty in a project. Client satisfaction is how well it is meeting client expectations. Time performance is a measure of how well the team is meeting the time schedule. Budget is a measure of how close to budget the project is running. Give each project a ranking of green, yellow, or red. Green represents a project that is on schedule and budget with little risk and an 80 percent or better client satisfaction score. Yellow represents a project that is within certain tolerances (10 to 20 percent) of time and budget schedules and has moderate risk and 50 percent or better client satisfaction ranking. Red represents a project that is out of these tolerances. The summary dashboard may only display the top two projects in the company, whereas the sub-dashboard for the applications group will show all projects sorted by size or importance.

- *Customer satisfaction:* Relative level of customer satisfaction within the organization; for example, satisfaction with the help desk, escalation procedures, problem resolution, system enhancement requests, availability of IT staff, quality of personnel, and so on. A satisfaction survey is typically the source for customer satisfaction scores.

- *People development:* Represents the degree to which the organization is executing its personnel development plan. Questions are answered as to how the IT organization is developing its people. Are the skills available in-house to execute projects? Is the attrition level average or increasing? Create metrics that are most important to the organization based on current environment. Examples of metrics for this area include attrition, average tenure, training days used versus available, average salary of IT personnel, skills availability, resources available, promotions for the current quarter, bonuses achieved, and number of individual performance objectives achieved.

Develop Dashboards by Area

After developing critical metrics for each IT area, each area should have its own one-page dashboard. These one-page dashboards are used to manage the personnel responsible for each respective area (e.g., operations manager receives the infrastructure and operations dashboard). Providing specific dashboards to the teams helps align their performance to the metrics deemed important by the IT director.

Define Target Performance for Each Metric

For each metric, define *target* performance. There are several ways to determine target performance. For example, is 98 percent uptime a reasonable target or is 99 percent required? There are three ways to set the target. If a service level agreement is already in place with the business users, this is the quickest way to set the target (it may still need to be reassessed). Essentially, begin to measure what was agreed on when the service levels were first negotiated. The second way to determine the target is to gather benchmark statistics about the metric to determine good performance in similar companies. For example, if statistics point to 99.4 percent uptime as average performance for all companies, that may be an appropriate level to achieve. Finally, the third way to determine the target is to negotiate with users. For example, manufacturing may actually need 99.9 percent uptime to meet business requirements. Setting targets based on agreement between the IT organization and the key business units is equivalent to developing a service level agreement.

Gather benchmarks of comparable performance for related companies within the industry from research groups like Gartner Group or Meta who collect and aggregate such information. These benchmarks can provide a guideline for assessing the IT department performance in comparison to companies of the same size and type of business. For example, in areas where the IT department is significantly underperforming other companies, recognize and note the gap, determine potential causes, and develop recommended actions to correct. In areas where the IT department is significantly overperforming other companies, note the overperformance and identify the area as a potential for decreasing the service level if the cost savings are attractive.

Develop Summary Dashboard

After the subdashboards are developed, distill the top two to three metrics for each area to create the summary dashboard. This is called the *IT dashboard* and is communicated to senior management. An example is shown in Exhibit 16.2.

Baseline Current Performance

The next step for the IT director is to document current performance. Objective metric results (hard quantitative metrics) should be collected from the most direct source (e.g., help desk system for help desk metrics).

Subjective metrics should be collected via survey(s) for all representative stakeholder groups. The surveys should include the following:

- Description and purpose of the survey.
- Fields for collecting stakeholder group differences (e.g., IT specialist versus business unit customer).
- Importance rating for each metric on a defined scale (e.g., 1 to 5) indicating the importance of the topic, service, or metric to the stakeholder.
- Performance rating for each metric on the same scale as previous point.

For the subjective measures, the following specific figures should be analyzed for each metric:

- *Mean of importance:* If this is higher than the mean for all metrics combined, the metric has relatively higher importance to the stakeholders. If this is lower than the mean for all metrics combined, the metric has relatively lower importance.
- *Standard deviation of importance:* A low standard deviation indicates agreement throughout the organization on the level of importance. Conversely, a high standard deviation indicates disagreement on the level of importance.
- *Mean of performance:* If this is higher than the mean for all metrics combined, it can be concluded that performance is better than average. If this is lower than the mean for all metrics combined, it can be concluded that performance is below average.
- *Standard deviation of performance:* A low standard deviation indicates agreement throughout the organization on the level of performance. Conversely, a high standard deviation indicates disagreement on the level of performance.
- *Gap of importance is a measure comparing IT personnel's view of importance versus business customer's view of importance for the topic, service, or metric:* If the gap is low, the IT department has a relatively strong understanding of the customer's priorities. Conversely, if the gap is high, the IT department may not have a full grasp of the business needs.
- *Gap of performance between IT specialists and business customers:* If the gap is low, the IT department has a fairly strong understanding of

its current performance. Conversely, if the gap is high, there is a strong disconnect between IT's perception of its performance versus the business community.

Based on these analyses, subjective performance metrics can be prioritized on the relative importance and perceived performance (see Exhibit 16.4). Areas with high importance and low performance indicate critical performance deficiencies and need the highest level of attention. Areas with low importance, but a relatively high level of performance, should receive the next level of priority because there may be some potential for cost savings. The remainder of the metrics can be addressed on a case-by-case basis.

Based on this prioritization, performance targets should be set for metrics in the highest priority problem areas. Targets can be set based on an absolute improvement, absolute percentage improvement, or relative percentage improvement to the average. In addition to high and low targets, specific bands can be set for low, medium, and high ranges for each metric, indicating performance tolerance ranges.

Develop Management Process for Data Collection, Analysis, and Reporting

In parallel with the baseline survey, ongoing processes for data collection, analysis, and reporting should be established to ensure that (1) the measurement program is integrated into the IT business process, (2) the program does not become overly burdensome in terms of data collection efforts and

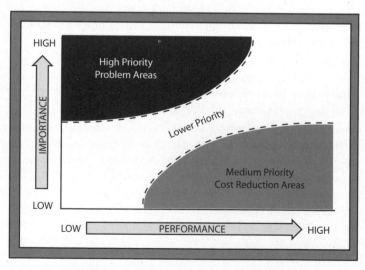

Exhibit 16.4   Subjective Metric Prioritization

costs, and (3) the program is effectively launched and communicated to the rest of the organization.

For all objective metrics, document the data collection process and identify the following:

- Method of collection.
- Frequency of collection.
- Person who performs collection.
- Method of transfer of data to the analyst.
- Duration of history to be preserved.

For subjective metrics, a survey should be designed based on the baseline survey. Care should be exercised developing the survey to ensure that the most appropriate questions are being asked at the right frequency, using the best methods available to capture an accurate response. Surveys should be no longer than absolutely necessary to capture the data needed—generally 5 to 10 minutes in duration for the person filling it out. Pay attention to format and accuracy. Inaccurate responses, at best, hinder the measurement effort and, at worst, make the measurement effort a complete failure. Fortunately, a manager does not need a degree in statistics or survey design to build an effective survey that captures an accurate response. Numerous short papers and books address this topic from a practical and useful standpoint. Many of the IT research houses provide guidance in developing user feedback surveys. Additionally, some firms specialize in conducting these surveys for companies.

Beware of mistakes commonly made with surveys:

1. Not repeating the survey in the frequency stated.
2. Failure to explain the purpose of the survey.
3. Making the survey too long, burdensome, or over-complicated.
4. Failure to report the results of the survey to all stakeholders.
5. Failure to use statistically scientific approach to surveys.

A single analyst, who is responsible for leading the measurement analysis and reporting, should collect the survey results along with the objective metrics. It should be this person's job to verify and validate the data to ensure that major errors do not creep into the analysis. Following collection, the data need to be analyzed to develop useful information for decision making. There are many methods for digesting and aggregating the data; however, the most basic and effective methods include gap analysis and trend analysis.

Using gap analysis, the analyst examines the absolute difference between the current performance point and the target. Depending on the targets set, the analyst determines whether each particular key performance indicator is within a good, fair, or poor state. Using trend analysis, the analyst can identify how the state is changing over time by referring to data collected on previous survey dates. The trend can also be reflected on the IT dashboard using additional codes or colors.

When performing trend analysis, the following specific figures should also be analyzed for all the subjective (survey) metrics combined into one group for IT personnel and another for business customers:

- *Correlation of importance and performance for business customers:* A high level of correlation indicates a high level of business customer satisfaction. If this figure is dropping over time, there may be changing customer needs, or performance is falling off for the more important needs.
- *Correlation of importance between IT specialists and business customers:* A high level of correlation indicates that IT specialists understand the needs of business customers. If this is decreasing over time, the IT department probably needs to gain more insight into the nature of changing business needs.

Additional analysis techniques include regression analysis, factor analysis, and perceptual analysis. These advanced techniques can be used to develop an in-depth understanding of causal factors, relationships between metrics, and gaps in questioning. These techniques require more advanced training or outside help in statistics and quantitative measures. They are best left to larger organizations that can collect more extensive information and justify the expense of using a statistician or statistics training for the staff for conducting some of the analyses.

The information obtained through the analysis should be entered into an appropriate reporting program such as Microsoft Access or Excel. Significant gaps and trends should be noted and graphs prepared that illustrate the measurements in a simple, yet effective, manner.

A report should be generated on a regular interval as data is collected and analyzed. Depending on the complexity and needs of the organization, the collection and reporting frequency can range from weekly to quarterly. In many cases, the team will set an interval similar to the standard financial reporting cycle. At a minimum, most organizations should measure performance semiannually.

Hard copies of the dashboard should be posted in prominent places in the IT department so that everyone is aware of the current status of the IT organization's performance. Similar to a thermometer used to motivate people during a fund-raising drive, an IT dashboard motivates people in an IT department to improve performance and calls attention to exemplary performance. Soft copies should be distributed to all relevant parties, including:

- IT steering committee members.
- IT organization employees.
- Senior management team.

- Business process managers.
- Any end user who completed a survey.

To encourage communication of the business relevance of information technology throughout the company, some of the key performance indicators and results should be shared via internal newsletters or marketing materials. Finally, a soft copy should be available on the company's intranet for easy viewing by any company employee. Chapter 12 contains additional information on effective communication between IT and the business.

Reassessment of the Measurement Program

While it is important for the IT director to identify particular deficiencies in the organization from the measurement process, it is equally important to include the information in all major decision-making processes. This information should become the baseline for developing and justifying both operating and capital expenditures on a regular basis. After all, if a proposed investment in technology is not going to fulfill a specific business need, why should the investment be made?

The same applies in reverse. If an investment should *obviously* be made, shouldn't the investment's value be reflected in the organization's key performance indicators? The measurement program should be adjusted often enough to ensure that the measurements reflect the needs of the business units but not so often that historical comparisons become impractical. The historical trend of various KPIs is important to understand how changes in the organization are being reflected in the business user's views of importance and performance of various aspects of the IT organization.

The measurement and evaluation program provides a key point in the overall IT planning and management process and should provide critical inputs into the IT planning and budgeting process (see Exhibit 16.5). Feedback from the regular planning and evaluation can help improve the overall efficiency of the IT organization by:

- Identifying projects whose priority has shifted (either higher or lower) since the project was started.
- Identifying projects whose relevance has shrunk so much that elimination may be the best option.
- Helping define required service levels appropriately.
- Helping set appropriate time lines for projects and initiatives.
- Providing guidance when considering whether to buy, build, or outsource particular initiatives.
- Helping identify costs to serve particular populations in the organization and sizing services to cost effectively serve them.

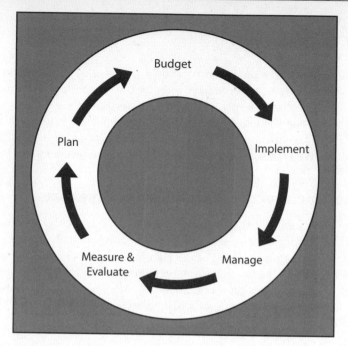

Exhibit 16.5   IT Planning and Management Process

The outputs of measurement and evaluation should help guide the organization in a continuous cycle of improvement—including improvement of the measurement process itself. As the organization grows and changes, so do the needs of various stakeholders of the IT department. To accommodate these changes, re-assess the measurement program to determine where additional information should be collected or to see where existing metrics are inadequate.

Evaluate and Take Action

The IT director will now be in position to take action based on the metrics through the following steps: analyze performance data to develop a snapshot of performance expressed in terms of key performance measures, analyze variance from expected target, and develop understanding into drivers of performance and causal relationships (for overreporting or underreporting, the schedule is the same).

Recognize and reward individuals for positive performance. Address underperformance through remedial action. Update strategy, planning, and budget processes to reflect new information. Raise performance targets to reenforce emerging objectives.

IT Metrics

Depending on the particular situation, some metrics are more relevant than others for improving IT performance. One of the critical components of the dashboard, discussed in the previous section, is selecting the appropriate measures. IT metrics can be categorized as objective metrics or subjective metrics. This section provides a starting point for selecting metrics.

Objective Metrics

Objective metrics are quantifiable facts about an organization that are easily observable or calculated and can be meaningfully compared to those in similar organizations. There are several advantages to including these metrics in a measurement program:

- *Free from bias:* While user satisfaction may be influenced by measurement techniques and nuances of survey questions, hard metrics, like the number of IT employees per IT user, are unbiased.
- *Ease of collection:* These figures are usually collected as part of regular accounting or system management, so they usually involve little additional labor or planning to collect.
- *Comparability:* Most of these figures can be readily compared with similar organizations in other companies or within an industry using benchmarks.

There are literally dozens of objective metrics that can be easily collected and recorded about an IT organization. While many of these metrics may be interesting, there are actually only a few dozen that are useful in achieving the ultimate objective of any program. In the planning stage of instituting a measurement program, it is crucial that the managers select only those metrics that will be useful in helping the manager improve performance. The value of the program can be seriously diluted if time is spent collecting, analyzing, or reporting statistics that do not help in decision making.

The actual metrics for a specific organization depend on the size of the IT group, organizational structure of the company, industry, growth rate, and many other circumstantial variables. Generally, however, we have found that there are some metrics useful in nearly every circumstance. These metrics are listed in Exhibits 16.6 through 16.12.

Subjective Metrics

Subjective metrics are figures compiled from feedback of stakeholders in the company. The majority of these metrics are used to measure customer

METRIC	COMPONENTS
I/T spending as percent of revenue	• Total enterprise IT spending divided by same period company revenue.
I/T spending as percent of gross margin	• Total enterprise IT spending divided by same period company gross margin.
I/T operations as a percent of I/T spending	• Spending on I/T operations divided by total enterprise IT spending.
I/T spending per employee	• Total enterprise IT spending divided by total number of employees in the company.
I/T employees as a percent of total employees	• Total I/T employees plus outsourcing employees dedicated to supporting company plus I/T contractors divided by total company employees.
I/T capital budget as a percent of revenue	• I/T capital budget divided by total company revenue.
Administrative costs as percent of total I/T cost	• I/T administration budget plus business support services plus service planning costs divided by total I/T budget.
I/T senior management span	• Number of I/T senior managers divided by total IT employees.
Number of layers	• Average number of layers between an entry-level I/T professional and the I/T Manager or CIO.
Percent of staff with less than 12 months of experience	• Total IT staff with less than 12 months' experience divided by total IT staff.

Exhibit 16.6   Objective Management Metrics

satisfaction but also include information to quantify what is sometimes termed as *alignment* between IT and the business units. There are several advantages of using subjective metrics for measuring IT:

- Ability to quantify business needs (e.g., functionality, reliability, responsiveness, system quality, cost effectiveness) and relative priorities of different groups throughout the organization.
- Ability to quantify the department's performance against specific needs.
- Ability to customize specific measures to particular aspects of the business.

METRIC	COMPONENTS
Total annual cost per seat	• Desk-top support staff plus tech support staff plus network connectivity plus printer support plus initial desktop preparation and delivery to user plus one-time purchased software licenses plus basic desktop maintenance (licenses, support, etc.) divided by total end users.
Desktops per employee	• Total number of desktops divided by total number of employees.
Total desktop support ratio (desktops per support FTE)	• Total desktops divided by total number of help desk personnel plus total number of desktop support, install, move/add/change (internal and outsourced) personnel plus total number of tech support staff plus total LAN management and administration staff plus total asset management-related staff.
Help desk staff per seat	• Total number of internal help desk staff plus total number of outsourced help desk staff divided by total end users.

Exhibit 16.7 Desktop Metrics

There are also some disadvantages to using subjective metrics:

- Not only must subjective surveys be meticulously planned, but the administration and collection of the feedback is laborious.
- Because questions can be specific to each business and usually are heavily customized, there is no reliable way to benchmark the metric results within an industry or across industries.

Subjective metrics should always be measured using two dimensions: expectation and performance. Performance of any service organization is relative to its customers' expectations. It is the differences between expectations and performance where much of the value of measurement can be found.

We generally group subjective measures as follows:

- Suitability, accessibility, reliability, and security of systems.
- Functionality of applications.
- Efficiency of completing projects.
- Service levels.
- Responsiveness to business requirements.

METRIC	COMPONENTS
First call resolution	• Percentage of calls resolved on the first call.
Average time to resolve trouble ticket	• Average time to resolve a trouble ticket from initial call to problem resolution.
Call queue waiting time	• Average wait on help desk call.
Call abandoned rate	• Percentage of help desk calls abandoned while on queue.
Length of help desk call	• Average time spent by user on a help desk call—includes time on Level 1 and Level 2.
Average reaction time	• Time between first call or message and the time it takes to reach someone live.

Exhibit 16.8   Help Desk Metrics

These are typically measured through carefully designed questionnaires, administered by administrators and third parties, and conducted through various media such as the Web, intranet, phone, and paper.

Periodic IT Health Check

In addition to performing regular ongoing measurement of objective and subjective measures to evaluate the performance of the IT organization, a major organizational health assessment should be performed every 12 to 18 months to evaluate the overall fitness and effectiveness of the organization. Additionally, all new IT directors should perform an IT health assessment during the first 90 days in the position. This assessment should cover every major IT area to identify potential problems that may have gone undiscovered through regular measurement or observation. The areas covered should include:

- Organization.
- Infrastructure.
- Applications.
- Budget/costs.
- Vender agreements.
- Operations.
- Processes.

METRIC	COMPONENTS
Telecom cost per employee (annual)	• Basic telephone service plus equipment plus labor/support plus telephone usage (local/long distance) plus data network divided by total employees.
Telecom as percent of I/T cost	• Basic telephone service plus equipment plus labor/support plus data network plus telephone usage (local/long distance) divided by total enterprise IT spending.
Telecom cost as percent of total revenue	• Basic telephone service plus equipment plus labor/support plus data network plus telephone usage (local/long distance) divided by total revenue.
Network availability	• Total hours network is available divided by total available hours for the period.
Total data cost per user per year	• Call center costs plus calling card costs plus toll-free number costs plus remote access data costs divided by total number of end users.
Data network cost per minute of use	• Communications lines maintenance, support divided by total minutes used.

Exhibit 16.9   Network and Telecommunication Metrics

- IT demand management processes.
- Project management practices.
- Communication networks.
- IT standards.
- Financial and risk management practices.
- Measurement and quality control.
- Overall IT planning practices.

For *each* of these areas, the assessment should evaluate:

- Overall health of the area according to objective and subjective benchmarks.
- Adequacy to service the current and future organization.
- Relative position to industry best practices.
- Overall cost effectiveness.

METRIC	COMPONENTS
Total cost per MIPs	• All costs (hardware, software, labor) for processor, DASD, tape, HSM, mainframe printing, disaster recovery, dedicated software, and services plus cost of production scheduling plus cost of data center operations plus cost of security and availability plus cost of host platform technology plus cost of asset management divided by total MIPs.
Total mainframe FTEs per MIPs	• Total mainframe FTEs including all operations and systems programming/management personnel, including: —Production scheduling. —Data center operations. —Security and availability. —Host platform technology. —Asset management. • All divided by total mainframe MIPs.
Total operators per MIPs	• Number of operations staff divided by MIPs managed.
System programmers per MIPs	• Number of systems programmers divided by MIPs managed.
Mainframe availability	• Total hours system available divided by total available hours during same period.
Hardware cost per gigabyte	• Total processor costs divided by total gigabytes of storage space.
Cost per printed page	• Total cost for mainframe printing (including application and end-user printing) divided by total printed pages.

Exhibit 16.10   Mainframe Metrics

In considering all the areas, the assessment should provide:

• Opportunities for cost-effective service improvements.
• Opportunities for cost savings.
• Recommendations and action plan for improvement.

Generally, the assessment should be performed by a capable analyst or an outside consultant who has expertise in evaluating the IT departments of

METRIC	COMPONENTS
User support ratio	• Total number of users divided by total midrange support FTEs.
Midrange availability	• Total hours system available divided by total available hours during same period.
Midrange hardware cost per gigabyte	• Total processor costs divided by total gigabytes of storage space.
Applications per processor	• Total applications divided by total server processors.

Exhibit 16.11   Midrange Metrics

organizations similar in size and scope. The consultant should follow a standard methodology for performing the assessment while interviewing personnel, auditing systems, examining documentation, and observing functions in the department. Specific time lines should be set for interviews, analysis, and deliverables. At a minimum, deliverables should include:

- *Statement of work:* Explains the areas to be addressed by the assessment, methods to be used, people to be involved, time lines, deliverables, costs, and so on.
- *IT assessment:* Includes the full assessment covering the overall health, cost effectiveness, adequacy, and relative position of each area to best practices.
- *Strategic recommendations:* Describes specific opportunities for service improvements and cost savings and prescribes specific recommendations, along with an action plan for implementing the recommendations over a given period with specific resources.
- *Executive summary:* Summary of the entire assessment and strategic recommendations for the executive leadership team, board of directors, and outside investors.

In addition to performing this study on an annual basis, it should also be performed immediately before or after major events that will significantly affect the structure of the organization, such as a merger, acquisition, spin-off, divestiture, joint venture, restructuring, major geographic expansion, or major project affecting many internal systems (CRM or business process outsourcing).

The study generally takes three to six weeks and involves significantly more resources than the regular ongoing measurement and evaluation

METRIC	COMPONENTS
I/T custom application costs	• Application development cost plus application maintenance cost.
Overall applications support percentage	• Total number of IT staff providing application development and maintenance services divided by total number of IT staff.
Application portfolio by age	• Number of applications older than 3 years (set timeframe) divided by total number of applications.
Retirement rate for applications	• Number of applications retired in last 12 months.
Percent of package applications in application portfolio	• Total number of packaged applications divided by total number of applications.
Programmer to lead ratio	• Number of programmers divided by number of team leads.
New application development spend as percent of total application spend	• Cost for development of new applications divided by total cost for development and maintenance of all applications.
Application enhancements as percent of total application spend	• Cost for development of system enhancements divided by total cost for development and maintenance of all applications.
Application support and maintenance as percent of total I/T cost	• Applications support and maintenance cost divided by total enterprise IT budget.
Application maintenance and support as percent of total application spend	• Cost of application maintenance divided by total cost for development and maintenance of all applications.
Application maintenance distribution	• Concentration of maintenance FTEs per application.
Application maintenance support ratio	• Total number of applications maintenance staff divided by total number of applications.

Exhibit 16.12   Application Metrics

program. Therefore, this type of study should be commissioned using the same practices that would be used for purchasing any major professional services project.

At the conclusion of the project, the consultant should conduct a workshop with the IT steering committee to discuss the results and recommendations. This four- to six-hour workshop should provide the management team with a strong understanding of the current effectiveness of the IT department, where it needs to be in the future, and the most cost-effective and timely path for reaching that future point.

The report should then be used by management as the basis for a medium-term IT strategic plan, which may affect every area within IT. Because of this, the strategic plan should be widely distributed and communicated to all stakeholders who are normally involved in the IT measurement and evaluation process.

RESOURCES

www.iqpc.com: The International Quality and Productivity Center. Provides practical information on IT metrics.

www.metricnet.com: Provides benchmarking data.

Gartner Measurement Services Group: Provides benchmarking data.

Robert S. Kaplan and David P. Norton, *The Balanced Scorecard: Translating Strategy into Action* (Boston: Harvard Business School Publishing, 1996).

META Group: Provides benchmarking data.

Arthur Money, D. Remenyi, and Alan Twite, *Effective Measurement and Management of IT Costs and Benefits,* 2nd ed. (Boston: Butterworth-Heinemann, 2000).

Margaret Tanaszi, *IT Value Metrics and Measurement: What's IT Worth to Corporate Success?* (Framingham, MA: International Data Corporation, 2002).

Ed Yourdon, *IT Measurement: Practical Advice from the Experts,* International Function Point Users Group (Reading, MA: Addison-Wesley, 2002).

NOTES

1. Thomas J. Peters and Nancy K. Austin, "Passion for Excellence" (New York: Warner Books, 1986).
2. Thomas Hoffman, "IT Investment Model Wins Converts," *ComputerWorld* (August 5, 2002).
3. Deborah Asbrand, "IT Metrics for Success," *Information Week* (August 17, 1998). All rights reserved. Reprinted with permission.

17

IT Steering Committee

Disagreement produces debate but dissent produces dissension. Dissent . . . means originally to feel apart from others. People who disagree have an argument, but people who dissent have a quarrel. People may disagree and both may count themselves in the majority. But a person who dissents is by definition in a minority. A liberal society thrives on disagreement but is killed by dissension. Disagreement is the life blood of democracy, dissension is its cancer.

—Daniel J. Boorstin, U.S. historian[1]

This chapter introduces the IT steering committee, a group composed of the IT director and senior managers organized to assist the IT group in making key technology decisions impacting the company. The IT steering committee is a group of senior executives and representatives from business units and functions across the company that meets regularly to give input on IT direction, communicate company business objectives, remove impediments to IT success, and approve IT priorities, spending, and projects.

The chapter is organized in four sections. The first provides background and an overview of the IT steering committee concept. The second explains the purpose of the group. The third discusses the appropriate membership in the committee, and the fourth discusses committee operations. As with other tools discussed in this book, IT managers should determine the best approach to implement the concept and modify the membership makeup and operating variables to accomplish most effectively the primary objectives in their company.

Why This Topic Is Important

As Daniel Boorstin wrote, "Disagreement is the life blood of democracy, dissension is its cancer."

Throughout this book, we have emphasized the costs of an ineffective IT department—overspending, failed projects, heterogeneous costly environments, unhappy business users, low morale in IT, poorly run operations and applications, and improper use of scarce corporate resources. The most valuable approach for tackling the issues that we have highlighted in this book is a cooperative, communicative relationship between IT and the business units it serves. The IT steering committee is the tool through which the communication and cooperation between IT and the business units can be established and perpetuated. The IT steering committee provides a venue in which IT can communicate issues, status, obstacles, and priorities to the company, while the company can ensure that overall corporate investments are flowing to the highest priority initiatives, and that business roadblocks to IT effectiveness are demolished. Most importantly, the IT steering committee promotes a healthy, cooperative relationship between the business and IT, instead of the backbiting, contentious, finger-pointing, dysfunctional tar pit that is so often encountered.

IT departments suffer from common stereotypes such as self-absorbed, technology-focused introverts with weak communications skills, who are disconnected from the business, its priorities, and the big picture. Accurate or not, this stereotype can naturally lead to defensiveness in IT and promote a hostile, uncooperative attitude. Compounding the issue is the utility nature of IT operations, where performance is only noticed if it is absent. Often, IT managers and staff lack business experience in general, and specific knowledge of their company's business priorities and operations. The IT director frequently lacks the corporate political capital to effectively represent the IT group and sell initiatives to senior executives or defend the IT group when its performance appears to be poor.

On the other hand, staff working in sales, marketing, and other functions and business units are usually not technology experts, and are often disinterested in learning even the basics. Technology can be intimidating, or at best, appear overly complex to nontechnical staff. Many executives still have their assistants print their e-mails to read on paper, and users are often impatient when dealing with complex, sophisticated systems. Business users intimidated by technology often translate those feelings to the IT department as aggravation or disinterest.

The rapid changes in technology and business priorities that are a natural part of any company only increase the need for discussion and communication. It is easy to understand how the business-IT relationship can become strained.

Most often, there is no set mechanism that forces IT and business to communicate with the appropriate frequency and depth. Typically, the IT director and the corporate officer in charge of IT (most often the CFO) meet periodically to review plans and progress. Perhaps once a year at budgeting and strategic planning time, a presentation is made by the IT director to the senior management team. This informal, infrequent, and narrow communication is a major cause of IT departments getting "off-track." The business doesn't understand what IT can accomplish and abandons it, or worse, commissions their own duplicate IT department inside their business unit. The steering committee, with its carefully selected membership and frequent, well-planned, structured agenda meetings forces the key business departments and IT to communicate routinely, properly setting priorities and expectations, and provides an effective two-way communication avenue for a traditionally communication-challenged relationship.

Throughout this book, we present substantial evidence supporting the argument that if an organization fails to monitor and supervise information technology investment decisions and operations, it fails to achieve the corporate strategic objectives and, thus, fails to gain competitive advantage through IT. Implementing the ideas in this chapter enhances the communication flow between the business and IT, as well as ensures that the business and IT are together setting IT priorities and investment levels. The result will be the avoidance of many of the IT perils we have covered previously.

Specific topics covered in this chapter include:

- The IT steering committee concept, purpose, and benefits.
- Optimizing IT investments and priorities across the company by implementing the IT steering committee.
- Establishing an IT steering committee.
- Responsibilities of the IT steering committee.
- Selecting participants for the IT steering committee.
- How to effectively operate the IT steering committee.
- How to improve and focus communication between IT and executives and between business units and functions.

IT Steering Committee Concept

The IT steering committee is composed of senior IT management and senior business leaders who meet on a regular schedule to review, discuss, prioritize, and resolve IT projects, issues, and strategy. Used properly, the IT steering committee is one of the most effective tools for creating a high-performance IT department. The steering committee conveys business priorities to IT so that IT management can direct resources to the highest value business functions in real time. The committee provides approval, oversight, and high-level steering of projects, as well as finalizes project priorities based on IT demand management analyses. It also reviews proposed operating and capital budgets, IT operations service levels, and IT performance metrics. The committee has the senior level membership and authority to facilitate the resolution of any roadblocks to IT effectiveness. Perhaps the most important responsibility of the committee is to improve communication and relationships between key business personnel and IT managers, facilitating better informal communication between groups outside of the committee. This chapter outlines the typical charter, responsibilities, membership, and ongoing operations of a properly functioning IT steering committee.

Exhibit 17.1 illustrates the communication flow and outcomes of the committee.

Purpose of an IT Steering Committee

Life without an IT steering committee is tough for both the business and the IT department. There are very few senior-level advocates for the IT department, and the business suffers by not achieving the benefits of an effective IT department. Typically, the IT plan is recreated annually, at which time the IT director presents the IT strategy for the next 12 months. The IT director highlights the initiatives the department has accomplished and will accomplish. The pages are littered with technical project upon technical project. "We must upgrade to Microsoft Office 2000; we are upgrading the servers; we are implementing an AR/AP patch" are typical projects listed as a strategic initiative. Senior management listens for an hour, and unless there is a controversial application being implemented, the meeting ends, the IT

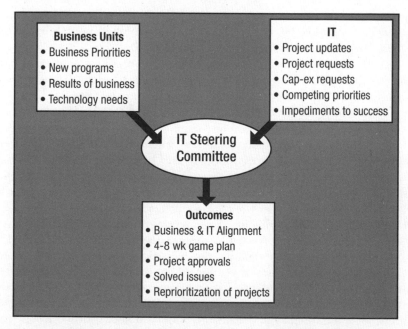

Exhibit 17.1 IT Steering Committee Communication Flows

director goes away, and everyone meets again the following year. Interim meetings are only called in the worst case, when a high-profile application being implemented is behind schedule and hundreds of thousands of dollars over budget. In these meetings, the business managers, entangled in a seemingly endless maze of technical obfuscations, throw up their hands and ask the IT manager to come back in a month with a comprehensive explanation of all the things that caused the implementation to go awry.

Further, the IT department, while being highly accountable to the senior executive who owns IT, shows very little accountability to the rest of the business. At one of our client companies, IT reported to the CFO, and the accounting department received the undivided attention of the IT department while the vice president of sales and marketing had met with the IT director three times in four years and had no idea if the sales IT initiatives were being driven by IT, or when they would be completed.

In the same company, the executive in charge of distribution logistics felt that the system enhancement request process used by the IT department was confusing and onerous. Additionally, new functions and features for the warehouse system would be developed and demonstrated, but there would be no design input from his team except when creating the original requirements specification. This led to rework when features were not developed that supported the warehouse team properly. When a new stock-keeping-units based work release function was rolled out, several variables for releasing the wave were not available. The developers went back to the drawing board for several weeks to correct the functionality. Most business unit leaders in companies where IT has limited direct accountability to the business have similar tales.

In another client company, a financial services provider, senior management was disappointed by the lack of vision and technology strategy being shown by the IT department. A host of questions were left begging by the IT communications gap: What new technologies need to be rolled out to support customers in the future? What are fast-moving competitors doing with technology to better support their customers and reduce costs? What tools should employees use to improve productivity? Infrequent business-IT strategy planning sessions and a lack of proactive agenda-setting by IT are other common symptoms of poor leadership and communication that is solved by the proper implementation of the IT steering committee.

In another client environment, an accounting financial analyst was working on selecting package software to support the accounting function. The analyst had met with five vendors and had them completing request for proposals (RFPs) at considerable vendor expense, conducting system demonstrations, and providing installation and licensing quotes. Simultaneously, the IT department was commissioned to review ERP packages to replace legacy systems, including finance and accounting applications. Neither group realized that the two competing package selection projects were taking place.

After we helped senior management inventory the full list of IT-related projects across the company, the duplicate, disconnected effort was discovered.

Implementing an IT steering committee helps IT ensure that they are providing the best value for the business, as well as ensuring that the business is working to remove any obstacles to the success of the IT department within the organization. Working together, IT and the business unit can eliminate the situations described above and throughout this book. The steering committee helps:

- Align technology and business strategy.
- Provide broad inspection and assessment of progress against company IT goals.
- Facilitate communication of business and project priorities.
- Build relationships between IT and business communities.
- Manage overall implications and tradeoffs of project priorities and business activities based on business rationale and IT capacity.
- Convert dissention to disagreement.

There are several interesting acid tests to perform in companies experiencing business-IT disconnects. One test involves submitting a contrived help desk request to solve a business mission critical-systems problem. For instance, a salesperson can send a message to the IT help desk to report that a printer is not working and note that it needs to be fixed quickly so that sales can get a quote or proposal out to a waiting customer. The test should measure how rapidly the IT department sends an initial response to repair the printer—in this case, examines the printer and determines that nothing is wrong. If the time elapsed is greater than four hours total for both answers, the company has a prioritization issue in the IT operations area. Clearly, a company cannot drive revenues if salespeople can't get quotes or proposals out the door to customers, and every minute that goes by is at best leading to a dissatisfied client. IT departments that understand the business impact of downtime to various organizations know that attending to customer-impacting problems is a high priority and repair delays mean lost revenue for the company.

Another simple test is to select two business units or functions in the company, and ask the top manager in those units the following questions:

- How often do you meet with the IT director to discuss priorities for your business unit?
- When did you have an informal meeting with the IT director (lunch, dinner, water-cooler conversation)?
- How many projects is IT working on for you at this moment? What is the top project? When will it be completed?

The answer to the first question should be greater than four times per year. Further, the IT director and top managers should be interacting on an informal basis frequently, outside of their formal status and planning meetings. The IT director should also respond to the final question. If the business unit leader and IT director high-value projects don't match, or the completion target dates differ, then there is a clear communication gap between IT and the business.

Benefits to the Company

At the company level, the benefits from implementing an IT steering committee are significant. First, the entire business provides direct and more frequent input into IT decisions, spending, and priorities. Second, increased scrutiny will result in better progress toward long-term goals. Third, the committee builds a team that backs IT and cooperates with IT, instead of blaming and castigating it. Last and foremost, the committee helps ensure that precious corporate effort and capital is not wasted on unnecessary projects or hardware.

Benefits to the Business Units

The business unit and functional department levels gain access and representation on the IT steering committee, which ensures that users from across the business have a voice in IT decision making. Business units also gain an understanding into the priorities of IT and how they are linked to the priorities within each business unit or function. They understand and help correctly set priorities—items that are of significance to the business and not unilateral priorities set by the IT department.

Benefits to IT Management

The IT director benefits by receiving direct, clear feedback from the most important constituencies on the performance of IT on a regular basis. Additionally, the IT director receives focused input in setting priorities, ensuring that the IT team is working on the correct set of projects and issues. It also reduces the occurrence of *canceled project phenomenon.*

The canceled project phenomenon is a result of misalignment in business priorities. For instance, the IT department may decide to implement an expensive terminal server solution, which allows applications run on a centralized server accessible by cheap desktop computers, thus simplifying end-user desktop support. IT gets internal approval, purchases the hardware and software, and installs the system. To attain approval, IT convinces business users that the system will increase the speed and longevity of their computers. When the system is finally deployed, the inevitable problems are encountered. Because IT has not properly defined and set end-user expectations, the first users see the new product, try it, and hate it because it's slower than anticipated and certain key features are missing. The users complain to management, management complains to senior management, and what could have been a successful project is shut down.

The committee helps ensure that business and IT are in tight linkage throughout any system rollout, and provides a forum for building IT relationships with the business decision makers. When impediments to successful completion of initiatives are encountered, the business and IT will work in partnership to remove them. Finally, it ensures a "no surprise" environment and minimizes potential for negative backlash.

Benefits to the IT Department

Members of the IT department benefit greatly by receiving more frequent and meaningful feedback on initiatives and service levels from senior management. IT teams can be frustrated by the start-and-stop nature of poorly chartered projects. Improved direction setting and feedback that minimizes the canceled projects benefits everyone in IT. Periodically, members of the IT department will present information to the steering committee; this provides those individuals with greater exposure to senior executives than they received before. The team will also have a satisfaction and sense of achievement that comes from finishing high-priority, high-return business projects and making a larger impact on the company. Last, it ensures that the team has better representation from influential senior managers in the corporation.

Objective of the IT Steering Committee

The primary responsibility of the steering committee is to provide IT direction setting. At the decision-making level, the IT steering committee is responsible for 12 key activities:

1. Review on an ongoing basis the IT strategic plan to ensure that it is consistent with the overall corporate direction.
2. Review (and approve or reject) all proposals for information systems package implementation or application development that cost more than a specified amount, depending on company size and authorization guidelines. The IT steering committee prescribes the required format of the information technology proposals, business case format, including a cost/benefit analysis and projects financial value calculation. (See Chapter 15 for details).

3. Consistent with IT Demand Management principles, manage the information systems project portfolio, set priorities for the development of the business information systems development, allocate the necessary resources, and monitor the progress of each project against objectives, time lines, and budgets.

4. Provide guidance and approval for capital expenditures over the IT director's spending authority. Sets authority levels by company size and company economic condition. At one extreme, the level can be set at zero and the ITSC review all capital expenditures. More realistically, the number is several thousand dollars. The committee can then review capex over $10,000 with final authorization provided by the executive with capex authority, given the amount and the recommendation of the steering committee. See Chapter 13 on IT budgeting.

5. Assist with allocation of IT and business unit resources for IT projects.

6. Resolve issues impeding high-priority projects. Key issues that are blocking the progress on projects are discussed in the meeting. Members debate the issues and offer resolutions. If issues cannot be resolved within the committee, the key stakeholders can meet off-line and provide a later update.

7. Approve use of all outside technology vendors by all business units. The committee should review new technology vendors and provide approvals.

8. Provide ongoing oversight of key projects (e.g., over $25,000 or longer than a certain duration).

9. Review project change requests requiring $10,000 or more capital. The ultimate responsibility for sign-off of project change orders is the executive who owns IT and the business unit or function involved.

10. Discuss any major business initiatives that may impact systems.

11. Approve IT standards proposed by IT (see Chapter 6).

12. Conduct post implementation systems reviews and IT effectiveness assessments that are independent of the IT department; the findings and recommendations of the review are presented to the committee with a response from the IT department.

The IT director has the responsibility to make the following preparation before each meeting:

1. Prepare an appropriate agenda that covers the decisions to be made and status updates to be provided.

2. Create project status reports for high-priority projects, including an outline of progress, percent complete versus percent of project budget spent, major issues, and change requests.

3. Aggregate all IT capital expenditures that should be reviewed by the steering committee for delivery to the steering committee prior to meeting.

4. Develop list of key questions or issues to discuss with committee members.

5. Create IT demand management/project prioritization schedule update.

In addition, the IT director's management responsibilities between meetings are as follows:

1. Approve IT projects and all initiatives/projects with an IT component that fall under the steering committee threshold.

2. Aggregate IT capital expenditures, ensuring the steering committee considers viable expenses.

3. Approve and assist with allocation of IT resources to initiatives/projects with an IT component.

4. Resolve minor issues impeding projects or support.

5. Screen projects before they are brought to the steering committee.

6. Evaluate change requests that fall under the steering committee threshold.

Membership of the IT Steering Committee

The IT steering committee is composed of 5 to 10 company managers who can provide the most comprehensive, company-focused input into the IT decision-making process. The committee should be composed of a cross-section of business function and business unit leaders with a high stake in the productivity and effectiveness of IT. The typical committee includes the following members:

- IT director.
- The person IT director reports to (typically the CFO, COO, or CEO). This person chairs the steering committee.
- CEO or COO (if different from above).
- One to three business function leaders or super users (accounting, HR, etc.).
- One to three business unit leaders or super users (influential business unit heads or their direct reports).

Lower-level analysts in the IT department should be brought into meetings to present specific project updates, but then leave the meeting; they should not be part of the steering committee.

At some client steering committee meetings, the senior management team intentionally leaves out CEO participation to ensure that his or her participation does not unduly sway decisions or recommendations from the committee. In these cases, the CEO is usually presented summaries of recommended decisions for final approval.

Roles and responsibilities on the ideal steering committee are outlined in the following section.

Structure of the IT Steering Committee

The IT steering committee is composed of a chairperson, secretary, scribe, and members. The chairperson of the IT steering committee is usually the senior executive who ultimately owns the IT function. In most midsize companies, this is the CFO. In larger companies, it may be the COO or CEO. Whoever the IT director or CIO reports to is the *chairperson*. In some large companies, the CIO may be a senior executive at the same level as, for example, the CFO. If that is the case, the CIO should serve as chairperson.

The actual members and member composition change over time according to business requirements and staff changes. Passage and approval of issues/recommendations can be based on the chairperson's decision or a majority vote. Organizations should determine what works best for their specific situation.

Roles and Responsibilities

- *Chair:* The chairperson is the leader of the IT steering committee:
  —Leads the IT steering committee, selects members, and directs the agenda.
  —Manages typical meeting functions—calls meeting to order, arranges for minutes to be taken and distributed before meetings, builds consensus, summarizes results and decisions.
  —Is generally the ultimate arbiter, tie-breaker, and final decision maker, depending on the topic.
- *Secretary:* The secretary is responsible for administration of the group:
  —Produces the agenda.
  —Organizes the meeting (finalizes time and location).
  —Acts as the chair in the chairperson's absence.
  —Records minutes of meeting.
  —Prepares and distributes meeting materials in advance.

—Distributes minutes after meeting.

—Monitors and reports status on meeting action items and open issues.

—Manages time in the meeting

- *Scribe:* The scribe is responsible for meeting notes (in small commit-tees, this position can be combined with the secretary); often this role is filled by the IT department administrative assistant.
- *Members:* Members are responsible for giving input and comments on issues:

    —Prepares and participates in meetings by reviewing agenda and meet-ing material before the meeting.

    —Considers issues and implications presented.

    —Participates in meeting discussions and decisions.

    —Represents the business unit or function.

Often busy business unit managers ask a trusted deputy to serve as their proxy on the steering committee. This should be avoided where possible; for the steering committee to have credibility and clout, as well as for the busi-ness unit area to be well represented, the committee should be composed of top company decision makers. An alternative approach to suggest is to have the business unit manager deputize their proxy, and have that person attend only the meetings that the business unit manager cannot possibly make. In every case, the CEO or COO should be made aware of consistent attendance problems to avoid the above issues.

Operating the IT Steering Committee

The steering committee meets on a regular schedule and covers the follow-ing topics at each meeting:

- Reviews critical issues affecting IT productivity.
- Reviews status of projects.
- Approves new projects/capital expenditure requests.
- Assesses IT priorities; re-prioritizes approved projects when appropriate.
- Approves proposed vendor relationships.

Exhibit 17.2 is a sample agenda. Each of the agenda topics is described in more detail in the following sections.

The steering committee, at the outset, may be forced to meet as fre-quently as once per week to purge the backlog of issues, stalled projects, and project-prioritization work. Over the longer term, the IT steering committee should not have to meet more frequently than once every two weeks. The committee should meet, at a minimum, once per month.

AGENDA ITEM	DESCRIPTION
Review issues	IT director presents priority issues.
Review status on projects	Team members present progress on milestones.
Approve new projects/ Capital expenditures	Business units provide business case. IT director presents capacity.
Assess priorities	Present competing objectives. Allocate resources as appropriate.
Approve proposed vendor relationships	Business unit or IT presents business justification.

Exhibit 17.2   Example IT Steering Committee Agenda

Reviewing Critical Issues

The first item to discuss is the top three to six issues that are hampering or hindering progress in IT. The issues are prepared for the committee to consider, along with potential resolutions and specific actions that IT and business managers can take. Project issues are covered in the next agenda item, so these issues should be non-project issues. For example: Issue 1—the company has been plagued by its third e-mail virus in the past three months. Should IT spend the resources and capital to increase prevention of viruses? It is important that business users on the committee weigh in on this question. If the virus caused no negative impact on the business, why spend the extra resources to get rid of all viruses? On the other hand, if the viruses are causing substantial business interruption, that input will be provided. The committee may then commission the IT department to develop recommendations for correcting the problem.

Often the IT department recommends solutions to issues that the business may not care about. Now the CIO or IT director can understand what issues are causing the largest business impact. The desired outcome is to have for each of the top issues (1) a resolution, (2) an action plan, or (3) a request for additional data.

Reviewing Status of In-Process Projects

The next step is to review the status of current high-priority IT projects (in prioritized order).

- *List of projects:* This lists all IT projects currently underway and includes the following attributes for each project: priority, target completion date, milestones, percent of hours worked as a total of estimated hours, and percent of project complete. Projects can be segmented into red (problem), yellow (caution/warning), or green (no problems or ahead of schedule).

- All red and yellow projects should be discussed; if time permits, the committee can review green project status updates.
- Any existing project in which the scope is changing from the original project plan needs a change request form completed. This form details the modification from original project design specification and allows the committee to determine whether the change is necessary, and any additional implications of the change.
- Existing project and applications should follow these change process steps:
  —Project champion (typically a line of business representative) completes preliminary sections of the change request form and submits it to IT.
  —IT works with the project champion to identify project scope, high-level design, IT requirements, schedule, and business rationale (cost and project financial value).
  —The completed change request form and schedule are submitted to the CIO/IT director.
  —The CIO/IT director reviews the change request.
  —Action is decided by the CIO depending on threshold limits. If moved to the committee, members may individually review and investigate issues before the meeting.
  —If approved by the CIO, the project champion and IT present the project to the committee using the project change request form and associated material (project schedule, project definition, etc).
  —ITSC discusses project proposal and determines appropriate action.
- *Outcome:* Each discussion on red projects should result in one of the following outcomes: (1) actions to be taken to correct the problem with follow-up at the next IT steering committee meeting, (2) a decision to kill the project, or (3) assignment of an independent resource to validate and verify the project issues and present at the next IT steering committee meeting.

Approve New Projects/Prioritization and Assess Capital Expenditure Requests

New project proposals should be completed and reviewed by the IT steering committee. The key is to prioritize new project proposals relative to existing projects. Each proposal should contain the following information:

- Project champion (typically a line of business representative—the person who completes preliminary sections of the project proposal form and submits it to IT).

- Description of project and scope, business reason for the project, the cost, the team, the time line, and the return on investment anticipated. Appendix items can include high-level design, IT requirements, and project plan.

The process to get project proposals in front of the committee includes having the champion complete the project proposal and submit it to the IT director/CIO. The IT director reviews the proposal and may request additional information. The CIO should approve proposals under a certain size in advance. Proposals over certain threshold should go before committee for approval. After approval, the project will be added to the approved projects list for further prioritization by the committee (see Chapter 15).

- *Outcome:* The IT steering committee should decide for each project proposal to either: (1) approve and move forward with project, (2) decline project, or (3) request additional information and decide at next meeting.

Capital expenditure requests for hardware are also reviewed and approved by the committee. The process is identical to the project proposal requests. The level of IT spending can be increased or decreased by loosening or tightening constraints on approval. Capital expenditure approvals by the IT steering committee help ensure that IT funds are being spent on investments that deliver appropriate value to the business.

Assessing IT Priorities

The committee will assess priorities periodically (at least once a quarter). The IT demand management and prioritization process is detailed in Chapter 15. During this segment of the meeting, review the updated priority list and discuss any issues with the current priorities.

The committee will also approve proposed vendor relationships, discuss proposed new vendors, and approve changes to current vendor contracts or terms.

Summary

The IT steering committee is a critical component of the effective IT department. The process described here increases and improves communication between IT and the business. The IT steering committee ensures buy-in of strategic IT decisions and projects by the business and upper management. Additionally, the discipline helps curb spending on unnecessary technology and IT projects, as well as helps enforce the disciplines and approaches covered throughout this book.

Steering committees can fail if they do not have the right charter, membership (both makeup and skill set), organization (run effectively with support from the culture), authority, processes, and attendance. Therefore, merely going through the motions is not enough. Committee members must be engaged and active to ensure that the steering committee is effective.

Sometimes, the name *committee* alarms the organization and brings out the cynical skeptics who dislike the connotation of the word. If *committee* is a negative term in the organization, the name can easily be changed to advisory group, board, council—any name that is appropriate; the most important step is creating the group and using it effectively.

The initial meetings may run long and feel like there is too much content to discuss; however, after the backlog of issues is cleared, subsequent meetings can focus on only the high-priority IT issues and projects and can be both rapid and successful. Over the long run, the committee can usually take the meeting frequency down to once every two to four weeks.

RESOURCES

K. Doughty, "Auditing the Implementation of the IT Strategic Plan," *EDP Auditing Journal* (New York: Auerbach, 1998).

K. Doughty, "Auditing Project Management for IS Developments," *EDP Audit, Control and Security Newsletter* (New York: Auerbach, 1996).

Mary Hayes, "IT Cuts Boost Productivity," *Information Week* (June 17, 2002).

NOTE

1. Daniel J. Boorstin, *The Decline of Radicalism: Reflections on America Today* (New York: Random House, 1969).

IT Toolkit

The tools to him that can handle them.

—English Proverb

This chapter introduces the electronic copy of the management tools that are helpful to the IT director in executing the approaches and methodologies covered in this book. We hope they are as useful to you as they have been for us.

The templates, links, and files provided are intended as a guide to provide a head start and to help drive critical thinking on the subjects. The tools must be refined for usage within any organization, and the specific circumstances being addressed.

The files are included on the accompanying CD-ROM, and are organized by chapter.

About the CD-ROM

The files on the enclosed CD-ROM are saved in Microsoft Excel 97 and Microsoft Word for Windows 97. In order to use the files, you will need to have spreadsheet software capable of reading Microsoft Excel 97 files and word processing software capable of reading Microsoft Word 97 files.

System Requirements

- IBM PC or compatible computer
- CD-ROM drive
- Windows 95 or later

- *Microsoft Word for Windows 97 or later or other word processing software capable of reading Microsoft Word for Windows 97 files.
- **Microsoft Excel 97 or later or other spreadsheet software capable of reading Microsoft Excel 97 files.

*For users who do not have Microsoft Word for Windows 97 on their computers, you can download the free viewer from the Microsoft web site. The URL to the viewer is:

http://office.microsoft.com/downloads/9798/wdvw9716.aspx

This download is for users who don't have Word; it allows them to open and view Word 97 documents. The URL to the download is:

**For users who do not have Microsoft Excel on their computers you can download the free viewer from the Microsoft web site. The URL to the viewer is:

http://office.microsoft.com/Downloads/2000/xlviewer.aspx

Use of the program with an earlier version of Microsoft Excel or other spreadsheet software might result in some formatting and display anomalies that we cannot support.

The Microsoft Excel 97/2000 Viewer is recommended for use with a stand-alone computer that does not have Microsoft Excel installed. This product allows the user to open and view Excel 97 and Excel 2000 spreadsheet files. The viewer is not suitable for use on a server.

Using the Files

LOADING FILES
To use the files, launch your spreadsheet or word processing software. Select **File, Open** from the pull-down menu. Select the appropriate drive and directory. A list of files should appear. If you do not see a list of files in the directory, you need to select **Word Document (*.doc)** or **Microsoft Excel Files (*.xls)** under **Files of Type.** Double click on the file you want to open. Use the file according to your needs.

PRINTING FILES
If you want to print the files, select **File, Print** from the pull-down menu.

SAVING FILES
When you have finished editing a file, you should save it in a new directory on your C:/ drive by selecting **File, Save As** from the pull-down menu.

User Assistance

If you need assistance with installation or if you have a damaged disk, please contact Wiley Technical Support at:

Phone: 201-748-6753
Fax: 201-748-6450 (Attention: Wiley Technical Support)
URL: www.wiley.com/techsupport

To place additional orders or to request information about other Wiley products, please call (800) 225-5945.

For information about the disk see the **About the CD-ROM** section on page **477.**

CUSTOMER NOTE: IF THIS BOOK IS ACCOMPANIED BY SOFT-WARE, PLEASE READ THE FOLLOWING BEFORE OPENING THE PACKAGE.

This software contains files to help you utilize the models described in the accompanying book. By opening the package, you are agreeing to be bound by the following agreement:

This software product is protected by copyright and all rights are reserved by the author, John Wiley & Sons, Inc., or their licensors. You are licensed to use this software on a single computer. Copying the software to another medium or format for use on a single computer does not violate the U.S. Copyright Law. Copying the software for any other purpose is a violation of the U.S. Copyright Law.

This software product is sold as is without warranty of any kind, either express or implied, including but not limited to the implied warranty of merchantability and fitness for a particular purpose. Neither Wiley nor its dealers or distributors assumes any liability for any alleged or actual damages arising from the use of or the inability to use this software.

(Some states do not allow the exclusion of implied warranties, so the exclusion may not apply to you.)

Index